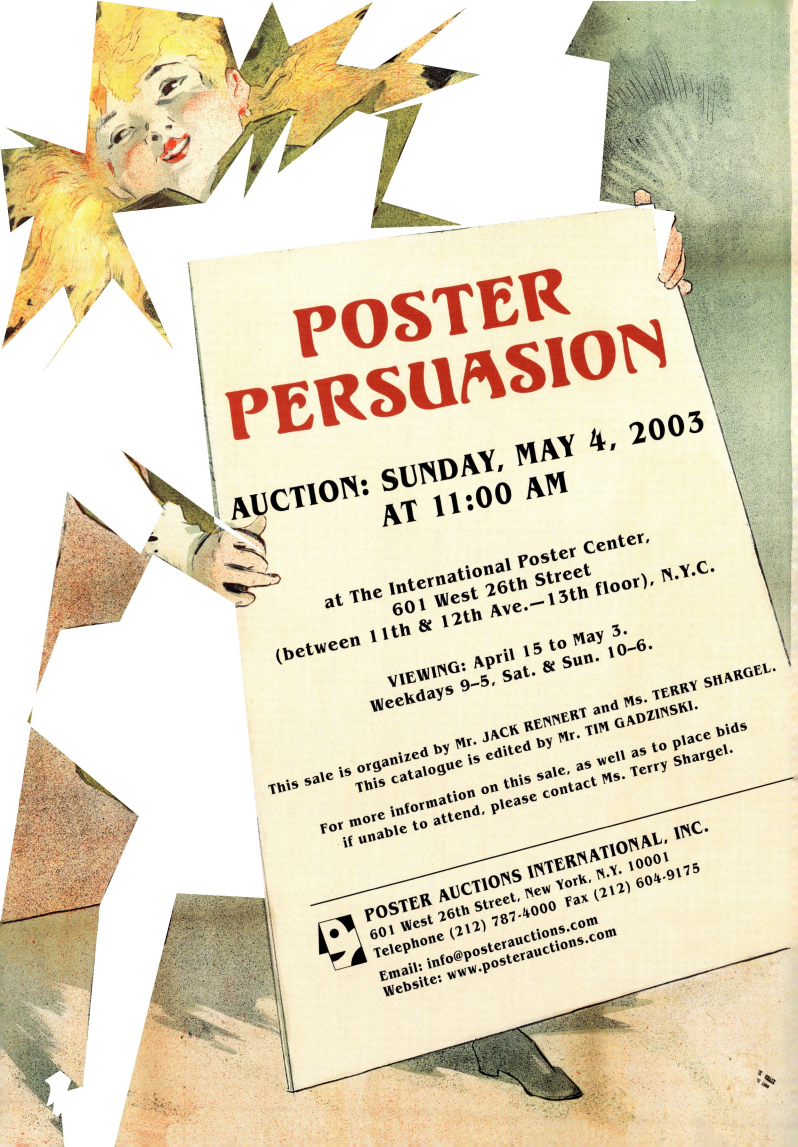

# POSTER PERSUASION

## AUCTION: SUNDAY, MAY 4, 2003 AT 11:00 AM

at The International Poster Center,
601 West 26th Street
(between 11th & 12th Ave.—13th floor), N.Y.C.

VIEWING: April 15 to May 3.
Weekdays 9–5, Sat. & Sun. 10–6.

This sale is organized by Mr. JACK RENNERT and Ms. TERRY SHARGEL.
This catalogue is edited by Mr. TIM GADZINSKI.

For more information on this sale, as well as to place bids
if unable to attend, please contact Ms. Terry Shargel.

**POSTER AUCTIONS INTERNATIONAL, INC.**
601 West 26th Street, New York, N.Y. 10001
Telephone (212) 787-4000  Fax (212) 604-9175
Email: info@posterauctions.com
Website: www.posterauctions.com

# CONTENTS

---

# ACKNOWLEDGMENTS

I am most grateful to the many individuals who have given their full support and assistance to us in the preparation of this POSTERS PERSUASION sale. First and foremost, our thanks to the 83 consignors in 11 States and 7 foreign countries who entrusted their finest works to us for this very special occasion.

Our staff has been materially helpful in all aspects of this auction, and I wish to especially single out the work of my associate, Ms. Terry Shargel. Our editorial department was headed once again by Mr. Tim Gadzinski who is responsible for the lively and incisive text in this book. Helping with many of the administrative aspects were Ms. Julie Press and Mr. Xavier Serbones. Mr. John Greenleaf and Mr. Edward Haber handled all the computer matters. And, finally, a special personal note of thanks to Barbara Rennert, who helps and encourages in countless ways.

We take great pride in making all our annotations as complete and accurate as possible, and we are helped enormously in this task by being able to call upon very knowledgeable colleagues throughout the world. Helpful in answering our many questions for this book were

Ms. R. Brook, Mr. Clark Chu, Mr. Chester Collins, Mr. William W. Crouse, Ms. Erin Foley, Mr. Ron Keats, Ms. Laura Kotsis, Mr. Andrew Krivine, Mr. Baltazar Macias, Dr. Maura Mansfield, Mr. Howard Sigman, Dr. Rene Wanner and Mr. Christophe Zagrodzki.

In the production of this catalogue, I was again fortunate to be able to call on the talents and devotion of fine craftsmen: Mr. Gunter Knopf is our very able photographer; the staff of Harry Chester, Inc. was in charge of design and production, and I especially want to thank Ms. Susannah Ing; all aspects of printing and binding were again handled by Cosmos Communications and I am especially indebted to Ms. Judy Lamm of their large and able staff.

Public relations is, as always, most ably directed by Mr. David Reich.

To all of them and to all the others who offered help, suggestions and encouragement, many thanks.

—Jack Rennert

---

## CONDITIONS OF SALE

We call your attention to the Conditions of Sale printed on the last pages of this book. Those bidding at this sale should first familiarize themselves with the terms contained therein.

---

## OUR NEXT SALE

We are pleased to announce that the PAI-XXXVII sale of rare posters will be held on Sunday, November 9, 2003.

Consignments are accepted until July 15, 2003.

---

## BID WITH CONFIDENCE—EVEN IF YOU CANNOT ATTEND

If you cannot attend the auction of May 4, please use the Order Bid Form on the next-to-last page. It should be mailed or faxed to arrive at our office no later than Friday, May 2. Note that all illustrations in this book are of the item being sold—we never use stock photos.

Jack Rennert—License 0797440

# AMERICAN SILENT FILMS OF THE 1920s

To say that the posters in this collection are extremely rare is something of an understatement when you consider that in most cases they represent the only remaining visual trace of the existence of these films—period.

Hailing from a brief period in the Golden Age of American cinema—between 1922 and 1926 to be precise—these designs capture a fleeting glimpse into an era when Hollywood was the epitome of glamour and glitz. The works seen here, however, provide an alternative to the big studio epics inundating the public of the era and represent the day-to-day, nuts-and-bolts production of outfits striving to create a niche for themselves in the shadow of the Big Boys. And this includes the Famous Player-Lasky studio, which in time would become major cinematic players themselves—Paramount and Columbia. These were the independents, following their artistic aspirations with the assistance of unknown actors and stars past their primes. This was the "real tinsel" of Hollywood, the working craftsmen hoping to fill the cracks left by the major studios.

Yet the posters for these second-string films, more so than the films they promoted, offer an array of outstanding artistic variety. Whereas a major studio advertisement almost exclusively featured the star-oriented, happy-ending clinch of lovers, here we're given the refreshing sweep of images under no such celebrity-centric restraint.

Regrettably, Hollywood never made much of an effort to preserve its heritage while there was still time. Many films were either mercilessly destroyed or simply left to their fate—to slowly deteriorate and disintegrate in storage vaults. These posters, though by no means household names or Generation-X touchstones, remain as a testament to the fleeting nature of artistic expression, as well as an enduring beacon in the service of independent promotional artistry.

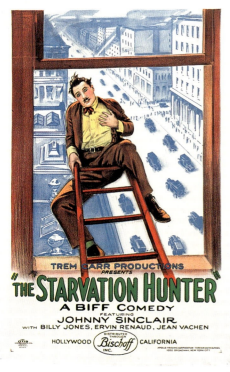

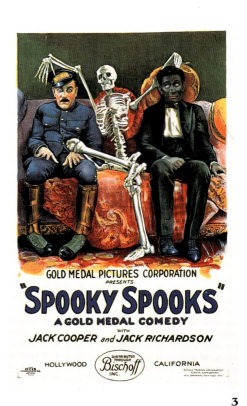

1                                                  2                                                  3

**1. The Starvation Hunter.** 1925.
26³/4 x 40¹/2 in./68 x 103 cm
Otis Lithograph Co., Cleveland
Cond B+/Slight tears and stains at edges.
Starved for attention perhaps. Nary a trace remains of the illustrious career of Johnny Sinclair, but judging from the illustrative antics seen in this promotion for "The Starvation Hunter" we can safely assume that Mr. Sinclair was more than willing to place himself in harm's way to elicit a chuckle from an audience—even if it meant having a coronary in the process. Regardless of the staying power of this low-rent Buster Keaton's career, the remaining poster is a tribute to promotional panache. The film was obviously a loose take-off of "The Salvation Hunters," a relentlessly grim melodrama by Joseph von Sternberg. One wouldn't think that the subject matter was ripe for parody, but more than a few people of the time thought that the pathos were being troweled-on a bit too thickly in von Sternberg's film, so it's probable that this is the aspect of the movie being spoofed. Since then, incidentally, "The Salvation Hunters" has become one of the all-time classics of silent cinema.
**Est: $1,000-$1,200.**

**2. Hollywoudn't.** ca. 1925.
26¹/2 x 40¹/2 in./67.3 x 103 cm
Otis Lithograph Co., Cleveland
Cond B–/Slight tears and stains at folds and edges; paper loss upper right border.
Johnny Sinclair is at it again, providing more comical daring-do in the pursuit of cinematic hilarity. Though no plot synopsis could be unearthed for this apparently Western-flavored farce, it's pretty clear from this and every other poster in this Silent Film section that it really wasn't a question of what "Hollywouldn't" do in order to increase the flow of cash into their coffers. More a matter of whatever Hollywood would or could.
**Est: $1,000-$1,200.**

**3. Spooky Spooks.** ca. 1926.
26¹/2 x 40¹/2 in./67.3 x 102 cm
Otis Lithograph Co., Cleveland
Cond B/Slight tears and stains at folds and edges.
It's doubtful judging from the macabre vignette on display here that "Spooky Spooks" drew its inspiration from the Eubie Blake jazz classic of the same name. However, what remains a bit scary are some of the less politically correct interpretations for the film's title. All minstrelry aside, the skeletal antics of comedy team Cooper and Richardson displays a willingness to indulge in the time-honored horror/comedy tradition exploited by the cinematic populace from Abbott and Costello to Jack Nicholson to Sam Raimi.
**Est: $1,200-$1,500.**

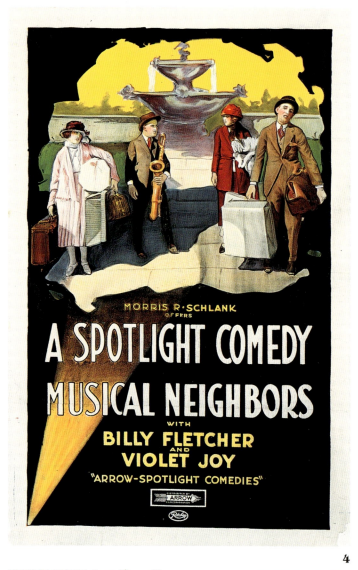

## SILENT FILMS (continued)

**4. A Spotlight Comedy/Musical Neighbors.** ca. 1926.
$26^3/_4$ x $40^1/_2$ in./68 x 102.8 cm
Ritchey Litho. Corp., New York
Cond B/Tears and stains, largely at folds and edges.
Things would appear to be a bit discordant at the
moment in the lives of these "Musical Neighbors." But
if our instincts are correct, we'd bet cents to saxo-
phones that a harmonious conclusion awaits our couple of couples in this particular Spotlight Comedy. And
you have to admit that it takes nerve to make a film
called "Musical Neighbors" in the silent era!
**Est: $1,000-$1,200.**

**5. Fliver Track's.** ca. 1924.
$27^3/_4$ x $41^3/_4$ in./70.4 x 106.3 cm
American Show Print Co., Milwaukee
Cond B/Slight tears at folds and edges.
You might not guess it looking at this rifle-toting doo-
fus, but George Ovey was the star of more than two-
hundred one-reel comedies. He certainly doesn't
inspire a great deal of confidence in a tracking vein,
but therein, ladies and gentleman, lies the formula for
fish-out-of-water hilarity. Ovey, though by no means a
household name, carved out a decent niche for himself as a film actor, working in such diverse works as
vampire movies and as the Plum Pudding in a 1933
version of "Alice In Wonderland," an adaptation that
also featured W. C. Fields as Humpty Dumpty and
Cary Grant as the Mock Turtle.
**Est: $1,000-$1,200.**

**6. Roomers Afloat.** ca. 1926.
$26^1/_2$ x $40^1/_2$ in./67.3 x 102.8cm
Otis Lithograph Co., Cleveland
Cond B+/Slight tears and stains at folds and edges.
Jack Cooper and Jack Richardson team up once more
for a high-seas romp with a title that once more conjures up a story line that the tastes and standards of
the time most certainly wouldn't have allowed.
Undoubtedly more innocent than the titular wordplay

would lead a contemporary mind to believe—though
the languorous undergarment pose doesn't exactly
help—one has to wonder if this film wasn't a candi-
date for early residence in the Celluloid Closet.
**Est: $1,000-$1,200.**

**7. The Riding Rascal.** 1926.
$40^1/_2$ x $79^1/_4$ in./103 x 201.2 cm
Morgan Litho. Co., Cleveland

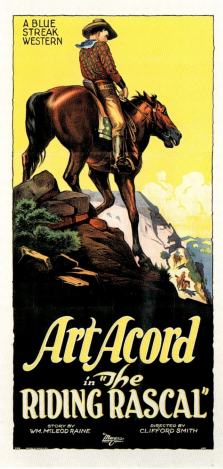

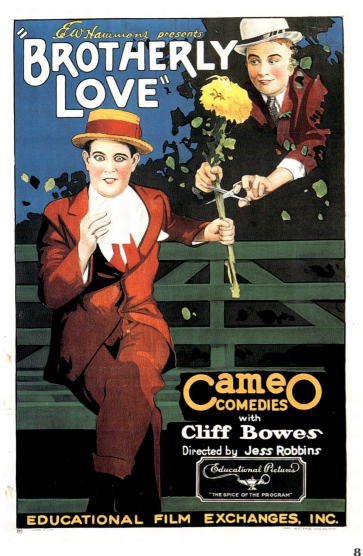

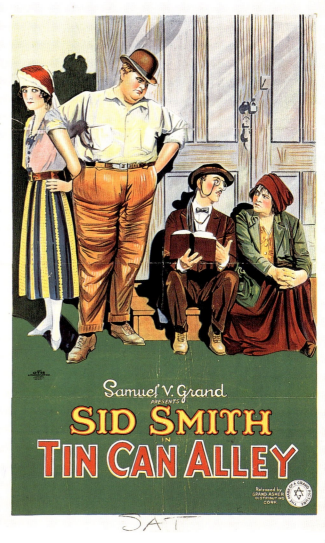

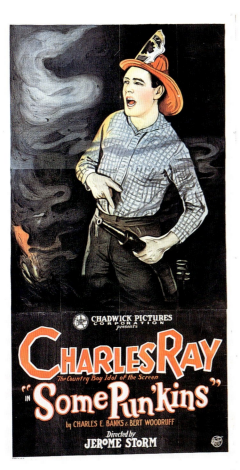

Cond B+/Slight tears at folds and edges.
Even though the plot of "The Riding Rascal" may have been what can best be described as a formula western, this 3-sheet Big Sky evocation far surpasses the limitations of the film it accompanied. Art Acord stars as a Texas Ranger who goes undercover to ensnare a band of rampaging cattle rustlers. Posing as a simple-minded homesteader, the thieving band sets him up as a scapegoat, convincing some of the ranchers that Acord is the rustling mastermind. Regardless of the hackneyed script, the inevitable climactic showdown contains one of the wildest shoot-outs ever staged for such a routine western. Art Acord (1890-1931) was the real deal, a genuine Oklahoman cowboy who became a star in the some of the earliest westerns and serials after considerable work in rodeos, Wild West shows and as a stuntman. When sound arrived, his career ended, as his voice didn't register well enough to satisfy the experts. He explored other lines of work, including bootlegging, which led to his arrest. After making bail, he fled to Mexico, where in 1931 he was found dead in his hotel room, aged only 41, a victim of cyanide poisoning.
**Est: $1,400-$1,700.**

**8. Brotherly Love.** ca. 1925.
27³/₄ x 40⁷/₈ in./70 x 103.7 cm
Acme Litho. Co., N.Y.C.
Cond B/Slight tears at folds and edges.
Vaudeville star Cliff Bowes gets top billing in "Brotherly Love", a comedy whose openly naive promotional material reflects that the "All's Fair in Love and War" policy is a sound one for striking comedy gold. Bowes had been around comedies since the early days of Keystone, where he can be spotted, briefly, in such farces as Chaplin's "Caught in a Cabaret" and Chester Conklin's "A Tugboat Romeo". Rarely seen in features, Bowes came into his own in the "Cameo Comedies" of the mid-'20s, usually playing befuddled young men.
**Est: $1,200-$1,500.**

**9. Tin Can Alley.** ca. 1924.
26¹/₂ x 40³/₈ in./67.2 x 102.5 cm
Otis Lithograph Co., Cleveland
Cond B/Tears and stains at folds and edges.
Aside from this assemblage of character types upon whose skeptical ears fall a preacher's message of heavenly rewards, nothing could be uncovered with regard to the down-on-their luck exploits of "Tin Can Alley". It's interesting to note the modified Star of David used as the calling card for the Grand-Asher distribution house, an insignia that in all likelihood would be deemed too politically-charged a moniker for the today's advertising climate, but in its day stood for "The Mark of a Grand Picture."
**Est: $1,200-$1,500.**

**10. Some Pun'kins.** 1925.
40³/₄ x 77¹/₄ in./103.5 x 196.2 cm
Butts Litho. Co., N.Y.
Cond B+/Slight tears at folds and seams.
A 3-sheet homage to rural firefighters isn't precisely what pops to mind when you hear the title "Some Pun'kins," but it certainly piques one's interest. The story, whose name was at one time a rustic expression of admiration derived from the word "pumpkin", goes like this: Lem, portrayed by Charles Ray, plays the son of a pumpkin farmer with two hobbies—tinkering around with firefighting inventions and admiring the local ingénue. His worldlier rival is helping his father to corner the pumpkin market. However, when Lem comes to the rescue with one of his inventions when his rival's house catches on fire, the father of his adversary helps Lem to market his father's turnips and even blesses the union of Lem and his beloved. In actuality, this was the kind of rural yarn that real country folk disliked, seeing as it typically portrayed them as boneheaded simpletons. This type of fare even prompted a show-biz reporter to coin the now-immortal *Variety* headline, "Stix Nix Hix Pix."
**Est: $1,200-$1,500.**

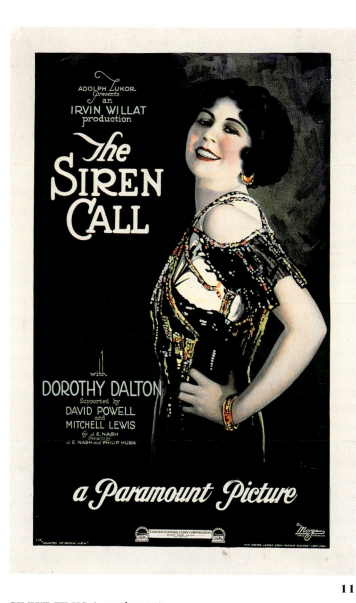

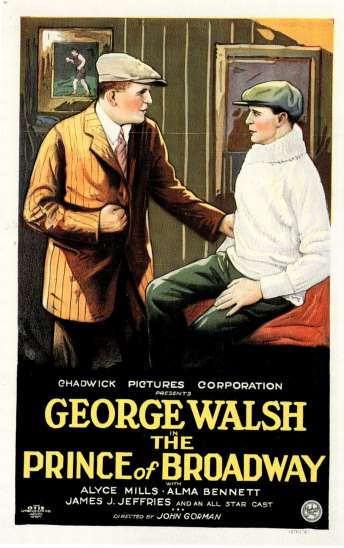

11

12

## SILENT FILMS (continued)

**11. The Siren Call.** 1922.
27 x 40⅞ in./68.5 x 103.7 cm
Morgan Litho. Co., Cleveland
Cond B+/Horizontal folds; tears at paper edges.
Seeing as "The Siren Call" is set in Alaska, it might be best to classify it as a north-western. Dorothy Dalton stars—and quite naturally graces the promotional material with vivacious candor—as Charlotte, the popular performer in an Alaskan music hall with no shortage of admirers, including a prospector and a trapper. The problem is that she's secretly married to a crooked gambler. To make matters worse, zealous reformers burn down the music hall, causing Charlotte and her husband to flee to another town, where they open a store. Many twists and turns occur, naturally causing Charlotte to face the perils of many a heroine, including abandonment, attempted rape, murder in self-defense and the revelation of true love. In the end Charlotte ends up in the arms of the prospector, while her ne'er-do-well husband has the good graces to be killed by wolves in the wilderness to make everything legitimate for the happy couple.
**Est: $1,000-$1,200.**

**12. The Prince of Broadway.** 1926.
26⅜ x 40¾ in./68 x 103.4 cm
Otis Lithograph Co., Cleveland
Cond B/Stains and restored tears at folds and edges.
It looks as if someone's about to get smacked in the chops if they don't listen up and fly right. And to be honest, this uncommon vision of straightforward masculinity sums up the plot of "The Prince of Broadway" to a point. You see, boxing champ George Burke, played by George Walsh, enjoys celebrating each winning bout with a vigorous night on the town, a practice that earns him the titular sobriquet. His carousing finally catches up with Burke when he finally enters the ring with a hangover and is knocked out cold. Because she

still sees great promise in him, Burke's childhood sweetheart, Nancy, sends him to a farm owned by one of her current admirers to dry out and get back in fighting shape. Naturally, the jealous admirer sabotages the champ's efforts until Nancy shows up to personally supervise George's comeback. And as you might have already guessed, under her guiding hand, he regains his title and the love of his youth. The film, adapted from director John Gormon's unproduced play of the same name, is notable for the appearance of several real-life boxers of the period in cameo roles.
**Est: $1,000-$1,200.**

**13. Lure of the Wild.** 1925.
26¼ x 40½ in./66.7 x 102.8cm
Otis Lithograph Co., Cleveland
Cond B/Unobtrusive folds; stains and paper losses in margins.
Man's best friend, played here by a ubiquitous canine credited as "The Wonder Dog" but known in the business as Lightning, is there to protect and serve in "The Lure of the Wild." This "Pulse-Throbbing Tale of Primitive Passion" begins as Jim, a western settler, convinced of his wife Agnes' infidelities with a man named Gordon, takes his daughter and heads for the Canadian wilderness. Gordon, who has actually been unsuccessful in his attempts to seduce Jim's wife, hires an unscrupulous ruffian—seen through the window in the poster—to follow and kill Jim. With her father gone, the little girl is left in the care of his faithful dog, Shep, and a trapper friend named Poleon, who promptly sends for the girl's mother. Gordon, cad that he is, tries to kill the mother as well, but the faithful Shep goes after him and forces him off a cliff to his death. In a rather peculiar twist, Poleon proposes to Agnes so that her daughter and Shep can have a happy new home. An ending that couldn't be more Hollywood if it tried.
**Est: $1,000-$1,200.**

13

**14. A Fight to the Finish.** 1925.
40⅞ x 77¾ in./103.7 x 197.5 cm
Otis Lithograph Co., Cleveland
Cond B+/Slight tears and stains at folds and edges.
Perfection Pictures arrives at pugilistic promotional perfection with this 3-sheet advertisement for "A Fight

**14**

**15**

**16**

**17**

him that he's just whipped the state's championship boxer, and naturally offers to train him as a professional boxer. Unfortunately, when the showdown with the champ arrives, Jim gets drugged and loses the match. When he discovers how the champ sealed his victory, he takes him out once more with bare knuckles, reconciles with his father and even—surprise, surprise—gets the girl of his dreams in the bargain. Despite the fact that the film was about fighters, the real star was the love interest, Phyllis Haver, a tall, vivacious blond born in Kansas. Breaking into the business as one of Mack Sennett's Bathing Beauties, she became a popular fixture of the silent era, retiring in 1929 after marrying a genuine Manhattan millionaire.
**Est: $1,200-$1,500.**

**15. Fair Week.** 1924.
40$^{1}$/$_{2}$ x 79 in./102.8 x 200.7 cm
Morgan Litho. Co., Cleveland
Cond B+/Slight tears at folds.
This spotlit 3-sheet convergence of glittering sophistication and bumpkin politesse draws our attention to "Fair Week," a Paramount release that recounts the account of two crooks, masquerading as evangelists, who arrive in a small Missouri town during a local fair with plans to rob a bank while their fellow conspirator, billed as "Madame LeGrande" performs a balloon stunt. The scheme is upset when Slim, a rotund village jack-of-all-trades portrayed by star Walter Hiers, discovers that the little girl he found abandoned years before and has been taking care of ever since is the illegitimate daughter of the phony "Madame." As one might expect, everything reconciles nicely and Slim even wins the heart of a gal that was on the verge of eloping with one of the would-be burglars.
**Est: $1,200-$1,500.**

**16. The Great Sensation.** 1925.
40$^{1}$/$_{2}$ x 77$^{3}$/$_{4}$ in./103 x 197.5 cm
Otis Lithograph Co., Cleveland
Cond B/Slight tears at folds.
Perhaps "The Great Sensation" of the title refers more to the spectacular cliff diving audacity on display in this 3-sheet poster rather than to the film itself. Check out this scenario and see if you don't agree. Jack, scion of a wealthy family, falls for a pretty socialite, but

as is the norm in the movies, he doesn't want to approach her as a rich heir because he just wants to be loved for who he is and not for the piles of money he keeps at home. Fortunately, the girl of his dreams is also pretty well-off and just happens to be in the market for a chauffeur. If you guessed that she hires Jack, you get a gold star. There ensue the expected complications, the climax of which is that Jack recovers his love interest's mother's jewels, stolen by a phony " captain" who has been courting her. The scene seen in the poster is apparently the promise of a "great sensation," where Jack saves his sweetheart from drowning. Stunning poster, mediocre movie.
**Est: $1,200-$1,500.**

**17. The Unchastened Woman.** 1925.
40$^{1}$/$_{2}$ x 77$^{3}$/$_{4}$ in./102.8 x 197.5 cm
Otis Lithograph Co., Cleveland
Cond B+/Slight tears and stains at folds and edges.
This 3-sheet seduction must certainly have raised a few eyebrows when it hit the streets on its promotional way. You wouldn't know it from the poster or the title, but "The Unchastened Woman" was actually a three-hankie tear-jerker. And a remake to boot, helped in no small part by the casting of Theda Bara, the one-time sensation and creator of the "vamp" prototype, now in the twilight of her career. The "Unchastened" story begins as a woman, played by Bara, is about to tell her husband that she is going to have a baby. However, she finds him in the arms of his secretary and decides not to disclose her pregnancy, but instead hightail it to Europe. When she hits the Continent, she keeps the gossip columnists busy with charades of wild behavior that they eagerly gobble up. She even goes so far as to bring home a young architect that she has been sponsoring under the guise of a more salacious association. Of course, her husband has since tired of his chippy secretary and is actually quite jealous of his wife's new liaison. Deciding to confront her in the midst of her sordid affair, he pays an unexpected visit, but instead of catching her with a lover, he finds her taking care of the baby she now presents to him as his son. That tears it and finally the reconciliation we have been waiting for arrives.
**Est: $1,700-$2,000.**

to the Finish," the tale of a millionaire who is forced to tell his spoiled playboy son, Jim, that he has lost his fortune in an attempt to get the lad back on the straight and narrow. While out hunting for a job, Jim witnesses a hooligan insulting a woman and promptly knocks him out cold. The damsel in distress informs

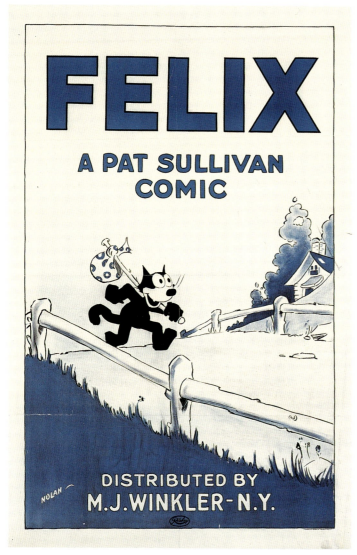

## SILENT FILMS (continued)

**18. Felix.**
Artist: **Nolan**
26³/₄ x 41 in./68 x 104
Ritchey Lith. Co., N.Y.
Cond B–/Tears and stains at folds and edges.
"Felix the Cat, the Wonderful, Wonderful Cat!" So
begins the theme song for one of the most enduring
images from the world of newspaper comic strips that
made its way to the big screen, the small screen and
even accompanied Charles Lindbergh as his lucky
mascot on his historic transatlantic flight. This black-
and-white hobo feline was created by Pat Sullivan
(1888-1963), but primarily drawn by Otto Messmer
from the early 1910s on. Messmer had his hand in on
the creation of more than eighty single-reel cartoons,
animated with a wonderfully free imagination, acknowl-
edging the origin of the figure in a drawing, and making easy transitions into the surreal—for example,
Felix readily detaches his own tail and uses it as an
implement or in self-defense. Though many of the
early silent cartoon art is lost to the ages, a number
of hard-core Felix fans ensured that he endured. As a
matter of fact, there are two silent cinema houses in
present-day Los Angeles that start every program with
a Felix the Cat cartoon.
**Est: $1,400-$1,700.**

**19. Mutt and Jeff/A Stretch in Time.** 1926.
27³/₄ x 41 in./70.5 x 104 cm
Miner Lith. Co., N.Y.
Cond B/Slight tears at folds and edges.
Mutt and Jeff originated in 1907 as a newspaper comic
strip, drawn by Bud Fisher. A precursor to Laurel and
Hardy, they were two working-class everymen—drink-
ing, gambling and getting in hot water with their wives.
It actually began as a solo act when Fisher began draw-
ing a daily comic strip called "Mr. Mutt." Soon after, he

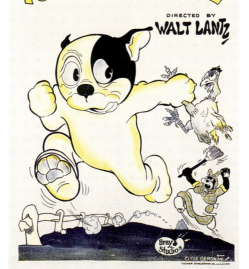

added the diminutive Mr. Jeff, and "Mutt and Jeff" was
born. Mutt was a tall, lanky man with a penchant for
the ponies, while Jeff looked like the Monopoly man
after a lost weekend. In brief, affable losers, guys you'd
see playing the lottery daily at 7-11. A fellow news-

paper cartoonist, Raoul Barre, transferred the strip to
the screen in 1913, where it did very well for thirteen
years. This particular precipice-fraught episode happens to be the very last one from the fall of 1926.
**Est: $1,000-$1,200.**

**20. For the Love o' Pete.** 1926.
26³/₄ x 41 in./68 x 104 cm
Tucker Scheuerman Co., L.I.C., N.Y.
Cond B/Slight tears at folds and edges.
Walter Lantz got his first job in the animated cartoon business when newspaper tycoon William Randolph Hearst opened an animation department within his Cosmopolitan Pictures. By 1922, Lantz had switched to the John Randolph Bray studio, created by one of the earliest pioneers in the cartoon business, originator of the first recurring movie cartoon character (General Heeza Liar). With Bray, Lantz wanted to get his own series going. The idea of a boy and his dog appealed to him, so he started a series with a mongrel whose name was Weakheart. It didn't find much of an audience, so he switched to a clown and Pete the Pup. The final incarnation was a hobo with Hot Dog, seen here in his very first loveably nefarious appearance. Hot Dog lasted for about two years, but still didn't quite make the grade. Lantz finally hit the jackpot in 1940 with Woody Woodpecker—and the rest is history.
**Est: $1,000-$1,200.**

**21. The Perfect Clown.** 1925.
26¹/₂ x 40¹/₂ in./67.3 x 103 cm
Otis Lithograph Co., Cleveland
Cond B+/Unobtrusive folds; slight tears and stains in margins.
Though his name is lost on most, Larry Semon, star of "The Perfect Clown," was once an enormously popular entity and for a brief moment enjoyed the highest salary in filmdom other than Chaplin. He did it by sheer frenzied pacing and non-stop mayhem; he was perfectly willing to wreck a hundred automobiles for a single laugh. Taking his cue from Mack Sennett's Keystone Cops, he piled on wild chases without justification or motivation. When the public tired of such broad slapstick by the mid-1920s, Semon found himself unable to adjust and his moment in the spotlight faded. The "Perfect" plot is the usual series of absurd coincidences strung together to justify thrills and mad chases, that coincidentally, have nothing to do with the peculiar wacky disc jockey seen on the poster; Semon, in fact, plays a broker's clerk in this particular vehicle. Perhaps the most interesting thing about the movie is the political incorrectness associated with Semon's black sidekick—nicknamed "Snowball" in the film, the actor actually used "G. Howe Black" as his professional screen name.
**Est: $1,000-$1,200.**

# FRENCH TRAVEL POSTERS

Almost without exception, these 71 French Travel posters place their focus on travel destinations. Some are realistic, some slightly romanticized, but all revolve around the thrill of arrival, the exuberance of the immediately unfamiliar. In some cases, such as with Alo, Dorival and Fraipoint, these visions are painterly, yet involving, while in other cases they verge on the graphically pure and stylized, as is the case with Bouchaud and Broders. Another approach to marketing travel is to portray the excitement of travel itself rather than the place said transport takes us; for that, one would have to visit the works of artists like Cassandre (see Lots 210-216), because in this section, destination is king.

France benefited in three respects in the destination poster. First and foremost from exceptional graphic artists. Secondly, tourist destinations from mountains to seashore, which were—and remain—the envy of French and international visitors. And third, railway companies that were on the forefront of marketing techniques, most especially when it came to the exploitation of the poster medium.

22

23

24

**ANONYMOUS**

**22. Forges-les-Eaux.**
29⁷/₈ x 41⁵/₈ in./75.8 x 105.7 cm
Imp. Parisienne Emile Lévy, Martinez, Paris
Cond A–/Unobtrusive tears at edges.
Ref: Train à l'Affiche, 70
It's the mineral waters—that hydrogen-and-oxygen panacea primed to combat anemia and depression, not to mention stomach and kidney problems—that are being touted in this uncredited design for Forges-les-Eaux, but the scenery isn't bad either. And by that I'm not exclusively talking about the Belle Epoque eye-candy with a glass of the stuff at the ready. The lively Normandy spa town is situated in the heart of the Pays de Bray countryside, surrounded by woods and parkland.
**Est: $1,200-$1,500.**

**23. Ascenseurs de Notre-Dame.**
34³/₈ x 50¹/₂ in./87.3 x 128.2 cm
Barlatier & Barthelet, Marseille
Cond B/Restored tears at folds.
Ref: PAI-XXIV, 84
The Notre-Dame cathedral in the old port city of Marseilles is a flashy 19th-century relative of Sacré Coeur in Paris, with a similar hilltop location. This poster promotes the two-minute ride up the hillside with a promise wrapped in a wide red ribbon: "one of the most beautiful panoramas in the world." The claim is not overstated: The vista stretches from the hinterland mountains to the sea and provides superb coastal views of nearby islands. Colorful pennants flying from the pavilion assure the whole family of worthwhile fun in the open air.
**Est: $1,200-$1,500.**

**24. Criel-Plage.**
28 x 41¹/₈ in./71 x 104.4 cm
Imp. Gentil-G. Largeau, Paris
Cond B+/Unobtrusive folds.
A spectacular aerial view of the Criel "Dream Beach," located at the very edge of where the land meets the sea on France's northwest coast at the lower Seine tributary. Located, as one might expect, in Normandie's Criel-sur-Mer, the seaside resort has plenty to boast about—an abundance of trout for the fisherman, plenty of crab, shrimp and mussels for those who choose to scour the tidal pools, a spectacular casino with rooftop garden. But what's highlighted here is really the true selling point: location, location, location, all at the foot of Mont-Joli-Bois (quaintly translated: "Pretty Woods Mountain"), a scant three hours from Paris and a relative Northern Railways stone's throw from Dieppe.
**Est: $1,200-$1,500.**

**25**

**27**

## ALO (Charles Hallo, 1884-1969)

**25. Mazamet.**
29¹/₈ x 40⁵/₈ in./74 x 103 cm
Imp. Serre, Paris
Cond A–/Slight tears in bottom text area.
Ref: Alo, p. 107; PAI-XXXIV, 233
Hallo, a Beaux-Arts-trained painter, is perhaps best known for his 100-odd posters for the French railways and the following three posters more than adequately demonstrate why his talents were such a frequently sought commodity in locomotion circles. Much like d'Alesi, Alo wasn't fond of including actual trains in his railroad promotions, preferring to sell the benefits of destination over the amenities of transport. This particular locomotive-free regional rail promotion from Alo takes us for a ride in an open touring car along a vertiginous ridge above the picturesque industrial town of Mazamet, placidly nestled into one of France's most spectacular landscapes, the Massif Central's Tarn gorge.
**Est: $1,200-$1,500.**

**26. Formentor-Ile Majorque.** ca. 1929.
24¹/₈ x 39 in./61.3 x 99 cm
Imp. Lucien Serre, Paris
Cond A/P.
Ref: Alo, 134; Color of Spain, p. 85; España, 1009
Exceptionally delicate handiwork evokes both atmosphere and locale in this Alo poster for the rail/ship collaborative, departing from Marseilles and responsible for delivering the happy passenger into the golden bosom of Majorca, the largest—and quite possibly the most beautiful—of Spain's Balearic Islands, situated in the Mediterranean. Though the inhabitants speak their own dialect of Catalan, its mild climate and beautiful scenery have long made Majorca a popular resort; tourism is, in fact, its primary industry.
**Est: $1,200-$1,500.**

## BAC (Ferdinand Bach, 1859-1952)

**27. Saint-Quentin-Plage.** 1897.
31 x 46 in./78.7 x 116.9 cm

**26**

**28**

Imp. Courmont Frères, Paris
Cond B/Unobtrusive tears at folds and margins.
Ref: Train à l'Affiche, 30
A haughty bathing beauty and her faithful servant are used as the primary bait to entice the viewer to consider the latest bathing hot spot on the French side of the

English Channel. It's not only the sandy beaches being extolled here, but also the real estate. Once deposited by the Northern Railroad, Bac's poster makes it clear that land is available for purchase upon which a villa or chalet could be built to the owner's specifications.
**Est: $1,400-$1,700.**

30

32

29

31

### JOSE BELON (?-1927)

**29. Lamalou-les-Bains.** ca. 1905.
29¼ x 41 in./74.2 x 104 cm
Imp. E. Baudelot, Paris
Cond A.
Ref: Train à l'Affiche, 88; PAI-XXXIV, 250
The women's pool at a fashionable spa is the featured attraction in this poster for a railroad destination. Belon was a painter whose designs, often in a humorous vein, were regularly exhibited in various French galleries between 1910 and the year of his death, 1927. His posters are not numerous, but always interesting.
**Est: $1,200-$1,500.**

### LEON BENIGNI (1892-?)

**30. Brides-les-Bains.** 1929.
24⅝ x 39½ in./62.5 x 100.4 cm
Editions d'Art, Paris
Cond A.
Ref: Golf, p. 4; Train à l'Affiche, 250; Montagne, p. 186;
    Deco Affiches, p. 101; Voyage, p. 50;
    Chemins de Fer, 118; PAI-XXXI, 299
For the PLM (Paris-Lyon-Méditerranée) railway, geometric mountains frame and focus our attention on two women—one *sportive*, the other *à la mode*, both *très chic*, as befits guests at this "elegant woman's spa." (Another version of the poster refers discreetly to weight and liver problems.) Christophe Zagrodzki names Benigni among those Art Deco travel posterists (led by Cappiello and Domergue) whose "elegant and mannerist design derives from fashion illustration, and who like using feminine grace as an argument in favor of this or that resort" (Train à l'Affiche, p. 76).
**Est: $3,000-$3,500.**

### HERVÉ BAILLE (1896-1977)

**28. Côte d'Azur.** 1949.
24⅜ x 39⅛ in./62 x 99.3 cm
Éditions Hubert Baille, Paris
Cond A/P.
France's Azure Coast—AKA The French Riviera—is such a happy place that even the sun has to smile. And with all the beautiful people that consistently converge on the fabulous international playground, what precisely does this happy ball of incandescent gas have to frown about? At least that's how Baille sees it in his promotion for the French Rail Society and sun-baked frivolity.
**Est: $700-$900.**

**33**

**34**

**35**

## FRENCH TRAVEL POSTERS (cont'd)

### GEORGES BLOTT

**31. Spa.** 1899.
28³/₄ x 41⁵/₈ in./73 x 106 cm
Imp. L. Geisler, Paris
Cond B–/Tears and stains at folds and edges.
Ref: Wallonie, 22
"Two ladies walking in the Spa woods form the essential tableaux. Behind them, a view of the city—where one distinguishes the church and the pouhon Pierre-le-Grand (Peter the Great spring)—indicating that the scene must be located on the promenade of the *Montagnes russes*, which overhangs the boulevard des Anglais. These two elegant creatures both wear flowered hats. The first, a blonde in a black dress, slides her glove past the text in order to draw our attention to it. Her partner, in a pink dress and with black hair, presents a water glass which, when placed in the center of the image, calls to mind Spa's thermal vocation. An informative text, in decorative framing, announces the various activities of the season of Spa's summer, as well as the railroad schedule between Paris and Spa. The elegant climate of the poster effortlessly recreates the spa-esque environment of the belle epoque. . . . Realized in a direct three-colour photo-offset process on zinc, it can be regarded as a very technically-advanced process when compared to the majority of the other publicity of the time" (Wallonie, p. 19).
**Est: $1,000-$1,200.**

### MICHEL BOUCHAUD

**32. La Plage de Monte Carlo.** 1929.
31 x 47 in./78.8 x 119.4 cm
Tolmer (Paris)
Cond A–/Slight creases at edges. Framed.
Ref: Tolmer, p. 81; Karcher, 408; PAI-XXXI, 314
Beach scenes in true Art-Deco style are uncommon—and this is one of the best. The figures are stylized and the scene cubist, with decorative details and dramatic colors.
**Est: $4,000-$5,000.**

### EUGÈNE V. BOURGEOIS (1855-1909)

**33. Chemin de Fer de Paris-Lyon-Méditerranée.**
ca. 1899.
26¹/₂ x 38¹/₄ in./67.2 x 97 cm
Ateliers Hugo d'Alesi, Paris
Cond A–/Slight tears at paper edge.
Ref: Marseille, p. 34

**36**

Bourgeois' sextet vignette promotion for the PLM railroad demonstrates his skill as artist—not to mention why these talents secured his services to the d'Alesi printing house, seeing as d'Alesi's work as a posterist ran in very similar vein. The six stops on the Paris-Lyon-Méditerranée route—Paris, Mont Blanc, Dijon, Marseille, Montpellier and Cannes—are laid out in all their sweeping touristic grandeur. "The quality of this employee of the Seine Prefecture made people take notice when his canvases were first presented at the 1874 Salon des Artistes Français. Eugene Bourgeois regularly displayed his works featuring sea and landscapes and it's always a pleasure to find an artist with such rare powers of observation, a faithful brush and precision" (Marseille, p. 101).
**Est: $1,200-$1,500.**

**37**

### ALBERT BRENET (1903-?)

**34. Aeromaritime.** ca. 1950.
24 x 38 in./61 x 96.5 cm
Imp. Mon-Louis, Clermont-Ferrand
Cond B+/Slight tears and stains at paper edges.
Ref: Negripub, 68
"Ebony Hercules, the fantasmatic glorification of the black body made flesh in its reference to antiquity (one also reads elsewhere of the 'Ebony Venus') celebrates the purity of the lines of the seaplane of the *Aéromaritime*" (Negripub, p. 61). Perhaps the greatest achievement of Brenet's allegorical promotion for the airborne branch of the Chargeurs Réunis travel service is that it lends a thrilling shot of the exotic to the flying boat pictured above the chiseled archer on its way to some African destination, a dose of the thrillingly unfamiliar coupled with straight-arrow dependability.
**Est: $1,400-$1,700.**

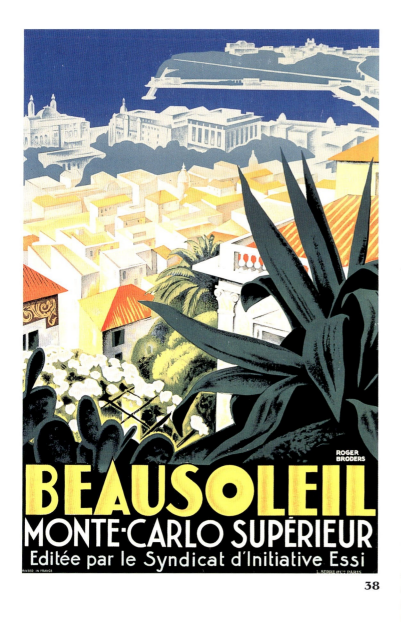

38

39

## ROGER BRODERS (1883-1953)

**35. Lac d'Annecy.**
24⁵/₈ x 39³/₈ in./62.8 x 100 cm
Cond A.
Ref: Broders/Travel, p. 68; Broders, p. 65B;
   Montagne, p. 182; PAI-XIX, 220b
Peaks and poplars overlook Lake Annecy in the French Alps, some thirty miles south of Geneva. The boat is the *France*, the largest and most elegant of a fleet of Annecy steamboats; launched in 1909, the pleasure boat could carry seven-hundred sightseers on its awning-covered deck.
**Est: $1,200-$1,500.**

**36. Glacier de Bionnassay.** ca. 1930.
24⁵/₈ x 39³/₈ in./62.5 x 100 cm
Cond B/Restored tears at edges.
Ref: Broders/Travel, p. 65; Broders, p. 74A;
   Montagne, p. 259; PAI-XXVII, 108
The PLM operated narrow-gauge electric trains, largely geared to sightseers, high amid the splendors of the French Alps; and speaking of gears, note the toothed middle rail for the rack-and-pinion traction on steep grades. This image advertises the train from the town of St. Gervais to a great glacier flowing down from Mont Blanc. As usual, Broders adds interest by framing the view with a characteristic local element—in this case, the jagged mouth of a tunnel.
**Est: $1,200-$1,500.**

**37. La Côte d'Azur/Ses Montagnes.** ca. 1930.
24³/₄ x 39³/₈ in./62.8 x 99.8 cm
Imp. Lucien Serre, Paris
Cond A–/Slight creases at edges. Framed.
Ref: Broders/Travel, p. 66; Broders, p. 87;
   Affiches Azur, 272; Affiches Riviera, 122;
   PAI-XXXIV, 260
"The unique charm of this highland and its attraction to tourists is illustrated by a poster by Broders . . . though not the first of the mountains of the Côte d'Azur, it sums up . . . their austere nature, majesty and difficulty of access; snowy peaks for winter sports; greener, more welcoming valleys, and the typical, high-perched village, affording cool summer repose. Finally, a car emerges from a tunnel to remind us of the many excursions one can make on the new road network" (Affiches Azur, p. 226).
**Est: $1,500-$1,800.**

**38. Beausoleil.** ca. 1928.
23⁵/₈ x 35¹/₈ in./60 x 89 cm
Imp. Lucien Serre, Paris
Cond A–/Slight tears at edges.
Ref: Broders/Travel, p. 34; Broders, p. 95;
   Affiches Azur, 189; Affiches Riviera, 100;
   PAI-XXIX, 234
Beausoleil, just uphill from Monte-Carlo and outside the border of Monaco (its casino is visible in the left distance, its palace compound on the peninsula beyond), was developed in 1904 for vacationers, residents and resort workers who couldn't find or afford accommodations in Monaco itself. Broders

shows us a Mediterranean Eden of terraced houses, tile roofs and lush vegetation and flowers. If this is second best, we'll take it.
**Est: $1,500-$1,800.**

**39. Sainte-Maxime.** 1928.
24¹/₄ x 39¹/₈ in./61.5 x 99.3 cm
Imp. Art et Tourisme, Paris
Cond A–/Unobtrusive fold.
Ref: Broders/Travel, p. 14; Broders, p. 85A;
   Voyage, p. 39 (var); Image de Mer, 88;
   Railway Posters, 136; Affiche Réclame, 96;
   Affiches Riviera, 42; PAI-XXXIV, 263
To advertise this resort on a stretch of the French Riviera called the Cote des Maures, or Moorish Coast, Broders directs our gaze past palms and bright orange sails and across a deep-blue bay, toward yellow and white buildings fronted with a whimsically pink beach. All gloriously summery—though the text assures us it's beach weather all year-round. Alain Weill points out that Broders sometimes uses "a process close to the technique of paper cutouts. Sainte Maxime remains his masterpiece of this category. The palm leaves, the sea, the beach, the sails, are nothing but non-underlined flats. Here again Broders is able to express, as by magic, the light of the Mediterranean—light—always light" (Broders/Travel, pp. 13-14). The poster was reissued in a smaller format the following year, and again eight years later for the SNCF, the national railroad into which the PLM and others were consolidated. The poster's endurance attests to its quality.
**Est: $2,000-$2,500.**

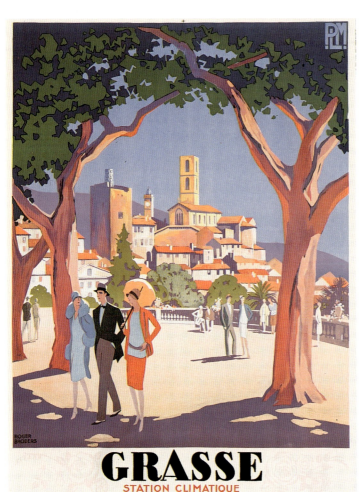

## FRENCH TRAVEL/BRODERS (cont'd)

**40. Grasse.** 1927.
29⁷/₈ x 41³/₄ in./76 x 106 cm
Imp. Lucien Serre, Paris
Cond A–/Unobtrusive tears at top edge.
Ref: Broders/Travel, p. 25; Broders, p. 89;
Affiches Riviera, 63; PAI-XXXI, 317
This PLM poster features stylish vacationers enjoying
a sunny terrace in the Alpes Maritimes resort of Grasse,
overlooking the Côte d'Azur (Cannes is a scant 10 miles
away). The Old City rises behind like a man-made
mountain, crowned by the ancient cathedral. Delicate
coloring evokes the delicious mixture of southern
warmth and the chill of the mountains; one virtually
shares the rarefied air.
**Est: $2,000-$2,500.**

**41. Grenoble/Services Automoblies.** ca. 1922.
31 x 42¹/₄ in./78.8 x 107.4 cm
Imp. Daudes Frères, Paris
Cond A.
Ref: Broders/Travel, p. 58; Broders, p. 59; PAI-XIX, 193b
For the Grenoble region, the PLM once more advertises
its automobile service on the Alps Route—though we
are, in all fairness, shown a train snaking along a spec-
tacular cliffside above the Isère valley and the town.
Subtle, watery greens, blues and purples predominate.
**Est: $1,200-$1,500.**

**42. Le Mont Blanc/Chamonix.** ca. 1924.
30⁵/₄ x 42¹/₄ in./78.2 x 107.3 cm
Imp. F. Champenois, Paris
Cond A–/Slight tear at bottom paper edge.
Ref: Broders/Travel, p. 59; Broders, p. 70; PAI-XXIX, 237
Broders' travel posters are typified by an elevated viewpoint, and he brings them to vivid life by including
foreground figures with whom we can identify and
whose panoramic view we share. Here, they're hikers
taking in the glorious view of the verdant Chamonix
and the snow-capped peaks and sheer slopes of Mont-
Blanc behind.
**Est: $1,700-$2,000.**

**43. Thonon les Bains.** 1929.
24 x 39 in./61 x 99 cm
Imp. Lucien Serre, Paris
Cond B+/Unobtrusive tears.
Ref: Broders/Travel, p. 69; Broders, p. 65A;
PAI-XIX, 201
White-peaked Alps in the distance are echoed by the
white "peaks" of the sails in this lovely design for a
spa-resort on the French shore of Lake Geneva.
**Est: $1,200-$1,500.**

**44. Mont-Revard/Les Sports d'Hiver.** ca. 1927.
30 x 41¹/₂ in./76.2 x 105.4 cm
Imp. Lucien Serre, Paris
Cond A.
Ref: Broders/Travel, p. 81; Broders, p. 77A; PAI-XIX, 205a
A wonderful winter-paradise panorama is presented for
our frigid enjoyment in this strong design.
**Est: $1,700-$2,000.**

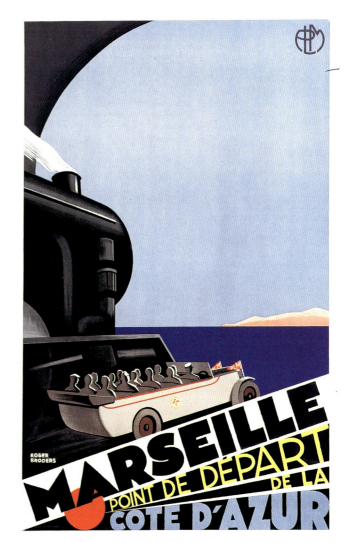

**45. Marseille/Côte d'Azur.** ca. 1929.
24⁵/₈ x 39³/₈ in./62.5 x 100 cm
Imp. L. Serre, Paris
Cond A.
Ref: Broders/Travel, p. 36; Broders, p. 82;
    Train à l'Affiche, 241; Voyage, p. 38;
    Affiche Reclame, 82; Deco Affiches, p. 95;
    PAI-XXXII, 206
The message here is that the Marseilles rail terminal
is the departure point for other destinations along the

Côte d'Azur—by PLM limousine, if passengers so wish.
The sleek simplification of forms and the way that the
angled text works into the design, serving as the "road"
up which the car and train travel out of the tunnel and
to the sea ahead of them, makes for a powerful design.
**Est: $2,500-$3,000.**

**46. Le Tour du Cap Course.** 1923.
29³/₈ x 41¹/₂ in./74.6 x 105.4 cm
Imp. Cornille & Serre, Paris
Cond B+/Slight tears at top and bottom edges.

Ref: Broders/Travel, p. 20; Broders, p. 98A;
    PAI-XIX, 200b
Via his innumerable touristic talents, Broders whisks
us away to Corsica. We pass an idyllic village on Cap
Corse, the peninsula at the northern tip of the island.
The greenery, pink roofs and hazy blue hills against
the bright ochre sky evoke a heartbreaking Mediterranean sunset. The image was reproduced as a postage
stamp in 1935.
**Est: $1,400-$1,700.**

## ROGER BRODERS: The Master's Methods

As Alain Weill points out in the new book, *Roger Broders—Travel Posters*, Broders dedicated
"himself to poster art during a ten year-span, between 1922 and 1932 . . . Very rapidly he
developed a system—a sort of tool box—which he uses at will, according to the task at hand.
When dealing with a single landscape—especially a mountain scene—he constructs his pictures in three grounds: The foreground, his view point, propped on the text, practically always
appearing at the bottom of the poster, rises above the middle distance, thus allowing for a
depth of field. Trees are added to increase these effects of perspective—a technique he uses
in masterly fashion. The foreground is almost always done in dark hues, which serve to
enhance and draw the attention of the viewer to the center, a valley, where according to the
criteria of his commission, he will draw a town or a village, in a lighter shade.

"Finally the background, where the deciphering of the picture ends, represents the mountains,
which draws upwards the gaze of the viewer. This system works perfectly and can be adapted
to any setting . . . Broders' approach from the start remains descriptive. He strongly uses color
side-by-side to convey the general atmosphere, the light at the time of the day or of the season he has chosen to evoke" (pp. 5-12).

**47**

**48**

**49**

## V. CHECA

**47. Bagnères de Bigorre.** ca. 1900.
30 1/8 x 44 7/8 in./76.5 x 114 cm
Imp. Chaix, Paris (not shown)
Cond B/Tears at folds.
Correct me if I'm wrong, but aren't you supposed to go to thermal resorts to relax? Though the calming environs seem to be working wonders for the feminine half of this horseback riding duo, the man still seems like he might need to soak for a while longer. Located in the High Pyrenees region, the locale promises equilibrium amidst nature—fortuitously sheltered from the winds, Bagnères-de-Bigorre, the vibrant tiny capital of the High Adour valley constitutes an ideal vacation resort.
**Est: $1,200-$1,500.**

## E. COSSARD

**48. Col de Bavella/Corse.** 1928.
24 1/2 x 39 1/4 in./62.2 x 99.7 cm
Imp. J. E. Goosens, Lille
Cond A.
Ref: Train à l'Affiche, 91
Not merely satisfied to bring the intrepid traveler to where their rail network could realistically reach, the PLM enterprise offers automotive excursions in Corsica, the mountainous French isle of the Mediterranean. Located in the southern region of the island, the rocky Bavella massif is the backbone of the isle, with a pass at 1218 meters and an immense forest that makes this place one of the most curious and beautiful of the isle. It's a place where colorful forms and light transport us into a world of enchantment and mystery, accentuated by the wind which, over time, has bent the Laricio pines into strange forms verging on the supernatural. These porphyry peaks, called "Needles," dominate the dawns and the twilights of the Bavella Pass. Not the destination for those preferring elegant architecture and a convenient casino, but a rewarding one nonetheless.
**Est: $1,000-$1,200.**

## GEORGES DARASSE

**49. Vittel.**
28 3/8 x 40 1/2 in./72 x 103 cm
Imp. Moullot, Marseille
Cond B/Restored tears.
A dainty tipple of the purest restorative waters points the way to Vittel, a spot easily accessed thanks to the good people of the French State Railway. And you won't find any forcefully stated claims in Darasse's text, simply the panoramic sprawl of a well-established

**50**

**52**

restorative destination. It's interesting to note the somber inset of Vittel's "grande source"—an inclusion that reminds the viewer that for all its scenic allure, health is an issue never to be looked upon lightly.
**Est: $1,200-$1,500.**

## DAVID DELLEPIANE (1866-1932)

**50. Provence.**
29 5/8 x 42 in./75.2 x 106.7 cm
Affiches Moullot Fils Aîné, Marseille
Cond A–/Unobtrusive tears at edges.
It wasn't that long ago that the American public was being literally exhorted to spend "A Year in Provence." Though hardly contemporary in nature, Dellepiane's design lucidly displays why that might not be such a bad idea: Mediterranean Moustiers and the amphiteater city of Sainte Marie; the towering Sainte Baum Massif; St. Remy, haunt of van Gogh and Nostradamus, six kilometers from the village of Les Baux with its winding road through what Dante described as the "Val d'enfer;" the bustling and beautiful seaside tri-

fecta of Toulon, Sicié and Tamaris. Utilizing his talents as both a portraitist and an evocative landscape artist, Dellepiane conveys a combination of heartfelt romanticism and rustic practicality.
**Est: $1,200-$1,500.**

## GEORGES DORIVAL (1879-1968)

**51. Chemins de Fer de l'État.** ca. 1912.
29 1/4 x 41 1/2 in./74.2 x 105.4 cm
Imp. Cornille & Serre, Paris
Cond A.
Ref: PAI-XXXIV, 361 (var)
Lying in a magnificent setting on the east bank of the Rance estuary opposite Dinard, Brittany's walled town of St. Malo is one of France's greatest tourist attractions. A previously-seen variant noted the network of six-hundred lakes that create the sandy expanses of the Emerald Coast, the name given to the picturesque stretch of Brittany from Cancale to Val St. André. But rather than try and incorporate any of these beaches into his design, Dorival gently sets us down on a wis-

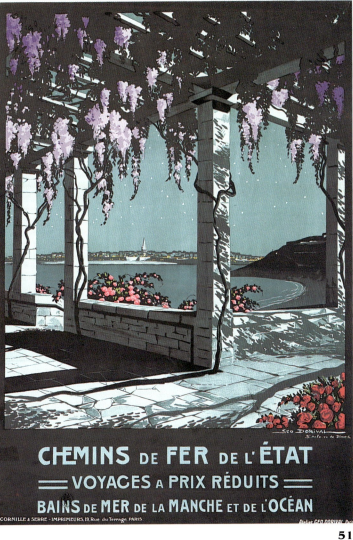

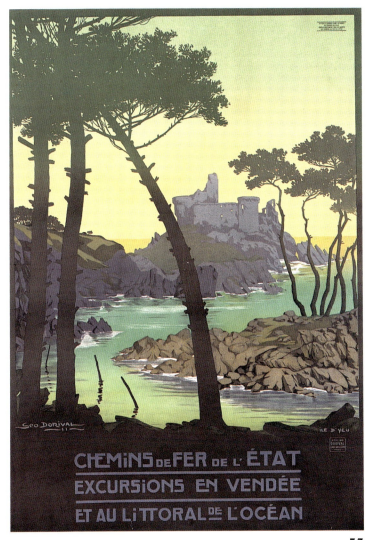

**51**

**53**

**54**

**55**

shrubbery, the leisurely teeming scene lays the popular weekend and holiday destination at our feet, the sun-splashed vista featuring the promontory-situated old walled upper town gracefully lording over the bathing beach, promenades and casino.
**Est: $1,200-$1,500.**

**53. Chemins de Fer de l'État/Ile d'Yeu.** 1911.
$28^3/_4$ x 41 in./73.2 x 104 cm
Imp. F. Champenois, Paris
Cond B+/Slight tears at folds and edges.
It appears as if it were a pebble detached from some distant lost continent, an island of light emerging from the majestic Atlantic, deploying its sorcerer's sites over the limpid waters that enclose it and serve as its shelter. The Breton island of Yeu, an island of contrasts, whose shores played host to an array of bold seafaring pioneers—Phoenicians, Greeks and Celts—not to mention barbarian raiders. Yeu's wild coast offers an imposing chaotic universe, made up of vertical cliffs, deeply cut out coves, at the bottom of which small beaches spread out, encircled by belts of reef, caves and deep valleys, and crowned by "Le Vieux Château" on its rocky outcropping. A rare destination, rich in tradition and savage beauty. And Dorival created a rare and intense travel design as befitting as the locale it proffers to the pent-up would-be traveler.
**Est: $1,400-$1,700.**

**54. Hyères.** 1914.
29 x $41^1/_8$ in./73.5 x 104.4 cm
Imp. Cornille & Serre, Paris
Cond B−/Restored tears.
Ref: Affiches Riviera, 30
Though renowned for its palm-lined boulevard, this Dorival promotion for the Côte d'Azur's southernmost resort gives play to all of the sun-sated vegetation awaiting the city-spent tourist in the Riviera getaway, as well as giving textual mention to the various coastline treasures easily attainable upon arrival.
**Est: $1,000-$1,200.**

teria-draped balcony under a canopy of stars with a dreamy view of St. Malo, the former sleepy fishing village turned smart summer resort, as seen from across the Rance from Dinard. A view, easily obtained, by the way, by the service of the French State Railway.
**Est: $1,200-$1,500.**

**52. Granville.** 1912.
$29^3/_4$ x $41^1/_4$ in./75.5 x 104.8 cm
Cornille & Serre, Paris

Cond B/Slight tears and creases, largely near edges.
Framed.
Ref: PAI-XXXII, 298
Another idyllic Dorival vision, this time for the Basse-Normandy resort town of Granville in Western France. Partially framed with a Broderish sprig of flowering

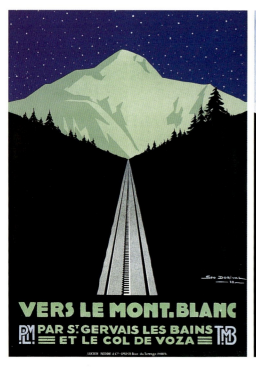

## FRENCH TRAVEL/DORIVAL (cont'd)

**55. La Mare de Cricqueboeuf/Normandie.**
24¹/₄ x 38³/₄ in./61.5 x 98.4cm
Imp. Lucien Serre, Paris
Cond A.
Ref: Chemins de Fer, 84; PAI-XXXIV, 360 (var)
Dorival's graceful wizardry of transferring place to poster is evidenced in a design promoting the seaside rail network that just so happens to provide service to Normandy's Cricqueboeuf, with its coastal highlight—the mussel-bound reef known as the Banc du Ratier—shelved in favor of the village's scenic pond and ivy-covered church. Not much in the way of locomotives, but how you get to all this serenity matters very little, as long as you take note of the travel services' names at bottom. In addition to his graphic appeal, Dorival was also known for his work as a sketcher and decorative artist, as well as serving as the director of *l'Art et la Mode*.
**Est: $1,200-$1,500.**

**56. Vers la Mont-Blanc: Three Posters.** 1928.
Each: $29³/₈ x 41 in./74.5 x 104 cm
Imp. Lucien Serre, Paris
Cond A.
Ref: Alpes, 43; Train à l'Affiche, 104; Voyage, p. 35
Dorival's classic of minimalist grandeur. Why waste time displaying a quaint dwarfed hamlet or detailed geo-graphic and verdant details when a simplified, almost childlike vision of the most renowned massif of the French Alps will do the trick nicely. Add in a silhouetted conifer forest and the funicular track that will provide the means for transport and you've arrived at a travel poster par excellence. The only way to improve on the subtle perfection of the design would be present it in its three solar variants—dawn/dusk, daytime and evening shade—which is precisely what we've done.
**Est: $3,000-$4,000.** (3)

## MAURIUS FORESTIER

**57. PLM/The French Riviera.**
24³/₄ x 39⁵/₈ in./63 x 100.7 cm
Cond A-/Unobtrusive tears at edges.

Forestier's design intended to attract the British urbanite to the languorous florid embrace of the Riv-iera for the PLM couldn't be any clearer: gloom versus radiance, pollution versus palms, repression versus rejuvenation. Everything is summed up with stark concision and the only real question that would appear to remain unanswered is what time the next train leaves the station. *Rare!*
**Est: $1,200-$1,500.**

## TSUGUHARU FOUJITA (1886-1968)

**58. Normandie.** 1958.
23³/₄ x 38³/₄ in./60.3 x 98.4 cm
Editions Paul-Martial, Paris
Cond A-/Slight tears at top and bottom edges.
Japan-born Foujita was famous for his paintings of women and cats. Towards the end of his life, he con-verted to Christianity, adopted Leonard as his first name and devoted himself to painting religious scenes. Though still fairly secular in nature, there's an air of spirituality breezing through the artist's promotion for the French National Railways service to Normandy, a quiet, virtually solemn whisper to wander for those in need of a bit of meditative peace and quiet away from the urban maelstrom amidst the farmland, forests and gentle hills of northwest France.
**Est: $1,000-$1,200.**

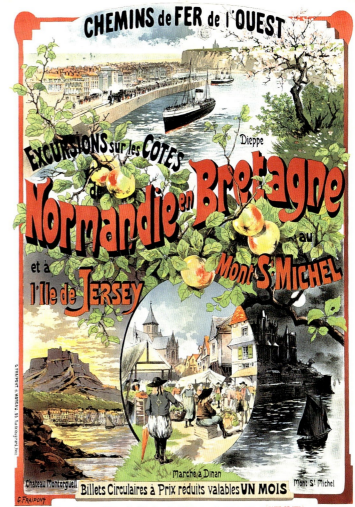

**60**

**61**

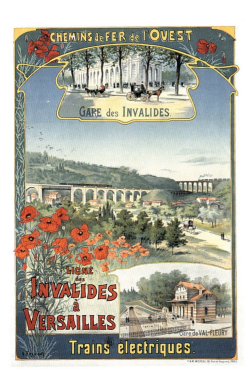

**62**

**63**

## GUSTAVE FRAIPONT (1849-1923)

**59. Chemins de Fer du Nord/P.L.M.**
$29^5/8$ x $41^3/4$ in./75.2 x 106 cm
Cond B/Slight stains and tears at folds and edges.
Two very different destinations—an urban architectural/
commercial Belgian hub and a Swiss center of sophistication naturally nestled betwixt mountains and water.
The common thread? Both are easily attainable destinations thanks to the combined efforts of the P.L.M. and

Belgian Northern Railways. Brussels-born artist Gustave
Fraipoint was a painter and illustrator in Paris, where he
collaborated on *Le Courrier Français* and other revues.
He also created numerous posters, largely for the
French rail, with most of them between 1891 and 1896.
He was named a Knight of the Legion of Honor in 1892.
**Est: $1,200-$1,500.**

**60. Enghien les Bains.** ca. 1891.
$28^3/8$ x 42 in./72 x 106.7 cm
G. Fraipont et Moreau, Paris
Cond B+/Slight tears at folds.
Ref: DFP-II, 368
This Northern railroad's poster emphasizes the recreational aspects of the lake resort near Paris over its
therapeutic aspects. And much as he did in another
promotion for the destination around the same time
(*see PAI-XXI, 181*), Fraipont focuses on the picturesque lake with its swans and irises.
**Est: $1,400-$1,700.**

**61. Normandie en Bretagne.** 1890.
$28^7/8$ x $41^1/2$ in./73.4 x 105.4 cm
G. Fraipont et Moreau, Paris
Cond B+/Slight tears at folds.
Apples and apple blossoms offset the imposing
architectural and commercial aspects of this Western
Railway promotion for Norman and Breton excursions,
effectively softening both monolithic structures and
urban bustle that some might not perceive as ideal
getaway alternatives.
**Est: $1,200-$1,500.**

**62. Chemin de Fer de l'Ouest/Invalides à Versailles.**
1904.
$27^7/8$ x $40^1/4$ in./70.8 x 102.2 cm
F & M. Moreau, Paris
Cond B/Slight stains and creases.
Ref: Train à l'Affiche, 4
A poster with a slightly different angle towards luring
the viewer: Certainly everyone would consider Versailles
to be a desirable destination, but what's the best
method to get there? Well, if you take Fraipont and the
Western Railroad's advice, the Gare des Invalides on
Paris' Left Bank is the way to go. It's interesting to see
a train promotion that celebrates itself and the ostensibly brief journey that it makes to its destination with
poppy-strewn aplomb. Another interesting inclusion is
the mention of the line's use of electric trains.
**Est: $1,200-$1,500.**

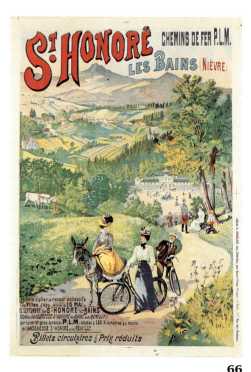

**66**

**64**

**65**

**70**

**67**

**69**

### FRENCH TRAVEL/FRAIPOINT (cont'd)

**63. Royan.** 1898.
$30^5/8$ x $45^3/8$ in./78 x 115.2 cm
Imp. Victor Billaud, Royan
Cond B+/Slight stains at folds.
Though it seems like a commonplace event today, the act of taking a dip in the ocean wasn't something one was likely to see in France before 1815. But once the practice of "sea bathing" got started, Royan took immediate strides towards becoming the most famous sea resort of the Charente-Maritime, with this new fashion launched in Royan by the inhabitants of Bordeaux. But it was during the Belle Epoque that the resort's popularity truly intensified, due in large part to the State Railway and the completion of the Grand Casino Municipal, at that time the largest casino in France. As the poster states, Royan played host to 100,000 visitors per summer at the time of its produc-

tion, a trend that would continue well into the 1900s. Fraipont's design does wonders at laying the treasures of Royan out for us, most especially in the shadowy intrigue of the nighttime casino.
**Est: $1,200-$1,500.**

**64. Royan sur l'Ocean.**
$31^1/2$ x $47^1/4$ in./80 x 120 cm
Imp. Victor Billaud, Royan
Cond B+/Slight tears and stains at folds.
Ref: DFP-II, 367
Fraipont certainly had a way with Royan. He once again sets his sights on calling attention to France's "Most Frequented" Atlantic coast resort, with a touch more attention paid to its beachtime aspects, as well as showing off Royan's more family-oriented nature.
**Est: $1,200-$1,500.**

### GÉACHE

**65. Arcachon.** 1896.
$28^1/2$ x $41^5/8$ in./72.5 x 105.7 cm
Imp. Demachy, Pech, Bordeaux
Cond B/Restored tears at folds.
Ref: Train à l'Affiche, 67
Comedic musical performances. Concerts day and night. Nonstop games. Pine forest excursions. Regattas. Bike races. Hunting. Fishing. Tennis. Golf. An aquarium and a casino. Oh yeah, and a majestic seaside location, well known for sailing and splashing about. Why state all of this up front. Well, chances are that one could easily miss the all-inclusive nature of the resort thanks to Géache's charming seaside scene featuring a sibling pair becoming much better acquainted with the local oceanic inhabitants. Arcachon, a popular seaside resort in southwest France's Landes region was born of the salt air, the scent of the pine forest, the arrival of the Central and Orleans railway, and the entrepreneurial foresight of the Pereire brothers.
**Est: $1,000-$1,200.**

## L. GEISLER

**66. St. Honoré les Bains.**
$29^7/_8$ x $42^3/_8$ in./75.8 x 107.6 cm
Raon-L'Etape, Paris
Cond A–/Slight stains at edges.
Geisler lays it all at our feet for the PLM's round trip service to the "City of Water": flirtatious encounters, family promenades, automotive accessibility, cyclic meanderings, burro excursions, far-reaching bucolic calm, and of course, the spa that acts as a magnet for the recreationally curative. To be honest, we can't be certain that Geisler is the artist or chief printer behind this poster; but, with results as exhilarating as this, credit can be given to Geisler in whatever role he played.
**Est: $1,200-$1,500.**

## GREIF

**67. PLM/Les Alpes et Le Jura.**
$24^1/_4$ x $39^3/_8$ in./61.5 x 99.8 cm
Editions Fortin, Paris
Cond A–/Slight stains at edges.
Ref: PAI-XXVI, 313
In this promotion for PLM's 120 destination points for winter fun in the Alps and Jura mountain ranges, the artist gives us a couple having the time of their lives—and they haven't even begun to ski. A charming example of selling the pleasure of time in the mountains, instead of the mountains themselves.
**Est: $1,500-$1,800.**

## ANDRÉ HARDY (1887-1986)

**68. St. Aubin s/ Mer.** 1936.
$24^1/_4$ x $39^3/_4$ in./61.6 x 101 cm
Rotophot, Paris
Cond A.
Ref: Train à l'Affiche, 202
This beach resort on the Mother-of-Pearl Coast—refered to here as "The Iodine Queen"—lures the potential wave-bent wanderer for the French State Railways with a beach ball toting bather as she skips away invitingly down the strand. Though this couldn't possibly have been a consideration for Hardy when he designed his poster, it's interesting to note that the breaking clouds can also, in hindsight, be seen as the gathering storm of World War II and the D-day invasion that would cast quite a different shadow over the sands upon which this carefree soul playfully gambols.
**Est: $1,400-$1,700.**

## ROLAND HUGON (1911- )

**69. Air Fer.** 1936.
$24^1/_4$ x $39^1/_4$ in./61.6 x 99.5 cm
Editions Paul-Martial, Paris
Cond A–/Slight tears at edges.
Ref: Train à l'Affiche, 295; Air France, p. 127;
    PAI-XVIII, 312
A joint Air France-French Railways poster offers combined tickets and convenient connections: "You leave one, you board the other." Train tracks are brilliantly photomontaged into the swathe the plane cuts across the lettering.
**Est: $1,000-$1,200.**

**70. 8 Jours de Neige.** 1938.
$24^3/_8$ x 39 in./62 x 99 cm
Editions Paul Martial, Paris
Cond A–/Slight scratch in ski.
Hugon's career is closely linked to advertising agent, Paul Martial, "that lover of beautiful printing and of modern typography and layout . . . for whom (Hugon) conceived a whole gamut of advertising material in a style perfectly in accord with the ideas of his employer" (Train à l'Affiche, p. 79). The perfect union of designer to subject is in full effect in Hugon's slick Art Deco creation for the French National Railway Society, whose prescription of "8 days of white snow, one year of rosy cheeks" comes across as anything but frigid despite the chilly setting.
**Est: $1,200-$1,500.**

## SUZANNE HULOT

**71. Dieppe.** ca. 1930.
24 x $38^7/_8$ in./81 x 98.5 cm
Imp. Jules Simon, Paris
Cond A. Framed.
Ref: Ref: Train à l'Affiche, 205; PAI-XXIX, 413
A popular resort on the Normandy coast of the English Channel, Dieppe has all the amenities of a high-class watering spot and is the nearest seaside resort to Paris—a scant 112 miles—easily attainable within two hours by train, a fact graciously provided by the State Railway and Dieppe's Office of Tourism. It's a favorite vacation destination and Hulot's design brings out the sun-dappled best of the beach, teaming with city dwellers unleashed from their workday routines into the the golden light of leisure.
**Est: $1,500-$1,800.**

72

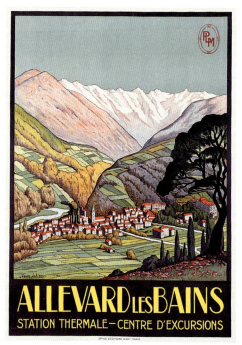

73

74

76

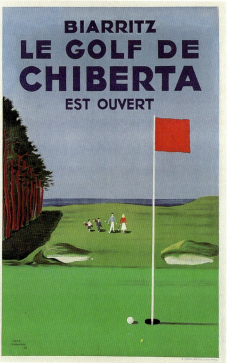

78

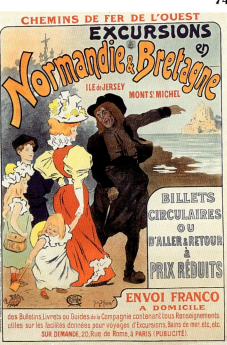

79

## FRENCH TRAVEL POSTERS (cont'd)

### LUCIEN-HECTOR JONAS (1880-?)

**72. Aix-Les-Bains.** 1933.
24³/₈ x 39 in./62 x 99 cm
Imp. H. Chachoin, Paris
Cond A.
Ref: Le Tennis; Montagne, p. 238; PAI-XXXI, 490
Jonas, a painter known for his historical subjects and genre scenes, is called into service by the PLM railway for its southeastern French resort destination of Aix-les-Bains. Caesar himself oversees the opening of newest thermal establishment through the sepia mists of time as the blue-and-white smart set head for the beach. As the town's alum and sulfur springs have been used since Roman times in the treatment of respiratory ailments and rheumatism, the poster provides a stunning marriage of artist to subject matter, which clearly demonstrates that everything classically old is new again.
**Est: $1,200-$1,500.**

### JEAN JULIEN

**73. Allevard les Bains.**
30⁵/₈ x 42⁵/₈ in./77.8 x 108.4 cm
Office d'Editions d'Art, Paris
Cond A–/Slight creases in bottom text area.
The quaint hamlet situated in the French Alps' Belledonne massif certainly doesn't go for the hard sell—realizing that the benefits of their thermal spa aren't precisely going to be a draw for the party crowd, Julien lays down a patchwork quilting of countryside and wide-open serenity to extol the restorative quietude of the PLM destination.
**Est: $1,400-$1,700.**

### JULIEN LACAZE (1886-1971)

**74. Vittel.**
24³/₈ x 39¹/₄ in./62 x 99.7 cm
Art & Publicité, Paris
Cond B+/Restored tears at top paper edge.
Ref: Golf Posters, p. 25

"Vittel might have remained a simple market town if Louis Bouloumié, an opponent of prince Louis-Napoléon Bonaparte, didn't have to nurse his deteriorating health in Contrexéville as a result of prison and exile. His dilapidated stomach wouldn't tolerate the water prescribed for his digestion, so he tried some of those which flowed in the near-by prairie of the Vittel commune. He found it so good that he bought the fountain, including the surrounding land, and in 1854, undertook the construction of the town's first thermal establishment" (Montagne, p. 116). Thank goodness the site didn't dwell in obscurity or we never would have had the opportunity to take in this splendid example of the many fine travel posters that Lacaze produced for the French Railways from 1910 to 1930. And though its health benefits are well publicized, the Eastern Railway wants to remind you that if a golf holiday is something on your agenda between mid-May and mid-September, Vittel might just be the ticket you were looking for.
**Est: $1,500-$1,800.**

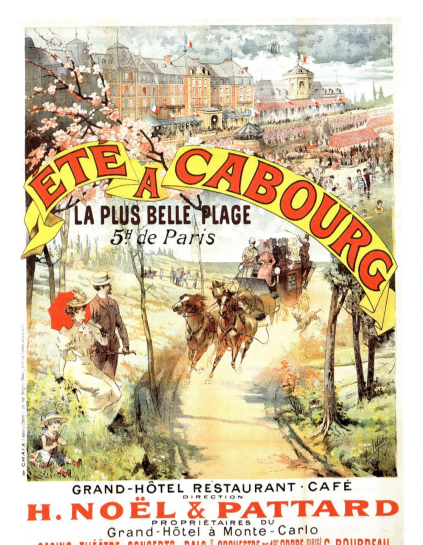

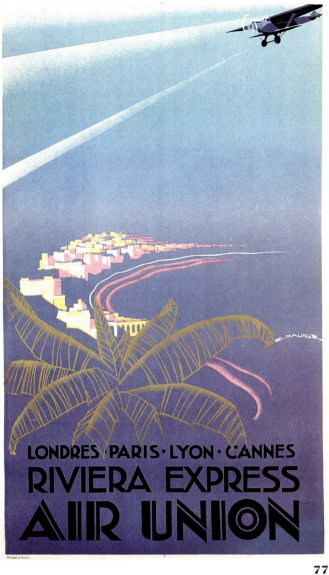

75

77

## LUCIEN LEFEVRE (ca. 1850-?)

**75. Été a Cabourg.** 1893.
38 x 55⁵/₈ in./96.5 x 136.2 cm
Imp. Chaix, Paris
Cond B/Slight tears and stains at folds and edges.
Ref: Train à l'Affiche, 41
Cabourg, Queen of the Flower Coast—located two hours from Paris now, five hours at the time of this posters production—is valued as an all-seasons resort, a real favorite with both couples and families. As late as 1853, Cabourg was a humble fishing village, but shortly thereafter, plans went into effect to make it the latest "sea-bathing" hotspot. And whereas most of the posters in this travel section promote train travel, Lefèvre's creation shows something a little different—the dramatic arrival of new summer guests by coach. While only producing posters since 1893, Maindron wrote in his 1896 book that Lefèvre, who received his training from Chéret, was mapping out an active career in which he was showing not only much promise, but an individual style whose work to date could only be judged as "outstanding" (pp. 82-83).
**Est: $1,500-$1,800.**

**76. Excursions en Normandie et Bretagne.** 1894.
33³/₄ x 47¹/₂ in./85.7 x 120.8 cm
Imp. Chaix, Paris
Cond B+/Unobtrusive folds.
Mont. St. Michel has been called "The Wonder of the Western World" and is an extraordinary sight, its rich and influential history combining with its glorious architecture to make it the most splendid of all French

abbeys. And Jersey, though not given much graphic due, is an isle thick with flowers with an impressive religious and cultural allure of its own. Lefèvre combines these elements with other Channel landmarks on the Norman and Breton coast, creating a travel promotion for France's Western Railway that is at once haunting and openly inviting.
**Est: $1,400-$1,700.**

## EDMOND MAURUS

**77. Air Union/Riviera Express.** 1932.
22⁷/₈ x 37³/₄ in./58 x 96 cm
Création Publix, Paris (not shown)
Cond A-/Slight tears at edges. Framed.
Ref: Affiches Riviera, 19; Air France, p. 27
An inspired Art Deco image from a designer whose few posters leave us wishing we had—and knew—more. The land, the sea and the sky intertwine in Maurus' design for Air Union and its Riviera service, a fantastic mélange well suited to the ethereal haze of both early passenger flight and intoxicating relaxation. The year following the production of this poster, Air Union, along with several other major French airlines, would combine to create Air France.
**Est: $2,000-$2,500.**

## JACK MAXWELL

**78. Le Golf de Chiberta.** 1948.
31¹/₈ x 47¹/₈ in./79 x 119.6 cm
Imp. B. Sirven, Toulouse
Cond A.

Ref: Golf Posters, p. 33; PAI-XXVII, 505
For anyone who has ever felt the serene thrill of driving a tee shot straight down the center of a well-manicured fairway in the midst of sun-drenched serenity, we bring you this impeccable vision used to announce the opening of the Biarritz Chiberta golf course. As this peppy twosome in the company of His and Hers caddies kick-off their day on the links, one can't help but be captivated by the gently rolling emerald expanses of Chiberta, as well as by the chipping virtuosity of the unidentified golfer who has left their approach shot scant inches from the cup.
**Est: $1,700-$2,000.**

## GEORGES MEUNIER (1869-1942)

**79. Normandie & Bretagne.** 1896.
29¹/₂ x 41³/₈ in./75 x 105 cm
Imp. Chaix, Paris
Cond A-/Slight tears at edges.
Ref: DFP-II, 591; Maitres, 31; Meunier, 30; PAI-XXX, 570
Granted, this promotion for the Western Railway highlights Norman and Breton excursions to both the Channel island of Jersey and Mont St. Michel at both tourist and reduced round-trip fares. But it shouldn't come as a terrible shock that the swarthy Norman tour guide singles out the French destination over the British option to this colorful matron and her brood, though the youngest member of the family looks as if she'd be just as happy chasing crustaceans up and down the shore as going on a greater adventure.
**Est: $1,400-$1,700.**

**81**

**82**

**86**

**87**

**84**

## RENÉ PEAN (1875-1940)

**81. Grand Casino de St. Malo.** 1905.
$34^7/8 \times 48^1/2$ in./88.6 x 123.2 cm
Imp. Chaix, Paris
Cond B–/Tears and stains at folds; restored losses
upper corners.
What a racy little number from Pean, a promotion for
the "Queen of the Beaches" on the "Emerald Coast"
that manages to be downright sexy without crossing
over into objectionable territory. And though the
municipal casino and the ramparts of the walled town
—including the cathedral of Saint Vincent—serve as
wonderful background material, it's the vivacious
bather in red that has our full attention, directly engaging the viewer as if preparing to draw them directly
into the poster's seaside shenanigans.
**Est: $1,500-$1,800.**

**82. Paris à Londres.** 1903.
$27 \times 42^1/8$ in./69 x 107 cm
Imp. Chaix, Paris
Cond A–/Slight tears and stains at paper edges.
Rather a different approach from the previous Pean
design, not to mention a world away from the Pal
poster advertising the exact same rail link (*see* No. 80).

## PAL (Jean de Paléologue, 1860-1942)

**80. Paris à Londres.** ca. 1899.
$30^7/8 \times 47^1/4$ in./78.4 x 120 cm
Imp. Paul Dupont, Paris
Cond B+/Unobtrusive folds.
In his mind, every commission provided Pal with an
opportunity to insert one of his pulchritudinous
females. Now, on the surface, this advertisement for
the Western and Brighton Railways calls our attention
to the economic and rapid service between the two
European capitals, but was it really necessary to go to
London to get a pineapple. Since Pal lived there, you'd
imagine he would have come up with something, shall
we say, perhaps a bit more British. And maybe I just
need to get out more, but it seems a little suspicious
that this Pal lass just also happens to be carrying a
basket of melons. Though it's pure speculation, it
would seem that Pal was indulging in a little graphic
slang as well as promoting rail travel.
**Est: $1,500-$1,800.**

Whereas the prior creation was all fresh-faced French
exuberance, this poster is all British business, from
the pipe-smoking coachman making his way through
the sepia cityscape dominated by the silhouette of St.
Paul's cathedral down to the detailed schedule and
fare information. Pean was a pupil of Chéret, working
under him at the Chaix printing firm. He specialized in
theater and cabaret posters from around 1890 to 1905.
After being among the first to produce posters for the
fledgling movie industry, he faded into obscurity.
**Est: $1,200-$1,500.**

## GEORGES REDON (1869-1943)

**83. Boulogne S. Mer.** 1905.
$29^1/8 \times 41^3/8$ in./74 x 105 cm
E. Marx, Paris
Cond B+/Slight tears at lower left corner.
Ref: Gold, 138; PAI-XXXII, 480
Unless you choose to bury your head in the sand and
naively believe that the posters of the Belle Epoque
were created for purely artistic reasons, this design
revels in an advertising axiom that has firmly been in
place from Day One: Sex Sells. It could hardly matter

**83**

**85**

**88**

that the only thing exposed on this fulsome bathing beauty is her arms—her blissful expression as she luxuriates in the lapping waves pounds the message home with about as much subtlety as a sack full of doorknobs. And even if you weren't a woman praying that a trip to this seaside resort would have the same orgasmic effect on you, Redon's design doubtlessly caught the eye of many pedestrians, who once caught, could move onto the text and the familial cameo of non-carnal recreational activities. As effective a design as it is blatant.
**Est: $1,700-$2,000.**

### PABLO PICASSO (1881-1973)

**84. Côte d'Azur.** 1962.
25⁷/₈ x 39¹/₄ in./65.6 x 99.6 cm
Imp. Mourlot, Paris
Cond A/P.
Ref: Czwiklitzer, 177; Affiches Azur, 31; PAI-XXIX, 581
Picasso opens a window onto the Riviera, permitting the viewer, at least graphically, to wallow a while in the balmy breezes and lucid colors of the sun-sated paradise. One of the aspects of Picasso's genius—be it in posters or paintings—that is altogether awesome is his ability to create permanence and vitality from a few, relatively-harried series of brushstrokes, evoking whatever he chooses with the facility of doodling. Two versions of the design exist, the other being a "Cannes" specific variant.
**Est: $700-$900.**

### F. PRODHOMME

**85. Versailles.**
28¹/₈ x 40⁷/₈ in./71.5 x 103.7 cm
Lith. Cornille & Serre
Cond B/Slight tears at paper edges.
Prodhomme invites the passerby to step into the fairy tale that is Versailles, the formerly insignificant French village made legendary by Louis XIV's court and palatial inclination. The palaces and gardens actually get little more than textual consideration in this fantastic poster that focuses on the Festival of Night and its magical waters, a Technicolor dream reminiscent of classic Disney animation.
**Est: $1,000-$1,200.**

### ROGER SOUBIE (1898-1984)

**86. Route des Pyrénées.** ca. 1914.
28⁵/₈ x 41⁵/₈ in./72.7 x 104 cm
Imp. E Baudelot, Paris
Cond A. Framed.
Ref: Montagne, p. 28; PAI-XXXV, 468
The travel service Compagnie du Midi advertises an

open-air motor coach service in the Pyrénées. Seen here negotiating the Aubisque Pass and offering a vertiginous panorama from the Ger peak, the touring bus looks rather insignificant contrasted off the rise of the towering cliff, which is precisely, one suspects the desired impact.
**Est: $1,200-$1,500.**

**87. Les Aiguilles d'Arves.**
30 x 41³/₄ in./76.2 x 106 cm
Imp. Cornille & Serre, Paris
Cond B/Slight tears at top and bottom edges.
Though other peaks pop to mind when the French Alps are mentioned, Soubie sets to paper this awe-inspiring vision of the Aiguilles d'Arves range's three towering summits situated in the southern France, the gateway to the Piedmont region and northern Italy. Soubie is best known for movie posters, but he produced some lovely travel posters as well. Most impressive here is how the artist's use of flattened perspective allows him to give his canvas an incredible depth in the manner of, though far more detailed than, Japanese woodblock prints—although apparently not quite enough room to roam for the bovines at bottom who leave the frame for textually greener pastures.
**Est: $1,000-$1,200.**

### MAURICE TOUSSAINT

**88. Paris à Londres.**
28 x 40¹/₂ in./71 x 103 cm
Cond B–/Restored tears at folds and edges.
More promotion that casts London's industrial atmosphere in a sepia tone, though not in nearly as somber a light as Pean (see No. 82). And though we're given ample fare and schedule information for the Brighton and French State Railways' cooperative, it's the landmarks that are truly intended to entice the French wanderer—Big Ben, Westminster Abbey and the Parliament Buildings, all seen from an awesome Thames point of view.
**Est: $1,000-$1,200.**

**90**

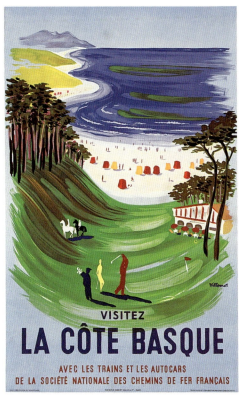

**91**

## FRENCH TRAVEL POSTERS (cont'd)

### A. TRINQUIER-TRIANON

**89. Paramé.**
29 x 41 in./73.6 x 104 cm
Imp. Courmont Frères, Paris
Cond B/Slight tears at folds.
Ref: PAI-XXX, 667
Trinquier-Trianon emphasizes the all-inclusive patronage of a getaway destination, a now-defunct seaside summertime resort known in its day as "The Queen of the Beaches." Set within a tasteful framework of what appears to be ornate kelp, Daramé's hotel/casino looms large behind the frolicsome bathers, a group conspicuously—and decorously—free of male swimmers. Apart from the posters he left behind, nothing is known about the artist.
**Est: $1,500-$1,800.**

### VICTOR VASARELY (1908-1997)

**90. Domremy/La Lorraine.** ca. 1936.
24³/₈ x 39 in./61.8 x 99 cm
La Technique Publicitaire, Paris
Cond A–/Slight tears at bottom edge.
Ref: Train à l'Affiche, 285
A rather peculiar travel design from Vasarely for the Lorraine town of Domremy. Virtually all the elements seem to glow from within, from the sheep to the flowering trees to the background architecture. As mysterious as this might appear to those not in the know, a bit of digging reveals the reasoning behind the radiance. You see, Domremy is the birthplace of Joan of Arc and the structure set amidst the pastoral quietude is the Basilica of Bois Chenu, situated one-and-a-half kilometers from the where the village stands. Begun in 1881 and consecrated in 1926, it is built on the spot where Joan heard her " voices ". The corona around the building is explicable as well: though pictured during the day, the basilica is floodlit every evening and majestically dominates the Meuse valley.
**Est: $1,000-$1,200.**

### BERNARD VILLEMOT (1911-1989)

**91. La Côte Basque.** 1953.
24¹/₄ x 39¹/₈ in./61.5 x 99.2 cm
Editions Hubert Baille, Paris
Cond A–/Slight tear at bottom edge.
Ref: Train à l'Affiche, 324; Villemot, checklist, 89;
PAI-XVII, 533
Villemot's death in 1989 left a real void in French poster art; for over 30 years, he had been the finest French posterist, unsurpassed at setting the right mood with just a few simple lines and bold colors. For example, this travel poster for the Côte Basque on France's Atlantic coast. It looks as if he couldn't have spent more than an hour painting it; however, if you're a Bernard Villemot, perhaps you need no more than an hour to describe an inviting beach, hills and golf course in a few fresh, easy sweeps of blue, green, red and yellow.
**Est: $1,500-$1,800.**

**92. Sports d'Hiver/France.** 1954.
24³/₈ x 39¹/₈ in./61.7 x 99.4 cm
Imp. S. A. Courbet, Paris
Cond B+/Unobtrusive folds and creases.
Ref: Villemot, p. 58; Voyage, p. 13; Montagne, p. 13;
PAI-XXXV, 498
A cross-hatching of skiers against a glacier-blue wintery landscape. An irresistable invitation to winter sport lovers from the master of simplified forms and solid, high-contrasting colors.
**Est: $800-$1,000.**

**92**

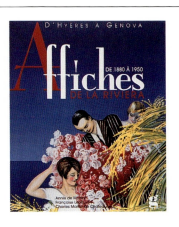

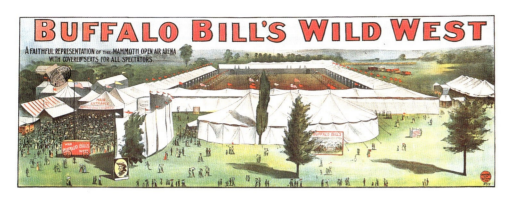

**93**

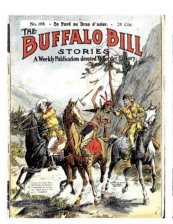 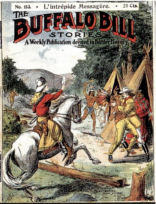 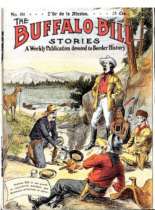

**94**

**95**

## ANONYMOUS

**93. Buffalo Bill's Wild West/A Faithful Representation.** 1905.
40 x 14³/8 in./101.5 x 36.5 cm
Weiners, London
Cond B+/Slight tears at fold.
Truly impressive. Most designs that arrive at our doorstep featuring the exploits of Buffalo Bill and his Congress of Rough Riders feature precisely that—sharp-shooting, cavalry charges, recreations of events

both perilous and astonishing on a grand scale, not to mention the sheer ethnic diversion the Wild West would trot out in any locale. But one aspect of the show that never really gets that much play is the sheer enormity of the venue that Cody required in order to present his lavish spectacle. Here, however, is the exception to the rule: a poster that focuses on the tent metropolis that housed the show. The text proclaims this to be "A Faithful Representation of the Mammoth Open Air

Arena," boasting "Covered Seats to all Patrons" to boot. Saying that is one thing, but backing up a claim with fine lithographic detail is quite another—note the billboard at center that's dwarfed by the neighboring mammoth tent, as well as the giant poster portrait of Buffalo Bill in the bottom left-hand corner.
**Est: $2,000-$2,500.**

**94. Buffalo Bill's Wild West/Incident Maritime.** 1905.
40 x 30¹/4 in./101.6 x 76.7 cm
Imp. Weiners/Ch. Wall, Paris
Cond B+/Slight tears and stains, largely in margins.
Ref: Buffalo Bill, 89 (var); PAI-XXXII, 10
"The United States Treasury Department's Life-Saving Service stationed small crews along the country's coast to aid in the rescue of ship-wrecked persons; this spectacle . . . glorified the 'Heroes of Storm and Wreck' and, by means of a beach apparatus drill, showed how these brave men established communications with wrecked vessels and thus rescued their passengers. . . . (It) becomes clear that what one sees in the arena is the action shown inside the ornate borders to the left and right. The text of the program is instructive and interesting: 'What they (the members of the Life-Saving Service) do in the arena is but a repetition of what these very brave men have repeatedly done in the line of their regular duty, when the temperature is below zero, in the teeth of a tremendous gale, on a lonely beach, where the surf ran mountain high. The firing of the shot carrying a line over the mast of the doomed vessel; the planting of the sand-anchor and connecting a hawser from it to the mast by means of the shot-carried line; the rigging of the breeches-buoy on the hawser and working it to and fro, over the surf, with the rescued mariners—all these are, like everything else in the Wild West, 'the real thing'" (Buffalo Bill, p. 14). Of course, a pulse-pounding dramatic interpretation of one such potential real-life tempest never hurts. *This is the French version.*
**Est: $1,700-$2,000.**

**95. The Buffalo Bill Stories: Ten Issues.**
Each: 8³/8 x 10⁵/8 in./21.2 x 27 cm
Ref: PAI-XXXV, 39 (var)
*10 complete issues, in overall good condition, with slight staining on covers and edges slightly soiled.* The text in all of the publications is in French, but the cover titles are in English, all with the subtitle: "A Weekly Publication devoted to Border History." The dime-novels, published by Street & Smith in New York, represented one of the most significant tools responsible for the canonization of William Cody into the lexicon of contemporary mythology. "Buffalo Bill and his national entertainment were the first to effectively capitalize on the merchandising of the Wild West, with dime novels, souvenir books, . . . programs . . . The art of slick promotion owes a great deal to Cody's master promoters and merchandisers" (Buffalo Bill/ Legend, p. 3).
**Est: $1,000-$1,200. (10)**

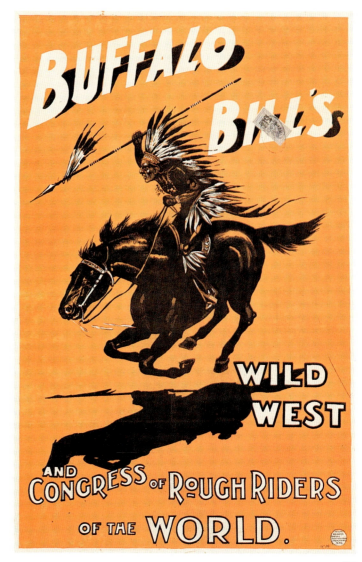

## ANONYMOUS (continued)

**96. Buffalo Bill's Wild West.** 1905.
Artist: **Arthur Jule Goodman (?-1926)**
20$^1$/$_4$ x 30 in./51.5 x 76.2 cm
Imp. Chaix, Paris
Cond A–/Slight tears at edges.
Ref: PAI-XXIII, 173 (var)
This fine Sepia-toned portrait of Chief Walks Under
The Ground was "drawn from life" by Goodman (no
relation to the A.J. Goodman Cody's oldest sister
Julia married), a Cleveland-born painter commis-
sioned for many of the show's posters. His portrait of
Cody, made for his fan King Edward VII of England,
now hangs in Buckingham Palace. Chaix, France's
leading theatrical lithographer at the turn of the century,
was one of the Wild West Show's two main French
printers. *This is the French version.*
**Est: $2,000-$2,500.**

**97. Buffalo Bill's Wild West.** 1905.
18$^1$/$_2$ x 28$^1$/$_2$ in./47 x 72.4 cm
Imp. Weiners/Chas. Wall, Paris
Cond A–/Unobtrusive folds.
The Native Americans in the Wild West posters (and in
the show itself) were always treated with great respect.
They were given top billing, along with the cowboys,
and portrayed in the posters with an air of dignity, be
it through warm, stoic portraiture, or, as seen here, as
a fearsome, though not grotesquely exaggerated
nemesis in the battle for Plains' supremacy. Cody
insisted that only authentic tribe members participate
and that the material in which they appeared be historically accurate and respectful.
**Est: $1,700-$2,000.**

**98. Huron County Fair.** 1916.
27$^7$/$_8$ x 42 in./70.8 x 106.7 cm
Fair Publishing, Norwalk, Ohio
Cond A–/Unobtrusive folds.
Much like their counterparts at Donaldson Litho. in
Kentucky (*see* PAI-XXX, 217 & XXXIII, 158) the Fair
Publishing House of Norwalk, Ohio, promotes their
lithographic rural homespin with a "sample full sheet
poster" that, were it not for the sample stamp inked
at the center of the poster, would do quite nicely to
whatever county affair one might choose to promote.
**Est: $1,000-$1,200.**

**99. King Pin Tailoring: Three Posters.** ca. 1914.
Each: 17$^1$/$_2$ x 21 in./44.5 x 53.3 cm
Sterking-Smythe Company, Chicago
Cond A–/Slight stains in borders. On display boards.
A tony trio of advertisements for a purveyor of fashion
with a pithy name, a penchant for a clever turn of a
promotional phrase and an utmost dedication to style.
Whether you're a "Toppy Dresser" in need of a trendsetting chapeau or a fashion plate looking to impress
in a three-piece suit, King Pin could satisfy your tailoring needs. And seeing as they weren't slouches in the
promotional department, it comes as no surprise that
they provided verso space for fabric samples.
**Est: $700-$900.** (3)

**100. Barnum & Bailey/Joie & Jupiter/Oxford.** 1903.
39 x 30$^1$/$_4$ in./99 x 77 cm
Imp. Courmont Frères, Paris
Cond B/Slight tears, largely at vertical fold.
Ref: PAI-XIV, 24
Horses taking on the hurdles, both mounted and rider-
less, are featured in this Barnum and Bailey design
provided by Strobridge Lithography to the Courmont
Frères firm. The one-sheet, which looks quite a bit
like two half-sheet posters put together, provides the

prowess particulars of Joie, Jupiter and Oxford, three
of Barnum & Bailey's esteemed stable of "High
Jumpers." It's interesting to note the dress and riding
style of the woman atop the gelding Oxford—even
though she's a circus performer, she still rides side-
saddle in the ankle-length skirt that was then *de rigeur*.
**Est: $1,400-$1,700.**

**99**

**The Barnum & Bailey Greatest Show on Earth**

JOIE & JUPITER, LES FAMEUX PONEYS-SAUTEURS
Avec un Record de 2 Metres 12% en Hauteur et de 9 Metres N
Longueur par dessus Deux Haies de 1 Metre 30 cent ½.

OXFORD LE CHAMPION-SAUTEUR en longueur et en hauteur

**LES PLUS GRANDIOSES & PLUS FASCINANTS SPECTACLES DU MONDE**

**100**

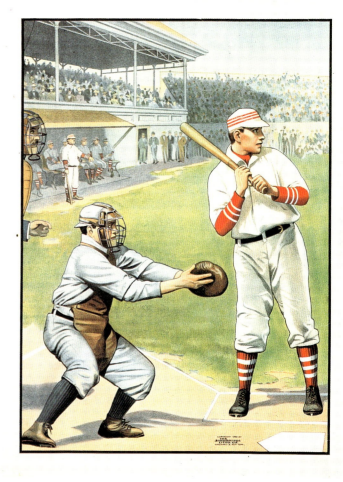

**101**

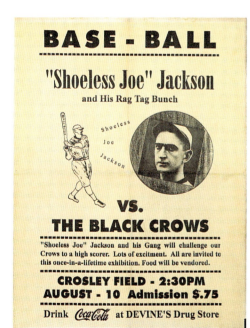

# BASE - BALL

## "Shoeless Joe" Jackson
### and His Rag Tag Bunch

Shoeless Joe Jackson

## VS.

## THE BLACK CROWS

"Shoeless Joe" Jackson and his Gang will challenge our
Crows to a high scorer. Lots of excitment. All are invited to
this once-in-a-lifetime exhibition. Food will be vendored.

### CROSLEY FIELD - 2:30PM
### AUGUST - 10 Admission $.75

Drink Coca-Cola at DEVINE'S DRUG STORE

**102**

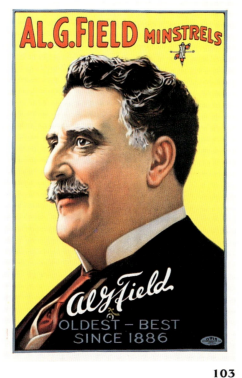

**AL.G.FIELD MINSTRELS**

*Al.G.Field.*

OLDEST - BEST
SINCE 1886

**103**

dal disrupted the sport. Shoeless Joe Jackson, whose
lifetime batting average is the third highest in the history of the game, and seven Chicago White Sox team-
mates—"eight men out" they were to be called—were
accused of throwing the 1919 World Series. The eight
were cleared in court, but banned from pro ball—Jackson included, though he was to maintain his innocence until his death. He did continue playing for
several years, leading a "Rag Tag Bunch" on "barn-
storming" tours against bush-league outfits like these
Black Crows in Cincinnati. But in 1923 he was caught
sneaking back into higher-paid leagues by playing
under a false name; after serving several days in jail,
he hung up the mitt for good and retired to the dry-
cleaning business. Two great American institutions are
represented here—baseball and Coca-Cola, whose
logo hasn't changed, even if the recipe has.
**Est: $1,700-$2,000.**

**103. Al. G. Field Minstrels/Al. G. Field.**
27¼ x 41 in./69.2 x 104 cm
Otis Lithograph Co., Cleveland, Ohio
Cond A–/Slight stains at folds.
One of the best-known minstrel impresarios was Al G.
Field of Columbus, Ohio. As stated on this poster, he
founded the Al. G. Field Greater Minstrels in 1886,
presenting an annual tour that would kick off at the
State Fair in Columbus, and then fan out over the Mid-
west, East and South. Vaudeville and burlesque would
ultimately bring an end to what was America's first
indigenous forms of mass entertainment, but Field
would be remembered as a consummate showman,
capable of putting together a show of spectacular proportions. And here, we actually are afforded a look at
the man behind popularizing this oft-debated diversion in a rare and humanizing poster portrait.
**Est: $1,400-$1,700.**

**101. Batter Up!** 1905.
18½ x 24¼ in./47 x 61.6 cm
Strobridge Litho., Cincinnati, Ohio
Cond A–/Slight scrape at top. Framed.
Hold on. Something's wrong with this picture. Where
are all the glaring advertisements that should be
pasted on every available inch of open space in this
ball park? Where are the luxury boxes and amusement
park diversions? Where are the Rally Monkeys? Could
this be what baseball looked like when the game mat-
tered more than the business it generated? How unfortunate that so much of the game's easy grace has all

but disappeared in a maelstrom of corporate sponsor-
ship and league mismanagement. A wonderfully sim-
plistic and straightforward lithographic vision of an
emerging American staple that treats its subject with
the dignity and respect it deserves.
**Est: $1,700-$2,000.**

**102. Base-Ball/"Shoeless Joe" Jackson.** ca. 1925.
18 x 23½ in./45.6 x 59.7 cm
Cond B+/Slight tears at folds.
Ref: PAI-XVII, 71
Back when a hyphen still disrupted "base-ball," scan-

**104**

**105**

**106**

## ANONYMOUS (continued)

### 104. Al. G. Field Minstrels/Nick Hufford.
26³/₄ x 40¹/₈ in./68 x 103.2 cm
Otis Lithograph Co., Cleveland, Ohio
Cond A–/Unobtrusive folds.
Ref: PAI-XXXIII, 142
Regardless of one's adherence to political correctness, advertising Nick Hufford—one of the Field cavalcade of stars, shown in this before-and-after "blacking up" pairing—as "One Loose Page From The Book Of Fun" is textbook chicanery at its finest.
**Est: $1,400-$1,700.**

### 105. Neil O'Brien Super Minstrels/Jack Weir.
20¹/₄ x 28¹/₄ in./51.4 x 71.7 cm
Strobridge Litho, Cincinnati, Ohio
Cond B/Some stains.
A previously seen poster refers to Neil O'Brien as the creator of "progressive minstrelsy" (*see* PAI-XXXIV, 143). Too bad that this oxymoronic-sounding movement wasn't better documented because it seems to have eluded the historians' pen. However, this Strobridge creation serves to remind us that even though we may never know how this forward-thinking vision of cultural mimicry may have manifested itself, Jack Weir was definitely a part of it, seen here embracing his inner minstrel.
**Est: $1,200-$1,500.**

### 106. Neil O'Brien Super Minstrels/Matt. Keefe. 1915.
20 x 29³/₄ in./50.8 x 75.5 cm
Strobridge Litho, Cincinnati, Ohio
Cond B+/Slight tears and stains in borders.
Another member of the progressive Neil O'Brien troupe—a yodeler by the name of Matt Keefe. Chances are likely that this distinctive looking fellow donned black-face when it came time to share the talent that earned him the "America's Greatest" title with an appreciative audience. But as seen here without an application of burnt cork, he certainly brings an aura of class to a rather rambunctious art form.
**Est: $1,200-$1,500.**

### 107. The Girl Raffles. 1906.
18¹/₄ x 27³/₄ in./46.3 x 70.6 cm
Strobridge Litho, Cincinnati
Cond A.
The bottom dialogue in this graphic peek into the early-20th century theatrical scene is quintessential tough talk on parade: "We'll get you for this!"/"Well, he's got you now!" Hokum so unfiltered it almost makes you want to stand up and cheer. Oh, that tomboy Raffles has done it again, naturally with the assistance of her handsome beefcake sidekick, whose name might as well be Chinworth McStud. It is, none-

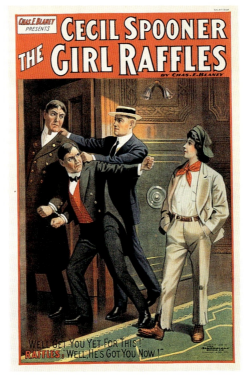

**107**

theless, a pleasant alternative to see a woman as the brains behind a crime-fighting team. Cecil Spooner, the actress who brought Raffles to life, was a minor star, working on-stage, in early film and extending her career into television with appearances on "The Lone Ranger." She also was a dancer of some renown, performing a suspiciously Loie Fuller sounding number called "The Kaleidoscope."
**Est: $1,000-$1,200.**

### 108. Under Southern Skies.
40⁷/₈ x 80¹/₂ in./103.8 x 204.5 cm
Metropolitan Printing Co., New York
Cond A.
Ref: PAI-XXXII, 28
Lottie Blair Parker, the author of the melodramatic theatricality being advertised in this 3-sheet poster, is probably best remembered for the film version of her play "Way Down East"—casually mentioned as part of the text here—starring Lillian Gish and directed by D. W. Griffith. However, the playwright was apparently never at a loss for the dramatic, as is evidenced by this overwrought wedding day encounter used to promotional ends for her latest, "Under Southern Skies." Perhaps Ms. Parker's intent was to work her way around the compass with tales of women wronged,

**108**

but that answer is lost to history as "East" stands as her sole documented work.
**Est: $1,500-$1,800.**

### 109. McIntyre and Heath. 1913.
40 x 83⁵/₈ in./101.6 x 212.4 cm
Strobridge Litho. Co., Cincinnati
Cond A–/Slight tears at folds.
The stage is a fickle mistress. For even though you may have packed 'em in during your time in the limelight, the constant influx of new talent almost guarantees that you will be all but forgotten to the bulk of future generations. Such would be the case of McIntyre & Heath, an influential dance team—seen here in 3-sheet portrait form from the later days of their careers—

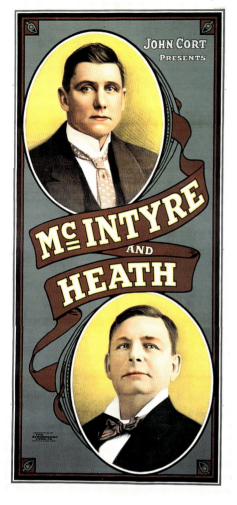

**111**

**109**　　　　　　　　　　　　　　　**110**

**112**

whose names ring no celebrity bells save in the minds of the most academic. But that wasn't always the case. James McIntyre (1857-?) of Kenosha, Wisconsin and Thomas K. Heath (1852-?) hailing from Philadelphia joined forces in the spring of 1874 in San Antonio, Texas. The well-known minstrel combo popularized a dance move known as the syncopated "buck and wing" —a maneuver derived from a boisterous, spontaneous jig done by poor Irish immigrants in the Carolinas— with McIntyre even going so far as to say that it was Heath and he that had introduced the buck and wing to American audiences. McIntyre told a reporter that he had learned it by "watching Negroes in the South soon after the Civil War." The dance was done to a tune called "Rabbit" and the team introduced the number at Tony Pastor's Theater in New York in 1879. Never one to shy away from bragging rights, McIntyre also claimed that this was the first time ragtime had been presented on the legitimate stage.
Est: $1,500-$1,800.

**110. The Girl From Utah.** 1914.
40 x 83⁷/₈ in./101.6 x 213 cm
Strobridge Litho. Co., Cincinnati
Cond A–/Slight tears at folds and seams.

It's hard to imagine, but this 3-sheet piece of good-natured promotional fluff touts a show that would permanently alter the face of the Broadway musical. Though it hardly seemed like an earthshaking event, "The Girl From Utah" provided an entry onto the Great White Way for one of its greatest composers. The play, an amusing trifle that traced the adventures of an American girl who flees to London rather than become a rich Mormon's latest wife, was immensely popular in Great Britain and imported into the States by Charles Frohman. But, seeing as British high society rarely arrived at a theater until intermission, London musicals of the period typically saved their best material for the last act. These shows needed revision for New York audiences, who would arrive for the first curtain and leave early if the proceedings didn't live up to expectations. Frohman hired Jerome Kern and lyricist Herbert Reynolds to write five new numbers for the lackluster first act. Their delightful ballad, "They Didn't Believe Me," with a fresh melody that defies time, became a tremendous hit. When Julia Sanderson and Donald Brian introduced Kern's song, they became one of the most popular stage duos of their time with a sound that pointed to the future of the Broadway musical.
Est: $1,500-$1,800.

**111. Rose Marie.**
39⁷/₈ x 79¹/₄ in./101.2 x 201.2 cm
Taylors Printers, Wombell-Yorks
Cond A–/Unobtrusive folds.
An uncredited design that stunningly captures the Great White North spectacle and musical theater schmaltz of *Rose Marie*, the Arthur Hammerstein adaptation of the same-named operetta by Rudolf Friml, Otto A. Harbach and Oscar Hammerstein II, an immensely popular play that originally opened on September 2, 1924 at Broadway's Imperial Theater and ran for 558 performances. The story of a gal and her Mountie (a small character in the stage version that was expanded for the movie) is probably best known from the 1936 film adaptation, highlighted by the most memorable pairing of "America's Singing Sweethearts," Jeanette MacDonald and Nelson Eddy, and their glorious "Indian Love Call" duet. And with classically cheesy lines such as Mr. Eddy introducing himself to Ms. Mac-Donald with a hale and hearty, "Your dream prince, reporting for duty," that's precisely as it should be.
Est: $1,700-$2,000.

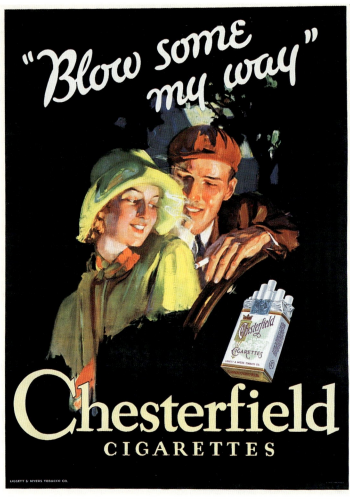

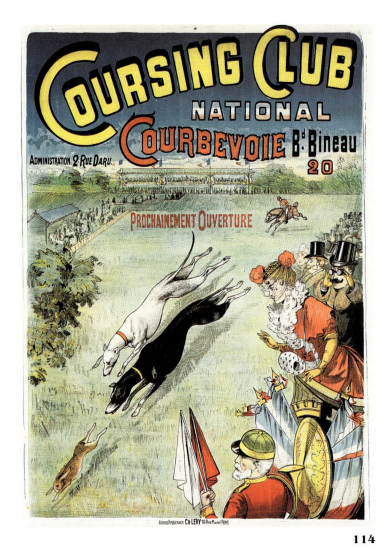

113

114

## ANONYMOUS (continued)

**112. Hart Schaffner & Marx: Five Posters.** 1910.
Artist: **S. N. Abbott**
Each: 15⁵/₈ x 23 in./39.6 x 58.4 cm
Cond A/P. Slight tears and crease at bottom of one
image.
Ref: PAI-XXVI, 118 (var)
From first glance, it's easy to see that Abbott's five
vibrant designs for Hart, Schaffner & Marx—the "Makers
of Fine Clothes for Men"—weren't concerned in the
least with showing the style of clothing available to the
consumer. No, he was more concerned with setting
the proper tone, showing the classical tie between
fashion and society—to underscore the solid tradition
and quality of the wearer and the clothes he chooses
to wear. With military proposals, colonial stability and
intriguing dramatics, as well as with more to-the-point
beach and evening wear scenes, Abbott implicitly infers
that success, it would seem, as well as a certain clothing line, are two things that are never out of style. *Rare!*
**Est: $3,000-$4,000.** (5)

**113. Chesterfield Cigarettes/"Blow Some My Way".**
30⁵/₈ x 41 in./77.8 x 104.2 cm
Cond A–/Unobtrusive folds.
Ah, the sweet smell of secondhand smoke. Well, one
really can't blame this uncredited designer retained by
the Liggett & Myers Tobacco Co. for romanticizing smoking in an era where the benefits of a nicotinic lifestyle
were more often than not touted as the healthy choice.
As always, Chesterfield comes across as the drag for
the in-crowd, the cigarette for anyone who was anyone.
**Est: $2,000-$2,500.**

**114. Coursing Club.** ca. 1898.
35 x 48 in./88.7 x 122 cm
Imp. Ch. Lévy, Paris
Cond A–/Unobtrusive folds.
Posters for early organized greyhound races are quite
rare, and this action-packed promotion for the Coursing Club at Courbevoire paints quite the lithographic
picture of canine competition. It's quite a match-up,
although one can't help but feel a bit sorry for the live

115

bunny bait being used in the days prior to its elec-
tronic hare-apparent.
**Est: $2,000-$2,500.**

**115. Corsets Baleinine Incassables.**
23¹/₂ x 31¹/₄ in./59.8 x 79.4 cm
Imp. Oscar Mayer, Paris
Cond B+/Slight tears at folds and edges.
At the turn of the century, all women wore corsets,
whether they were generously proportioned or as
skinny as a beanpole. Here we have a belle of the
epoque cinching herself in with a smile with a corset
whose stays are made out of unbreakable whalebone
for "softness, elegance, and long wear."
**Est: $800-$1,000.**

116

**116. Concert Périco.**
15 x 23¹/₈ x 38 x 58.7 cm
Imp. Eugène Verneau, Paris
Cond B+/Slight tears at folds and edges. Framed.
As close to Chéret as you can get without changing
your name to Jules. The designer—identified with a
"J. P." monogram—obviously knew how the popular
tastes of the day were running and was commissioned
to promote this lesser cabaret with the same sort of
breezy aplomb that would have cost considerably
more coming from a better known posterist. Still, all

**118**

**117**

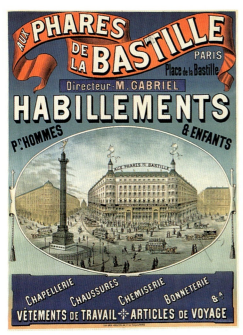

**119**

**121**

Der Elefanten-Gott „Jenny"

Anbetung des Wunder-Elefanten „Jenny"
im Jenny-Tempel in Tangore

**120**

the elements are precisely in place: lyric grace, flirtatious revelry, a promise of humor and a mention of
the weekday prices for refreshments.
Est: $1,200-$1,500.

**117. Cycles Gladiator.** ca. 1895.
53 x 38¹/₂ in./134.6 x 97.8 cm
Imp. G. Massais, Paris
Cond A–/Restored lower margin. Framed.
Ref: Bicycle Posters, 42; Petite Reine, 47; Ailes, p. 11;
    Musée d'Affiche, 22; Reims, 154; PAI-XXXIII, 33A
This is, without question, one of the most sensational
designs for a bicycle ever created, yet the artist hid his
name—the outlines of his initials can barely be seen
in the lower right corner. Even Alexandre Henriot, the
great collector who organized the huge 1896 poster
show at Reims, was unable to credit him. Many of the
Gladiator posters proclaimed the bike to be "Sans
Egale"—without equal. The same can be said when
comparing this design to the thousands of other bicycle posters of the period.
Est: $20,000-$25,000.

**118. Wilson Tullet.** ca. 1889.
17³/₈ x 22⁷/₈ in./44.2 x 58.2 cm
Imp. Charles Levy, Paris
Cond B+/Unobtrusive folds.

You'd think that historians would have been consid-
erate enough to at least remember the existence of
Wilson Tullet. I mean, just look at him for Pete's sake
—he doesn't even break a sweat as he stands cockily
atop a ball that's balanced on a trapeze that's suspended high above the circus itself. Even if that's a
bit of lithographic braggadocio, it seems like such a
stunt would be worth mentioning even if it happened
within the confines of the Big Top. Also, take note of
the various implements of equilibrium that have been
woven into the name of the "Aerial Genius."
Est: $1,200-$1,500.

**119. Aux Phares de la Bastille.** ca. 1896.
28⁷/₈ x 38⁷/₈ in./73.5 x 98.8 cm
Lith. Van-Geleyn, Paris
Cond A–/Unobtrusive folds. Framed.
Ref: PAI-XXX, 355
A wonderful Paris street scene from the 1890s—as
much a vivid document for the pre-automotive lifestyle
of the City of Lights as it is a great poster for the Aux
Phares de la Bastille department store clothing sale it
was created to bring to the attention of the pedestrian
public. And if the proof is in the poster, that's where
everyone who's anyone is headed.
Est: $1,400-$1,700.

**120. "Jenny"/Der Elefanten-Gott.**
32¹/₄ x 45 in./82 x 114 cm
Cond B+/Slight tears and stains at edges.
Although she might appear a tad terse in this poster,
Jenny was doubtlessly a benevolent elephant god,
overseeing her acolytes with compassion and wisdom.
Seen as she exits her temple located in the South
Indian capital of Thanjavur, this pachyderm is deified
grace incarnate. Sadly, even though the elephant has
always been a huge draw to the circus going public, no
specific reference to either the initially-identified artist
"H. H" nor Jenny herself could be found.
Est: $1,200-$1,500.

**121. Hurtu/Cycles Français.**
39¹/₂ x 52³/₈ in./100.3 x 133 cm
Imp. Charles Verneau, Paris
Cond A–/Slight tears at edges.
An advertisement for the Hurtu brand of pedal pow-
ered transport that states right up front that Hurtu is the
"French bike." You'd literally have to be blind not to
notice that was the gist of the uncredited designer's
promotional thrust—from the sedately bustling Champs
Elysées to the Arche de Triomphe to the fashionably
pristine cyclist, everything is as Francophilic as could
be. In addition to a socially-aware setting, the design
also makes mention of the fact that Hurtu bicycles
were exhibited out of competition in the Liege 1899
Universal Exposition—a major distinction—and were in
fact members of the jury.
Est: $1,500-$1,800.

122

123

124

125

## ANONYMOUS (continued)

**122. Fête des Fleurs.** 1891.
34⅝ x 47⅝ in./88 x 121 cm
Imp. Ch. Lévy, Paris
Cond A–/Unobtrusive folds.
An evocative, lively, colorful Belle Epoque image for a floral festival in Paris' Bois de Boulogne. This fragrant event, whose profits went to the less fortunate citizens of Paris, was something of a precursor to the Rose Bowl's "Tournament of Roses" parade, with its star attraction being a procession of blossom-decorated vehicles. 1891 was quite a year for the Lévy printing firm: In addition to producing this lovely anonymous design, this was also the year when they printed Toulouse-Lautrec's classic "Moulin Rouge" poster.
**Est: $2,000-$2,500.**

**123. Remington.** 1908.
38⅛ x 58 in./97 x 147.2 cm
O. de Rycker, Bruxelles-Forest
Cond B+/Slight tears at folds.
Ref: PAI-XXVI, 122
A secretary gazes down affectionately at her new Remington Standard 10 typewriter, both radiating confidence in the glow of the afternoon sun. The front-stroke machine, introduced in 1908, replaced the less efficient, more troublesome under-stroke design of earlier models.
**Est: $1,500-$1,800.**

**124. La Italo Argentina.**
Each: 14 x 20¼ in./35.5 x 51.5 cm
Scherrer Hnos., Buenos Aires
Cond A–/Slight stains at edges.
These two in-store displays for an Argentine line of carbonated soft drinks proves that a pretty face goes quite a bit further down the path of selling a product than the product itself. In fact, they don't even bother with any sort of lithographic refreshment. The allegorical message couldn't be any clearer: Regardless of whether your tastes ran more towards the unbridled fire of a gypsy or the refinement of a sophisticated socialite, Italo Argentina had a beverage suited perfectly to every individual.
**Est: $1,000-$1,200.** (2)

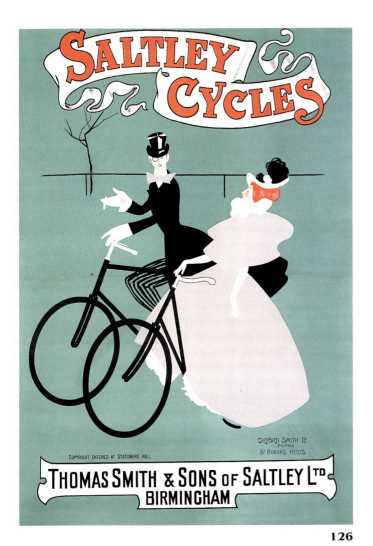

**126**

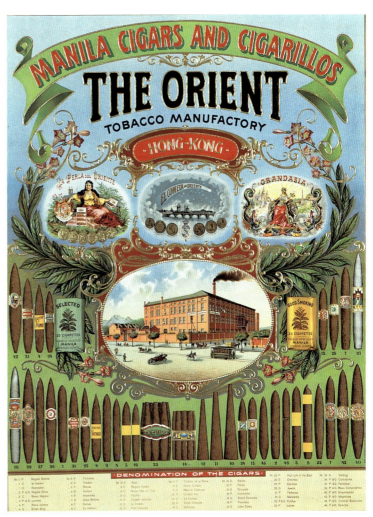

**127**

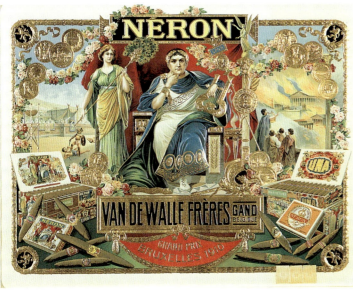

**128**

The manufacturers of the Saltley bicycle obviously weren't into promoting the technical specifics of their pedal-powered transport. What they were going after was the sense of sophistication and class that came with riding a Saltley. And they achieved their goal in spades thanks to this uncredited designer, who places his pedaling sophisticates in the center of a sparse 2-sheet jade landscape as they put more effort into their detached attitudes than they do into powering their rides onward. *Rare!*
Est: $5,000-$6,000.

**127. Orient Tobacco.**
25 x 31$^1/_2$ in./63.5 x 80 cm
Gebr. Klingenberg, Detmold (Germany)
Cond A–/Slight stains at edges. Framed.
Ref: PAI-XXXIV, 204
Gold embossing gives this promotion for the Orient Tobacco firm a 3-D effect, lending the Manila leaf nicotinic indulgence an even greater sense of opulent sophistication. With metal strips top and bottom and their Hong Kong factory presented as the centerpiece of the tobacco concern, forty-six different types and sizes of cigars are shown on the poster, with each name shown at the design's bottom—names like "British King," "First Cheroots," "Little Dukes" and "Pearl of the Orient."
Est: $2,000-$2,500.

**125. Derby Dog Biscuits.**
23$^3/_8$ x 18$^1/_4$ in./59.2 x 46.3 cm
R. Allen & Son, Nottingham
Cond A–/Slight tears at edges. Framed.
A canine's work is never done. But if you're employed by a clown whose going to work you and your fellow puppy jumpers on your routines regardless of location and time of day, it's good to know that he's got the good sense to entice you with the treat that's literally going to have you jumping through hoops: Greensmith's Derby Dog Biscuits. An amusingly peculiar point of purchase board with hanger still in place.
Est: $1,200-$1,500.

**126. Saltley Cycles.**
55$^1/_2$ x 79$^3/_8$ in./141 x 201.5 cm
Oxford Smith, St. Albans
Cond B/Tears, largely at paper edges and folds.

**128. Néron/Van de Walle Frères.** ca. 1911.
31$^1/_4$ x 23$^3/_4$ in./79.3 x 60.3 cm
Hermann Schött, Rheydt
Cond A. Framed.
Ref: PAI-XXIV, 5
This poster's virtue is its sheer excess. One feels that if this Belgian cigar firm could have staged a full Roman triumph for winning the grand prize at the 1910 International Exposition in Brussels, it would have. The brand name alone could hardly go further in associating the cigar with arrogant power and luxury; one almost imagines Nero (*Néron*, who here looks remarkably like a later emperor, Napoleon, in the portrait by Gérard), lighting up off some burning bit of Rome and inhaling both cigar and city with satisfaction. Vignettes of his infamous recital and of gladiatorial combat fill what little space remains between the cigars, garlands and medals whose heavy gold embossing creates an extraordinary three-dimensional effect.
Est: $2,000-$2,500.

**129**

**130**

**131**

**132**

**133**

**ANONYMOUS (continued)**

**129. Radine/Passage Jouffroy.**
23³/₄ x 31 in./60.2 x 79 cm
Imp. Ch. Levy, Paris
Cond B/Slight tears and stains, largely at edges.
You'd imagine that since the J. O. Radine emporium, located at 41 Passage Jouffroy in the heart of Paris' fashionable 9th arrondissement, is the "central depot for every Russian article" that the pictured shop might receive a bit more poster play than being relegated to the upper right quadrant. Still, the detail paid to the shop in minutia is magnificent, as is the overall sumptuous impression left by the design.
**Est: $1,200-$1,500.**

**130. Régénérateur de Mme. S. A. Allen.**
32 x 45³/₈ in.81.3 x 115.3 cm
Strobridge Lith. Co., London
Cond B+/Slight tears at folds.
Now that is a serious head of hair! And though we have no real way of knowing whether or not this is Madame Allen herself displaying the effects of her hair regenerator—a product, by the way, that promises to "return bleached or color-treated hair to the luster and beauty of its youth"—it's a sure bet that this nearly-photographically rendered coif sent more than a few tress-challenged consumers bolting for the shelves of their nearest beauty emporium. It's important to note that although the credit for this poster is given to Strobridge London that there was never a Strobridge printing plant set up in England, merely a sales office.
**Est: $1,500-$1,800.**

**131. Veuve Amiot.**
14³/₈ x 19¹/₂ in./36.5 x 49.6 cm
Lith. G. Bataille, Paris
Cond A–/Slight creases at edges.
Ref: PAI-XXX, 357
Not only does this devastating Byzantine Delilah want the inhabitants of France to drink deep from the chal-

ice of Veuve Amiot sparkling wine she delicately proffers whilst sitting pretty in mosaic grandeur. No, she wants to break into the Chinese market as well. There are two basic techniques used by every marketing division attempting to get a handhold in a foreign market: find sounds from the language in question which most closely approximates the name of the product or brag about how great the company is in terms a particular country will appreciate. Veuve Amiot has chosen the latter: the four characters at left, from top to bottom, promote the long-standing tradition of the enterprise ("eternity"), its prosperous nature ("abundance") and the appeal of a product not produced at home ("Western Company").
**Est: 1,000-$1,200.**

**132. Bouillie "G. Marquès".**
31 x 46⁷/₈ in./78.7 x 119 cm
Lith. J. Javanaud, Angoul∏me
Cond B/Slight creasing; tears at folds.
There's no sign of smut in this G. Marquès fungicide pulp poster, just a beautiful pastoral lifestyle graced

with the porcelain doll beauty of a lovely French farmer's daughter secure in the fact that her grapes are sure to remain mildew-free. A highly persuasive poster for a highly decorated product.
**Est: $1,500-$1,800.**

**133. Da Capo Zigaretten.** ca. 1916.
34⁵/₈ x 46¹/₂ x 88 x 118.2 cm
J. Aberle, Berlin
Cond A.
Once upon a time in Germany, a state trust controlled the import of cheap tobacco from various foreign sources that was then allocated to manufacturers who made the cigarettes in-country in order for them to be labeled "German." This monopoly's practice earned the product a lousy reputation. Da Capo cigarettes, however, wants the nicotinic consumer to know that they purchase their own tobacco, making it "trust-free" and quite obviously superior. And they do so without a single smoldering piece of evidence, opting instead to display the standards of a united nation of smokers.
**Est: $800-$1,000.**

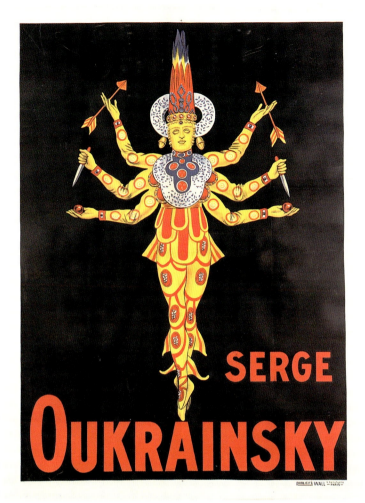

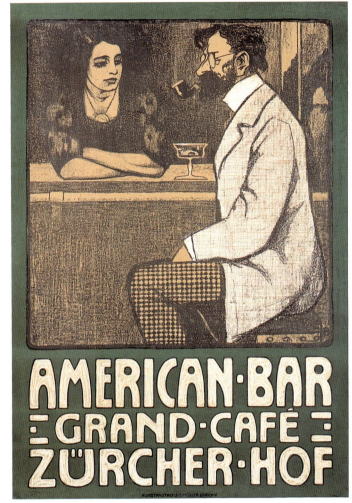

**134**

**135**

**136**

**137**

### 135. American Bar.
25$^7$/$_8$ x 39 in./65.7 x 99 cm
J. C. Müller, Zurich
Cond B+/Unobtrusive tears at edges and in bottom
text area.
More known for their banking community than visiting
Yankee esquires, the poster for Zurich's American Bar
associates drowsy decadence with serious consumption, commingling to create an atmospheric nod to
top-shelf sedation. *Rare!*
**Est: $2,200-$2,800.**

### 136. Gran Show de la Risa.
29$^1$/$_4$ x 43$^1$/$_8$ in./74.3 x 109.5 cm
Cond A–/Slight tears at folds and edges.
Why mince words when you have a cavalcade of comedic luminaries in poster portrait format to promote
your film compilation? Why not just tell it like it is?
That's just what this anonymous designer did, letting
the name of the "most extraordinary program of comic
shorts presented to date"—the "Big Laugh Show" in
case their was any doubt—speak what the Spanish-
speaking film-going public already expected from the
likes of Charlie Chaplin, Laurel and Hardy, Harold Lloyd
and many, many other less-remembered funny men.
**Est: $1,000-$1,200.**

### 137. Gothard Express/Wagons-Lits. 1927.
25$^1$/$_2$ x 39 in./64.7 x 99 cm
Orell Fussli, Zurich
Cond B+/Slight tears and stains.
Ref: Wagons-Lits, 185
Not precisely what one imagines when thoughts of
train travel drift through the one's mind. And that
would decidedly be the point of this swank black-and-
brown parlor-on-the-ties design from the Swiss Federal
Railways and the Wagons-Lits Company for their opulent Pullman service aboard the Gothard Express. A
wonderful slice of elegant 1920s travel.
**Est: $1,500-$1,800.**

### 134. Serge Oukrainsky.
47 x 63 in./119.5 x 160 cm
Publicité Wall, Paris
Cond B+/Restored margins.
Ref: Philips I, 24
Serge Oukrainsky (1885-1972) and Andreas Pavley
were co-directors and choreographers of the Pavley-
Oukrainsky Ballet, based in Chicago, from 1916 to
1931. Theirs was a ballet style full of theatricality and
many of their performances featured bacchanals and
Oriental opulence. And this poster reflects that pro-
pensity: It's Oukrainsky as deity Dagon in the baccha-
nalia from the opera *Samson et Dalila* who is seen in
this extravagant work. It's not inconceivable that
Oukrainsky, who often designed the costumes and
sets, also designed this poster.
**Est: $1,700-$2,000.**

**138**

**139**

IMP. GERIN, DIJON-PARIS

**140**

**141**

## ANONYMOUS (continued)

**138. Anchor Line.** ca. 1925.
$19^5/_8$ x $25^5/_8$ in./50 x 65 cm
American Lithography Co., N.Y.
Cond B/Slight tears and stains at paper edges.
The Anchor Line, Scotland's oldest steamship company, enlists the seafaring solidity of the *Caledonia* to promote their Glasgow to New York run. Sailing on her maiden voyage less than two weeks after her completion in 1925, the *Caledonia* could carry over one-thousand-six-hundred passengers in her three classes of accommodations. In September of 1939, the British government converted the ship into an armed merchant cruiser and renamed her the *Scotstown*. Less than one year later, on June 13, 1940, the *Scotstown* was torpedoed and sunk by the German sub, U-25, taking six lives to the bottom with her.
**Est: $1,400-$1,700.**

**139. Phoscao.**
$47^1/_8$ x $63^1/_2$ in./119.6 x 161 cm
Imp. J. E. Goossens, Lille
Cond B+/Unobtrusive folds; slight stains at edges.
A stylish and blissfully unharried promotion for Phoscao, a powerful restorative beverage that's as sweet as it is beneficial. Just a wonderful promotion that does very little in the way of product placement, but more than makes up for it with its grace and allusion to attainable lifestyle through precise consumerism. *Rare!*
**Est: $2,000-$2,500.**

**140. Terrot.**
$30^3/_8$ x $46^1/_4$ in./77 x 117.3 cm
Imp. Gerin, Dijon-Paris
Cond A–/Unobtrusive folds.
What need is there be for textual overstatement when an image could create all the bragging rights a product would ever want? Such is the case in this Terrot promotion—created by an artist solely identified with the initials "T.D.T"—featuring a spiffy rider hitting the open Art Deco road atop his motorcycle of choice. The Terrot company was a successful manufacturer of bicycles

during the 1890s, but the firm really came into its own with motorcycles as of 1901, remaining in business until the 1960s with one of the best makes in France.
**Est: $800-$1,000.**

**141. 6th Commemorative National Equestrian Exhibition/Tokyo.** 1928.
$21^1/_4$ x $30^3/_8$ in./54 x 77 cm
Nissel Printer
Cond B+/Slight tears and stains at edges.
An equestrian nearly as chiseled as his steed trumpets

in the eight-hour National Horse Exhibition at Tokyo's Daikiren Armory with well-defined Grecian sensibilities. The event, sponsored by the Imperial Horse Racing Society and the Imperial Equestrian Society, was also supported by the Ministry of Agriculture and Forestry and the Ministry of War. With the auspices of the military involved, this striking design takes on another altogether nationalistic layer. The following year,1929, was the 3rd year of the reigning Showa Emperor, known in the West as Hirohito. Japan had already defeated Russia in the Russo-Japanese war,

alb. jarach et p. chambry

**142**

**143**

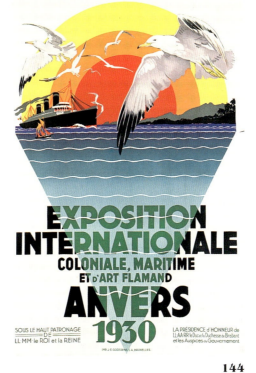

**144**

**145**

becoming the first Asian nation to defeat a modern Western nation. The military factions in Japan were already in control, and expansion into China was seen as crucial to Japan's economic survival. The Japanese army was firmly entrenched in Korea, Taiwan, portions of China and poised to invade Manchuria. After centuries of isolation, Japan had played a rapid game of "catch-up" with the West. They took the best the West had to offer: education and naval technique from the British; medicine, government and army technique from the Prussians, which still depended on cavalry. The horse was an essential and valuable vehicle of war, and Japan would put it to good use in their expansion into the continent.
**Est: $1,000-$1,200.**

**142. Notre Agenda est Paru.** 1927.
29¼ x 10¾ in./74.2 x 27.2 cm
Alb. Jarach et P. Chambry
Cond B+/Vertical fold. Framed.
Metallic gold ink gives this Art Deco design for a 1927 date book by Jarach & Chambry a special appeal and sets it apart as the perfect organizational accoutrement for the smart set.
**Est: $1,500-$1,800.**

**143. Stoewer/8 Zyl.** ca. 1928.
34½ x 46⅛ in./87.7 x 117 cm
Kunstanstalt Weylandt, Berlin
Cond A.

In 1899, the Stoewer brothers, Bernhard Jr. and Emil, recognized the automobile's great future, even though at that time it was regarded as a plaything of the wealthy. Bernhard took control of the technical side, while Emil handled commercial concerns. Until their departure from the company in the 1930s, the brothers made all the decisions concerning the development of their company and, through their trendsetting policies regarding new models, were the driving force behind its rapid growth in the early years. The special thing about the Stoewer concern is that it never was a huge producer, but instead opted to maintain a manageable size. It shone through with technical innovation rather than sheer numbers and this is what makes it interesting to the contemporary motor enthusiast. In 1928, the Stoewer G14 touring car was introduced. Along with their competitor's Horch models, they were the first 8 cylinder German cars.
**Est: $1,200-$1,500.**

**144. Exposition Internationale/Anvers.** 1930.
39⅜ x 58¾ in./99.4 x 149.4 cm
Imp. J. E. Goosens, Bruxelles
Cond B+/Unobtrusive tears at folds.
Ref: PAI-III, 9 (var)
An intriguing fan-shaped design for the Belgian Railways' service to the 1930 Antwerp International Exposition and its focus on colonial, maritime and Flemish

art. Contrasting realistically-conceived seagulls off a splashy, sun-striped concoction, the uncredited designer manages to strike a delicate balance between commerce and conceptualization. *This is the larger format.*
**Est: $1,400-$1,700.**

**145. Learn Esperanto.** 1930.
15 x 22¼ in./38 x 56.5 cm
Cond A.
Esperanto, the artificial language introduced in 1887 and intended by its inventor, Dr. Ludwig L. Zamenhof of Poland, to ease communication between speakers of different languages has never gained any form of widespread international acceptance, though it is taught at schools and universities throughout the world. It is also seen by its practitioners to be an intrinsic element in the banishment of class rule, a language able to break through the barriers of nationalism and oppression. The S.A.T., or "Sennacieca Asocio Tutmonda," a non-nationalist world organization, promotes its global congress with the assistance of hulking envoy of socialist labor, an icon from which the star of universal communication is emitted with single-color clarity. The six letters that appear in the bottom left corner are a tad mysterious: They could be the initials of a collaborative trio of artists, or perhaps they could stand as a textual shorthand for those in the Esperanto know.
**Est: $1,400-$1,700.**

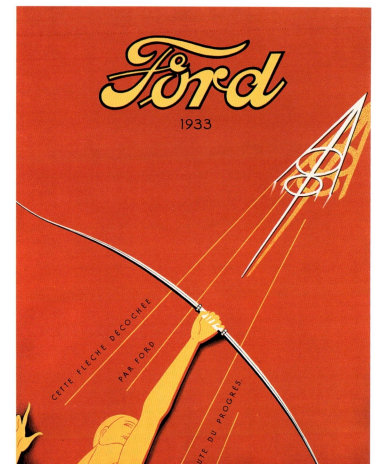

146

147

152

## ANONYMOUS (continued)

**146. Ford 1933.**
30$^1$/$_2$ x 46 in./77.4 x 116.7 cm
Draeger, Paris
Cond A.
Ref: PAI-XXXIV, 158
"Ford lets fly this arrow to show the road of progress."
And what precisely, you may ask, is this evolutionary
automotive indicator? Why that would be the V-8
engine, introduced in 1932, and anonymously shot
forth here for the following year's model with striking
Art Deco classicism. Ford was the first company in
history to successfully cast a V-8 engine block in one
piece. It was many years before Ford's competitors
learned how to mass-produce a reliable V-8; in the
interim, the car and its powerful engine became the
darling of performance-minded motorists worldwide.
**Est: $4,000-$5,000.**

**147. Castrol.**
40$^1$/$_2$ x 26$^3$/$_4$ in./103 x 67.8 cm
Pub. Gianoli & Valentin
Cond B/Slight tears at vertical folds and edges; image
　　　　and colors excellent. Framed.
Ref: Auto Show III, 111; PAI-XXX, 253
While best known for their automotive lubricants, Castrol has produced a wide range of products and services for the past 100 years. Charles Cheers Wakefield
not only set the foundations of a company committed
to premium quality, high performance and leading
edge technology, he was one of the first marketers,
using publicity and promotion to spread the name of
Castrol worldwide. One such tool is seen here in this
point-of-purchase display, which in its advertising days
would have been mounted on board with two vertical
folds to allow it to stand, but has since been mounted
on paper and linen. Announcing that Castrol has been
instrumental in creating "The Open Road To The Pleasures of Tourism," all vehicular uses for the oil are laid

out for the consumer to see, from autos to airplanes,
motorcycles to motorboats, with the entrance to the
tunnel framing it all perfectly.
**Est: $1,500-$1,800.**

**148. Horse Super Cigarettes.** ca. 1935.
335$^1$/$_4$ x 49$^3$/$_4$ in./89.6 x 126.2 cm
Cond A–/Slight tears at edges.
Ref: PAI-III, 202
What a strikingly powerful image for what was undoubtedly a potent tobacco product. Not only have prices
risen from the fifty-cents-a-pack days of this poster—
not to mention an acute awareness of the health risks
involved with this particular habit—but you can't help
but appreciate how current cigarette promotions seem
downright timid in the face of this crimson equine.
**Est: $1,000-$1,200.**

**149. Visit Cuba.**
20$^3$/$_4$ x 28 in./52.7 x 71 cm
Artes Graficas, Habana
Cond A.
Despite the contemporary political malaise between
the United States and the republic of Cuba—with the
continuous rumors of lessened sanctions never mate-
rializing—it was not that long ago that the largest of the
West Indian islands was the Caribbean vacation destination of choice for many Americans, due in large part
to its geographic proximity (a scant ninety miles from
Key West) and a reputation as a hedonistic bastion of
tropical indulgence. This wonderful pre-Castro photomontage design—with photo credit given to C. M.
Zoehrer—doesn't play up these more wanton pleasures,
choosing instead to focus on the welcoming, friendly
faces that one is likely to encounter. And in this less-
politically charged era, it's interesting to note that the
Cuban Tourist Office maintained an office in Miami.
**Est: $700-$900.**

**150. Cadours/4e. Circuiti International.** 1952.
30$^1$/$_2$ x 45$^7$/$_8$ in./77.4 x 116.5 cm
Imp. Chabrillac, Toulouse
Cond B/Slight tears and stains, largely at edges.
Ref: PAI-XXXII, 108
An unusual head-on perspective distinguishes this
design by an unknown artist. The blue car appears to
be a Simca Gordini, with a red Ferrari on its heels.
This particular Formula Two race was won by Louis
Rosier in a 2-liter Ferrari.
**Est: $1,700-$2,000.**

## VANY D'AROCHE

**151. Boites-Lumière.** 1905.
30 x 45$^5$/$_8$ in./76.2 x 116 cm
Moulot Fils, Marseille
Cond B+/Slight tears at folds.
Art Nouveau allegory in its most dulcetly persuasive
form. For this brand of illumination, d'Aroche lures the
viewer with a transparently-veiled corporal embodiment of industrial innovation prettily perched atop an
ever-turning technological wheel, and then surprises
them with the inclusion of decoratively tweaked luna
and polyphemus moths, whose beauty seems to owe
as much to Tiffany glass as it does to Mother Nature.
And so as these moths are drawn to flame, so are we
to the advertising brilliance of Boites-Lumière.
**Est: $1,500-$1,800.**

## MARCELLIN AUZOLLE (1862-1942)

**152. Banyuls-Trilles.**
61 x 46$^1$/$_4$ in./155 x 117.5 cm
Imp. G. Dupuy, Paris
Cond B+/Slight tears at edges.
Now, I'm no prude, but does it look like this young lady
really needs another cocktail? Though his intentions
may not be the purest, the gent topping off her glass

**148**

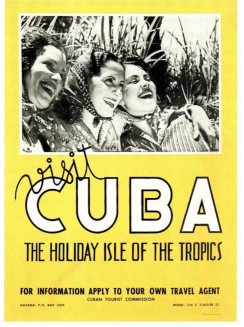

**149**

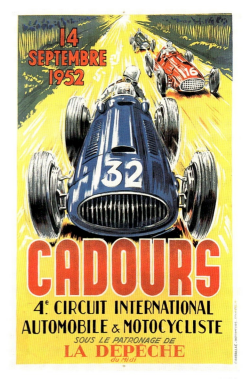

**150**

**153**

**151**

**154**

with Banyuls-Trilles, a wine beverage augmented with quinquina, would definitely appear to adhere to the tenet, "Candy is dandy, but liquor is quicker." Auzolle remains someone of whom we know little. The Bibliothèque Nationale has 34 of his posters dating from 1898 to 1927, but they're missing his best-known work: the 1895 poster announcing the opening of the world's first movie house, the Lumière Brothers' cinématographe (see PAI-V, 7).
Est: $2,000-$2,500.

### BAC (Ferdinand Bach, 1859-1952)

**153. Scala/Yvette Guilbert.** 1893.
$29^{1}/_{2}$ x $77^{1}/_{2}$ in./75 x 196.8 cm
*Hand-signed watercolor and ink maquette on paper.*
*Framed.*
Ref (All Var): DFP-II, 30; Reims, 213; Abdy, p. 103;
 Maitres, 19; PAI-VI, 18A
A lovely maquette for one of the three posters designed for Yvette Guilbert by her lifelong friend Bac, the German-born illustrator, posterist and writer whose real name was Bach. In addition to subtle tonal shifts and the addition of the venue's name, the most striking difference between conceptual artwork and poster completion is the softening of Guilbert's features in the poster, a choice which is perhaps slightly more

aesthetically pleasant, but in turn, robs the entertainer of populist character. Yvette opened at the Scala on September 29, 1893, having signed a record-price two-year contract with the large theater on the Boulevard de Strabourg. *Also included with this lot is a framed Maitres plate of the poster.*
**Est: $8,000-$10,000.** (2)

### BACHUS

**154. Lido.**
33 x $46^{3}/_{8}$ in./83.7 x 117.8 cm
Kunst in Druck, München
Cond A.
A captivating convergence of elements adds a hedonistic subtlety to this promotion for the Bavarian Lido bathing beach in Seeshaupt. Nothing overt, mind you, seeing as no overly salacious advances can be taken from this beach ball tossing cutey and her Lake Starnberg environs. But when a place is named after the spit of sand bounding the Venetian lagoon known for its carnal revels and when the posterist who created the design's name is suspiciously close to that of Bacchus, the Roman god of wine and carousal, one can't help but wonder if things were perhaps a bit racier than they appear.
**Est: $1,000-$1,200.**

**155**

**156**

**157**

## HERVÉ BAILLE (1896-1977)

**155. 21e. Salon des Humoristes.** 1928.
15¹/₂ x 23¹/₄ in./39.5 x 59 cm
Imp. H. Chachoin, Paris
Cond B+/Slight tears and stains at edges.
An eagerly anticipated Parisian event, this exhibition of humorous paintings, drawings and illustrations took place every spring from 1907 on at the Gallery La Boëtie. This year, Baille was tapped to bring the humorous word to the public and he did so with delicious irony, if not subtlety. Having a husband heft his, shall we say, Rubenesque spouse in order for her to nail-up a picture of a svelte, openly nude woman being chased by a snake isn't the precise equation for marital bliss. But having their Scottie look on with barely-contained enthusiasm for the impending disaster elevates the entire piece to a whole new voyeuristically comedic level.
**Est: $1,200-$1,500.**

## PAUL BALLURIAU (1860-1917)

**156. Fête des Tuileries.** 1892.
35⁷/₈ x 51 in./91 x 129.5 cm
Imp. G. Bataille, Paris
Cond B/Restored tears at folds.
An interesting design for the annual fair held at the Jardin des Tuileries, the park that links the Louvre to the Place de la Concorde in Paris. Flowers and reveling women are prominent, all to raise funds for poor Russian immigrants in France. Balluriau, a regular contributor to *Gil Blas*, executed several of the posters to promote the former chief's lurid tales in *Le Journal*.
**Est: $1,200-$1,500.**

## ADRIEN BARRÈRE (1877-1931)

**157. Mona Païva.** ca. 1918.
27³/₄ x 44³/₄ in./70.5 x 113.7 cm
Imp. Robert, Paris
Cond B/Slight tears at folds.
Barrère is well known for his portraits of French stage personalities ca. 1900-1910. He also produced many film posters, especially for Pathé. His caricature-like treatments and flat colors yielded delightful and witty designs—yet their depth and sensitivity often transcended caricature. Here, we are treated to a stylishly exotic and flirtatiously vibrant profile of Mona Païva, a dancer and courtesan that created something of a scandal during the early part of the 20th century with a series of seminude photos taken of her as she danced at the Acropolis. *Rare!*
**Est: $1,200-$1,500.**

**158. Mlle Polaire dans Le Visiteur.** 1911.
46³/₄ x 61³/₄ in./118.7 x 156.8 cm
Affiches d'Art Robert, Paris
Cond A.

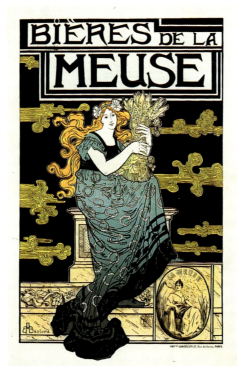

**159**

Despite this gripping bit of Barrère hoopla, *Le Visiteur* was nothing more than a ten-minute one-reeler most likely done as a response by Pathé to a rival studio's series starring Mistinguett and their desire to have a music-hall star of their own. And what a choice they made—Polaire, nee Emilie Bouchaud in Algiers, whose tiny-waisted/ample-bosomed figure coupled with her refusal to wear rigid corsets or bustiers brought her quite a bit of censure. Fortunately for Polaire, she had the talent to back up her look and she became a super-luminary. What we're being treated to here is a so-called "apache dance," with the faux-Native American label finding its way into popular French slang via Western dime novels and short films with the term "apache" coming to denote a streetwise Parisian tough guy.
**Est: $2,000-$2,500.**

## MARC AUGUSTE BASTARD (1863-1926)

**159. Bières de la Meuse.** 1896.
19¹/₄ x 19 in./49 x 73.6 cm
Imp. Lemercier, Paris
Cond A–/Slight tears and stains at edges.
Ref: DFP-II, 51; Reims, 218; Litfass-Bier, p. 120;
    PAI-XXIII, 135

**160**

This poster was created a year before Mucha's design for the same beer company (*see* No. 442), and it's constructive to compare the two. Both include the firm's logo, a cameo representing the goddess of the Meuse River; and in both, the figure in the cameo is elaborated and enlarged as the main figure, an enchanting beauty bedecked with poppies and barley stalks to represent the region and the product. But the similarity ends there: Bastard's design is formal and almost stilted; the type intrudes awkwardly, and the model on the pedestal is cold, statue-like. Mucha's maiden, on the other hand, is warm, sensuous and beckoning, with an exotic flavor that is altogether captivating; and the typography is integrated to make the message harmonious and clear. It is the difference between competence and inspiration. A decorator, painter and designer, the Swiss artist Bastard worked in many media, including furniture, painting, rugs and books. *This is the smaller format.*
**Est: $1,400-$1,700.**

158

161

162

163

in the mid-1890s and no one has ever uncovered any significant particulars for him. However, his small oeuvre was distinctive enough to create a following for the artist's work, both at the time he was active and at present. *This is the larger format.*
**Est: $2,000-$2,500.**

**162. Grands Magasins de Pygmalion/Jouets.** 1896.
$32^3/4$ x $47^1/4$ in./83.2 x 120 cm
Imp. B. Sirven, Toulouse-Paris
Cond B+/Slight tears at folds and edges.
Ref: Chaumont/Exposons, p. 30; PAI-XXVII, 284
Named for the Greek legend of a statue brought to life, this Yuletide advertisement for the French department store's toy department demonstrates how easily they too can turn fantasies into joyous realities. The riotous mob of trinket-laden tots couldn't be more pleased, much to the chagrin of their harried mother or guardian, who appears in the background, a hapless victim of unbridled exuberance.
**Est: $1,700-$2,000.**

**163. Acatène Métropole.** ca. 1893.
$34^1/8$ x $48^7/8$ in./86.7 x 124.2 cm
Imp. Kossuth, Paris
Cond B/Restored tears, largely at folds.
Ref: Reims, 223 (var); Maindron, p. 120 (var);
    PAI-XXXIII, 13
When women were still required to wear long skirts, even when biking, there was always the danger of getting tangled up in the chain drive. The Métropole here advertises its chainless model, driven by a spunky brunette. An earlier version of the poster advertised the Seddon tire which came as standard issue with the bicycle (*see* PAI-VII, 379) and which advertised the Marie bicycle outlet at the indicated address; here, Marie's name has been obliterated by overprinting, the address is unchanged and it touts the American-made G & J brand used with this model. The unsigned image must have been quite successful, for not only was it used in the two aforementioned versions, but also as part a poster-within-a-poster design for the company (*see* PAI-XX, 379).
**Est: $1,700-$2,000.**

## OTTO BAUMBERGER (1889-1961)

**160. Jelmoli/Orient-Teppiche/Grands Magasins.**
1916.
$35^1/8$ x $50^1/4$ in./89.2 x 127.6 cm
Gebr. Fretz, Zürich
Cond B/Restored tears, largely at edges.
Ref: Baumberger, 32; Margadant, 373; PAI-X, 96
For an oriental rug sale at the Jelmoli department store in Zurich, Baumberger gives us an exotic rug weaver at work. And by choosing to depict the artisan in an appealingly rustic fashion, the artist transforms his design into a handy piece of graphic folk art.
**Est: $1,200-$1,500.**

## LUCIEN BAYLAC (1851-1913)

**161. Grand Manège Central.** 1894.
$34^5/8$ x $48^7/8$ in./88 x 124 cm
Imp. Chaix, Paris
Cond B/Slight tears at folds.
Ref: Bicycle Posters, 32; DFP-II, 913; Reims, 226;
    PAI-XXXIV, 248 (var)
"Manège," a term carried over from equestrian schools, was in this case a bicycle riding school; in the early days, people actually paid to have someone teach them how to ride bikes, and these places did a lively business. This poster, highlighted by its fresh, vibrant colors, looks like an outright imitation of Chéret, and is unsigned. Baylac created only a dozen or so posters

## LUCIEN BAYLAC (continued)

**164. Electricine.** 1895.
$33^{1}/_{2}$ x $48^{1}/_{4}$ in./85 x 122.5 cm
Imp. Chaix, Paris
Cond B/Slight tears and stains at folds.
Ref: DFP-II, 54; Wine Spectator, 22; PAI-XXVII, 283
Baylac worked under Jules Chéret and the Master's influence is clearly evident in his designs. Other than that fact, the artist remains a bit of an enigma, known to us solely from the ten posters he produced during the span of one year between 1894 and 1895. "Electricine was an ordinary lamp kerosene whose manufacturer wanted to make use of the awe in which electricity was held at the time by naming its product after it, and claiming it gave light every bit as bright" (Wine Spectator, p. 22). This lovely letter writer is more preoccupied with the sharpness of her quill than the lighting conditions, clearly illuminating the effectiveness of the product.
**Est: $1,700-$2,000.**

## BELIGOND

**165. 24 H du Mans.** 1961.
$14^{3}/_{4}$ x 23 in./37.5 x 58.4 cm
Imp. Thirillier
Cond A–/Folds show.
Though we're shown the #12 car—an experimental Ferrari entry—as it roars its way through the grueling twenty-four hour Le Mans endurance test, it was actually the #10 car that would take the checkered flag, another Ferrari, covering almost 2,782 miles at an average speed of 116 miles-per-hour. 1961 represented the fifth Ferrari victory at Le Mans, who put three cars in the first three positions. The #12 car—even though it retired in the thirteenth hour of the race—was historic in that it was the prototype of the future GTO. Despite some aerodynamic and engine problems, the car displayed amazing potential.
**Est: $1,000-$1,200.**

## G. K. BENDA (Georges Kugelmann)

**166. Mlle Napierowska.** ca. 1910.
$46^{3}/_{8}$ x $62^{5}/_{8}$ in./118 x 159 cm
Cond B–/Slight tears and stains at fold.

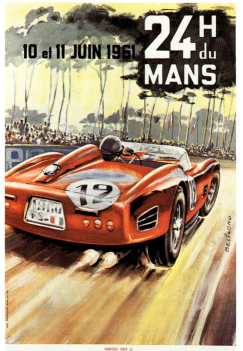

Ref: PAI-XXIII, 77
Big black eyes, a Bohemian charm, and a presence generated not least by her weight made the Polish-born actress/dancer Stacia Napierowska a star in a film career lasting from about 1909 through the late Twenties. Her name, indeed, is bigger than the film's in this poster for *L'Etoile du Genie*, a story of "the cruel life" by the great producer Ferdinand Zecca and

director René Le Prince. The costume and the column behind her suggest a classical Greek setting. Benda produced only a few posters, almost all for figures in the entertainment field, but they comprise a consistently impressive body of work. He was a painter whose portraits, landscapes and still lifes were exhibited in the major Paris Salons between 1907 and 1921. *Rare!*
**Est: $1,700-$2,000.**

**167**

**169**

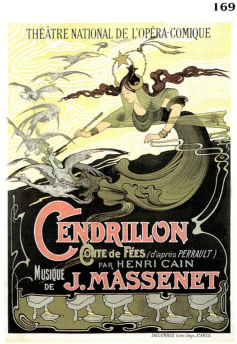

**170**

**171**

**172**

## EMILE BERCHMANS (1867-1947)

**167. Chaudfontaine/Fête de Jour et Nuit.** 1896.
39³⁄₈ x 27³⁄₈ in./100 x 69.5 cm
Imp. A. Benard, Liège
Cond B–/Restored tears at folds and edges.
Ref: DFP-II, 988; Reims, 1435
Berchmans was one of the first artists from the Walloon region of Belgium to devote himself to posters. He exhibited some of his decorative designs at *La Libre Esthétique* in 1895, and the following year he started to produce posters, marked by their use of simple lines and flat color planes. His approach for promoting this all-day Belgian charity event is simple enough: post a sophisticated and attractive Art Nouveau philanthropist and more people like her—and those that aspire to her social status—are sure to follow. *Rare!*
**Est: $1,500-$1,800.**

## ROGER BERCKMANS (1900-?)

**168. Heyst & Duinbergen.**
24¹⁄₈ x 39 in./61 x 99 cm
O. de Rycker, Bruxelles
Cond A–/Unobtrusive tears at folds and edges.
Ref: PAI-XII, 96
A happy beach scene with a mother and child sharing a color-coordinated day of fun in the sun with their trusty beach umbrella, all set against an achingly blue sky. Without an iota of pretense, Berckmans' strong brilliant colors emphasize the feeling of sunshiny day good times.
**Est: $1,200-$1,500.**

## PAUL BERTHON (1872-1909)

**169. Les Boules de Neige.** 1900.
23 x 18 in./58.3 x 45.8 cm
Imp. Chaix, Paris (not shown)
Cond A. Framed.
Ref: Berthon & Grasset, p. 106; Gold, 201;
    PAI-XXXIII, 214a
"Of all the posterists who also designed decorative panels, Berthon was perhaps the best qualified to do a series on flowers personified as women since his women are so flower-like—delicate creatures, so light as to nearly be ethereal, seen in the softest of focus and tinged with the gentlest of pastel hues. The flower here is a variety of white rose; the woman a shy, soulful spirit passing by in our dreams" (Gold, p. 137).
**Est: $1,500-$1,800.**

**170. Le Livre de Magda.** 1898.
15¹⁄₂ x 22³⁄₄ in./39.3 x 57.8 cm
Imp. Chaix, Paris
Cond A. Framed.
Ref: DFP-II, 66; Berthon & Grasset, p. 97;
    Timeless Images, 29; PAI-XXXI, 305
An advertisement for a book of poetry by Armand Silvestre. One may doubt whether the poems themselves were as lyrically lovely as Berthon's ethereal, Art Nouveau illustration of a nude forest nymph, who seems—her hair especially—part of the landscape. "Berthon's small but characteristic body of work . . . epitomizes the Art Nouveau style on paper" (Berthon & Grasset, p. 8).
**Est: $2,000-$2,500.**

**171. Revue d'Art Dramatique.** 1897.
20 x 25¹⁄₂ in./51 x 64.8 cm
Imp. Bougerie, Paris
Cond A–/Slight tears top paper edge.
Ref: Berthon & Grasset, p. 99; PAI-XIV, 119
For a theatrical journal, Berthon gives us a design in trademark warm shades of green and brown. Note the indication at bottom that this poster is for sale at the Arnould print shop. Most of Berthon's posters and decorative panels were available there for about 3 francs each.
**Est: $2,000-$2,500.**

## EMILE BERTRAND

**172. Cendrillon/J. Massenet.** 1899.
23¹⁄₂ x 31¹⁄₂ in./59.6 x 80 cm
Imp. Devambez, Paris
Cond A.
Ref: French Opera, 35; Theaterplakat, 48;
    Spectacle, 649; Gold, 155; PAI-XXX, 103
"For Massenet's musical version of Cinderella, Bertrand evokes an eerily haunting twilight mood, animated by a fairy directing a flock of geese. Art-Nouveau ornamentation throughout the design brings the elements of this admirable composition together in a memorable image" (Gold, p. 109). Active primarily around the turn of the century, Bertrand, a member of the Société des Artistes Français, was an engraver and painter who exhibited his works at several of their Salons.
**Est: $1,200-$1,500.**

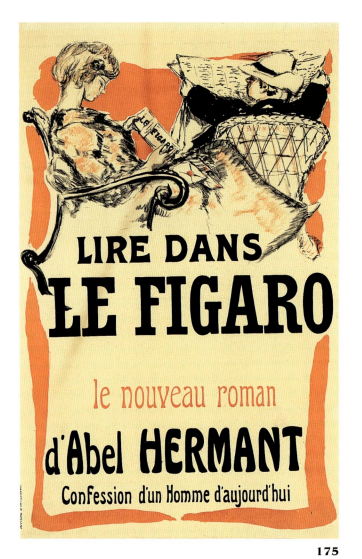

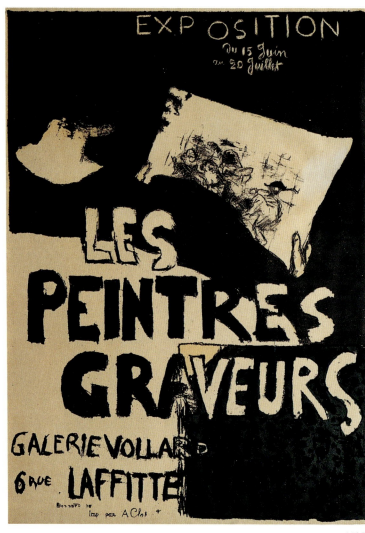

175

176

173

174

**CARLO BISCARETTI DI RUFFIA**
**(1879-1959)**

**173. Anisetta Evangelista.** 1925.
39¹/₄ x 55¹/₈ in./99.6 x 140 cm
Lit. Doyen, Torino
Cond A.
What can you say about a drunken monkey? Especially if the simian in question is getting looped on an anis-flavored liqueur. I mean, if it was banana-infused, well

then that would be understandable. He certainly seems to enjoy it though. And the peculiarity of the image is precisely what the Evangelisti firm was banking on to get their dessert tipple firmly lodged in the viewer's mind. A founder of the Museo dell'Auto-mobile in Turin, Biscaretti was an industrial designer who produced only a handful of posters, most of them for the automotive industry between 1920 and 1930.
**Est: $1,700-$2,000.**

**V. BOCCHINO**

**174. Lefèvre-Utile.** 1911.
26⁵/₈ x 20³/₈ in./67.7 x 51.7 cm
Imp. F. Champenois, Paris
Cond A.
Ref: Art & Biscuits, 26; Art du Biscuit, front & back
  inside covers; Alimentaires, 160; Gold, 58;
  PAI-XXXIV, 256

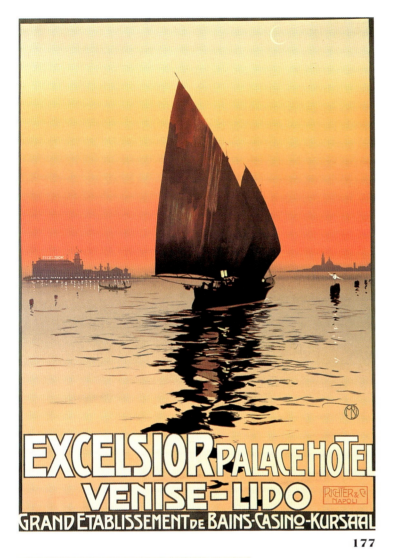

"Among the most enlightened companies of its day, Lefèvre-Utile sought many ways to popularize its products, among them posters prepared by top artists. Here, we see an assortment of decorative boxes and toys the company used to attract youthful clientele, some of whose adorable members are obviously responding to the bait—an equally sure lure for mothers interested in pleasing their offspring" (Gold, p. 42). Bocchino's several designs for Lefèvre-Utile had a wholesome

feel about them; he was the Norman Rockwell of the biscuit world as this image makes clear.
Est: $1,500-$1,800.

## PIERRE BONNARD (1867-1947)

**175. Le Figaro.** 1894.
$14^7/_8$ x $22^7/_8$ in./37.8 x 58 cm
Cond A. Framed.
Ref: Marx, 70; Bouvet, 78; DFP-II, 81; PAI-XVII, 119
Bonnard was primarily a printmaker, illustrator and painter; his poster output is few, but never fails to engage the viewer's interest. This one announces the serialization of a new novel in the pages of *Le Figaro*. Bonnard's signature is placed, rather oddly, on the back of the man's chair.
Est: $2,500-$3,000.

**176. Les Peintres Graveurs.** 1896.
$18^3/_4$ x $25^3/_4$ in./47.6 x 65.4 cm
Imp. A. Clot (Paris)
Cond A. Framed.
Ref: Marx, 40; Bouvet, 38; Ives, 23; DFP-II, 78;
      Modern Poster, 8; Gold, 184; PAI-XXXIII, 228
We look over the shoulder of a prospective buyer in this poster advertising an exhibition at Vollard's gallery—22 prints by artists from the group that called themselves the Nabis, including Vuillard, Vallotton and Bonnard himself. The exhibition was staged to publicize the portfolio "Album des Peintres-Graveurs," which contained the same prints and was simultaneously issued in a small edition of 100 sets by Vollard.
Est: $2,500-$3,000.

## MARIO BORGONI (1869-1936)

**177. Excelsior/Palace Hotel.**
$34^3/_4$ x $48^1/_4$ in./88.3 x 122.5 cm
Richter, Napoli

Cond B+/Slight tears at folds and edges.
After attending Naples' Institute of Fine Arts, Borgoni dedicated himself to lithographic production, collaborating with the Richter firm to create a remarkable number of posters. Working in many styles yet specializing in tourism posters, Borgoni frequently used the feminine figure to lure the viewer's eyes to his designs. Another element to be found in his works is the use of a frame to open a window onto voluptuous landscapes. This is the approach he takes to promote Venice's Excelsior Palace Hotel in this beautiful design highlighted by the fine Richter lithography. Instead of graphically trying to recreate the splendor of the deluxe destination of the pampered European beach crowd—though he is kind enough to include it as a background element—his sumptuous gradations of sunset colors over the canals of Venice serve as more than temptation enough to attract those for whom grey cityscapes have lost their charm. Though now a member of the Westin family, when the Excelsior was built, it was the world's biggest resort hotel, and its presence helped to make the Lido fashionable. *Rare!*
Est: $3,000-$4,000.

## JEAN BOUCHAUD (?-1942)

**178. Afrique Occidentale Française.** 1946.
$30^7/_8$ x $46^1/_4$ in./78.3 x 117.3 cm
Damour Publicité, Paris
Cond A–/Slight tears at edges.
An aridly evocative design promoting travel to what was then called French West Africa and is now, among other countries, Benin. Though published by the Ministry of the Colonies, very little in the way of colonial condescension enters into the picture, simply an effective reflection of daily indigenous life, executed with vivid artistry and a radiant palette.
Est: $1,700-$2,000.

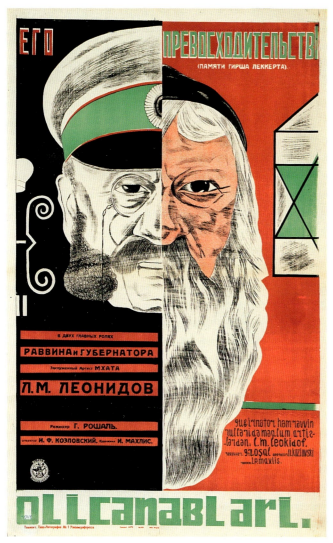

## FIRMIN BOUISSET (1859-1925)

**179. Chocolat Menier/Eviter les Contrefacons.**
   ca. 1895.
38¹/₈ x 54 in./97 x 137.2 cm
Imp. Charles Verneau, Paris
Cond B-/Restored tears. Framed.
Ref (All Var but Karcher & PAI): DFP-II, 85; Reims, 237; Maindron, p. 42; Musée d'Affiche, 49; Weill, 75; Masters 1900, 75; Chocolate Posters, Cover & p. 20; Karcher, p. 75; PAI-VIII, 277
Most frequently, Bouisset's design of this young female graffiti artist shows her scribbling "Chocolat Menier" on the blank slate of a wall she has happened upon. In this lesser-seen, later version, the young girl is writing "Eviter les Contrefacons" ("Avoid Substitutes"). Regardless of version, the seductive charm of the composition remains, making it one of the most appealing posters by this artist who frequently used children as his theme.
**Est: $3,000-$4,000.**

**180. Garden Prayer.**
21¹/₈ x 35¹/₂ in./53.7 x 90.2 cm
Cond A.
In what would apparently appear to be a continuation of a decorative panel series Bouisset began with his Salon des Cent design (see PAI-VII, 358), the artist sets out to compare and contrast the flower of youth with an abundantly-floral Art Nouveau evocation. Here, as opposed to the Salon des Cent design which is a bit more feral, Bouisset manages to combine two disparate ingredients to a breathtaking end—innocent reverence and blossoming sensuality.
**Est: $1,200-$1,500.**

## DMITRI A. BULANOV

**181. Ego prevoskhoditel'stvo (His Excellency).**
   1927.
26³/₄ x 42³/₈ in./68 x 107.6 cm
Belgoskino, Tashkent
Cond B+/Slight tears at folds and edges.
Ref: PAI-XXXI, 325
Released in the U.S. as *Seeds of Freedom*, this film is

one of several during the period that dealt with the dilemma of Soviet Jews. It was inspired by the real-life tragedy of Hirsh Lekert, a Jewish shoemaker executed in 1902 for attempting to kill the czar's governor-general of the city of Vilna (today's Vilnius, capital of Lithuania) for his harsh treatment of the Jewish minority. In this adaptation, the governor of an unnamed city is killed, and the Jewish leaders fear that the entire Jewish community will be blamed and persecuted for the action. The conservative rabbi, played by distinguished stage actor Leonid M. Leonidov (he was also the assassinated governor), plans to send a delegation to the new governor pleading for mercy—even as his own daughter abandons her orthodox Jewish background to join the Communist rebels. Bulanov was a poster designer who was active in Leningrad in the 1920s and early 1930s. His split design underscores the film's central Jewish-Soviet conflict and Leonid's performance as the two opposing characters.
**Est: $2,000-$2,500.**

## MAX BURI (1868-1915)

**182. Sonderausstellung Max Buri.** 1913.
32⁷/₈ x 44 in./83.5 x 111.8 cm
J. E. Wolfensberger, Zurich
Cond A.
Ref: Plakat Schweiz, p. 191(var); PAI-XXV, 209
As a painter, Buri gained a reputation as a close observer of the Swiss rural scene, and it is therefore not surprising that in a poster for his own exhibition, he stays with his favorite theme. As may be expected, most of the paintings at this show celebrated various aspects of rustic life.
**Est: $1,000-$1,200.**

## BUTLER

**183. Buy Your Wife a Ford.**
27 x 41¹/₈ in./68.5 x 104.5 cm
The Akron Tire Display Co., Akron, O.
Cond B+/Tears and stains, largely at edges.
Ref: PAI-XXXIII, 242

You know that you're doing something right when all you have to do to advertise your product is show a steering wheel and reveal to the automotive public the name of the car that brought the smile to the engaging driver's face. And though the women of today's world might prefer to have a greater voice when it came down to purchasing their vehicular transport,

**184**

**185**

**186**

**182**

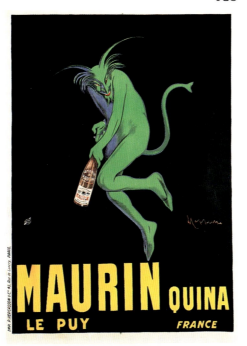

**187**

Cond A. Framed.
Ref: PAI-XXXIV, 270 (var)
Though a tad more strictly Byzantine than the bulk of his panels, this porcelain doll swathed in azure and fairly dripping with overindulgent ornamentation provides a luxuriant dose of Camps' femininity, the fall of her shawl with its exquisite peacock bauble lending an ideal Art Nouveau exclamation mark to the design. *This is the smaller format on paper.*
**Est: $1,200-$1,500.**

**186. Ricardo Aparicio.**
9¹/₈ x 19 in./23.1 x 48.3 cm
Imp. F. Champenois, Paris (not shown)
Cond A. Framed.
Ref: PAI-XXXV, 197 (var)
The Spanish wine producer Aparicio doubtless chose this image for imprinting because of the beautiful wide border of grapevines on the figure's scarlet dress. In further tribute to the autumn theme, Camps has included turning leaves and seasonal dahlias, and a reflecting pool shows us the warm colors of day's end. Our Lady of the Grapes—seen here before the addition of text—strikes a coy pose suitable for her remarkable jewelry. *This is the smaller format on paper.*
**Est: $1,200-$1,500.**

## LEONETTO CAPPIELLO (1875-1942)

**187. Maurin Quina.** 1906.
44¹/₂ x 62¹/₈ in./113 x 157.7cm
Imp. Vercasson, Paris
Cond B+/Slight tears at folds and edges.
Ref: Cappiello, 266; PAI-XXXII, 219 (var)
Well, you can't say that Cappiello didn't try to warn us. Granted, there's a little devilry in any alcoholic beverage, but when the infernal imp in question confronts the passerby with his smirking, smoldering eyes gleaming, and Cappiello renders the bottle of Maurin Quina face-out so that we can see that elephants are prominently displayed on the label of the fortified wine, you can be pretty sure that responsible consumption should be the order of the day.
**Est: $1,700-$2,000.**

there's something nostalgically sweet in the sentiment expressed and executed in this Ford design.
**Est: $2,000-$2,500.**

## GASPAR CAMPS (1874-1931)

**184. Tender Temptation.** ca. 1904.
9¹/₈ x 19 in./23.1 x 48.3 cm
Imp. F. Champenois, Paris (not shown)
Cond A. Framed.
Ref: PAI-XXXIV, 270 (var)
A dark-haired beauty in a peacock-feathered boa and a long, exquisitely-fringed green gown cradles a bird in a nest. Birds also adorn the borders. A superb Art Nouveau design, executed with meticulous workman-

ship. Camps, a Spaniard who spent most of his career in France, was one of a number of artists hired by the Champenois printing house to fill the void when Mucha left for America in 1904. Creating both advertising and decorative works, Camps eventually found his own groove—less graphic than Mucha and more akin to oil painting, marked by soft edges and shadings, as well as loads of kitschy sentimentality. *This is the smaller format on paper.*
**Est: $1,200-$1,500.**

**185. Balcony Bouquet.** ca. 1904.
9¹/₈ x 19 in./23.1 x 48.3 cm
Imp. F. Champenois, Paris (not shown)

**188**

**189**

## CAPPIELLO (continued)

**188. Cachou Lajaunie.** 1900.
38 x 54 in./96.5 x 137 cm
Imp. Vercasson, Paris
Cond A–/Slight stains at folds.
Ref (All Var but PAI): Cappiello, 231;
    Cappiello/St. Vincent, 4.10;
    Wine Spectator, 202; PAI-XXXIII, 253
This is Cappiello's first poster for Lajaunie breath
freshening pastilles ("indispensable for smokers").
His early style of flat planes and colors—rooted in his
experience as a caricaturist—is very different from the
more dimensional design we see in the second image,
done two decades after and printed by Devambez (*see*
No. 203). The client, Mr. Lajaunie, wrote glowingly to
Vercasson: "When you submitted the maquette of my
poster by Cappiello, I simply told you I was satisfied
. . . . Today (a year later) I appreciate it better still for
the originality of the design and the happy choice of
colors. This poster has truly contributed to the in-
creasing success of my candies. In France and
abroad, numerous collectors have asked me for a
copy, which proves to me the favor this poster has gar-
nered among the public and among connoisseurs"
(Cappiello, 231). *This is the Spanish version.*
**Est: $2,500-$3,000.**

**189. Corset Le Furet.** 1901.
39³/₈ x 54¹/₂ in./100 x 138.3 cm
Imp. Vercasson, Paris
Cond B+/Slight tears and stains at folds.
Ref: Cappiello, 238; Cappiello/St. Vincent, 4.8;
    Menegazzi-I, 465; PAI-XXXI, 332
A somewhat daring design by 1901 standards. This
corset, which "stays firm but doesn't restrain," promises
to give its wearer "the suppleness of the Orient with
the charm of France." One of Cappiello's earliest and
most appealing images.
**Est: $3,500-$4,000.**

**190. Poulain-Orange.** 1911.
47 x 62¹/₄ in./119.4 x 158 cm
Imp. Vercasson, Paris

**190**

Cond A–/Slight tears at folds.
Ref: Chocolate Posters, p. 31; PAI-XVI, 165
Cappiello previously prepared a poster for the Poulain
brand of cocoa with a little girl anointing the globe
with the beverage (*see* Chocolate Posters, p. 30). But
here it's an orange horse, for obvious reasons, in a
simple heart-tugging scene of a little tyke deprived of
her chocolate treat by a larcenous equine.
**Est: $2,000-$2,500.**

**191. Docteur Rasurel/"Sous Vêtements
    Hygiéniques".** 1906.
46¹/₂ x 62³/₈ in./118 x 158.5 cm
Imp. Vercasson, Paris
Cond B+/Slight tears at folds.

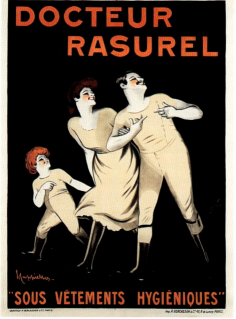

**191**

Ref: Health Posters, 26; Gold, 123; PAI-XXXIV, 278
Beginning in 1892, the newly-introduced one-piece
undergarments known as union suits gained an instant
widespread popularity. "Docteur Rasurel" was a trademark for a line of thermal underwear, slippers and other
textile products. "Cappiello shows his perfect mastery
of his art: using three contrasting colors, three figures
that seem to move as one, and three lines of text . . .
The whole posters evokes an impression of vitality and
energy . . . The comfortable benefits of wearing Rasurel
underwear seems to be confirmed by the contented
expressions of the three figures shown" (Health Posters,
p. 29).
**Est: $1,700-$2,000.**

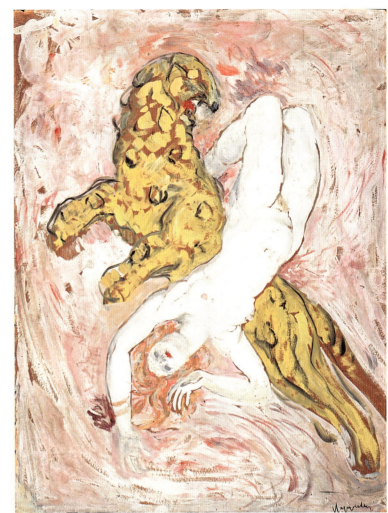

**192**

**193**

**194**

BISCOTINES UNION

MARQUE DÉPOSÉE

59. G.de Rue. ROUBAIX

PRODUIT DE SURALIMENTATION

**195**

the medium of promotion. However, it's difficult not to notice his artistic attributes in this circus artwork that may or may not have been intended for a lithographic end. In fact, more comparisons can be drawn to post-impressionistic works along the lines of van Gogh than to more familiar Cappiello designs such as Chocolat Klaus. Without a doubt, an impassioned sense of motion flows through this oil-on-board creation, a sensuality one is unlikely to encounter in the lion's share of Cappiello's poster designs. And quite a bit more sensual as well, not so much thanks to the presence of the naked female form, but for the sinuous feline entwinement in which she finds herself—savage yet languid, sensuous yet perilous. Superb and blissfully dramatic.
**Est: $12,000-$15,000.**

**194. Pneu Velo Lefort.** 1911.
15 x 22⁵/₈ in./38 x 57.3 cm
Imp. Vercasson, Paris
Cond B–/Several tears.
Ref (Both Var): Bicycle Posters, 79; PAI-XXV, 217
An original way to show how sturdy the tires are: the rats are breaking their teeth trying to gnaw through them. They are just too strong ("le fort") for the rascally rodents. A true Cappiello inspiration! *This is the indoor display format.*
**Est: $1,500-$1,800.**

**195. Biscotines Union.**
38³/₈ x 54 in./97.5 x 137 cm
Imp. Vercasson, Paris
Cond A.
Ref: Gourmand, p. 30; PAI-XXIX, 250
This hungry redhead couldn't care less that the cookie he's about to crunch into won medals at the Liège and Milan World Fairs. And anyone with a sweet tooth who's ever been in the grips of a snack attack can definitely empathize with his situation. Cappiello's exaggeration is wonderful—surely no consumer ever believed that the Union product was as gargantuan as portrayed, but the promise of big taste satisfaction comes across brilliantly.
**Est: $1,500-$1,800.**

charity event in the Bois de Boulogne. And thanks to Cappiello's effervescent mastery, we're all but powerless to follow her in.
**Est: $2,500-$3,000.**

**193. Untamed Tumble.**
30¹/₂ x 40¹/₄ in./77.4 x 102.2 cm
*Hand-signed oil on board.* Framed.
Much has been made, can be made and will continue to be made over Cappiello's significance to the world of advertising. But it's rather rare to hear someone expound on his virtues as a fine artist working outside

**192. Grand Kermesse de Charité.** 1903.
39¹/₈ x 54¹/₂ in./99.2 x 138.4 cm
Imp. Vercasson, Paris
Cond A–/Unobtrusive tears and creases at edges.
Framed.
Ref: DFP-II, 119; PAI-XXXI, 335
This golden lass, daintily carrying a hanging wicker basket of freshly cut flowers, whisks her way to a

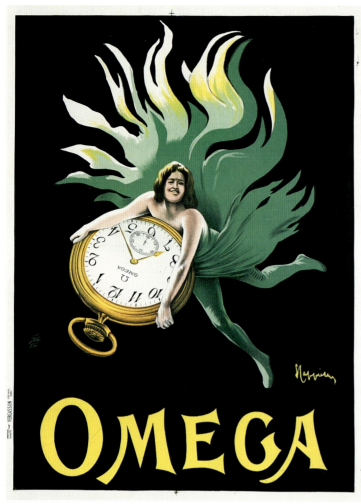

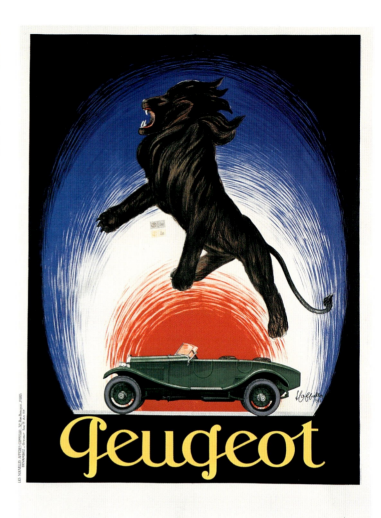

See also books & periodicals illustrated by Cappiello: *Les Contemporains Célèbres* (No. 584), *Miroir a Deux Faces* (No. 858) and *Le Rire* (No. 590).

## CAPPIELLO (continued)

### 196. Omega.
37 x 49 in./94 x 124.5 cm
Imp. Vercasson, Paris
Cond A–/Unobtrusive tears at edges.
The sprite representing Omega, somehow staying magically aloft despite the heft of the massive pocket watch in tow, adds a necessary touch of flamboyance to what would otherwise be just another everyday timepiece advertisement.
**Est: $2,500-$3,000.**

### 197. Peugeot. 1925.
46⁵/₈ x 62¹/₄ in./118.4 x 158 cm
Imp. Devambez, Paris
Cond A–/Unobtrusive folds.
Ref: Cappiello, 316; Auto Show I, 62;
    Auto Posters, p. 42; PAI-XXX, 260
Typical Cappiello exuberance: the French colors form a halo, while the trademark Peugeot lion springs for the skies. Grab attention and you'll make a sale. It's as simple as that. Or so Cappiello's facile talent would have us believe.
**Est: $2,500-$3,000.**

### 198. Veuve Amiot/Crémant du Roi. 1922.
47 x 62³/₈ in./119.4 x 158.6 cm
Imp. Devambez, Paris
Cond A.
Ref: PAI-XXXIV, 289
It appears as if we've come across this rouged monarch draped in his royal robes (*Crémant du Roi*) during a transcendent moment, carried away on the exquisite proboscis-tickling bubbles of Veuve Amiot sparkling wine. A convincing design of infinite charm that effortlessly persuades without sacrificing one jot of intimate amusement.
**Est: $2,000-$2,500.**

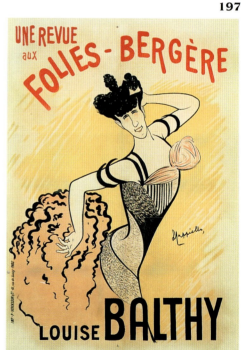

### 199. Folies Bergère/Louise Balthy. 1902.
39¹/₄ x 55 in./99.6 x 139.6 cm
Imp. Vercasson, Paris
Cond C+/Restored tears.
Ref: Cappiello, 215; Cappiello/St. Vincent, 4.2 (var);
    Wine Spectator, 182; PAI-XXXI, 50
"Louise Balthy (1869-1926), a remarkably talented performer who was trained in ballet but broke into show business with comic songs, which secured her an engagement at the Eldorado at the age of 17. A native of Bayonne near the Spanish border, she sometimes affected some Spanish mannerisms, and Cappiello makes it clear in this design. At the time he portrayed her, she was much in demand as a star of lavish revues and spectacles" (Wine Spectator). And if Cappiello graphically captured even half of Balthy's moxie, it's easy to understand why she commanded the attention of the City of Lights.
**Est: $1,700-$2,000.**

**200**

**201**

**202**

**203**

## 201. The Butcher.
21$^1/_4$ x 29 in./54 x 73.7 cm
*Signed watercolor and crayon maquette.* Framed.
In opposition to the previous design, this is straightforward Cappiello overindulgence, from the maniacally slicing butcher to the salami sizable enough to feed a small Third World country. Ever the genius of exaggeration, Cappiello doesn't fail in turning a trip to the butcher for cold cuts into a frenzied sausage siren song.
**Est: $4,000-$5,000.**

## 202. Cognac Monnet. 1927.
50$^3/_8$ x 78$^1/_8$ in./128 x 198.5 cm
Imp. Devambez, Paris
Cond A. Framed.
Ref: PAI-XXXIV, 286
"Sunshine in a glass" is the company's slogan, and Cappiello, with a charming literal-mindedness, depicts exactly that—and, of course, the pure black background makes it stand out prominently. The cognac firm was founded in 1905 by Jean Gabriel Monnet, and is today part of the Hennessy Corporation.
**Est: $4,000-$5,000.**

## 203. Cachou Lajaunie. 1920.
39$^3/_8$ x 59$^1/_8$ in./100 x 150.2 cm
Imp. Devambez, Paris
Cond A–/Slight creases at edges.
Ref: Cappiello, 291; Marques, p. 43;
     Health Posters, 222; PAI-XXXIII, 259
The smoker has just taken a Lajaunie breath freshener to counteract the effects of her cigarette, but it's her dress—with its large sequins in shades reminiscent of autumn leaves—that catches our eye. The product takes its name from the color of its tin—"jaune" is French for yellow—as well as the name of its inventor. "The pharmacist, Léon Lajaunie, set up his pharmacy in Toulouse. After developing several invigorating elixirs, he turned to cachou, as an aromatic for perfuming the breath whose strong flavor covered smoker's breath" (Health Posters, p. 169).
**Est: $1,700-$2,000.**

## 200. Aluminum.
23$^1/_2$ x 31$^1/_2$ in./59.6 x 80 cm
*Signed watercolor and crayon maquette.* Framed.
This and the following maquette are from the Devambez archives. The emphasis on the aluminum pots being held by a strong chef's hands are meant to indicate its solidity. The aluminum cookware promises economy and cleanliness, but the most significant element would seem to be Cappiello's creation of a solidly masculine image, an interesting approach considering that the product's primary demographic was feminine. Verging on the territory of the object poster, this design is cast in the metal of a mind forged in the fires of creative brilliance.
**Est: $4,000-$5,000.**

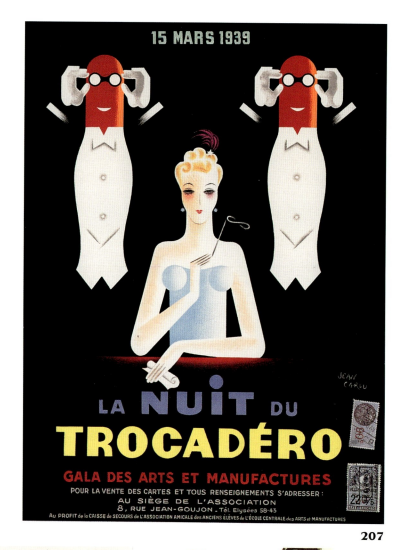

204                                                                                      207

## CAPPIELLO (continued)

**204. 26eme Salon des Humoristes.** 1933.
$30^7/8$ x $46^3/4$ in./78.5 x 118.7 cm
Imp. Devambez, Paris
Cond B+/Slight tears and creases.
Ref: PAI-XXIX, 254
Laugh and the world laughs with you. Cappiello had
designed the poster for the 1922 Salon (*see* PAI-XX,
166) and eleven years later, he was commissioned to
create the graphic promotion for the event once more.
Keeping things simple, we're shown a few of the many
faces of comedy, the pink bow of this duplicitous
joker tying everything up nicely, while at the same
time, providing the sole color present in the design.
*This is the larger format.*
**Est: $2,000-$2,500.**

**205. Bally Lyon/"Le Meilleur Marché Par La Qual-
ité".** 1933.
$43^7/8$ x $61^1/4$ in./111.4 x 155.6 cm
Imp. Devambez, Paris
Cond B/Restored tears in upper text.
Ref: Cappiello, 341 (var); PAI-XXX, 438
A year after Cappiello created this slick poster for
Bally, a contemporary critic used it as an example of
the artist's mastery in giving utilitarian objects special
treatment: "Even for Bally, where two different shoes
are pictured, Cappiello can't limit himself to a strict
interpretation. His subtle imagination doesn't give us
the shoes on feet; with unequaled elegance, he places
the man's oxford on a silken palm and holds the
narrow heel of the woman's pump in his fingers as if
it were a work of art" (Pierre Guéguin, in *Cappiello*,
pp. 154-5). Another version of the poster exists without the second line of text (*see* PAI-XXIV, 202).
**Est: $1,700-$2,000.**

## ALOIS CARIGIET (1902-1985)

**206. Baden.** 1943.
$35^1/2$ x $50^1/8$ in./90 x 127.3 cm
Wolfsberg, Zurich
Cond B+/Slight tears at horizontal fold.

205

Ref: PAI-XVIII, 217
A green-skinned, golden-haired forest or river nymph
and a deer friend sample the waters of Baden, billed
as "Switzerland's most mineral-rich thermal baths."
Carigiet was trained as a decorator and house painter,
but in 1923 went to work at an ad agency and drifted
into poster design, theater decor and mural painting.
He later also gained some fame as an illustrator of
children's books.
**Est: $1,000-$1,200.**

206

## JEAN CARLU (1900-1997)

**207. La Nuit de Trocadéro.** 1939.
$11^3/4$ x $15^1/2$ in./30 x 39.5 cm
Imp. Bedos, Paris
Cond B+/Unobtrusive tears at horizontal fold. Framed.
For this late-winter springboard into the revelrous night,
Carlu utilizes the flat black background to marvelous
effect, heightening the surreal presence of the abstracted
gentlemen of leisure, while firmly placing the attention
on one of the belles of the ball, whose lorgnette, coincidentally, hints at the amount of fun awaiting all comers.
**Est: $3,000-$4,000.**

**VILLE DE TURIN**

EXPOSITION INTERNATIONALE TURIN 1911
RÉUNION-CONCOURS INTERNATIONAL DES SAPEURS-POMPIERS
17-21 AOÛT 1911

**208**

**209**

**210**

immediately on the toasty side of an environmental duality. The Deville company is alive and well today; established in 1896, they now enter a third century as purveyors of functional, stylish comfort.
**Est: $2,500-$3,000.**

## GIOVANNI BATTISTA CARPANETTO (1863-1928)
**209. Ville de Turin/Exposition International des Sapeurs-Pompiers.** 1911.
55 x 78¹/₂ in./139.7 x 199.4 cm
Lit. Doyen, Torino
Cond B+/Slight tears at folds.
What an incredible 2-sheet image—we're graphically driven up to the scene of a raging fire as if we were part of the squad that was about to bring the blaze under control. An amazing—and quite large—poster for a Turin fire-fighting exposition. Carpanetto was primarily a painter, trained at Turin's Albertina Academy, who still managed to produce a good number of posters thanks to a firm grounding in lithographic technique. His works tend to resonate with allegorical grandeur and are sought after by collectors. Most especially in the Turinese area. Of historical importance, it should be noted that Carpanetto designed the first poster for Fiat automobiles in 1899. *Rare!*
**Est: $3,000-$4,000.**

## A. M. CASSANDRE (Adolphe Mouron, 1901–1968)
**210. Dubonnet/. . . à l'eau.** 1935.
14 x 10³/₈ in./35.5 x 26.3 cm
Alliance Graphique, Paris
Cond A–/Restored tears at corners. Framed.
Ref: Art Deco, p. 179; Cassandre/Suntory, 138; PAI-XXVII, 323
One of the many uses made of Cassandre's immortal 1932 Dubonnet figure is this small placard recommending Dubonnet with water and a touch of cassis or lemon: here, he's wearing green and the scene is framed in red.
**Est: $2,000-$2,500.**

**208. Chauffage Deville.** 1935.
30³/₄ x 47¹/₈ in./78.2 x 119.7 cm
Imp. Leon Nuez, Lille-Paris
Cond B/Slight tears at folds.
Ref: Carlu, 46
Carlu—along with Charles Loupot, A. M. Cassandre and Paul Colin—was one of the "gang of four" who led French advertising art between the wars, distinguishing themselves and their medium with almost everything they created. Here, Carlu creates a hieroglyph of stunning efficiency to promote Deville heaters. Combining a completely flattened perspective with stringent geometry and deeply imbued tonal evocation, the artist places us

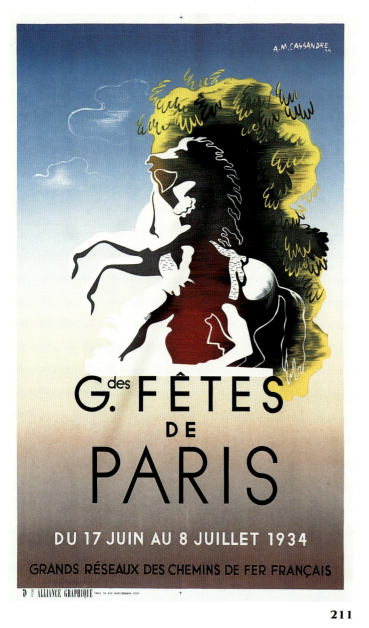

211

212

**211. Grandes Fêtes de Paris.** 1934.
24³/₈ x 39¹/₄ in./62 x 99.7 cm
Alliance Graphique, Paris
Cond A–/Slight tears at paper edges.
Ref: Brown & Reinhold, 46; Mouron, 116; PAI-XXXIV, 296 (var)
"Cassandre celebrates Paris—the Paris of tourists and sunny days in late
June when the statues in the parks are framed in foliage. His design has
all the spontaneous charm of a free-hand sketch" (Mouron, pp. 70-71).
*This is the smaller format.*
**Est: $5,000-$6,000.**

**212. Normandie/Service Regulier.** 1935.
24³/8x 39 in./62 x 99 cm
Alliance Graphique/L. Danel, Paris
Cond A.
Ref: Mouron, 56; Brown & Reinhold, 53; Cassandre/Suntory, p. 91;
   Weill, 345; Deco Affiches, p. 33; Moderno Francés, p. 194;
   PAI-XXXV, 230
An advertisement for the *Normandie* and her "First Arrival in New York
City on June 3 (1935)" touted that "The arrival in New York Harbor of the
gigantic super-liner *Normandie* will inaugurate a new era of transatlantic
travel. She will set new standards of luxury and speed, steadiness comfort
and safety . . . not merely the largest liner afloat (79,280 tons) . . . but in
almost every respect *a new kind of liner!*" And in almost every respect,
this Cassandre masterpiece was a new way of selling the glamour and
excitement of ocean liner travel. A deceptively simple, but impressive
design with the ship towering above us, a flight of small birds at bottom
giving the image as much scale and strength as the imposing hull itself.
The classic design appeared with several variants of text at the bottom;
this is the version with the ship's name emblazoned over its ports of call.
**Est: $12,000-$15,000.**

**213. Nord Express.** 1927.
29¹/₂ x 41¹/₄ in./75 x 105 cm
Imp. Hachard, Paris
Cond B/Slight tears at folds and edges.
Ref: Mouron, Pl. 10; Brown & Reinhold, 9; Cassandre/Suntory, 49;
   Deco Affiches, p. 27; Avant Garde, p. 162; Word & Image, p. 80;
   Art Deco, p. 77; Weill, 310; Affiche Réclame, 80; Modern Poster, 155;
   PAI-XXXIV, 295
This poster shows how well Cassandre understood that with rail travel,
you're selling the romance of far-off horizons and the sheer euphoria of
the physical experience—the geometry of the tracks, wheels, pistons and
mesmerizing perspectives. "Although the viewer's eyes are focused on
the rail, they are almost on the same level as the distant destination point.
Using this angle of view, the dynamic power, speed, and huge size of the
locomotive are expressed. Speed is emphasized by the extreme angle of
our perspective on the horizon. The destination of the train is skillfully
designated on the rail" (Cassandre/Suntory, p. 73).
**Est: $7,000-$9,000.**

**214. Etoile du Nord.** 1927.
29¹/₂ x 41³/₈ in./75 x 105 cm
Imp. Hachard, Paris
Cond B+/Unobtrusive tears. Framed.
Ref: Mouron, Pl. 22; Brown & Reinhold, 18, Pl. 10; Cassandre/Suntory, 48;
   Deco Affiche, p. 25; Avant Garde, p. 158; Timeless Images, 105;
   Weill, p. 199; Modern Poster, 154; Art Deco, p. 59;
   Moderno Francés, p. 161; PAI-XXXIV, 294
The *North Star* was the name of a Paris-to-Amsterdam express; Cassandre
gave it glamor by catching the purely sensual enjoyment of rail travel—the
rhythm of the wheels, the fascination of the endless perspectives of con-
verging tracks, and the North Star itself. A truly mesmerizing achievement.
**Est: $10,000-$12,000.**

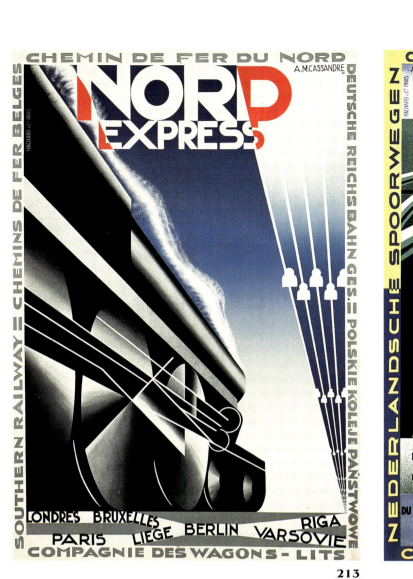

213

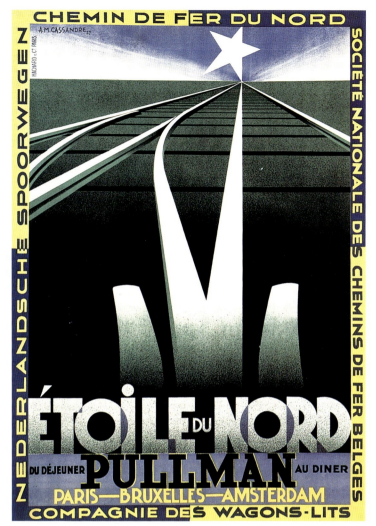

214

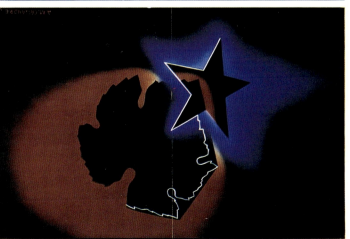

215

**215. Celestial Musing: Two Prints.** 1929 & 1932.
Each: 14$^{1}/_{4}$ x 9$^{1}/_{2}$ in./36 x 24.2 cm
Cond A/Usual vertical folds. Framed.
Even though he strays from his typically earthly terrain, Cassandre's perfectly at home lithographically pondering more celestial affairs in no way connected to advertising on any horizon. Whether it be the inner-gears of the galactic machine or luminary concerns, Cassandre's fantastical meanderings are a sleek escape from the mundane. These prints appeared in *Arts et Metiers Graphiques.*
**Est: $1,500-$1,800.** (2)

216

218

## A. M. CASSANDRE (continued)

**216. Sweepstake.** 1935.
$31^5/8$ x $47^5/8$ in./80.2 x 120.6 cm
Imp. L. Danel, Lille
Cond B+/Slight tears at folds.
Ref: Mouron, 54; Brown & Reinhold, 50;
  Cassandre/Suntory, 30;
  Moderno Francés, p. 191; PAI-XXI, 117
"The drama and excitement of a photo finish are stir-ringly depicted by the concentrated and overlapping form of two jockey's and horses crossing a finish . . . Cassandre evokes the feeling of blurred, blinding speed that is always associated with the neck-and-neck battle of a stretch run" (Brown & Reinhold, p. 18). There was also a larger and smaller format; this is the medium size.
**Est: $14,000-$17,000.**

## HENRI CASSIERS (1858-1944)

**217. Red Star Line/Services Réguliers Directs.**
  1907.
$24^1/4$ x $39^7/8$ in./61.6 x 101.3 cm
O. de Rycker, Bruxelles
Cond B/Restored tears at folds.
Ref: PAI-XXIX, 93
Though his name appears nowhere on the poster, the signature artistry of Cassiers blankets this design for the Red Star Line and its various North American desti-nations, all originating from the home port of Antwerp. The stark use of green and scarlet makes the on-deck vignette stand out with glaring clarity, nearly burning the image into the mind's eye with its singular gaze. Born in Antwerp, Cassiers became an aquarellist of note at an early age, placing his work at many exhibi-tions and earning himself various kudos. In the 1890s, he traveled as a roving magazine contributor. In poster work, he sticks close to his painterly roots, generally creating an evocative scene to which text is then added.
**Est: $1,200-$1,500.**

## CELLO

**218. Recta.** 1931.
$46^1/2$ x $62^1/2$ in./118 x 158 cm
Havas
Cond B+/Unobtrusive tears at folds.
When you're promoting a brand of men's linenwear that's more than capable of keeping up with the man on the move, it's best to enliven that product a bit—even if that means personifying it with little more than an energy-emitting logo. A great Art Deco image that shows that when it comes to promoting quality and tradition, it need not be a stuffy display. *Rare!*
**Est: $2,000-$2,500.**

## MARC CHAGALL (1887-1985)

**219. Die Zauberflote/Metropolitan Opera.** 1966.
$25^7/8$ x $39^7/8$ in./65.7 x 101.2 cm
Imp. Mourlot, France
Cond A/P.
Ref: Sorlier, p. 107; PAI-XXXIV, 304
This is one of two posters for the inaugural season of the new Metropolitan Opera at Lincoln Center. It ad-vertises the opening of February 19, 1967: Mozart's "Magic Flute" with sets and costumes by Chagall. Like its companion poster (*see* PAI-XXIX, 280), it borrows a detail from "The Triumph of Music," one of the two large decorations by Chagall that flank the entrance to the opera house. A native of Vitebsk, Russia, Chagall arrived in Paris in 1910 and soon made a name for himself in art circles with his somewhat surreal, poetic vision which seamed best suited for illustrating dreams. Almost all his posters are taken from paint-ings and prints (the print in this case was titled "The Bay of Angels") which were not originally created as posters, but many of them, because of their bold images and bright colors, turn out to make fine posters nonetheless.
**Est: $2,000-$2,500.**

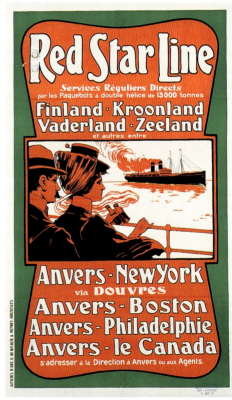

217

## A. CHAZELLE

**220. Blanche Bilbao.** 1926.
$46^7/8$ x 63 in./119 x 160 cm
Imp. H. Chachoin, Paris
Cond A–/Slight stains at edges.

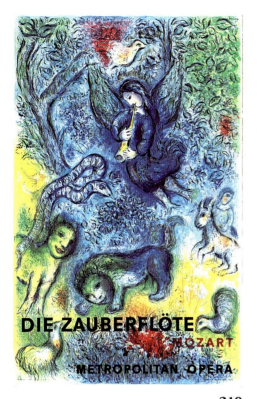

**219**

**220**

**222**

**223**

**221**

Isn't she sweet? It's a darn shame that no record of Ms. Bilbau's talents exist to back up this graphic supposition that only the most angelic of tones could have flowed from such a delicate instrument. Fortuitously, we are left with this tender Chazelle remembrance of this willowy blossom in full bloom.
**Est: $1,400-$1,700.**

These first three posters in our Cheret collection were all printed by the master at his own printing plant, before the 1881 merger with Imprimerie Chaix. They are especially rare and prized by collectors.

## JULES CHÉRET (1836-1932)

**221. L'Oncle Sam.** 1873.
17³/₄ x 14¹/₈ in./45 x 35.8 cm
Imp. J. Chéret, Paris
Cond A.
Ref: Broido, 228; Maindron, 197
There's nothing that invites either American patriotism or derision in this teeming Chéret etching-style design

for a "Quadrille Americain" being performed at the Théâtre de Vaudeville. Regardless of its musical content, this early "Uncle Sam" design is a unique Chéret discovery, possibly used as a program or song sheet cover. *Rare!*
**Est: $800-$1,000.**

**222. La Reine Indigo.** 1875.
21⁵/₈ x 29¹/₈ in./55 x 74 cm
Imp. J. Chéret, Paris
Cond A.
Ref: Broido, 48; Maindron, 43; French Opera, 45
"This was the first French production of Strauss's first operetta with Zulma Bouffar as the heroine, Fantasca. . . . The story is based on *Arabian Nights* motifs, and Strauss derived his popular '1001 Nights Waltz' from musical themes composed for *Indigo*. Feet seem to be dancing on the name of the composer, who, the poster proudly proclaims, is 'from Vienna'" (French Opera, p. xxiii). As one might expect, the operetta was first produced in Vienna, but soon became an international success. "Paris saw an obviously racier show: Romadour in Vienna was merely a high priest,

in Paris he was Chief of the White Eunuchs. 'The Blue Danube,' that irresistible waltz was dropped into the middle of the last act (sung in the wings by a chorus of sailors)" (Operetta, p. 114).
**Est: $1,500-$1,800.**

**223. La Tzigane.** 1877.
23¹/₂ x 31¹/₂ in./59.7 x 80 cm
Imp. J. Chéret, Paris
Cond A.
Ref: Broido, 10; Maindron, 11; French Opera, 46; Spectacle, 731; PAI-XXII, 265
Chéret's poster for the French rendition of Strauss' *Zigeunerbaron*, which opened at the Théâtre de la Renaissance on October 30, 1877, is one of his early works. It hasn't lost any of its vitality over the years and shows how advanced he was compared with the very few others who worked in the trade at the time. The boisterous scene features the ardent fellow in the blue uniform enjoying a dance with a beautiful woman scant moments before a fracas erupts courtesy of a jealous rival in red.
**Est: $1,500-$1,800.**

# JULES CHÉRET (1836-1932)

In 1880, some 15 years before the poster craze even started, art critic Karl Huysmans made the observation that there was a thousand times more talent in the smallest of Chéret's posters than there was in the majority of the pictures hung at the Paris Salon. He probably meant it most to startle some of the more complacent "Established" painters; it was nevertheless a very perceptive statement about a posterist who was still far from reaching his creative peak. What Huysmans saw is a quality that breathes from every Chéret poster: a vibrant, dynamic force that virtually compels you to stop, look and be enchanted.

Just how potent that force was can be estimated from Charles Hiatt's 1895 assessment: "Many have produced charming wall pictures: nobody, save Chéret, has made an emphatic mark on the aspect of a metropolis. Paris, without its Chéret's, would be Paris without one of its most pronounced characteristics; moreover, with its gaiety of aspect materially diminished. The great masses of variegated colour formed by Chéret's posters greet one joyously as one passes every hoarding, smile at one from the walls of every café, arrest one before the windows of every kiosque. The merits of the Saxoliéne lamp, the gaieties of the Moulin Rouge, the charms of Loïe Fuller, the value of a particular brand of cough-lozenges are insisted upon with good-humoured vehemence of which Jules Chéret alone appears to know the secret. Others, in isolated cases, have possibly achieved more compelling decorations, but none can pretend to a success so uniform and unequivocal."

"Chéret is utterly original," chimes in Charles Matlock Price in 1913, " generally subversive, and sometimes almost exasperating in an audacity which throws all precedent to the winds, and launches lightly clad female figures, floating–ephemeral as so many soap bubbles, sparkling, iridescent, and explosive. They seem evoked from airy nothingness, born of daring and fantastic gaiety, and seem joyously to beckon the beholder on with them in a madcap elusive chase after pleasure."

It was Chéret, the lithographic innovator, as well as the artistic and advertising genius, who formulated the technical means to produce posters in every shading of the rainbow with just three or four stones and thus, for the first time, taking the poster from the lithographic Stone Age and making the color pictorial poster an economically feasible marketing instrument. Moreover, as the little magazine *Poster Lore* stated in 1896, "It was not until Jules Chéret, the magician of the brush, began to design his posters with their startling color effects and odd originality, that poster designing attracted attention as a special branch of art."

He gave posters life and proved that they were art; and to top it off, he produced in a career spanning more than half a century, more of them than anyone else. Naturally, in his nearly 1,100 known designs, he had to hark back to similar themes; yet no Chéret poster is ever dull, stale or lacking in original creative spark.

Chéret was in every way a pioneer, an innovator, a mentor—the prophet of the poster.

***The 55 works of Chéret presented in this sale span the entirety of his career and represent one of the largest such collections ever exhibited and offered for sale.***

224

225

226

## JULES CHÉRET (continued)

**224. Tripes à la Mode de Caen.** 1881.
47⁷/₈ x 68 in./121.6 x 172.7 cm
Imp. Chaix, Paris
Cond B+/Unobtrusive folds.
Ref: Broido, 843; Maindron, 714;
    Gourmand, p. 19; PAI-XVIII, 120
The product may be tripe; the image certainly is not. True, it's not Chéret's most glamorous female figure—they came later and, anyway, one of those floozies wouldn't have been very believable stirring-up piping-hot helpings of tripe. For a shop selling the Norman specialty, this Norman cook in her classic cotton bonnet, is just the order.
**Est: $1,400-$1,700.**

**225. Mam'zelle Gavroche.** 1885.
22³/₈ x 31¹/₈ in./57 x 79 cm
Imp. Chaix, Paris
Cond A–/Slight stains at edges.
Ref: Broido, 53 & Pl. 1; Maindron, 47;
    Spectacle, 792; PAI-XXXV, 242
A colorful trifle for an Hervé comic operetta featuring the ample crinolined charms of this fetching conductor as she drums up business for her theatrical endeavors. She's facilely captured the attention of all the men in Chéret's graphic universe, and she achieves the same effect on the fleshier folk from our walk of life that can't help but glance her way.
**Est: $1,000-$1,200.**

**226. Oeuvres de Rabelais.** 1885.
35⁵/₈ x 47⁷/₈ in./85.3 x 121.7 cm
Imp. Chaix, Paris
Cond B/Slight tears at folds and edges.

Ref: Broido, 598; Maindron, 487;
    Maitres, 117 (var); DFP-II, 158(var);
    Reims, 448(var); PAI-XXVIII, 234 (var)
The illustrated works of Rabelais are being offered here at 15 centimes per installment, with the first five at a bargain 5 centimes apiece. To tempt the reader, Chéret supplies a lusty figure, with a sword strapped over his generous stomach, marching down the road in the company of a fulsome woman. A friar by the side of the road looks on with amusement at their hedonism. Small text at lower left tells us "It's better to write about laughter than tears" and admonishes us to live happily. Sagot, in his 1891 catalogue, sold most of Chéret's posters for three to five francs each; this image, however, had a selling price of 20 francs. It was rare even then, and Sagot declared it to be "a superb poster, one of (Chéret's) most beautiful." *This is the smaller, 1-sheet format.*
**Est: $1,400-$1,700.**

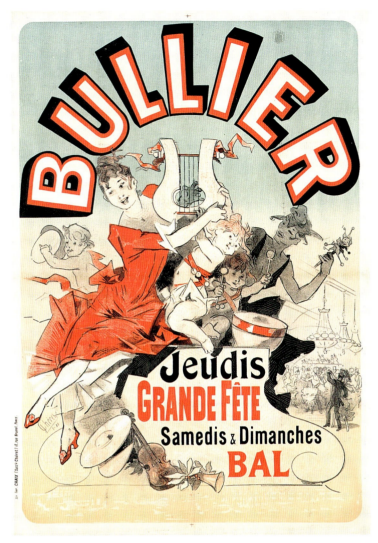

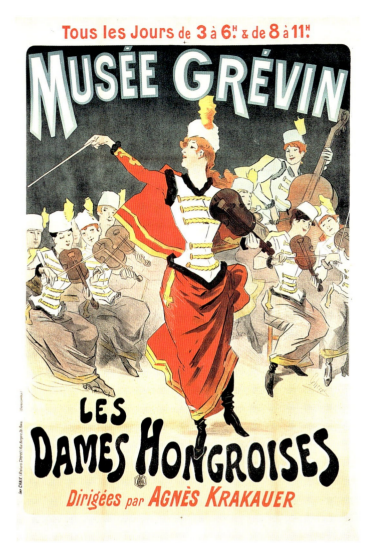

**227**

**228**

**229**

**230**

**227. Bullier.** 1888.
34 x 48³/₈ in./86.3 x 123 cm
Imp. Chaix, Paris
Cond B+/Slight tears and stains at folds.
Ref: Broido, 280; Maindron, 242; PAI-XXX, 461
In this poster for the dance hall favored by students of the Latin Quarter—lithographically very advanced for the time—Chéret uses an allegorical grouping of muses and cherubs, yet at the same time makes the figures quite contemporary in dress and dancing shoes.
**Est: $1,700-$2,000.**

**228. Musée Grévin/Les Dames Hongroises.** 1888.
33³/₈ x 48³/₄ in./84.7 x 124 cm
Imp. Chaix, Paris
Cond B+/Slight stains at folds.
Ref: Broido, 465; Maindron, 378;
  Wine Spectator, 9; PAI-XXII, 300
A Hungarian women's orchestra is led with great élan by a violin-playing conductor. The troupe's uniforms are styled in the manner of Hungary's elite dragoons.
**Est: $2,000-$2,500.**

**229. Nouveau Cirque/La Foire de Séville.** 1889.
34¹/₄ x 47¹/₈ in/87 x 119.8 cm
Imp. Chaix, Paris
Cond B+/Slight tears and stains at folds and edges.
Ref: Broido, 425; Maindron, 345; DFP-II, 177;
  PAI-XXV, 249
A lively pair of flamenco dancers accompanied by a guitar player announce a Spanish revue titled "The Fair of Seville" at the Nouveau Cirque.
**Est: $1,400-$1,700.**

**230. Bal du Moulin Rouge.** 1889.
16¹/₈ x 23³/₄ in./41 x 60.2 cm
Imp. Chaix, Paris
Cond B/Slight tears and stains at folds and edges.
Ref: DFP-II, 181; Broido, 310; Maitres, 53 (var); PAI-XXXI, 57
The Moulin Rouge, which virtually single-handedly created the cancan craze, opened its doors on October 6, 1889, and this is the historic poster for that very occasion. (The same image was used again for the 1892 season.) The donkeys are not Chéret's imagination—the two shrewd creator/promoters, Joseph Oller and Charles Zidler, actually had girls riding donkeys outside to attract attention to the place. That soon became superfluous, as all Paris came to gawk at the display of frilly female underthings by high-kickers like La Goulue, La Torpille, Miss Rigolette, Hirondelle and others, ushering in the Naughty Nineties in a swirl of petticoats. *This is the rare smaller format.*
**Est: $1,400-$1,700.**

**231**

**232**

## JULES CHÉRET (continued)

**231. Jardin de Paris/Fête de Nuit Bal.** 1890.
34$^1$/$_4$ x 48$^7$/$_8$ in./87 x 124 cm
Imp. Chaix, Paris
Cond B+/Slight tears and stains at folds.
Ref: Broido, 250; Maindron, 218; Maitres, 65;
    PAI-XXXII, 266
A flirtatious young woman enjoys the festivities along
with a swirl of other revelers at this café-concert next
door to the Pavillon de l'Horloge. Talk about painting
the town red: the night sky over Paris is positively
scarlet. Joseph Oller, owner of the Moulin Rouge,
took over the Jardin de Paris, which remained a popular nocturnal destination until it closed in 1914. *This
is the larger format.*
**Est: $2,500-$3,000.**

**232. Fête des Fleurs/Bagnères de Luchon.** 1890.
35$^5$/$_8$ x 48$^1$/$_8$ in/85.4 x 122.2 cm
Imp. Chaix, Paris
Cond B+/Slight stains at folds.
Ref: Broido, 485; Maindron 391; Maitres, 101; DFP-II,
    200; PAI-XXV, 246
A lovely young woman with a floral garland announces
the Flower Show in Luchon, an attractive and lively
town that is still one of the most fashionable resorts
in the French Pyrénées, with sulphurous and mildly
radioactive springs.
**Est: $3,000-$4,000.**

**233. La Closerie des Genets.** 1890.
33$^3$/$_8$ x 48$^3$/$_8$ in./84.7 x 123 cm
Imp. Chaix, Paris
Cond B/Slight stains at folds.
Ref: Broido, 667; Maindron, 554; Reims, 304;
    PAI-XXVIII, 238
*Le Radical* announces that it will start serializing the
previously unpublished novel "La Closerie des Genets"
in its upcoming issue. The original stage play from
which it was taken eventually was translated into English, under the title "The Willow Copse."
**Est: $1,200-$1,500.**

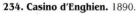

**233**

**234. Casino d'Enghien.** 1890.
40 x 51$^1$/$_4$ in./101.6 x 130.2 cm
Imp. Chaix, Paris (not shown.
Cond B/Restored tears and slight stains at folds.
Ref: Broido, 484; Maindron, 129; Maitres, 129
Though this Chéret mother/daughter hobby horse
steeplechase is as ebulliently breezy as can be, it's
important to note that it was intended to promote a
charity event for the victims of the volcanic eruption at

**234**

Fort-de-France, Martinique, a fact announced on separate text-only poster of the same size.
**Est: $2,000-$2,500.**

**235. La Diaphane.** 1890.
33$^1$/$_2$ x 48$^3$/$_4$ in./85 x 123.8 cm
Imp. Chaix, Paris
Cond B+/Slight tears and stains, largely at paper edges.
Ref: Broido, 931; Maindron, 773; Maitres, 121; PAI-XI,
    172
Sarah Bernhardt was not only a consummate artist, but
also a very good business person. She initiated what
is now a common practice: the celebrity endorsement.

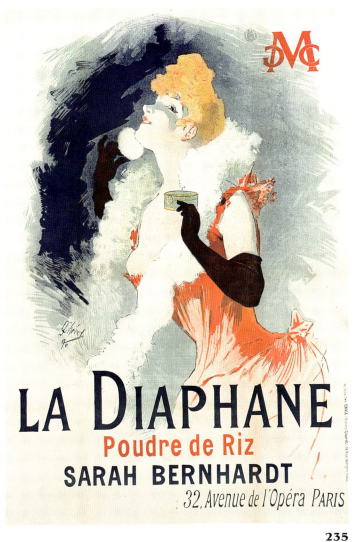

**235**

**236**

**237**

**238**

She first did this for La Diaphane face powder and later for Lefèvre-Utile biscuits (*see* No. 445).
**Est: $2,500-$3,000.**

**236. Yvette Guilbert/Au Concert Parisien.** 1891.
34¼ x 48³⁄₈ in./87 x 123 cm
Imp. Chaix, Paris
Cond B/Slight tears and stains at folds and edges.
Ref: Broido, 215; Maindrom, 188; DFP-II, 213; PAI-XXXII, 233 (var)

Chéret's concept of Ms. Guilbert appears to be at odds with that of most other designers: whereas he sees her as lighthearted and frothy, other posterists, generally, presented her with a far more serious, dignified demeanor. But then, Chéret saw all his women from a fairyland viewpoint, and infrequently allowed reality to interfere with his muse. *Rare proof before addition of "Au Concert Parisien" imprint at bottom.*
**Est: $2,500-$3,000.**

**237. Aux Buttes Chaumont/Exposition.** 1890.
33½ x 48 in./85.2 x 122 cm
Imp. Chaix, Paris
Cond B+/Slight stains at folds.
Ref: Broido, 706; Maindron, 588; DFP-II, 202; PAI-XXIX, 291

A flaxen-haired charmer in a short green dress bursts onto the scene wearing a sandwich board announcing a women's and girls' winter clothing sale. Who could resist such a lovely pitch?
**Est: $1,700-$2,000.**

**238. Le Courrier Français.** 1891.
33⅛ x 48³⁄₈ in./84 x 123 cm
Imp. Chaix, Paris
Cond B+/Unobtrusive folds.
Ref: Broido, 445, Maindron, 362; DFP-II, 216 (var); Reims, 316; Wine Spectator, 16 (var); PAI-XXVIII, 239

The original version of the joyous design, with the allegorical bow-and-arrow toting fairy tickling the face of a satyr with a quill, used to promote an art show arranged by the newspaper. This well-traveled design was used in several manners that very same year: it advertised a second art exhibition arranged by *Le Courrier Français*, it was used as a promotion for the newspaper without the appearance of text, it was sold in several editions as artwork for the home, and lastly, in a reduced format as a supplement to the magazine's March 28 issue. This would seem to be the rarest of all variants.
**Est: $2,000-$2,500.**

239

240

241

## JULES CHÉRET (continued)

**239. Libraire Ed. Sagot/Affiches-Estampes.** 1891.
$32^3/_4$ x $95^1/_4$ in./83.2 x 242 cm
Imp. Chaix, Paris
Cond B/Slight tears, largely at folds and seam. Framed.
Ref: Broido, 528; Maindron, 427; DFP-II, 218; Reims,
406; PAI-XXXV, 259 (var)
If the pretty lass with flowers seems a tad incongruous
advertising a book store, it's because the design was
prepared by Chéret for La Belle Jardinière (The Pretty
Gardener) department store. However, that store's
management, for unknown reasons, didn't like the
design; Sagot, a shrewd purveyor of posters and prints,
saw an opportunity to acquire a beautiful design at a
bargain price, and used it to advertise his first poster
catalogue, which he published in 1891. In fact, this
5-color poster, folded, came to subscribers with the
112-page catalogue: total 10 francs. It's one of the
loveliest of all Chéret posters, a sunny spirited design
in which the woman's face radiates the glow of youth
and vivacity.
**Est: $7,000-$9,000.**

**240. Elysée Montmartre/Bal Masqué.** 1890.
$33^1/_8$ x $94^1/_2$ in./84 x 240 cm
Imp. Chaix, Paris
Cond B/Slight tears at folds; water stains at bottom
edge.
Ref: Broido, 210; Maindron, 260; DFP-II, 190; Wine
Spectator, 13; Reims, 342;
Gold, 144 (var); PAI-XXVIII, 241
Very fresh colors highlight this 2-sheet Chéret delight.
"One of the big Paris dance halls advertises by showing a couple enjoying themselves with abandon. One
of Chéret's assets as a posterist was the way he gave
his figures motion; there is a swing and a rhythm in
his revelers that sweeps us right along with them. It's
hard to imagine one of Chéret's figures as a household drudge or seamstress; they seem to exist only
for the moment, heedlessly bound for pleasure alone.
The posters make you forget everything mundane—
and therein lies the master posterist's greatest talent"
(Gold, p. 100).
**Est: $2,000-$2,500.**

**241. Casino de Paris/Camille Stefani.** 1891.
$33^1/_2$ x $97^1/_2$ in./85 x 246.3 cm
Imp. Chaix, Paris
Cond A–/Unobtrusive tears at folds and edges.
Ref: Broido, 211; Maindron, 185; DFP-II, 214; Reims,
290; PAI-XXXI, 58
This is the two-sheet version of the poster promoting
Camille Stefani's appearance at the Casino de Paris.
She is poise personified, and somehow she maintains
that grace even amidst a swirl of tumbling jesters.
**Est: $3,500-$4,000.**

**242. Casino de Paris/Camille Stefani.** 1891.
$22^7/_8$ x $32^1/_2$ in./58.2 x 82.6 cm
Imp. Chaix, Paris
Cond B/Slight tears and stains at folds and edges.
Ref: Broido, 212; Maindron, 187; PAI-XX, 195
*This is the smaller, 1-sheet version of the previous
poster.*
**Est: $1,500-$1,800.**

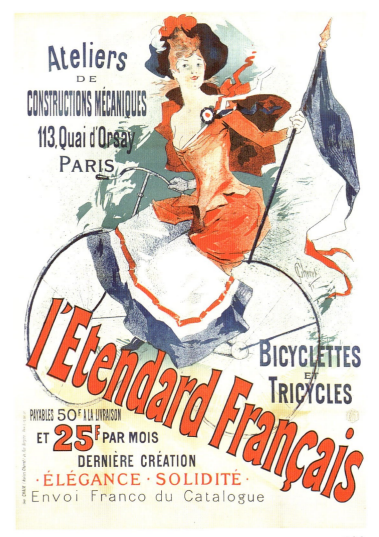

243

244

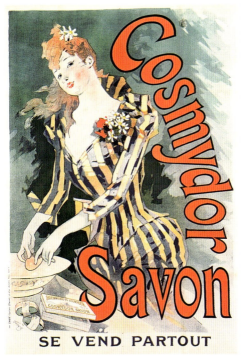

242

245

but we're not told for how many months! It is somewhat surprising that Chéret prepared only two bicycle posters during a 50-year career that encompassed the cycling craze, especially considering that his printing firm, Chaix, which was situated next to the large Clément bicycle company, produced many such posters.
**Est: $2,500-$3,000.**

**243. Alcazar d'Eté/Kanjarowa.** 1891.
34 x 48¼ in./86.5 x 122.6 cm
Imp. Chaix, Paris
Cond B+/Slight tears at folds.
Ref: Broido, 214; Maindron, 186; DFP-II, 215;
   PAI-XXX, 471
This performing paragon of femininity poised against a turbulent background of splashing blues was used to promote her appearance at both the Alcazar d'Été, as seen here, and the Casino de Paris (see PAI-XVI, 200).
**Est: $3,500-$4,000.**

**244. L'Etendard Français.** 1891.
33⁷/₈ x 47³/₈ in./86 x 121.5 cm
Imp. Chaix, Paris
Cond B/Slight tears and stains at folds.
Ref: Broido, 998; Maindron, 820; Reims, 345; DFP-II,
   219; Bicycle Posters, 52; PAI-XXXIII, 17
The bicyclist—appropriately in blue, white and red—holds the banner of the bicycle firm whose name means "banner" as well as "standard," both obviously implied in the design. The company offers a payment plan of 50 francs down and 25 per month thereafter—

**245. Cosmydor Savon.** 1891.
33⁵/₈ x 48¹/₂ in./85.3 x 123.2 cm
Imp. Chaix, Paris
Cond A–/Unobtrusive folds.
Ref: Broido, 938; Maindron, 777; DFP-II, 220;
   PAI-XXXIV, 385 (var)
A lovely poster for Cosmydor soap, featuring a model resplendent with exquisite, rich color. The flowers adorning her dress and hair underline the fresh beauty the soap ostensibly brings to her skin. *This is the larger format.*
**Est: $2,500-$3,500.**

## JULES CHÉRET (continued)

**246. L'Aureole du Midi.** 1893.
33⅝ x 48 in./85.4 x 122 cm
Imp. Chaix, Paris
Cond B/Slight stains at folds.
Ref: Broido, 975; Maindron, 805; Maitres, 237; DFP-II, 243; PAI-XXIX, 308
Perhaps to show that this lamp can be handled even by a child, Chéret allows a little towheaded tike to run around with it, while another one carries a canister of kerosene, cheerfully disregarding basic safety precautions. But we forgive him because the kids are just so darn cute, especially the one in the polka-dot dress.
**Est: $2,500-$3,000.**

**247. Musée Grévin/Pantomimes Lumineuses.** 1892.
34⅝ x 48⅝ in./88 x 123.7 cm
Imp. Chaix, Paris
Cond B+/Slight tears at folds.
Ref: Broido, 468; Maindron, 381; DFP-II, 227; PAI-XIX, 293
Emile Reynaud (1844-1918) was a science teacher who combined a primitive peephole viewing apparatus with a projector, and came up with strips of celluloid pictures in color, coming as close to inventing movies as anyone could. He even used perforations to advance the images. After obtaining a patent in 1889, he put on his first public show at the Musée Grévin on October 28, 1892. Between then and 1900, there were 12,800 performances attended by more than 500,000 customers. However, Mr. Reynaud brooded over the fact that by then, regular motion pictures, perfected by others, left him in virtual obscurity. One day in 1900, he took all his apparatus and slides and tossed them into the Seine. Eighteen years later, he died in a sanitarium, entirely forgotten by the world. At least we have this fine poster to remember him by.
**Est: $3,000-$4,000.**

249

250

251

**248. Bal du Moulin Rouge.** 1892.
35⁵/₈ x 49 in./89.7 x 124.4 cm
Imp. Chaix, Paris
Cond B/Slight tears and stains at folds and edges.
Ref: Broido, 309; Maindron, 253; DFP-II, 181; Maitres,
53; Reims, 275; Wine Spectator, 6; PAI-XXXIV,
310
*This is the larger format of the poster seen in Lot 230.*
**Est: $3,000-$4,000.**

**249. Grands Magasins du Louvre/Jouets, Etrennes**
1891.
33¹/₄ x 95¹/₄ in./84.5 x 242
Imp. Chaix, Paris
Cond B+/Slight tears at seam and edges.
Ref: Broido, 673; Maindron, 560; DFP-II, 203;
PAI-XXX, 496

A cascading 2-sheet image of overjoyed children with
the toys and gifts they've received from the Louvre
department store. Infectiously charming.
**Est: $3,000-$4,000.**

**250. Purgatif Géraudel.** 1891.
32³/₄ x 95³/₄ in./83.2 x 243.2 cm
Imp. Chaix, Paris
Cond B+/Unobtrusive folds. Framed.
Ref: Broido, 894; Maindron, 743; DFP-II, 221; Health
Posters, 273; PAI-XXX, 468

A lively *Chérette* is caught in a 2-sheet whirlwind of
blossoms and boxes of Purgatif Géraudel, a product
that promises "a fresh rosy complexion, excellent
digestion, physical strength, perfect health and regular
sleep"—all for only 1.5 francs per box. One is often
asked how much posters cost in their own day relative
to other commodities. The 1891 Sagot catalogue lists

this two-sheet poster for 3 francs—the cost of two
boxes of these miraculous little pills.
**Est: $3,500-$4,000.**

**251. Cacao Lhara/F. Mugnier.** 1893.
35⁵/₈ x 94⁷/₈ in./85.7 x 240.8 cm
Imp. Chaix, Paris
Cond B/Slight tears and stains at folds.
Ref: Broido, 864; Maindron, 730; DFP-II, 241;
PAI-XXX, 29

Mugnier's success bottling a cherry-flavored liqueur
called Bigarreau (*see* No. 268) eventually enabled him
to expand until he had the largest distillery in the Dijon
area. In this two-sheet design, the drink being advertised
is a chocolate-flavored one in Mugnier's prize-winning
line, and Chéret offers it to us from the hand of a
dark-haired temptress in a Spanish mantilla and shawl.
**Est: $2,000-$2,500.**

## JULES CHÉRET (continued)

**252. Olympia/Anciennes Montagnes Russes.** 1893.
$34^1/4$ x $48^3/4$ in./87 x 124 cm
Imp. Chaix, Paris
Cond B+/Unobtrusive tears at top paper edge; colors very fresh.
Ref: Broido, 345; Maindron, 278; Gold, 146; Maitres, 133; DFP-II, 225;
    Folies Bergère, 28; Masters 1900, p. 12; PAI-XXXIV, 329 (var)
With éclat and élan, to say nothing of a pair of cymbals, the ebullient,
unabashedly hedonistic sprite calls us to the Olympia to enjoy the "Russian mountains"—French term for the rollercoaster. The poster was used
for the opening of this new establishment, in April of 1893; it was one of
the first places in Paris that called itself a "music-hall," borrowing a word
from British show business. There was a bumpy ride as an added attraction to the usual stage spectacles, but to call it a rollercoaster was probably somewhat euphemistic. *This is the larger format.*
**Est: $5,000-$6,000.**

**253. Alcazar d'Eté/Louise Balthy.** 1893.
$33^1/2$ x $48^1/2$ in/85 x 123
Imp. Chaix, Paris
Cond B+/Slight tears and stains at folds.
Ref: Broido, 173; Maindron, 153; Spectacle, 828; PAI-XXIV, 231
Looking over her shoulder, the performer executes a nimble step. The
pointy-chinned Balthy (1869-1925) was a well-known interpreter of
humorous songs who had already become a headliner at the Eldorado at
the age of 17; later she worked at other cabarets, including the Scala, the
Bodinière and, here, at the Alcazar d'Été. Cappiello showed her, almost 10
years later, at the Folies-Bérgère (*see* PAI-XXXI, 50).
**Est: $2,500-$3,000.**

**254. Halle aux Chapeaux/Depuis 3F60.** 1892.
33 x $47^1/2$ in/83.8 x 120.6 cm
Imp. Chaix, Paris
Cond A. Framed.
Ref: Broido, 830; Maindron, 704; DFP-II, 231; Maitres 1900, p. 11; Wine
    Spectator, 17; Gold, 250; PAI-XXXIV, 319
One of the most appealing of several posters Chéret designed for this

**255**

**256**

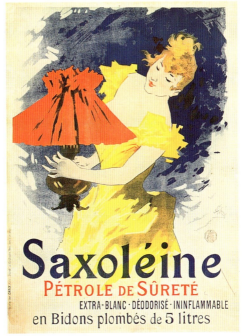

**257**

**258**

**256. Saxoléine.** 1900.
34 1/2 x 48 7/8 in./87.8 x 124 cm
Imp. Chaix, Paris
Cond A.
Ref: Broido, 957; DFP-II, 209; Wine Spectator, 20; PAI-
XXXIV, 332
Chéret's series for Saxoléine kerosene extended over
ten years and as many memorable designs. They all
show little more than a woman and a lamp, but they
constitute a virtual textbook on the use of the female
figure to sell a product. This poster is the only one in
the series in which a heater, rather than a lamp, is
shown, basking the surroundings in a comfy snug red.
*Rare variant without printer's name lower left.*
**Est: $2,500-$3,000.**

**257. Saxoléine.** 1893.
23 1/8 x 32 1/8 in./58.7 x 81.6 cm
Imp. Chaix, Paris
Cond B/Tears and stains at edges; image and colors
excellent.
Ref: Broido, 942; Maindron, 781; PAI-XXI, 135
One of the first of the distinguished Chéret kerosene
series. Here, a yellow dress and a red lampshade
create just the appropriate tone of warmth and lumi-
nosity. *This is the smaller format.*
**Est: $1,400-$1,700.**

**258. Saxoléine.** 1894.
33 1/2 x 48 7/8 in./85 x 124 cm
Imp. Chaix, Paris
Cond B+/Slight tears at folds and edges.
Ref: Broido, 948; Maindron, 787; DFP-II, 249;
PAI-VIII, 89 (var)
This young woman, who appears to be as much in awe
of her kerosene illumination as she is appreciative
for its presence, makes another lovely addition to the
Saxoléine parade of exalted domesticity.
**Est: $1,400-$1,700.**

fashionable Paris hat shop. The golden-haired child
trying on her bonnet is the star, although her mother,
in a fashionable red dress, gets only slightly lesser
billing. It's interesting to note that at the time when
you could buy a hat for 3.6 francs, this poster advertising it could be had for slightly less—3 francs—at
Sagot's and Arnould's print shops.
**Est: $2,500-$3,000.**

**255. Redoute des Etudiants.** 1894.
33 x 48 1/4 in./84 x 122.6 cm
Imp. Chaix, Paris
Cond A–/Slight tears at folds.
Ref: Broido, 291; Maindron, 247; Maitres, 85;
DFP-II, 245; PAI-XXXV, 256 (var)
One of the most ebullient of Chéret's always animated
scenes used to promote a student ball, with this rol-
licking trio coming at us with verve and gusto. *Rare!*
**Est: $7,000-$9,000.**

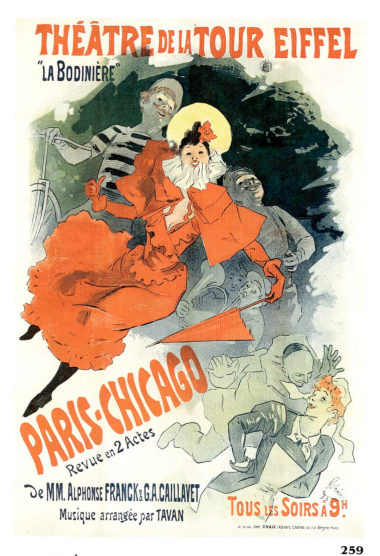

**259**

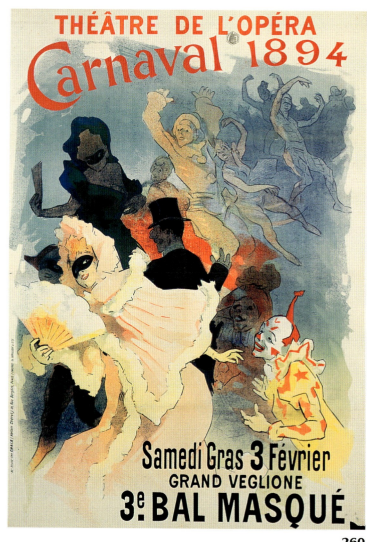

**260**

## JULES CHÉRET (continued)

**259. Théâtre de la Tour Eiffel/Paris-Chicago.** 1893.
$34^1/8$ x $48^1/2$ in./86.8 x 123.7 cm
Imp. Chaix, Paris
Cond B+/Slight tears at folds.
Ref: Broido, 273; Maindron, 239; DFP-II, 2379; PAI-XXXIV, 333
One of Chéret's carefree nymphs with no visible means of support advertises a revue at La Bodinière, an adjunct to the Théâtre de la Tour Eiffel; as always, everything has a feeling of breezy gaiety and lighthearted fun; anyone who'd inquire what the show was about would have been a grump who'd never come to see it anyway.
**Est: $3,500-$4,000.**

**260. Carnaval 1894/3e Bal Masque.** 1894.
$34^1/4$ x $48^1/2$ in./87 x 123 cm.
Imp. Chaix, Paris
Cond A–/Slight tears at folds.
Ref: Broido, 290; Maindron, 236; DFP-II, 236; PAI-XXV, 252
A very lively scene with assorted revelers invites us to the third masked ball of the 1894 season. The feeling of agitated movement is conveyed with a masterly perfection.
**Est: $6,000-$8,000.**

**261. Folies-Bergère/Emilienne d'Alençon.** 1893.
23 x $32^3/8$ in./58.4 x 82.2 cm
Imp. Chaix, Paris
Cond B+/Slight tears at folds.
Ref: Broido, 124; Maindron, 112; Maitres, 113; Spectacle, 1128; Cirque, 598
Emilienne d'Alençon was one of the desirable women of the French Belle Epoque stage that came to be known as the *Grand Trois*—a trio of famous courtesans that included Liane de Pougy and La Belle Otero. Though she studied acting at the Conservatoire for a relatively brief period of time, she became a sensation for an act that she developed at the Cirque d'Eté that she later reprised at the Folies Bergere to great acclaim—advertised with this Chéret poster, no less. Knowing as all fashionable women do that accessorizing is everything, d'Alençon dressed completely in pink—frothy taffeta with lace

**261**

**262**

trimming to be exact—"Raspberry Ice" was how writer Jean Lorrain described her. To complete her ensemble, she had a collection of performing rabbits that she dyed a particularly shocking shade of pink, topped off with ruffles, that she included as part of the act.
**Est: $1,500-$1,800.**

**262. Madame Sans-Gêne.** 1894.
$32^5/8$ x $48^3/4$ in./82.8 x 123.8 cm
Imp. Chaix, Paris
Cond A–/Slight tears at folds. Framed.
Ref: Broido, 670; Maindron, 557; DFP-II, 247; PAI-XXVI, 258

The newspaper *Le Radical* announces serialization of the classic story of a laundress who wheedles her way into high society. Chéret chose a moment when the girl is already a duchess; she stands in her splendid gown and ermine-lined cloak, receiving a note from a young officer at a writing table—Napoleon.
**Est: $1,200-$1,500.**

**263. Folies-Bergère/La Danse du Feu.** 1897.
$34^3/8$ x 49 in./87.3 x 124.4 cm
Imp. Chaix, Paris

# FOLIES-BERGÈRE

La Danse du Feu

**263**

## CHAMPS-ELYSÉES

Palais de Glace

**264**

Palais de Glace
Champs Elysées

**265**

Palais de Glace
Champs-Elysées

**266**

something new to her work . . . but with her latest creations, especially the fire dance and the lily dance, she was again enthralling the Paris public" (Fuller/Goddess of Light, p. 111). And so Chéret's poster did not need to name her—the performance title, "Dance of Fire," said it all.
**Est: $8,000-$10,000.**

**264. Palais de Glace.** 1896.
33$^1/4$ x 48$^5/8$ in./84.4 x 123.5 cm
Imp. Chaix, Paris
Cond A–/Unobtrusive tears at edges.
Ref: Broido, 368; DFP-II, 256; Wine Spectator, 19;
    Gold, 131; PAI-XXX, 158
The skater in the red-and-yellow striped skirt is one of the loveliest of the several designs that Chéret created for the Paris ice-skating rink between 1893 and 1900. And with the help of her partner—umbered by an eclipse of radiant beauty—creates a compelling vision of oppositional balance that couldn't possibly be more appealing. *Exceptionally pristine colors! This is the larger format.*
**Est: $8,000-$10,000.**

**265. Palais de Glace.** 1893.
16$^1/8$ x 23$^5/8$ in./41 x 60 cm
Imp. Chaix, Paris
Cond A–/Unobtrusive folds.
Ref: Broido, 36a; PAI-XXX, 161
With a turn of the head, this lithe skater lures the viewer into gliding along with her in this most-appealing—and quite probably most subtle—Chéret design for the Parisian ice palace in its "Courrier Français" incarnation.
**Est: $2,000-$2,500.**

**266. Palais de Glace.** 1894.
15$^3/4$ x 23$^1/2$ in./40 x 59.8 cm
Imp. Chaix, Paris
Cond A–/Unobtrusive folds.
Ref: Broido, 367; PAI-XXXIII, 281
The *Courrier Français* supplement of this magnificent Palais de Glace design features the charms of a skater whose sunny disposition all but melts the ice.
**Est: $2,000-$2,500.**

Cond B+/Slight tears at folds.
Ref: Broido, 128; DFP-II, 262; Abdy, p. 61;
    Gold, 168; PAI-XXX, 122
One of the most spectacular images ever created for Loïe Fuller, this poster also shines as one of the rarest and very finest posters ever produced by Chéret. Fuller's specialty gave Chéret license to indulge his penchant for depicting joyous motion to the fullest. Talk about "tripping the light fantastic"! "L'Estampe et l'Affiche" called it "a masterpiece of light and motion" (1897, p. 243). "Loïe Fuller's meteoric rise to fame is one of the oddest success stories of the 1890s. Coming from a small Midwestern town in the United States, . . . she

studied singing, dancing and acting . . . In one play, she noticed how the spotlights, with various color filters, created a rainbow effect on the material of her dress. Fascinated, she experimented with the effect, eventually working up a specialty dance wearing diaphanous materials on which the colored lights played with dazzling results" (Gold, p. 116). In the newly-published and quite revealing biography of the dancer, we read that: "the French had always taken Loïe more seriously than the Americans had, and they did so again after she reappeared at the Folies-Bergère on October 21, 1897. . . . She had maintained her fame by constantly adding

267

268

## JULES CHÉRET (continued)

**267. Arlequin au Lutte.** 1900.
10 x 13$^{1}$/$_{4}$ in./25.4 x 33.6 cm
Oil on board. Framed.
*Signed and dedicated to Ernest Maindron, the famed historian of poster art ("à mon cher ami E. Maindron").*
With his career as a posterist crowned by the Legion of Honor in 1890, Chéret devoted himself to decorative painting. At his easel every day, he was in the habit of giving his canvases away rather than exhibiting them. Writing of the works in 1986, Jean Forneris observes that their "chromatic palette, which systematically eliminates dark values. . . and . . . renders shadows by blue or green tonalities . . . without any doubt reminds us that Chéret has looked at impressionist painting in its maturity." And he obviously did a bit more than look, as this gamboling harlequin provides ample proof that regardless of Chéret's reputation as a master posterist, his talents extended far past the lithographic stones to the realm of the palette and the brush.
**Est: $20,000-$25,000.**

**268. Bigarreau.** 1895.
33$^{3}$/$_{8}$ x 95$^{1}$/$_{4}$ in./84.5 x 242 cm
Imp. Chaix, Paris
Cond B+/Slight tears at folds.
Ref (All Var): Boido, 875; DFP-II, 254; Reims, 276; PAI-XXXIV, 318

A young taster is sampling a finished product as the lass on the ladder picks this year's vintage of grapes to be transformed into Bigarreau liqueur. A somewhat off-beat, but most appealing two-sheet poster by Chéret. *Adding to the rarity, this specimen is hand-signed by the artist at lower right!*
**Est: $2,500-$3,000.**

**269. Le Punch Grassot.** 1895.
33 x 47$^{3}$/$_{8}$ in./83.8 x 120.2 cm
Imp. Chaix, Paris
Cond B/Slight tears, stains and creases, largely at paper edges. Framed.
Ref: Broido, 876; Maindron, 427; DFP-II, 218 (var); Reims, 406; PAI-XXXIII, 294 (var)
*Rare proof before letters.*
In this masterpiece of three-color printing, Chéret subordinates the details of draftsmanship to the overall sweep of the scene. The design itself is rarely seen—much less without text—with one of the artist's delightful women airily carrying a tray of Grassot's best.
**Est: $2,500-$3,000.**

**270. La Dentellière.** 1900.
34$^{1}$/$_{8}$ x 50$^{1}$/$_{4}$ in./86.6 x 127.6 cm
Imp. Chaix & de Malherbe, Paris
Cond A–/Unobtrusive stains at edges. Framed.
Ref: Broido, 65; PAI-XXXV, 252

For the 1900 World's Fair in Paris, Chéret created two decorative panels for the publisher Malherbe. *La Fileuse* (The Spinner—*see* PAI-XXXII, 250) has hair as soft, fluffy and fine as the wool she is turning into yarn for the weaver at the loom in shadows behind her. *La Dentellière* (The Lace-Maker), seen here, wears a ruffle of the frothy stuff she seems to produce without the slightest bit of effort. And, as is always the case for Chéret, neither of these ladies are precisely dressed for the tasks they are involved with. But what good is artistic license if it's never used.
**Est: $2,200-$2,600.**

**271. Pippermint.** 1899.
34 x 48$^{1}$/$_{8}$ in./86.3 x 122 cm
Imp. Chaix, Paris
Cond B/Slight tears, largely at folds. Framed.
Ref: Broido, 883; Maitres, 213; Wine Spectator, 2; DFP-II, 205; PAI-XXXIII, 289
Just by placing a dark area behind the figure and bathing her front in an orange glow, Chéret is able to suggest the cozy intimacy of a fireside scene to advertise this cool-tasting mint liqueur. Another subtle graphic touch is the way the woman's sleeve seems to form a nestling hood around her head. *This is the larger format.*
**Est: $1,700-$2,000.**

**269**

**270**

**271**

**272**

**273**

**272. Musée Grévin/Fantoches de John Hewelt.** 1900.
34³/₈ x 48⁵/₈ in./87.4 x 123.5 cm
Imp. Chaix, Paris
Cond A–/Slight stains and creases at edges. Framed.
Ref: Broido, 471; DFP-II, 267; PAI-XXXIV, 328
This is the before-lettering version of Chéret's charming
poster for *Les Fantoches*, a puppet-show extravaganza
staged at the theater of the Musée Grevin, a frequent
Chéret client—in fact, the design was so eye-catching
that it was also used to announce a Fête des Artistes at

the venue (*see* PAI-XV, 222). Some versions of the image
show the printer's name, while others, such as this, have
no text at all. With text or word-free, Chéret's fine
sense of composition and great lithographic skill shine.
**Est: $2,500-$3,000.**

**273. Grands Magasins du Louvre/Etrennes 1897.**
33¹/₄ x 47⁷/₈ in./84.2 x 121.6 cm
Imp. Chaix, Paris

Cond B+/Unobtrusive tears and stains at folds and
edges.
Ref: Broido, 674; DFP-II, 257; PAI-VIII, 80
Children and clowns are perfect subjects to show
rollicking fun and movement, and Chéret took full
advantage of that fact in all his designs for toy and
gift sales at various stores.
**Est: $1,700-$2,000.**

274

275

## JULES CHÉRET (continued)

**274. Théâtre de l'Opéra/Gd Veglione de Gala/
3e Bal Masqué.** 1897.
$33^{1}/_{2}$ x $48^{3}/_{8}$ in./85.2 x 123 cm
Imp. Chaix, Paris
Cond B/Slight tears and stains at folds and edges.
Ref (All Var but Broido & PAI): Broido, 299A;
    Maitres, 105; DFP-II, 263; Wagner, 48;
    Timeless Images, 10; PAI-XXII, 275
This design was used for four balls during the 1897
season at the Théâtre de l'Opéra; interestingly enough,
practically all sources document only the first, second
and fourth one, making this poster for the 3rd Ball the
rarest version. We don't know what the gentleman is
whispering to the ravishing beauty, but if it isn't a compliment, then he's not on the ball even if he's at the ball.
**Est: $5,000-$6,000.**

**275. Théâtre de l'Opéra/Carnaval 1896/Dernier
    Gd. Bal Masqué.** 1895.
$33^{7}/_{8}$ x $48^{3}/_{8}$ in./86 x 123 cm
Imp. Chaix, Paris
Cond A–/Slight tears at folds.
Ref (All Var): Broido, 293; Maitres, 9; DFP-II, 251;
    Reims, 528; PAI-XXXV, 254
Like virtually all of the posters Chéret did for the
dances at this theater between 1892 and 1897, the
design features a profiled woman in a billowing dress
looking out over her shoulder as a shadowy male
figure and other revelers dance around her. Chéret
would do a single design each winter and it would be
repeated with varying text throughout the season. For
1896, the charmer's dress is striped in two shades of
green and she gestures to her escort with a fan. It's
interesting to see how Chéret, reworking the same
visual ingredients, always keeps us interested.
**Est: $7,000-$9,000.**

## CHOPPY

**276. La Houppa.**
$46^{7}/_{8}$ x $62^{1}/_{2}$ in./119 x 158.7 cm

276

Imp. Choppy, Paris
Cond A–/Unobtrusive folds.
Ref: PAI-XXVII, 368
A radiant invitation to trip the light fantastic from La
Houppa, the vivacious entertainer who never appeared
on stage without her top hat, high-stepping her way
into our hearts in a flouncing gumdrop dress. Though
little is known of Choppy, he created at least one other
image for La Houppa, featuring her in the company of
her adorable furball hand-puppet sidekick, Fourtoutou
(*see* PAI-XXIV, 245).
**Est: $1,700-$2,000.**

278

## ALFRED CHOUBRAC (1853-1902)

**277. Fin de Siècle.** 1891.
$31^{1}/_{4}$ x $46^{1}/_{8}$ in./79.3 x 117.2 cm
Lith. F. Appel, Paris
Cond B+/Slight tears and stains at edges.
Ref: Maindron, pp. 54 & 55; Wine Spectator, Intro;
    PAI-X, 199a
To announce a new magazine, *Fin de Siècle*, Choubrac
depicted a young woman in a provocative posture
and skimpy costume. When the censors objected, the
publisher capitalized on it by publishing it anyway,

**277**

**279**

**280**

**281**

279. **Folies-Bergère/Ilka de Mynn.** ca. 1890.
$30^3/_4$ x $46^3/_4$ in./78 x 118.8 cm
Lith. F. Appel, Paris
Cond B/Restored tears, largely at folds.
Ref: Reims, 561; PAI-VIII, 309
The seductive artiste, in non-concealing gauzy attire, is depicted against a night sky, placing her respectfully amidst other luminaries and completed by a huge crescent moon. Other than her flesh tone, midnight blue and pale yellow are the only colors required. Sagot called it one of the finest works of Choubrac (No. 992) and charged his highest price—5 francs—for the artist's work. Choubrac was one of the pioneers of French poster art; in 1884, when Maindron published his first article on posters, he listed only nine active posterists known to him, and included the three poster artists whose work made up the first poster exhibition, held that same year in the Passage Vivienne in Paris: Alfred and Léon Choubrac and Jules Chéret.
**Est: $1,500-$1,800.**

**HOWARD CHANDLER CHRISTY (1873-1952)**

280. **The Spirit of America/Red Cross.** 1919.
$20^1/_8$ x $29^3/_4$ in./51 x 75.5 cm
Cond B–/Restored tears at folds and edges.
Ref: Darracott, 6
The American Red Cross, one of the nation's premier humanitarian organizations, was founded on May 21, 1881 in Washington, D.C. by Clara Barton and a circle of acquaintances. Barton had been inspired by the Swiss International Red Cross Movement while visiting Europe following the Civil War. During the First World War, the Red Cross staffed military hospitals and ambulance companies. Christy's humanitarian recruitment poster conveys a confident, upbeat postwar optimism.
**Est: $800-$1,000.**

with the objectionable section duly whited out and overprinted with the explanation that "this portion of the design was censored" (see PAI-X, 199b).
**Est: $1,500-$1,800.**

278. **Fin de Siècle.** ca. 1891.
$32^1/_4$ x $46^1/_4$ in./82 x 117.4 cm
Lith. F. Appel, Paris
Cond B/Slight tears and stains at folds and edges.
A far more demure Choubrac damsel is used to promote

the *Fin de Siècle* publication than what we have previously seen by the artist. Perhaps this was a follow up promotion, with the artist deciding that perhaps all the broo-ha-ha was an unnecessary distraction for a publication featuring such contributors as Emile Zola, Guy de Maupassant and Aristide Bruant. *Fin de Siècle* began publication in December 1890 and concluded in 1909.
**Est: $1,200-$1,500.**

**282**

**283**

## A. CLAEYS

**281. Breedene.** 1948.
24$^1$/$_4$ x 38$^1$/$_2$ in./61.5 x 97.8 cm
Leon Beyaert-Sion, Kortrijk
Cond A–/Unobtrusive tears.
With the harsh realities of the war now behind them, it was time to once more attempt to return to the normalcies of life, an existence concerned with thoughts of vacations rather than those of survival. And what better way than with an affordable little camping excursion to Belgian's Breedene sur Mer. Claeys' sunshine design lets the viewer know right up front—with both its French/Flemish text and a multinational display of pennants—that Breedene is the perfect destination. What a gorgeous beach. And more importantly, what a wonderful attitude.
**Est: $1,000·$1,200.**

## PLINIO CODOGNATO (1878-1940)

**282. Salvatore Castelli.** 1934.
38$^3$/$_4$ x 55$^1$/$_8$ in./98.4 x 140 cm
S. A. Parini Vanoni, Milano
Cond A–/Unobtrusive folds.
What a forceful image from Codognato for the Salvatore Castelli in-country shipping enterprise, its muscularly direct Art Deco assertiveness providing instant evidence that the firm can get whatever—and one must assume whomever—anyone might need to get from Point A to Point B with extreme immediacy, be that by land, sea or air. Codognato was one of the best Italian graphic artists of the 20th century, creating about 150 first-rate posters for commercial products, theater and sporting events. He is best known for his work for Fiat, Pirelli, Campari and Cinzano, as well as his auto racing posters. All his work is charged with motion that gives it a unique intensity.
**Est: $3,000·$4,000.**

**283. 1er Salon International de l'Aeronautique.** 1935.
27$^1$/$_4$ x 39$^1$/$_4$ in./69 x 100 cm
Cond B+/Unobtrusive folds.
Ref: Ali d'Italia, p. 85 (var)
Certainly the streaking aircraft is impressive, but it truly takes a back seat to the pillared avian iconoclasm on display, a message used to promote a Milanese international air show that is both stately and aggressive, much in keeping with the Italian political climate of the period. *This is the smaller format, with text in French.*
**Est: $6,000·$8,000.**

**284. Cicli "Jenis".**
38$^3$/$_4$ x 54$^1$/$_4$ in./98.4 x 137.7 cm
Lit. Sala, Milano
Cond B–/Restored tears in bottom text area and at folds.
What a peculiar concept: Although it's graphically obvious that the Jenis firm produces bicycles and bicycle parts—as well as the textually noted van manufacturing—the way these bikes and parts are spewed forth from the factory's infernic furnace makes it appear as if the bikes are falling apart as they're flung into the atmosphere. Codognato's fiery design does, however, achieve its primary mission—to make it hard to look away once he's secured the passerby's attention.
**Est: $1,200·$1,500.**

## PAUL COLIN (1892-1986)

**285. André Renaud.** 1929.
44$^3$/$_4$ x 61 in./113.7 x 155 cm
Imp. H. Chachoin, Paris
Cond A–/Unobtrusive slight tears at edges. Framed.
Ref: Colin, 39; Colin Affichiste, 74; Art Deco, p. 99;
    PAI-XXXIV, 340

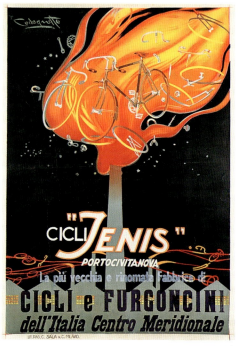

**284**

The two pianos that André Renaud simultaneously played look like a double exposure, but, like all the geometric "tricks" of Colin, they are deliberately drawn for maximum effect. And the effect that Colin seeks here—to overwhelm us with the wizardry of Renaud—is achieved by the sheer mass of the combined pianos.
**Est: $22,000·$28,000.**

**285**

**286**

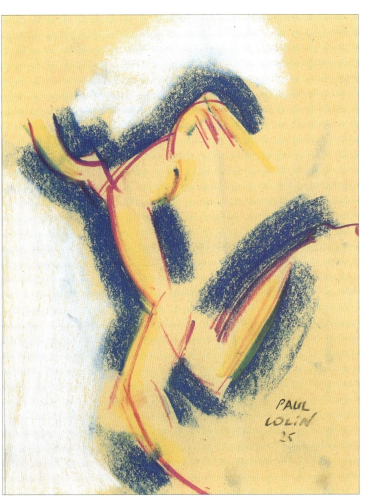

**287**

**286. Grand Guignol/Le Main de Singe.** 1930.
43⁵/₈ x 59 in./110.8 x 149.8 cm
Imp. H. Chachoin, Paris (not shown)
Cond B/Trimmed to image; restored losses largely in top text area.
Ref: Colin, 60; PAI-XXXI, 401
"Horror reigned at the Grand Guignol and people flocked in, not knowing or caring much about the plot of the play they were about to see, but taking comfort in the certainty that they were going to be frightened out of their seats" (Colin, p. 10). In this case the fright fest in question was one of the all-time horror classics, "The Monkey's Paw," a tale that all but created the phrase "Be careful what you wish for." "Asked about his unusual, almost photographic, treatment in this poster, Colin says: 'You can interpret Mistinguett or plays and actors in various ways, but for a drama whose sole purpose is to frighten, the poster itself must become terrifying and gruesome and this does require a realistic treatment'" (Colin, p. 10). Thus, he adds a rotary printing press to the arsenal of horror weapons.
**Est: $2,000-$2,500.**

**287. Jean Borlin.** 1925.
7¹/₄ x 9¹/₂ in./18.5 x 24 cm
*Hand-signed pastel and crayon maquette.* Framed.
Jean Borlin, the Swedish dancer and choreographer, who would go on to found and present the instantly-successful Swedish Ballet in Paris during the 1920 season of the Théâtre de Champs-Elysées, was something of a multi-disciplinarian, determined "to enlarge the field of ballet, and re-invigorate it, by bending to its service the newest tendencies in art, music, and literature, yet never allowing any of these elements to dominate the dance . . . Experiment succeeded experiment, each bolder than the last. . . . In after years, it is sometimes difficult to understand the clamour excited by certain productions, so often is the sensation of to-day the commonplace of to-morrow. But the pioneers are sacrificed on the altar of progress, and Borlin suffered from being in advance of his time. . . . (He) disbanded the 'Ballets Suédois' (in 1925), . . . but continued to give dance recitals both in France and abroad" (*Complete Book of Ballets*, by Cyril W. Beaumont, pp. 669 & 670). How appropriate then that this Colin pencil-and-crayon study eschews detail for impressionistic abstraction, putting the essence of Borlin's motion into colorbound focus without the distraction of pedestrian detail.
**Est: $3,000-$4,000.**

**289**

**291**

**292**

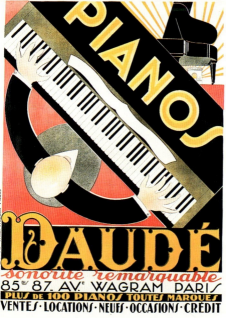

**293**

**288**

**PAUL COLIN (continued)**

**288. Liberty Knot.**
$16^{1}/_{2}$ x $10^{3}/_{4}$ in. 42 x 27.4 cm
Cond A–/Slight stains and creases. Framed.
The ties that bind. Historically, both diplomatically
and artistically, France has been bound to the United
States. From colonialism and nascent nation status,
through peace and conflict, this tandem of nations
has relied on one another even during the times
where they may not have precisely seen eye-to-eye.
Colin's spectacular silk-screen conveys the entire
spectrum of nationalistic emotions with a simple
twist—flags become ropes and ropes form an inextri-
cable knot of liberty, full of the implications that such
a condition would warrant: strength, determination
and solidarity, as well as tension and dependence.
**Est: $1,400-$1,700.**

**GISBERT COMBAZ (1869-1941)**

**289. Inauguration Hotel de Ville/Saint-Gilles.**
    1904.
$39^{3}/_{8}$ x $60^{1}/_{8}$ in/100 x 152.7 cm
O. De Rycker, Bruxelles
Cond B/Slight tears at folds and edges. Framed.
Ref: Brussels, 15; PAI-XXIII, 230
A bell-ringer announces the opening of the newly en-

larged City Hall of the St. Gilles commune in Brussels.
The pictorial ingredients—the woman, the fruit tree and
the sun—are elements that Combaz favored in his
series of posters for the society of La Libre Esthétique
(*see* PAI-III, 66-68), but they're combined here in a way
that is far less stylized than his usual manner. "This
representation echoes the words of a commemorative
poem by Lucien Solvay, which was also created for the
opening festivities: 'A palace that rises in the air, its
superb forehead crowned with azure and light, proclaims the triumphal effort of the work and proud
thought'" (Brussels, p. 68). Combaz was an Oriental
scholar, painter and graphic designer, as well as a
lawyer, often indicated by the "Me." (for "Maitre")
before his signature. *Rare!*
**Est: $1,500-$1,800.**

**A. COMETTI**

**290. Freia Chocolade.**
$43^{1}/_{2}$ x $49^{3}/_{4}$ in./110.5 x 151.6 cm
Affiches Camis, Paris
Cond B/Restored tears at folds.
This stork may have delivered this portly bundle of joy
in a slightly less corpulent state, but now it's payback
time. And what better remuneration than the sweet
reward of Norway's Freia chocolate. Today the Freia

enterprise is a member of the Kraft family's Norwegian
product line. Cometti left behind a large and worthy
body of work for Paris advertisers of the 1920s and 30s
(the Bibliothèque Nationale has 260 of his posters),
yet nothing is known about the artist himself.
**Est: $2,000-$2,5000.**

**DARTMOUTH WINTER CARNIVAL**

**291. Dartmouth Winter Carnival/Feb. 10-11 1939.**
Artist: **Dom Lupo**
$21^{3}/_{8}$ x 33 in./54.2 x 83.8 cm
Child-Walker School, Boston
Cond B/Slight tears at stains.
The flush of thrilling wintertime socializing pervades
Lupo's poster for the 1939 Winter Carnival. The social
scene of this particular Dartmouth weekend is chroni-
cled in *Winter Carnival*, a fictional filmed account of
the celebration. The plot follows the matinee-contrived
romance between a Dartmouth professor and his old
flame, a divorced duchess who had held the crown of
Winter Carnival Queen in her younger days. Regardless
of the saccharine contrivances, the film is an entertaining look at Winter Carnivals of yesteryear, one that not
only shows students meeting their dates at the train
station, but also footage of athletic events and black-tie
fraternity dances. Incidentally, Winter Carnival was

**290**

**295**

# THE SHIPS ARE COMING

UNITED STATES SHIPPING BOARD ⚓ EMERGENCY FLEET CORPORATION

**294**

named "one of the five objectionable pictures of 1939" by the Catholic Legion of Decency—a distinction shared by *Gone With the Wind* and *Of Human Bondage*.
**Est: $800-$1,000.**

**292. Dartmouth Winter Carnival/Feb. 6-7 1942.**
Artist: **Dom Lupo**
21¹/₂ x 33¹/₈ in./54.6 x 84 cm
Brett Lithographing Co.
Cond B/Slight tears and stains.
Dubbed in 1919 as "the Mardi Gras of the North" by National Geographic magazine, the Dartmouth Winter

Carnival is the oldest collegiate winter festival in the United States. Founded in 1910 by members of the Dartmouth Outing Club who wished to promote the then-fledgling pastime of recreational skiing, participants from nearby colleges trekked to Hanover, New Hampshire, attempting to defeat Dartmouth men at skiing and snowshoeing events. It didn't take long for the Dartmouth event to develop into the most celebrated college weekend in the nation. As is the case with the previous poster, this fresh-faced confetti-and-streamers take on the 1942 Winter Carnival has been laminated, most likely to protect them from the harsh northeast winter conditions.
**Est: $800-$1,000.**

## ANDRE DAUDE (1897-1979)

**293. Pianos Daudé.** 1926.
46¹/₂ x 62³/₈ in./118 x 158.5 cm
Publicité PAG, Paris
Cond A–/Unobtrusive tears and stains at edges. Framed.
Ref: Art Deco, p. 94; PAI-XXXI, 417
The creator of this stunning poster for the piano store on Avenue Wagram in Paris (still there today) is none other than the former president of the company. It is an inspired design: The diagonal placement of the piano instantly animates the entire scene, and the overhead view of the baldheaded pianist adds just the right note of humor.
**Est: $2,500-$3,000.**

## JAMES H. DAUGHERTY

**294. The Ships are Coming.** ca. 1918.
19³/₄ x 29⁷/₈ in./50 x 75.8 cm
Forbes, Boston
Cond B/Slight tears and folds at edges.
Ref: Wake Up America, p. 77
"By the summer of 1918, the Emergency Fleet Corporation had a great array of shipbuilding facilities under its direction, including the huge Hog Island shipyard near Philadelphia, which could launch seventy-eight ships at once. The country was fast approaching the goal of launching one-hundred ships a day, and it

reached a total of ninety-five on the fourth of July, the subject of an especially dramatic poster" (*Wake Up America*, p. 77). That poster, issued by the United States Shipping Board and Philadelphia's E.F.C., presents itself with nationalistic gusto, its fleet of gunmetal vessels surging in unbroken rows toward the fiery horizon that is Europe, accompanied by Daugherty's talon-bearing symbol of an heroic America. Daugherty served as a camouflage artist for the U.S. Navy at the onset of World War I. Given sheets of ship diagrams, he experimented with bright hues to observe the structure of color relations within the outline of a battleship. Using his vibrant palette and brilliant brushwork, he also created navy recruitment posters and publicity posters.
**Est: $800-$1,000.**

## ERNST DEUTSCH (1883-1938)

**295. Josma Selin.** 1916.
37¹/₈ x 49³/₄ in./94.3 x 126.4 cm
F. Kaiser, Wien
Cond B+/Slight tears and stains at folds.
Deutsch was a fashion designer born in Vienna and active also in Berlin and Paris. He moved to Hollywood in 1933 and became a set and costume designer under his nom-de-plume, Ernst Dryden. In a style typically reserved for his efforts focusing on fashion, this poster for an appearance by Viennese chanteuse Josma Selim calls upon an exuberant freeform quick sketch technique to bring out the performer's flirtatious best. Though he only receives textual mention as Ms. Selim's accompanist, Ralph Benatzky was actually the creative force of this duo destined to linger longer in the memories of the musically minded. He began his musical career as a lyricist and conductor in Munich before becoming the director of a cabaret in Vienna. Though you wouldn't know it from the design, Benatzky and Selim were married in 1914. Moving to Berlin in 1915, he began to concentrate on operetta composition. After Selim's death in 1930, Benatzky left Germany, moving to Paris, Vienna, Hollywood and Zurich. Apart from his stage music, Benatzky composed some film scores and is estimated to have produced over 5000 songs. *Rare!*
**Est: $2,000-$2,500.**

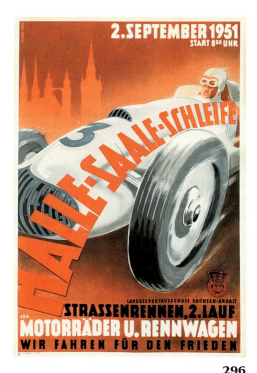

**296**

**297**

**298**

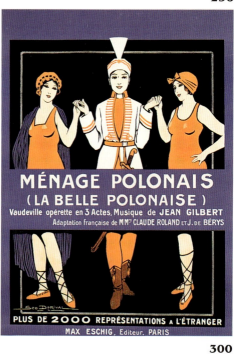

**300**

**302**

**304**

## DEWAG·WERBUNG

**296. Halle-Saale-Schleife.** 1951.
23¹/₂ x 33¹/₈ in./59.7 x 84 cm
Cond A–/Slight tears at edges.
The Dewag Agency places us precariously close to being in harm's way in this promotion for this German road race thundering its way through the Salle river valley. Set scant fumes away from the oncoming vehicle with the Marienkirche and Halle marketplace silhouetted in the background, the Saxon National Sport Committee takes a moment to very subtly politicize this event for both motorcycles and cars with the inclusion of one bottom line of text. With Berlin divided by a Cold War power play, the message resounds with surprising resonance: "We Drive For Peace."
**Est: $700-$900.**

## JEAN-GABRIEL DOMERGUE (1889—1962)

**297. Alice Soulié.** 1926.
47 x 63¹/₄ in./119.4 x 160.7 cm
Imp. H. Chachoin, Paris
Cond A–/Unobtrusive tear at lower right edge.
Ref: PAI-XXXII, 295
Domergue was a painter known for his high-style fashion drawings. His women are always sleek, elegant and smart. Blond cabaret performer—and rumored transvestite—Alice Soulié is no exception, with her rope of oversized pearls and sumptuous black feather fan.
**Est: $1,400-$1,700.**

## JEAN DON (1900-1985)

**298. Jane Marny.** 1930.
46³/₄ x 62³/₄ in./118.7 x 159.4 cm
H. Chachoin, Paris
Cond A.
Don was a prolific illustrator whose specialty was portraits and posters of celebrities of stage and film; otherwise, little is known of him. Here, for an appearance by French entertainer Jane Marny, he sets down a fresh-faced portrait, with a look that is at once a vision of blushing innocence and slyly-contained clear-eyed passion.
**Est: $1,200-$1,500.**

## GEORGES DORIGNAC (1879-1925)

**299. Salon d'Automne.** 1922.
46⁵/₈ x 62¹/₂ in./118.4 x 159 cm
Imp. J. Minot, Paris
Cond B+/Restored tears at folds and edges.

Throughout a long and lauded career that placed an emphasis on the naked female form, Dorignac utilized a carbonaceous technique to add a particular lustrous warmth and vibrancy that lent his works an additional dimension of accessibility. And he would not abandon that technique in his poster for the 1922 Autumn Salon—an event that was both lit and heated—of decorative arts, using the bronzed inverted image of the sculpture in hand to both reflect and infer a greater power at play behind the urges of the artistic.
**Est: $2,500-$3,000.**

## GEORGES DORIVAL (1879-1968)

**300. Ménage Polonais.** 1914.
23¹/₂ x 31¹/₂ in./59.5 x 80 cm
Cond A–/Slight stains at edges.
Dorival shows that he's more than capable of moving beyond the realm of travel posters (see 51-56) with this lighter-than-air confection for "Ménage Polonais," a seemingly gender-bending three-act vaudeville operetta that despite its "2,000 Performances Abroad" prior to its French premiere has left no trace of a plot to compliment its pretty poster performers.
**Est: $800-$1,000.**

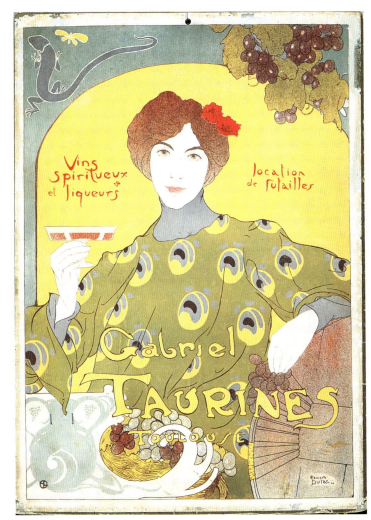

**299**

**301**

**303**

by wealthy American publisher and expatriot James Gordon-Bennett, in his Mercedes. Inspired by the designs of Montaut and Gamy, for some mysterious reason flip-flopped the colors of Jenatzy's vehicle, which had a fiery red chassis with a white number four on its grill. The English-born Eliott was a poster designer, printer and illustrator in the genre of motoring, horses and hunting. He also illustrated editions of Dickens, Jack London and other authors. Many of his prints and books are in the collection of France's Bibliothèque Nationale.
**Est: $1,200-$1,500.**

## G. FAVRE

**304. La Moto Peugeot.**
$30^3/4$ x $46^5/8$ in./78 x 118.4 cm
Affiches Gaillard, Paris
Cond B/Slight stains and tears at folds and edges.
Ref: PAI-XXXIII, 327
As he rounds a bend on his seaside tour, the speeding motorcyclist takes his gaze off the road in order to look the viewer straight in the eye, almost daring anyone to challenge him on the quality of his alabaster ride or his matching sense of fashion. The design makes excellent use of the shape of the rocks, echoing them in the offshore outcropping and even in the clouds puffing about the horizon, as well as the artist's magnificent choice of colors. Favre produced a large body of posters between 1927 and 1935, but he didn't have the consideration to leave us a little bio of some sort. The Bibliothèque Nationale has 44 Favre posters in its collection, all printed by Gaillard from 1928 to 1935; this image is not among them.
**Est: $1,200-$1,500.**

## EDMOND DULAC (1882-1953)

**301. Gabriel Taurines.** 1902.
$14^1/4$ x $19^5/8$ in./36.2 x 49.7 cm
Imp. B. Servin, Toulouse
Cond B/Slight tears and stains. Framed.
A very classy in-store display for a distributor of fine wines and spirits, by the bottle or by the cask, calling upon the stoic charms of a very accessible Art Nouveau temptress who proffers her chalice with direct Byzantine propriety. Toulouse-born Dulac was a well-known and accomplished illustrator.
**Est: $1,000-$1,200.**

## LEON DUPIN

**302. Chateau Roubaud.** 1931.
$38^3/4$ x 55 in./98.4 x 139.6 cm
Imp. Joseph-Charles, Paris
Cond A.
Little is known of Dupin. He was born about 1900; his poster output is slight but distinguished, most of it having been done at the Joseph-Charles plant from about 1929-1936. And this fine example of his Art Deco constructivist output, utilizing an abbreviated

minimalist triptych that makes Cassandre's work for Dubonnet seem extravagantly detailed in comparison. His shortcut from a blanched silhouette bearing the weight of the world on his slumped shoulders to tuxedoed bon vivant passes directly through a bottle of Chateau Roubaud rosé wine, demonstrating to the viewer that "la vie en rose" is only a sip away. The French wine producers are still a thriving enterprise. And in case you believe that it takes an artist who's a household name to produce an enduring image, just visit the company's website (http://www.chateau-roubaud.fr) and see what image greets you.
**Est: $1,200-$1,500.**

## HARRY ELIOTT

**303. Jenatzy/Mercedes/Coupe Gordon Bennett.**
ca. 1903.
$28^3/4$ x 11 in./73 x 28 cm
Cond A–/Slight tears and stains at edges.
Ref: PAI-XXVII, 41
Camille Jenatzy had great success in driving and designing racing cars at the turn of the century and in 1903, won the Gordon Bennet Cup, a race sponsored

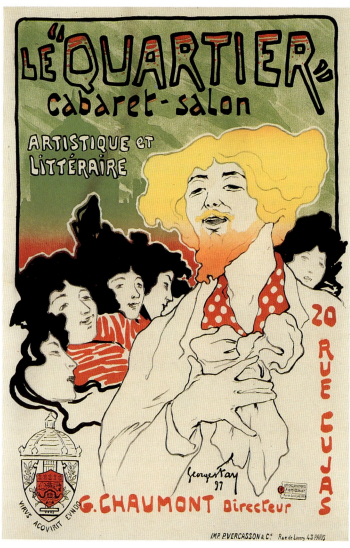

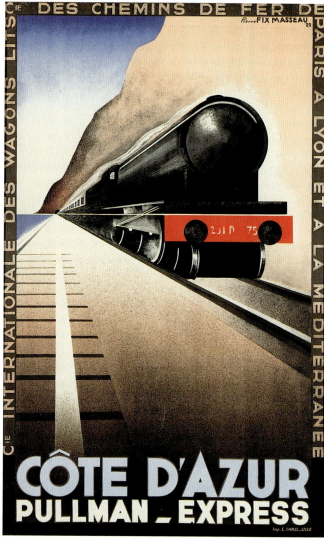

**306**

**309**

### FERNAND FAU (1858-1917)

**305. Salon des 100.** 1894.
16 x 25 in./40.8 x 63.5 cm
Typ. Chamerot et Renouard
Cond B/Slight tears at folds.
Ref: DFP-II, 330; Reims, 604; Salon des Cents, p. 34;
    Salon des Cents/Neumann, p. 67; PAI-XXXI, 623
The woman in a trailing blue print dress and a white
cape is so consumed by the artwork she's been
inspecting with her lorgnette that she seems to have
unknowingly dropped her exhibition catalogue. Fau
was a painter and illustrator of books; he contributed
to several journals like *Le Chat Noir* and *Le Rire*, produced only a handful of posters and participated in
performances at the "Chat Noir" cabaret.
**Est: $1,000-$1,200.**

### GEORGES FAY (?-1916)

**306. Le Quartier Cabaret-Salon.** 1897.
31 x 45³/₄ in./78.7 x 116.2 cm
Imp. P. Vercasson, Paris
Cond A–/Unobtrusive tears at horizontal fold. Framed.
Ref: DFP-II, 337; Schardt, p. 103; PAI-XX, 241
A flamboyantly bohemian type—Van Dyke beard,
unruly hair, red polka-dot scarf et al.—is being admired
by a bevy of young beauties who apparently frequent
the Quartier cabaret in the hopes of meeting someone
just like him. Little is known of Fay; he was killed at
the front in WWI.
**Est: $2,500-$3,000.**

### GEORGES DE FEURE (1868-1943)

**307. Le Diablotin.** 1894.
23³/₄ x 31 in./59 x 78.7 cm
J. Weiner, Paris
Cond B–/Slight tears and stains, largely at edges.
Ref: DFP-II, 345; De Feure, p. 27; Reims, 609;
    Presse, 41; PAI-XXXIII, 330
To advertise the Brussels-based illustrated literary
journal, *Le Diablotin*, de Feure gives us an assertive

**305**

female character and adds a dash of devilish wit, in
this, his first poster.
**Est: $1,700-$2,000.**

### HARRY FINNEY

**308. Le Figaro.** ca. 1895.
23¹/₂ x 33³/₈ in./59.7 x 84.7 cm
Imp. Chaix, Paris

**307**

Cond B+/Slight tears and stains at folds.
Ref: PAI-XXX, 497
"The Six Pages of Le Figaro," a Parisian newspaper, are
trotted out in a manner more befitting a Montmartre
revue than a journalistic endeavor. At the head of this
parade of curvaceous delegates appears a quill-sharp-
ening fellow who seems to be the amalgamation of all
the elements to which the paper aspires. Very curious.
Harry Finney was an artist and illustrator of English
descent with a humorous bent who executed the bulk
of his work from 1894 to 1896 while in Paris working
for *Le Rire*.
**Est: $1,200-$1,500.**

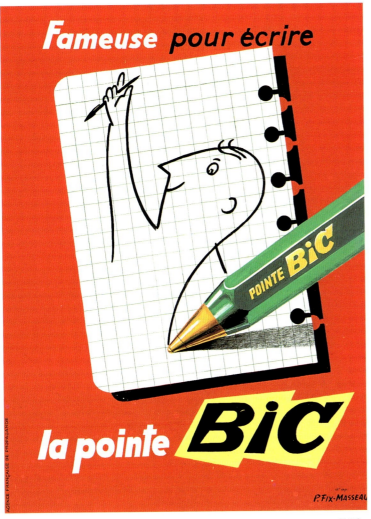

**310**

**312**

**308**

**311**

maker of fountain pen parts and mechanical lead pencils. At the same time, however, he saw the enormous potential of a disposable ball-point pen that offers both value and quality. Six short years later, he introduced his "BIC" ball-point to Europe. And a product that has become synonymous with the word "pen" itself emerged. Fix-Masseau gets write to the point with his maquette, showing the device "famous for writing" in the process of drawing an illustrated individual preparing to enter the inkish fray himself with the assistance of his BIC.
**Est: $1,500-$1,800.**

**311. L'Empire Réclame.**
$31^1/8$ x $47^1/8$ in./79 x 119.7 cm
Cond A.
Although a poster extolling the benefits of colonial imperialism might not be the most fashionable or politically correct graphics at the moment, it's impossible to not be held by the potent austerity of this Fix-Masseau creation, a poster sponsored by the Secretariat d'Etat aux Colonies and put out by the Secretary of Information, featuring France's best and brightest in the service of reclaiming the Empire.
**Est: $1,500-$1,800.**

**FOACHE**

**312. Clément.** ca. 1900.
$37^1/8$ x $53^7/8$ in./94.2 x 136.8 cm
Imp. Bourgerie, Paris.
Cond B+/Unobtrusive tears at folds.
Ref: Bicycle Posters, 65; DFP-II, 610; Schardt, p. 158;
   Dodge, p. 121; PAI-XXX, 1
This striking, highly decorative poster bothers little with the actual details of the bike, instead opting to emphasize pride of ownership via an allegorical figure (reminiscent of Nike of Samothrace, a famous figure in the Louvre) who holds the laurels won by the machine. Though it was thought to have been anonymously-created until recently, the authorship for this poster has been firmly attached to Foache, a turn-of-the-century illustrator of whom little is known.
**Est: $5,000-$6,000.**

**PIERRE FIX-MASSEAU (1905-1994)**

**309. Côte d'Azur/Pullman Express.** 1929.
$24^1/2$ x $39^1/4$ in./61.2 x 99.5 cm
Imp. L. Danel, Paris
Cond A. Framed.
Ref: Fix-Masseau, p. 5; Chemins de Fer, 113;
   Railway Posters, 132; Train à l'Affiche, 268;
   Affiches Azur, 14; PAI-XXVII, 405
"Fix-Masseau seemed particularly adept at putting the speed and power of locomotives to good effect in his graphic designs. This 1929 poster for the luxury Côte d'Azur Pullman trains of the PLM adopts a track-level

viewpoint to emphasize the streamlined 'windcutter' profile of the train engine" (Railway Posters, p. 112).
**Est: $8,000-$10,000.**

**310. Bic.**
21 x $28^1/4$ in./53.5 x 71.7 cm
*Hand-signed gouache and ink maquette.*
In 1945, Marcel Bich (1914-1994), who had previously been the production manager for a French ink manufacturer, purchased a factory on the outskirts of Paris and, along with partner Eduoard Buffard, became a

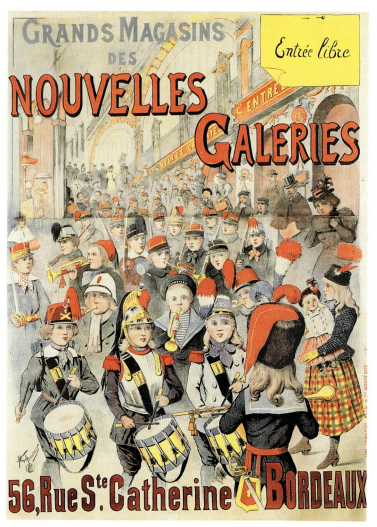

313

314

## G. DE FONRÉMIS

**313. Grands Magasins des Nouvelles Galeries.**
49¹/₄ x 66 in./125 x 167.6 cm
Imp. Demachy, Pech & Cie., Bordeaux
Cond B/Slight tears and stains at folds and edges.
Seeing as Fonrémis was a cavalry officer who created
lively illustrations in a military theme, it shouldn't
come as much of a surprise that he sounds the charge
to shop at Bordeaux's Nouvelles Galleries with this
pint-sized regiment, themselves comprising a future
army of potential consumers.
**Est: $1,700-$2,000.**

## LEONHARD F. W. FRIES (1881-?)

**314. Burger-Kehl & Co./PKZ.** 1917.
35¹/₄ x 49³/₄ in./89.5 x 126.5 cm
J. E. Wolfensberger, Zürich
Cond B/Stains and tears at edges; slight creases.
Ref: PAI-XX, 391
How to impress other strollers on an autumn afternoon:
a fitted navy coat and hat, pigskin gloves and walking
stick—from PKZ, of course. Although all archival and
museum information indicates that this design is the
work of Fries, another poster by the same artist done
in the same year exhibits a completely different style.
Whoever is responsible, he has accomplished a handsome, effective design—one of the very best in the
distinguished PKZ series. *Rare!*
**Est: $5,000-$6,000.**

## C. GADOUD

**315. Vins Camp Romain.**
47¹/₈ x 62⁷/₈ in./119.6 x 159.7 cm
Affiches Camis, Paris
Cond B+/Tear at upper-right corner; slight staining in
black background.
Ref: PAI-XXXIV, 380
Stylish Art Deco image of three centurions raising three
bottles of the product—red, rosé and white. With the
trademark "Roman Camp," the reference is obvious.
**Est: $1,700-$2,000.**

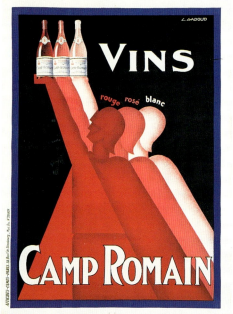

315

## STAN GALLI (1912– )

**316. United Air Lines.**
24⁷/₈ x 39³/₄ in./63.3 x 101 cm
Cond A.
We've been privy to a great number of sensational
European destination posters, but here's an American
work by Galli for United Air Lines that more than stands
up to its Continental rivals. Featuring the Big Sky mag-
netism of an unspecified western locale free from the

316

preoccupations and pollution of the citified, the airline
promotion puts forth its most valuable service—rapid
escape. Galli, a founding member of the San Francisco
Society of Illustrators, was elected into the national
Society of Illustrators Hall of Fame in 1981.
**Est: $600-$800.**

**317**

**318**

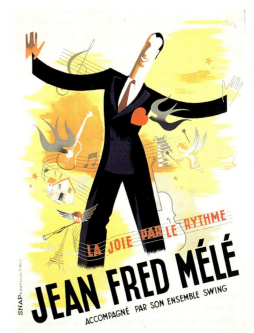

**319**

**320**

**321**

of music is facilely conveyed in this Gerale Art Deco design, most especially with the assistance of one of Mélé's fair-feathered fiends who just happens to be delivering a bright red valentine to him.
**Est: $1,200-$1,500.**

## P. GOBLET

**320. Plages Belgas.** 1925.
25 x 39 in/63.5 x 99 cm
Affiches d'Art C.L. Sips-Catoir, Bruxelles
Cond A–/Slight tears at folds.
Ref: Côte Belge, p. 23; PAI-XXIII, 143 (var)
Botticelli's Venus on a Belgian half-shell, the figure seems to be standing on top of the water rather than actually in it. Dressed very much of the moment with espadrilles to match her bathing suit and her swirling towel echoing the contours of the sunset clouds, she suggests why Goblet was much in demand as a posterist for the Innovation department stores. The lithographer was pleased with the job, too; he added his name, Jean Malvaux, at lower left. The poster was prepared for Belgium's National Society of Advertising and Film and printed, as seen here, in a bilingual French-Dutch version for Belgian use. In addition to a Spanish version (see PAI-XXIII, 143), it also probably appeared in other European languages.
**Est: $1,400-$1,700.**

## FERNAND-LOUIS GOTTLOB (1873—1935)

**321. 2e Exposition des Peintres Lithographes.** 1898.
31$^{1}$/$_{2}$ x 47$^{3}$/$_{8}$ in./80 x 120.3 cm
Imp. Lemercier, Paris
Cond A–/Unobtrusive tears and creases, largely at edges.
Ref: DFP-II, 392; Maitres, 219; Timeless Images, 31; Wine Spectator, 108; Femme s'Affiche, 99; Gold, 183 (var); PAI-XXXIII, 357
Although Gottlob was a versatile graphic artist, his output included very few posters. Fortunately, we have this one for an exhibition in which he was one of the participants. It's "a most interesting design, featuring a woman going through a display cradle of prints. The shadows on the front of her dress and the use of bright yellow in the background create the effect of back-lighting and give the scene an air of intimacy it would otherwise lack" (Wine Spectator, 108). And whether Gottlob planned it this way or not, the scarlet curtains and slender window mullions handily divide the top into areas that organize all the necessary information.
**Est: $1,700-$2,000.**

## GALY

**317. Cycles "Arion".** ca. 1908.
46$^{7}$/$_{8}$ x 63$^{3}$/$_{8}$ in./119 x 161 cm
Daudé Frères, Paris
Cond B+/Unobtrusive folds.
A poster as lyrical as the output of the Greek poet from which the bicycle in question draws its name. And what would a peddling promotion of the day be without the standard vehicular braggadocio—could there be any doubt that a socialite atop an Arion could outpace a Blériot VIII. What sets Galy's creation apart from other like-minded advertisements is his understated command of breezy decorum.
**Est: $2,000-$2,500.**

## GÉO

**318. Spa-Citron.**
39$^{1}$/$_{8}$ x 62$^{5}$/$_{8}$ in./99.3 x 159 cm
Imp. Gouweloos, Bruxelles
Cond A–/Slight tears at folds.

When someone is so dedicated to a citrus-filled life-style that they fashion their outerwear to manifest their inner tartness, the casual observer has to realize that this person knows their way around fruit-infused mineral water. And this plucky lass in the lemon dress is the perfect match for the Spa product, a refreshing insignia come to life against a flat azure background.
**Est: $1,200-$1,500.**

## N. GERALE (Gerard Alexandre, 1914-?)

**319. Jean Fred Mélé.** 1941.
46$^{5}$/$_{8}$ x 62$^{1}$/$_{2}$ in./118.4 x 158.8 cm
SNAP, Paris
Cond B+/Slight stains and creases, largely at edges.
Ref: PAI-I, 311
Singer and bandleader Mélé is shown in the company of his soaring swing ensemble, an orchestra metaphorically composed of birds and angels. Mélé looks spectacular in his dashing blue suit and his style

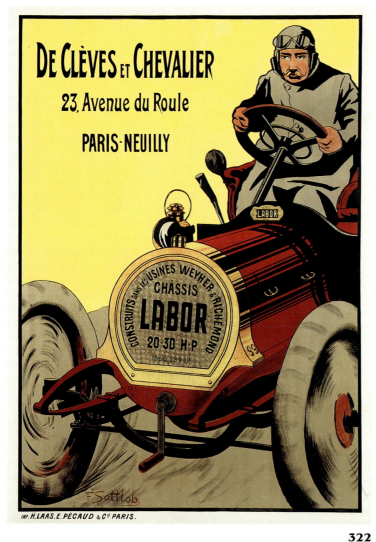

322

324

## GOTTLOB (continued)

### 322. Labor.
46 x 62⁵/₈ in./117 x 159 cm
Imp. H. Laas, E. Pécaud, Paris
Cond A–/Unobtrusive folds.
Ref: PAI-XXX, 267

If the name doesn't clue you in as to the very serious nature of this French automobile, then the expression on the driver's face lets the passerby know straight-away that Labor is the make for those who know that the automobile is not just some passing fancy, but a very solemn technological advance to be regarded with the proper respect. Maybe if they would have emphasized that responsibility doesn't have to preclude enjoyment they would have lasted more than five years in the market. But as is, the 4-cylinder, shaft-driven Labors were produced from 1907 through 1912 at the Weher and Richemond factory in both 20 and 30-horse power models from the designs of Cleves-Chevalier, who also served as their sales agent.
**Est: $2,500-$3,000.**

## JEAN-LOUIS FORAIN (1852-1931)

### 323. Deuxième Salon du Cycle. 1894.
81¹/₄ x 37 in./206.3 x 94 cm
Imp. H. Hérold, Paris
Cond B/Slight tears and stains, largely at folds.
Ref: DFP-II, 362; Maindron, p. 64; Maitres, 51;
    Bicycle Posters, 20; Wagner, 55; Abdy, p. 106; PAI-XXXII, 314

This is the largest of three formats of this engaging design depicting two charming cyclists on 2-sheets in the most delicate of pastels—yellow pink and light olive. This was a favorite of turn-of-the-century poster collectors; Maindron, a year after its publication, was unequivocal: "This poster is perfect."
**Est: $3,000-$4,000.**

## JAMES GARDNER

### 324. Aer Lingus. 1954.
39³/₄ x 24⁷/₈ in./101 x 63.2 cm
Ormond Printing Company, Ireland
Cond A.

Though the shamrock may have moved from the nose to the tail since the days of this poster's production, Aer Lingus has maintained their reputation for efficient, friendly and safe air travel. And Gardner takes the
classic approach of presenting a cutaway of the Vicker's Viscount craft in order to present the potential passenger with a lithographic approximation of their future traveling accommodations. Beginning in 1936 with one aircraft—a six-seat De Havilland 84 Dragon biplane —the airline, whose name is an Anglicization of the Gallic "aer loingeas", meaning "air fleet", took to the skies. And though this poster boasts of the turboprop airliner's four Rolls-Royce Dart propeller turbine engines, 1954 would also usher in a new age for Aer Lingus as they introduced 707 jet-prop planes into their fleet, as well as becoming an early pioneer in the carriage of passengers with special disabilities.
**Est: $1,000-$1,200.**

323

326

327

328

## EUGENE GRASSET (1841—1917)

**325. Encre L. Marquet.** 1892.
32¹/₄ x 47⁷/₈ in./82 x 121.6 cm
G. de Malherbe, Paris
Cond A–/Unobtrusive folds.
Ref: DFP-II, 404; Maitres, 158; Berthon & Grasset, p. 33;
    Musée d'Affiche, p. 52; Gold, 3; PAI-XXX, 76
This contemplative young woman looks into the distance, quill poised, as she ponders how best to translate her innermost thoughts to paper. Whatever her words, the fine ink she is using is sure to make the most of them. "Grasset adheres to the classic mode of portraying women as serenely composed and dignified. Only the fluttering hair and scurrying night clouds suggest any wild untamed thoughts" (Gold, p. 5). *This is the larger format.*
**Est: $2,000-$2,500.**

**326. Jeanne Darc/Sarah Bernhardt.** 1894.
29³/₈ x 46⁵/₈ in./74.7 118.4 cm
G. de Malherbe & H. A. Cellot/Imp. Draeger & Lesieur, Paris
Cond B/Slight tears and stains at folds.
Ref: DFP-II,399; Berthon & Grasset, p. 41;
    Murray- Robertson, p.111 (var); Abdy, p. 127;
    Plakat Schweiz, p. 210; Theaterplakate, p. 29;
    PAI- XXIII, 274
This bold design was commissioned for the opening of Sarah Bernhardt's appearance in the play at the Theatre de la Porte-St. Martin on January 3, 1890—but before it could be printed, the star requested changes, including a slightly different expression and less frizzy hair, which were accordingly made. Subsequently, however, Draeger also printed this rejected version, and it was sold through G. de Malherbe's art poster department.
**Est: $1,500-$1,800.**

**327. Jeanne Darc/Sarah Bernhardt.** 1894.
29 x 46³/₈ in./73.7 117.8 cm
G. de Malherbe & H. A. Cellot/Imp. Draeger & Lesieur, Paris
Cond B/Slight tears and stains at folds and edges.
Ref: DFP-II, 399A; Berthon & Grasset, p. 40
And voila! Star requests changes and changes are made. But other than the more austere expression and manageable hair, the Grasset poster remains unchanged from the previous design.
**Est: $1,500-$1,800.**

**328. Belle Jardiniere/1899 Calendar.**
14¹/₈ x 19¹/₂ in./36.2 x 49.5 cm
Imp. de Vaugirard, Paris
Cond A. Framed.
Ref: Rogers, p. 58; PAI-XXXII, 327
Grasset had already done an 1896 calendar for this big Paris department store with separate sheets for each month (*see* PAI-XXXII, 326); this time around, the entire year—and an array of flowers—was compressed onto a single sheet. A typical Grasset lass—flowing hair and Art Nouveau attire—is shown in a pose the artist frequently relied on: reaching for permissible fruits or flowers.
**Est: $1,400-$1,700.**

**329**

**330**

**331**

**332**

## GRASSET (continued)

**329. Froideur.** 1897.
32⁵/₈ x 32⁷/₈ in./82.7 x 83.6 cm
Cond A.
Ref: Berthon & Grasset, p. 68; PAI-XXIII, 268
This icy-visaged young woman, aloof and reserved among tall hydrangeas, is Plate V of the series of ten lithographs, paired in five different formats and sizes, published by G. de Malherbe as *Dix Estampes Décoratives* in an edition of 750 copies. "Each represented an attractive girl beside, or surrounded by, flowers or fruiting plants. Each is treated quite distinctly, the girl's hair forming decorative patterns which alternate with the formalised plants and the occasional glimpse of sky and clouds" (Berthon & Grasset, p. 64). The circle-shaped image forms a set with Jalousie, Plate IX (*see* following lot).
**Est: $2,000-$2,500.**

**330. Jalousie.** 1897.
31³/₈ x 33³/₈ in./80.6 x 84.7 cm
Cond A–/Slightly light-stained.
Ref: Berthon & Grasset, p. 69 (var); PAI-XXIII, 267
The mood or emotion communicated in each is different as well: Here, the young woman amidst the roses is suffering the pangs of jealousy. This is plate IX, paired with Plate V titled *Froideur* (coolness—*see* previous lot).
**Est: $2,000-$2,500.**

**331. Danger.** 1897.
24 x 31¹/₄ in./61 x 92 cm
Cond A.
Ref: Berthon & Grasset, p. 70; PAI-XX, 256
Although the theme of peril is expressed in this decorative panel through the torn clouds, the ravening wolf and even the strange fishhook pattern on the fleeing woman's dress, it's the odd—almost plummeting—angle that makes us feel her jeopardy most of all.
**Est: $2,000-$2,500.**

**332. Meditation.** 1897.
20⁵/₈ x 34³/₈ in./52.3 x 87.3 cm
Cond A.
Ref: Berthon & Grasset, p. 71; PAI-X, 248

Another of the ten plates published by Malherbe in an edition of 750 copies of the "Dix Estampes Décoratives" series, featuring the serious charms of an ideal-chasing young woman lost in the infinity of thought.
**Est: $2,000-$2,500.**

**333. Tentation.** 1897.
26⁷/₈ x 26⁵/₈ in./68.1 x 67.6 cm
Cond B–/Tears and stains in margins; light stained.
Ref: Berthon & Grasset, p. 68; PAI-IX, 280 (var)
This and the following lot show two tenderly drawn women representing feminine allure in this decorative set by Grasset, part of the "Estampes Décoratives" suite published by Malherbe. This Byzantine Eve holds forth a piece of forbidden fruit to some unseen Adam, who more than likely would be powerless to resist the charms of the Art Nouveau temptation.
**Est: $2,000-$2,500.**

**334. Coquetterie.** 1897.
27 x 27 in./68.5 x 68.5 cm
Cond B/Unobtrusive tears and stains in margins; light stained.
Ref: Berthon & Grasset, p. 69; PAI-IX, 280 (var)
This print was paired with the prior lot in the Malherbe-published decorative portfolio. However, it seems a bit unfair to label this flower plucking lass a "coquette" in light of other coquetry we've encountered along our lithographic path. Still, this subtly flirtatious trifle provides attractive ample distraction from otherwise drab surroundings.
**Est: $2,000-$2,500.**

**335. Extravagance.** 1897.
17¹/₂ x 50¹/₈ in./44.4 x 127.2 cm
Cond B/Unobtrusive tears in top and bottom margins; light stained.
Ref: Berthon & Grasset, p. 65; PAI-XXVIII, 325
The companion to "Bonne Nouvelle" (*see* PAI-XXVIII, 324) in the *Dix Estampes Décoratives* series. Here, the maiden wandering through the field of cockscomb indulges herself in a bit of extravagance, wielding a fan and lorgnette—two nonessentials where communing with nature is concerned.
**Est: $2,000-$2,500.**

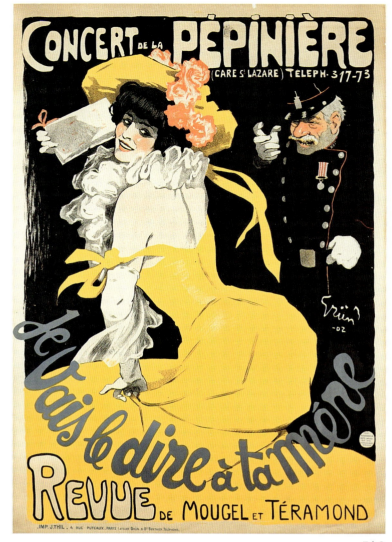

336

342

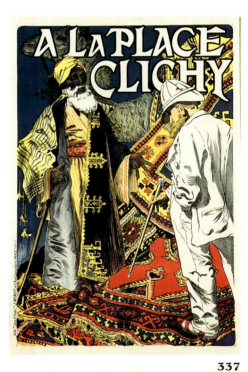

337

338

339

**GRASSET (continued)**

**336. L'Eventail.** 1900.
32 x 49¹/₈ in./81.3 x 126.6 cm
Imp. Chaix, Paris
Cond B/Tears, largely near edges.
Ref: Berthon & Grasset, p. 86; Gold, 205; PAI-XXX, 231
For the 1900 World's Fair in Paris, Grasset designed jewelry, stained glass, tapestries and two large lithographs, one named "The Parasol" (see PAI-XXXII, 328) and the other, seen here, titled "The Fan." As she peers out from behind her oversized fan, the coy temptress is either keeping a summery cool or flirting—or both.

Either way, her gaze is captivating.
**Est: $2,500-$3,000.**

**337. A la Place Clichy.** 1891.
45¹/₈ x 63 in./114.5 x 160 cm
J. Minot, Paris
Cond A. Framed.
Ref: DFP-II, 401; Reims, 683; Berthon & Grasset, p. 37; Maitres, 18; Wagner, 52; PAI-XVII, 470
Grasset did much to introduce the concept and practice of Art Nouveau in France. In fact, Grasset "brought Art Nouveau to the aid of the poster: it was to become a worldwide vehicle of the art of advertising. In France,

Grasset was the pioneer of an attempt, like that of William Morris in England, to reconcile art and industry . . . Interested as he was in all the applied arts, he came naturally to the poster" (Weill, p. 32). This detailed slice of exotica clearly illustrates the fact that the Place Clichy department store was the premiere importer of oriental merchandise, most-notably rugs. The oft used design went through several printings and editions, beginning in 1891. *This is the larger format.*
**Est: $1,700-$2,000.**

**H. GRAY (Henri Boulanger, 1858-1924)**

**338. Théâtre de l'Opéra/2eme Bal Masqué.** 1899.
37 x 49¹/₂ in./94 x 125.7 cm

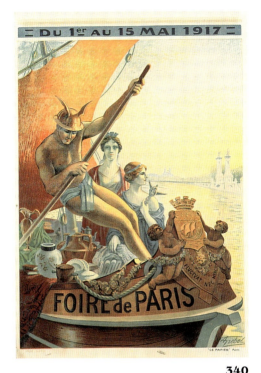

**340**

Marche des Midinettes—Paris Nanterre 1903

**341**

**343**

**344**

Affiches Camis, Paris
Cond B/Staining at folds and edges.
Ref: DFP-II, 422; PAI-XXXV, 330 (var)
A pulchritudinous harlequin beckons us to join the fashionably trendy throng already in attendance for the second Masked Ball of the season. This hippy jester must have brought them in in droves, as the Gray belle was used on at least one other occasion in the employ of the Opera for an orchestral evening under the direction of Charles Haring (*see* PAI-XXXV, 330). Gray started out as an illustrator and caricaturist; his work for such magazines as *Le Boulevardier*, *Le Boudoir* and *Paris Illustré* was signed with the nom-de-plume "Grivois." His diverse output also included menus, catalogues and costumes for the famous Paris music halls. He naturally joined in the poster mania of the 1890s under yet a new name, Gray.
**Est: $2,500-$3,000.**

**339. Trianon Concert.** 1898.
24$^1$/4 x 31 in./ x 61.6 x 78.8 cm
Affiches V. Palyart, Paris
Cond B–/Slight loss at left paper edge; tears at folds.
Ref: PAI-XXVIII, 331
A stock poster for the Trianon Concert, the café-concert built in the garden of the Elysée-Montmartre, shows two courtesans executing a pavane. Another version of this design lists the entire stock company of the establishment in the right panel (*see* PAI-IX, 298),

while another displays the talents of a female sword-play troupe in a poster-within-a-poster format (*see* PAI-XXVIII, 331); here—in a smaller format—the un-specified talents of a mademoiselle Gabrielle Lange are touted in the text panel. The detail H. Gray lavished upon the gowns of his poster women came naturally to the artist, as he was the costume designer for all the major Paris music-halls.
**Est: $1,000-$1,200.**

## A. GREBEL

**340. Foire de Paris.** 1917.
29$^3$/4 x 43$^1$/8 in./75.4 x 109.5 cm
"Le Papier", Paris
Cond A–/Slight tears at folds and edges.
The annual Paris Fair was a large international industrial exhibition which attracted not only manufacturers from around the world, but also posterists who vied for the honor of having their design selected as the official poster of the event. Grebel gives us a barge's-eye view of the city as we arrive via Seine, the Pont Alexandre in the background, our mercurial oarsman guiding us safely to shore, having handed off his caduceus to one of the two haunting allegorical envoys of commerce and craftsmanship with whom he shares his skiff. Not to keep things on an entirely ethereal level, the boat is laden with samples of the fair's potential wares.
**Est: $1,000-$1,200.**

## VILLY GREEN

**341. Marche des Midinettes—Paris Nanterre.** 1903.
29$^1$/2 x 21$^3$/4 in./75 x 55.3 cm
Cond A/P.
The Place Concord on the right bank of the Seine is the scene for this charming "March of the Shopgirls," a bubbling sea of humanity primarily populated with young liberated Parisians on the move. This lively street scene is enhanced by its pochoir treatment applied over lithographic printing.
**Est: $1,200-$1,500.**

## JULES-ALEXANDRE GRÜN (1868-1934)

**342. Concert de la Pépinière/Je vais le dire à ta mère.** 1902.
37 x 50$^7$/8 in./94 x 129.5 cm
Imp. J. Thil, Paris
Cond A–/Slight tears at paper edges.
Ref: Timeless Images, 18; Weill, p. 45; PAI-XXIV, 299
Declaring Grün "one of the most original talents of this time," Weill attributes his relative lack of celebrity to his subject: "If in his posters he had not treated mainly car-ousers and coquettes, with facility but without genius, he would be one of the greatest poster artists of the period: In fact he is the only one to use flat tints with-out outlines, allowing the paper itself to function as a design element, to compose scenes that are often of great graphic audacity" (pp. 43-44). Grün's joyful good humor is most evident here. The flirty woman is pay-ing not the slightest shred of attention to the police-man who springs from the background to threaten "I'm gonna tell your momma"—the title of this revue at the Pépinière.
**Est: $5,000-$6,000.**

**343. Scala/La Revue de la Scala.** 1905.
23$^1$/2 x 31$^1$/4 in./60 x 79.2 cm
Imp. Ch. Verneau, Paris
Cond A.
Ref: DFP-II, 238; PAI-XXXII, 338
One quickly learns to recognize the Grün characters: the impudent flirtatious women and the gentlemen bent on seduction—he is the undisputed master of this sort of music hall poster. Obviously pleased with Grün's formula, the Scala became one of his most loyal clients.
**Est: $2,000-$2,500.**

**344. Scala/Revue à Poivre.** 1903.
17$^1$/4 x 24$^3$/8 in./44 x 62 cm
Imp. Charles Verneau, Paris
Cond B+/Slight tears at stains and edges.
Ref (Both Var): DFP-II, 436; PAI-XXXIV, 392
For a 1903 revue at the Scala, Grün gives us one of his patented exuberant coquettes, barely able to contain her, um, excitement—naturally, all in bright scarlet. Ob-viously, as far as we're concerned, she's the one who puts the spice in the "Pepper Revue" advertised here. *This is the smaller format.*
**Est: $2,000-$2,500.**

345

346

**345. Bal Tabarin.** 1904.
$30^5/8$ x $46^1/2$ in./77.7 x 118 cm
Imp. Cornille & Serre, Paris
Cond B–/Restored tears.
Ref: Spectacle, 1334 (var); PAI-XII, 240
This is the rarely seen alternative design to the better known version (*see* PAI-XI, 243), in which the gentleman bringing up the rear was black. Whether the reasoning behind this change was racially motivated or not will never been known with complete surety. His reworking of the design, however, allowed Grün to indulge in one of his least subtle graphic oglings: the new member of the trio at left peers directly down the woman's dress, whereas the original gent didn't. Whichever version is on hand, it's certainly one of Grün's most jubilant Montmartre scenes.
**Est: $2,500-$3,000.**

**346. Société des Peintres-Lithographes/3ème Exposition.** 1901.
34 x $48^3/4$ in./86.4 x 123.8 cm
Imp. Chaix, Paris
Cond B+/Slight tears and stains, largely at edges. Framed.
Ref: DFP-II, 440; Phillips VII, 103
Though the majority of Grün's designs feature leering gentlemen and flirtatious coquettes, he indulges in his decorous muse in this poster for the third exhibition of the Society of Lithographic Artists. In an interview conducted a few years prior to the creation of this poster and featured in the March, 1899 edition of *The Poster*, Grün summed up his graphic goals as follows: "Since (1891), I believe that I have done about fifteen (posters), in which I have tried to find new and simple effects. Two or three colors are quite sufficient to produce something interesting. Black and white, with a touch of red or green . . . As for my subjects, I search for them always in the same places: in the theatres or café-concerts, for which I have done all my affiches" (p. 100). His shadings, as well as the inclusion of the society's monogram as part of the wallpaper, arrive at

349

350

a most appealing design featuring a lovely young patron studying her exhibition catalogue.
**Est: $3,000-$4,000.**

**ALBERT GUILLAUME (1873-1942)**

**347. Automobiles et Cycles Clément.** 1903.
$34^3/4$ x 50 in./88.2 x 127 cm
Imp. Minot, Paris
Cond B–/Slight tears, largely at folds. Framed.
Ref: PAI-XIX, 30
On an outlook point far above the twinkling lights of

Paris, two young ladies with their bikes come upon a sporty gentleman in his automobile of the same make. Two lanterns carried by the ladies help to light up the scene, but it's the fireworks erupting against the dark blue sky that provides a machine-age geyser of illumination to the vehicles' logo.
**Est: $2,500-$3,000.**

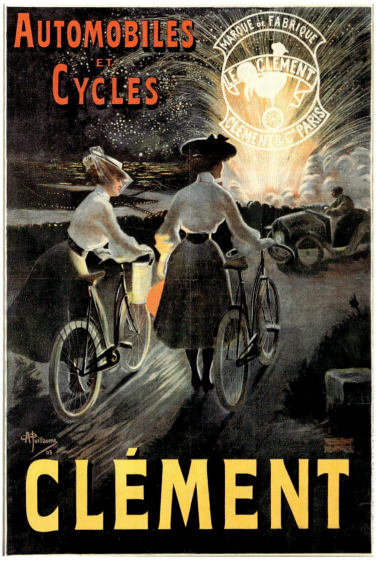

347

348

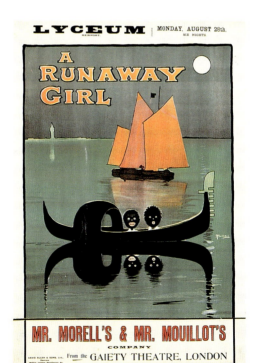

351

**GEO HAM (Georges Hamel, 1900-1972)**

**348. Monaco/23 Avril 1933.**
30 x 46¹/₄ in./76.2 x 117.4 cm
Imp. Monégasque, Monte-Carlo.
Cond A. Framed.

Ref: Auto Posters, p. 51; Deco Affiches, p.83;
     Affiches Azur, 333; Affiches Riviera, 259;
     PAI-XXXIV, 167

The 1933 event introduced a new practice, determining starting position by practice times, rather than randomly by lot. Design pioneer Enzo Ferrari set up what is considered the most distinguished team in Grand Prix racing, the Alfa Romeo group. This time around, the winner was still Achille Varzi in a French Bugatti T51, but Alfa Romeo took three of the next four places. Design-wise, we detect some of Falcucci's influence, but Ham, who spent much of his career on paintings and illustrations of cars and airplanes, obviously knows his craft at least equally well.
**Est: $6,000-$7,000.**

**349. L'Homme-Oiseau.** 1937.
15³/₄ x 21⁷/₈ in./40 x 55.6 cm
Imp. Air-Propagande, Paris
Cond A. Framed.

Icarus has nothing on this daredevil, here billed simply and accurately as "The Bird Man." You have to admire his spread-eagle, devil-may-care attitude, but it's incredible that would-be flyers have never ceased to be convinced that human flight on flapping wings is possible in spite of all the physical evidence. There was even an "Ally McBeal" episode that revolved around the premise! Though not mentioned specifically by name, it's likely that Ham executed this poster for an appearance by "American 'birdman' Clem Sohn . . . After jumping from an aircraft, he spread his webbed 'wings' and 'tail' and performed limited maneuvers in gliding flight, finally opening his parachute for a normal descent. On 25 April 1937, at Vincennes, France, the parachute failed to open properly and Sohn was killed" (History of Aviation, by John W. R. Taylor and Kenneth Munson, p.11).
**Est: $800-$1,000.**

**350. Fête de l'Aviation/Vincennes.** 1937.
38 x 59¹/₈ in./96.4 x 150 cm
P.A. Chavane, Paris
Cond A–/Slight creasing in bottom text area.
Ref: PAI-XXVI, 75

The master of French automobile posters turns here to a different milieu: an aviation fair at Vincennes held in conjunction with the 1937 World's Fair in Paris. The event—targeted at "the youth of France"—is represented by an heroic jumpsuited pilot calling the lads from their tame play with model airplanes to come and experience the excitement of the real thing.
**Est: $2,500-$3,000.**

**JOHN HASSALL (1868-1948)**

**351. A Runaway Girl.** 1899.
20 x 29⁵/₈ in./51 x 75.4 cm
David Allen & Sons, Belfast
Cond B+/Creasing and stains in margins.

Hassall started as an illustrator for the Daily Graphic and Punch before emerging as one of the best early British posterists. Much of his work was for the theater, especially frothy, slightly naughty musicals with titles like "The French Maid," "Little Bo Peep" and "The Shop Girl" (subtitled, to feminists' certain delight, "A Little Bit of Fluff"). His style tended toward bold outline and flat color, but could vary considerably. Despite a prodigious output of some 600 posters, Hassall still managed to spend some years as a farmer in Manitoba. And though the story line of the musical comedy hit "A Runaway Girl" most likely drifted from time to time into naughty territory, Hassall abandons his frothier ways for a dulcet Venetian night scene whose serene flow is utterly disrupted—in a rather comical manner—by a pair of caricaturistic minstrel cast members.
**Est: $1,000-$1,200.**

**352**

## PAOLO HENRI

**352. Braga Sisters.** ca. 1896.
$24^1/8$ x $32^3/8$ in./61 x 82 cm
Affiches Brondert, Paris
Cond A.
I'm certain that they never intended to blow their own horns, but was there anything that the Braga sisters couldn't do? Whether your tastes ran towards the athletic, the instrumental or the vocally adept, this sibling twosome could obviously deliver the goods, from arias to concertina concertos. Henri packs all of this talent onto a single sheet with attractive, uncluttered panache.
**Est: $800-$1,000.**

## ADOLFO HOHENSTEIN (1854-1928)

**353. Onoranze a Volta.** 1899.
$19^3/4$ x $41^1/2$ in./50.3x 105.3 cm
G. Ricordi, Milano
Cond B/Slight tears and stains, largely at edges.
Ref: Ricordi, 157; PAI-XXXIII, 374
Two young women with the symbols of manual labor (a shuttlecock and a washboard) place a wreath around the cameo of Alessandro Volta (1754-1827), to indicate their gratefulness for his electricity that liberates them from drudgery. The poster is for an exhibition of electrical products being held in honor of the 100th anniversary of the birth of Volta, the inventor of an instrument for measuring electricity (voltmeter), and the man who defined a single unit of it, a volt, as "the electron drive force which, when applied to the conductor with the resistance of one ohm, produces a current of one ampere." That so impressed Napoleon that he made him a count as well as a senator of Lombardy. *This is the smaller format.*
**Est: $1,500-$1,800.**

## LUDWIG HOHLWEIN (1874-1949)

**354. Wilhelm Mozer.** 1909.
$34^1/2$ x $47^3/8$ in./87.6 x 120.3 cm
Vereinigte Druckerein & Kunstanstalten, München
Cond A. Framed.
Ref: DFP-III, 1357; Hohlwein, 141;
   Hohlwein/Stuttgart, 23; Plakate München, 207;
   PAI-XXXIV, 400
This is one of Hohlwein's finest works, executed for the Munich delicatessen Wilhelm Mozer. The arrangement and colors are just perfect—and perfectly enticing. It is one of a series of his works which were basically still life images supported by robust typography.
**Est: $1,700-$2,000.**

**355. Stakato.** 1935.
$33^1/8$ x $48^1/8$ in./84.2 x 122.2 cm
Sonntag, München
Cond B+/Recreated right margin.
There's nothing abrupt or disjointed about this free-

**353**

**356**

spirited Hohlwein invitation to set the night ablaze at this pre-Lenten revelry at the Schniabinger Brewery, a musical shindig sponsored by a student organization from the institution of higher artistic learning that gives the ball its acronymic title: Munich's STatlichen AKAdemie der TOnkunst. A fiery Hohlwein vision, far more free than a great number of his designs, and one whose flat planes of vibrant color create a feeling of pyrotechnic flirtation. Weill comments that "Beginning with his first efforts, Hohlwein found his style with disconcerting facility; it would vary little for the next forty years. The drawing was perfect from the start: . . . nothing seemed alien to him, and in any case, nothing

**354**

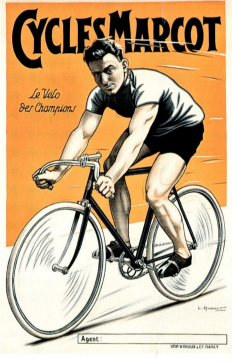

**357**

posed a problem for him. . . . His figures are full of . . . a play of light . . . that brings them out of their background and gives them substance" (pp. 107-110). *Rare!*
**Est: $6,000-$7,000.**

## A. HUGÉDÉ

**356. Cycles Malinge & Laulin.** 1896.
36 x $50^3/4$ in./91.4 x 129 cm
Imp. G. Paré, Angers-Paris
Cond B+/Restored tear at horizontal fold.
Is it a race or is it romance? This mobile encounter—courtesy of Malinge & Laulan bicycles—between a young domestic and a dashing courier may be nothing more than a passing fancy, but a bike that allows you to execute one's daily responsibilities while simultaneously broadening one's social horizons is a ride worth holding on to.
**Est: $1,000-$1,200.**

## L. HUSSON

**357. Cycles Marcot.**
$32^1/4$ x $48^1/4$ in./82 x 122.5 cm
Imp. V. Idoux, Nancy
Cond A.
As if you couldn't tell just from looking, the Marcot

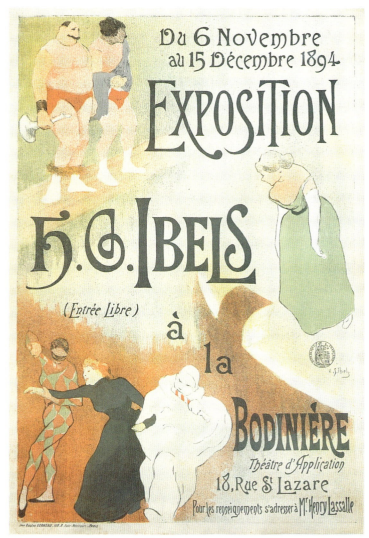

355

358

### E. MCKNIGHT KAUFFER (1890-1954)

**359. American Airlines/Boston.** 1953.
30 x 40 in./76.2 x 101.5 cm
Cond A/P.
Ref: PAI-XV, 316 (var)
Although he was a native of the United States, born in Montana, Kauffer spent most of his creative years in England. Returning home for the last fifteen years of his life, he designed posters in a New York studio, where his biggest clients were book publishers and American Airlines, for whom he designed some thirty posters in a period from 1948 to 1953. These clean designs in bright colors show his expert hand with simple, powerful travel images. For example, he respectfully deconstructs the American flag to make the Boston destination stand out in stark contrast, and includes a cameoed minuteman for good measure.
**Est: $1,000-$1,200.**

359

360

bicycle is "The Bike of Champions". Though the merest graphic basics are given to us in the Husson poster, we have to imagine that during its heyday, both the bike and its chiseled rider were visually identifiable enough to warrant the use of no further textual embellishment.
**Est: $1,400-$1,700.**

### HENRI-GABRIEL IBELS (1867—1936)

**358. Exposition H. G. Ibels à la Bodinière.** 1894.
15⁵/₈ x 22³/₈ in./39.6 x 56.8 cm
Imp. Eugène Verneau, Paris

Cond B+/Unobtrusive folds' slight stains at edges.
Ref: DFP-II, 475; Reims, 746; Maindron, p. 46;
    PAI-XXVII, 461
A member of the Nabi group of artists, Ibels shared with the others a stylistic debt to Gauguin, but diverged from their esoteric, symbolist interests, preferring to depict directly and honestly the popular life of the streets. Here for an exhibition of his own work, he selects three of his images of performing artists and interweaves the text around them.
**Est: $2,500-$3,000.**

**360. American Airlines/East Coast.** 1948.
30 x 40 in./76.2 x 101.5 cm
Cond A/P.
Ref: PAI-XX, 14 (var)
What if the assignment was to promote travel to an entire American region? Well, if you were Kauffer, you'd simply choose an iconographic envoy from that region's proud maritime heritage—in this case the United State's Eastern seaboard and a model-building tar—drop in a few cursive textual location and remind us that even when not traveling, the journey is never far from one's mind. Of course, it never hurts to drop in the logo of the company that commissioned your services.
**Est: $1,000-$1,200.**

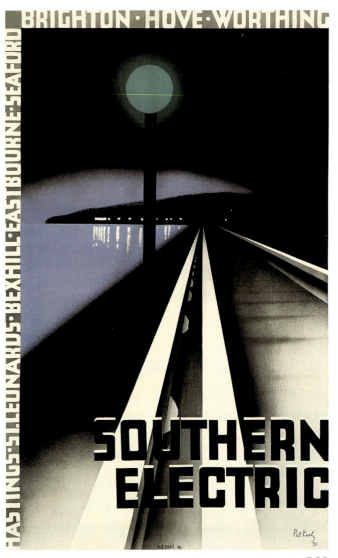

**362**

**363**

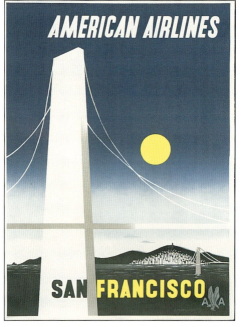

**361**

**364**

**E. MCKNIGHT KAUFFER (continued)**

**361. American Airlines/San Francisco.** 1948.
30 x 40 in./76.2 x 101.5 cm
Cond A/P.
Kauffer once more proves that a little can go a long way in the advertising department, providing us with an abstracted moonswept hint of the famed Golden Gate Bridge and the metropolis to which it provides access in this exemplar of promotional brevity for American Airlines.
**Est: $1,000-$1,200.**

**PATRICK COKAYNE KEELY (?-1970)**

**362. Southern Electric.** 1935.
24³/₄ x 39⁵/₈ in./63 x 100.7 cm
Cond B+/Slight tears at edges.
Ref: PAI-XI, 264
An impressive twilight Art Deco design with the moonlit rails disappearing in the shadows past the green signal light. Only a little wedge of blue daylight still remains.
**Est: $3,000-$4,000.**

**G. KIBARDIN**

**363. Lenin Flagship Dirigible Squadron.** 1931.
28¹/₄ x 41 in./71.7 x 104.2 cm
Cond B/Slight tears at folds and edges.
Ref: Iconography of Power, p. 157
A Constructivist design of powerfully iconoclastic proportions uses a photomontage treatment and an awesome grasp of balanced propaganda to deliver its message of strength through zeppelin supremacy. Executed in a dialect of Russian, Kibardin's poster exalts Lenin as the leading proponent of dirigible power, backing this up with an impressive gathering of the stratospheric behemoths above and an admiring proletariat throng below. Sporting names meant to inspire, the zeppelins run the gamut of monikers, from

Party legends ("Lenin," "Stalin" and "Voroshilov") to the ideological ("Truth" and "Collective") to the oddly complimentary ("Handsome Bolshevik").
**Est: $2,500-$3,000.**

**CHARLES KIFFER (1902-1992)**

**364. Fredo Gardoni/Pathé.** 1941.
47³/₈ x 62³/₄ in./120.5 x 159.5 cm
Cond B/Slight tears and stains at fold.
Ref: PAI-I, 318

Although Charles Kiffer is known primarily for his many fine posters of Maurice Chevalier, his poster output chronicles the entire French theatrical and music-hall scene for more than fifty years. For example, accordionist Fredo Gardoni might not be an entertainer discussed around the dinner tables of today's families, and yet Kiffer's design resonates with a vitality that the contemporary eye can connect to regardless of familiarity.
**Est: $1,700-$2,000.**

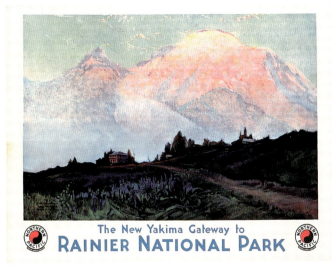

**367**

**369**

**365**

# SÜDBAHNHOTEL
## SEMMERING
### AUSTRIA

**366**

**368**

**365. Maurice Chevalier.** ca. 1948.
44³/₄ x 61¹/₄ in./113.6 x 155.5 cm
Imp. Bédos, Paris
Cond A.
Ref: PAI-XXXII, 377
One of the all-time great images associated instantly with its subject. Even without letters . . . straw hat at a rakish tilt, prominent lower lip—voila, Chevalier! Kiffer designed all of Chevalier's publicity from 1925 into the 1960s; this poster was issued for Chevalier's triumphant return from his extended American tour; no text was needed to alert the French public to the occasion —Kiffer's design said it all. *This is the larger format.*
**Est: $1,400-$1,700.**

# HERMANN KOSEL (1896-1985)

**366. Sudbahn Hotel.**
24 x 36³/₄ in./61 x 93.2 cm
Christoph Reisser's Söhne, Wiene
Cond A.
Ref: PAI-XXXIV, 409
The flattened perspective and isolated chill of Kosel's winter revelry lends additional grandeur to the already resplendent Südbahn Hotel and its shimmering Semmering environs. This romantic pass, with its steep limestone cliffs, craggy rocks, broad ridges and wide valleys, gained significance through the centuries as a first-class place to spend the night, even though it remained a difficult destination to reach, due primarily

to the gradients of the old pass road. However, the construction of the railroad created an explosive influx of tourism that changed the face of the region forever. The daring pioneer of all mountain railways, the Semmering Railway still enjoys the admiration of the world. With sixteen several-story viaducts, fifteen tunnels, one-hundred-forty-two vertical structures, one-hundred-twenty-nine bridges, artificial rock faces and supporting walls, it was amazingly built over a construction period of only six years. In 1882, the luxurious Südbahnhotel was built, and though it saw some rough transitions during the World Wars, the hotel reopened with all the amenities of its former magnificence in 1948.
**Est: $1,000-$1,200.**

# CARL KUNST (1884-1912)

**367. Bilgeri-Ski Ausrüstung.** ca. 1910.
30¹/₄ x 20¹/₈ in./76.6 x 51 cm
Reichhold & Lang, München
Cond A.
Ref: Voyage, p. 193; Takashimaya, 84; PAI-XXIX, 435
Kunst was not only a painter and graphic designer but also an enthusiastic mountaineer—a logical choice for this Munich ski equipment poster. A year or so later, he adapted the design for a ski equipment dealer in Berlin by simply adding a skier fastening his bindings and changing the mountains to snow-covered pines (*see* PAI-XVIII, 326).
**Est: $1,000-$1,200.**

# A. LAPUSZEWSKI

**368. Le Veuve Joyeuse.**
45³/₄ x 90⁵/₈ in./116.2 x 230 cm
Publicité Wall, Paris
Cond B+/Slight tears at folds.
Lapuszewski's shapely 2-sheet charmer and her entourage of suitors sweeps us back to the Parisian world of Franz Lehár's *The Merry Widow* and its high-kicking cancan girls, popping champagne corks, elegant ball gowns and secret assignations. The plot thickens as Baron Zeta, the cuckolded ambassador of the impoverished Balkan state of Pontevedro, seeks to prevent foreign suitors from securing the hand and fortune of the rich widow, Hanna. Naturally, being an operetta, all ends happily, but not before Hanna and her true love, Danilo, have led a merry dance or two.
**Est: $1,700-$2,000.**

371

373

## SYDNEY LAURENCE

**369. Rainer National Park/Northern Pacific.** 1932.
40 x 30³/₈ in./101.5 x 77.2 cm
Cond A.
A gorgeous poster for the Northern Pacific Railroad that essentially reproduces a Laurence oil painting of Mount Rainer at sunrise. Also used in their magazine promotions, the text that accompanied that particular version of the artwork spelled out exactly what awaited the potential traveler: "A new entrance to Rainer National Park, opens this summer—The Yakima Gateway. From Yakima, Wash., on the main line of the Northern Pacific to the Pacific Coast, guests are motored along a majestic avenue of orchards, rivers, canyons and forests to Sunrise Lodge—the most thrilling mountain trip imaginable." Sold!
**Est: $1,500-$1,800.**

**370. Northern Pacific/Alaska.** 1931.
30 x 40³/₈ in./76.2 x 102.5 cm
Cond A–/Slight tears at paper edges.
Ref: American Railroad, p. 85
"Alaskan artist Sydney M. Laurence, who led the life of a Jack London adventure-story hero, created what were perhaps NP's most compelling images. Gold fever had led him to Alaska in 1903, where he took up landscape painting after incurring injuries in a shipwreck. (General Passenger Agent Max) Goodsill acquired the rights to reproduce his paintings as posters and ads beginning in 1930. If more picture than poster, Laurence's luminous views of snowcapped peaks nevertheless conveyed a world of mystery and adventure. . . . *Off to the Potlatch*, which set Northwest Indians in a traditional dugout canoe sailing to a festival of giving, proved most popular; its poster version won first prize in a contemporary Boston exhibition" (American Railroad, p. 83).
**Est: $1,000-$1,200.**

## UMBERTO DI LAZZARO

**371. Crociera Aerea Transatlantica.** 1931.
38³/₄ x 55 in./98.4 x 139.7 cm
I. G. A. P., Roma
Cond B+/Slight tears at folds.

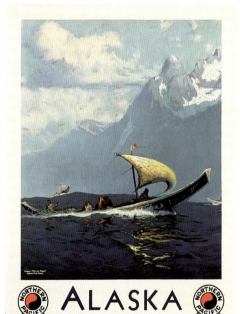

370

This pin-spotted global route as seen from on high is quite different from this artist's other promotion commemorating the 1931 massive Italian formation flight from Rome to Rio De Janeiro (see PAI-XXXI, 170) over South Atlantic waters, with the poster here created with straightforward Colorform clarity as opposed to the portrait-laden, shrunken perspective of the other design. This was the first of the Italian formation flights over the Atlantic Ocean—the second transpiring some two years later (see PAI-XXIX, 114)—that would effectively demonstrate—with a squadron of Savoia-Marchetti flying boats outfitted with Fiat motors, Manelli magnetos, spark plugs and batteries, Stanavo corroborators and sponsored in part by the Italo-American Petroleum

372

Industry of Genoa—how flight was rapidly shrinking the planet. Both missions were headed by the dashing Italian Air Minister, General Italo Balbo. After serving in World War I, Balbo joined the Fascist movement and in 1922 was one of the four top leaders of the March on Rome, which brought Mussolini to power. A general of the Fascist militia, he held several cabinet posts and efficiently developed aviation in Italy. Ironically, he was killed in 1940 when his plane crashed at Tobruk, Libya, apparently shot down accidentally by Italian

**374**

**375**

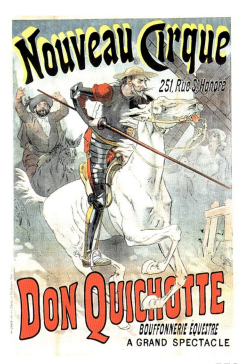

**376**

**377**

**378**

antiaircraft artillery. *This is the rare larger format.*
**Est: $3,000-$4,000.**

## LILDEN

**372. Paris/International Exposition 1937.** 1936.
24¹/₄ x 39 in./61.6 x 99 cm
Publimp-Nadal, Paris
Cond B–/Restored tears at folds.
A very fine photomontage invitation to the 1937 Paris International Exposition, a global event focusing on art and the technical aspects of modern life. Though the photographic elements keep everything on a nicely nationalistic level, the graphic shorthand keeps the relationship between the U.S. and France clearly on the radar.
**Est: $1,500-$1,800.**

## LUCIEN LEFÈVRE (ca. 1850-?)

**373. Electricine.** 1895.
33¹/₄ x 48 in./84.4 x 122 cm
Imp. Chaix, Paris
Cond B/Slight stains at folds.
Ref: DFP-II, 515; Reims, 807; Schardt, p. 87; PAI-XXXIV, 334
"Although Lefèvre's technique was very close to that of his teacher Chéret, his style was quite different . . . Whereas Chéret displayed an infectious vitality which

flowed right to his fingertips, the younger man was much more lyrical, much softer. Carefully and circumspectly the young lady with the flattering hairstyle sets down a lamp, which is lit by the brand of paraffin she is advertising, Electricine. With a dreamy look she touches the lampshade with her left hand, evoking an atmosphere of respectable, well-groomed domesticity" (Schardt, p. 96).
**Est: $1,700-$2,000.**

**374. La Bague Soleil.** 1891.
33³/₈ x 48 in./ 85 x 122 cm
Imp. Chaix, Paris
Cond B+/Slight tears and stains at folds.
Ref: DFP-II, 509; PAI-XXIII, 329
An advertisement for the jewelers Crespin & Dufayel features diamond rings and earrings—25 and 45 francs respectively—that "shine like the sun." The happy recipient seems to have received at least two from her generous beau.
**Est: $1,700-$2,000.**

**375. Grande Fête de Bienfaisance.** 1895.
33³/₄ x 48¹/₂ in./85.6 x 123 cm
Cond B/Slight tears and stains, largely at folds.
As they rush from the inferno that continues to blaze in the background, the indigenous populace of Martinique and Guadeloupe are free to fall into the benevolent embrace of a sympathetic Marianne, the angelic calling card for this charity event whose proceeds will

benefit the fire victims of the French territories.
**Est: $1,200-$1,500.**

**376. Nouveau Cirque/Don Quichotte.** 1892.
34³/₄ x 48⁷/₈ in./88.2 x 124 cm
Imp. Chaix, Paris
Cond B/Slight tears and stains at folds and edges.
Ref: Reims, 803; PAI-XXIII, 330
Parisians could expect all sorts of entertainment at the Nouveau Cirque. Here, Lefèvre advertises an equestrian version of Cervantes' tragicomic tale *Don Quixote*. We see the Man of La Mancha tilting at his imaginary windmills with fierce intensity. Neither his steed nor his companion Sancho Panza know quite what to make of it all.
**Est: $1,400-$1,700.**

**377. Café Malt.** 1892.
34 x 47³/₄ in./86.4 x 121.5 cm
Imp. Chaix, Paris
Cond B+/Unobtrusive folds.
Ref: Gold, 57; PAI-XXXIII, 414
"Instead of advertising properties such as aroma, flavor, and taste, this coffee brand takes a 'status' approach. The image of an upper-class maid pouring a cup from an elegant silver pot implies that the product is routinely served in the best social circles. Lefèvre worked at the Chaix printing shop where Chéret was his mentor, and he acknowledges his debt to him in every design" (Gold, p. 42).
**Est: $1,700-$2,000.**

**379**

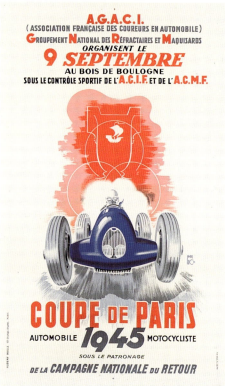

**380**

**382**

**385**

## FRANZ LENHART (1898-1992)

**378. Palace Hotel.** 1923.
$37^1/_2$ x $26^5/_8$ in./95.2 x 67.6 cm
J. G.M. Giaccone & Salucci, Firenze
Cond A–/Unobtrusive folds.
Rock-solid Old World opulence in the heart of Italy's South Tyrollean region along the Brenner Pass, a location that inspired Henrik Ibsen to create some of his greatest theatrical contributions. How unfortunate that Gossensass' fortress-like Palace Hotel didn't have the monolithic permanence of its graphic counterpart, seeing as the palatial lodging has faded from record, even though the region is still a thriving winter sport destination. Born in Bavaria, Lenhart studied in Italy and settled there permanently in 1922 to work and teach.
**Est: $1,500-$1,800.**

## M. LEROY

**379. La Guerre et Les Humoristes.** 1917.
55 x $38^7/_8$ in./139.6 x 98.7 cm
Imp. Lapina, Paris
Cond B/Slight tears and stains at folds.
The subtlety of this design for an exhibition of works by the combined Societies of Humorist Designers and Artists focusing on their work during wartime is a tad vexing. Does the winged gremlin-esque creature with the scissors represent the artists and their ability to

slice through all the political doublespeak to the heart of the matter through incisive wit? That's one interpretation, but there easily could be many more for this striking Leroy image. The exhibit certainly had sufficient credentials in the organizational department, seeing as the two creative entities in charge were headed by Jean-Louis Forain and Jules Abel Faivre.
**Est: $1,200-$1,500.**

## JEAN LUC

**380. Coupe de Paris.** 1945.
$39^1/_2$ x 63 in./99.9 x 160 cm
Hubert Baille, Paris
Cond B/Unobtrusive tears at folds.
With the war still very much in the memories of the Parisian populace, what better way to attempt to at least temporarily whisk away those troubled times and reestablish some form of reality than with thunderous barrage of automotive competition. Hence, the reinstatement of the Paris Cup, a sports car and motorcycle event—also known that year as the "Prisoner's Cup". Luc's head-on vision of the motor-minded competitor's need for speed muscularly plays itself out beneath the galleoned crest of the races' organizing bodies.
**Est: $1,200-$1,500.**

## E. CHARLE LUCAS

**381. Théâtre Athénée Comique/Mme Putiphar.**
$45^5/_8$ x $30^1/_2$ in./116 x 77.4 cm
Imp. Charles Verneau, Paris
Cond A–/Slight tears at edges.
Though not precisely modest, the titular character on display certainly cuts a diaphanously appealing figure. And though this gauzy temptress is costumed ideally to portray a siren at the Théâtre Athénée Comique, no record of this particular operetta exists to further the titillation. It must be assumed that the subject matter ran somewhat along the lines of the biblically-originated tale of Joseph and the wife of the Egyptian official whose treachery landed him in prison—seeing as her name, "Potiphar" is one vowel away from this languid theatrical femme fatale. But without evidence, this remains nothing more than speculation.
**Est: $2,000-$3,000.**

**382. L'Exposition du Théâtre et Musique.** 1896.
$28^3/_8$ x $48^5/_8$ in./72.2 x 123.5 cm
Imp. Chaix, Paris
Cond B+/Slight tears at folds.
Ref (All Var): DFP-II, 551; Reims, 817; Gold, 186; PAI-XXX, 238
A young woman holding up the masks of tragedy and comedy announces a four-month festival of theatrical and musical performances at the Palais de l'Industrie. The design is symmetrical, but provides a lovely contrast between the overwrought masks and the sly smiling visage of the delicate, bare-shouldered woman, accompanied by a branch of laurel, the Roman symbol of fame. Lucas, who signed all his posters E. Charle

383

384

386

Lucas, was born Charles-Louis Lucas. Unfortunately, little else is known about him. *This is the medium format.*
**Est: $1,500-$1,800.**

## PRIVAT LIVEMONT (1861-1936)

### 383. Absinthe Robette. 1896.
$31^1/2$ x $43^3/8$ in./80 x 110 cm
J. L. Goffart, Bruxelles
Cond A.
Ref: DFP-II, 1062, Maitres, 104; Belle Epoque 1970, 75;
    Timeless Images, 38; Wine Spectator, 80;
    Absinthe, p. 134; Masters 1900, p. 88;
    Absinthe Affiches, Cover & 105; Gold, 43;
    PAI-XXXII, 389
Livemont gives us a study in green, shading from chartreuse to olive, because "absinthe was known as The Green Fairy. It was a potent hallucinogen, which Livemont hints at by having the (figure) hold the drink in an attitude of mystic awe, as well as by the use of a strangely convoluted pattern in the background. A classic of inspired product promotion!" (Wine Spectator, 80). And thanks to Livemont's artistry, commerce is again serviced by unflinching female sensuality.
**Est: $7,000-$9,000.**

## PIERRE LOUŸS

### 384. Citroën. 1925.
$61^1/2$ x $87^1/2$ in/156 x 222.2 cm.
Imp. Chaix, Paris
Cond B+/Slight tears and stains; image and colors
    excellent.
Ref (Both Var): Auto Show II, 50; PAI-XXV, 65
Citroën is best known for his pioneering work with front-wheel drive, the so-called "self-leveling" suspension system, and full power brakes as a standard feature. André Citroën opened his first factory in 1915, and was the first to offer cars with all accessories standard, which was such an innovation that he sold six-teen-thousand cars before he could actually deliver a single one. In this colorful poster for the B-12 model, a lady is taking her family or friends for a ride past an imposing chateau. *This is the larger format.*
**Est: $3,000-$4,000.**

## BURKHARD MANGOLD (1873-1950)

### 385. Grosch & Grieff. 1910.
$32^5/8$ x $44^3/8$ in./82.8 x 112.7 cm
J. E. Wolfensberger, Zürich (not shown)
Cond A–/Unobtrusive tears at edges.
Ref: Mangold, 110; PAI-XXXII, 405
For the Lausanne merchant's annual white sale, Mangold dispenses with the typical fluttery of billowing blanched fabric and presents us with a pristine vase of newly-plucked daisies atop a contrastingly polka-dotted platform. As fresh an idea as the floral arrangement itself. Mangold, born in Basel, spent seven years in Munich (1894-1900) where he received grounding in the principles of the popular Jugendstil movement. He became involved with every facet of decorative arts, and after returning to Switzerland in 1900, he practiced many of them, including glassblowing, woodblock printing, illustration, painting and lithography. He produced some 150 posters, choosing his graphic style very carefully for each assigned message.
**Est: $1,400-$1,700.**

## JAN MARCOZ

### 386. Bountiful Harvest.
$9^1/8$ x 19 in./23.1 x 48.3 cm
Cond A/P.
Arboreal Byzantine splendor, very much in a Camps vein, yet exuding a gauzy diaphanousness all its own. The Marcoz decorative panel's perky plucker prettily promotes that beauty for beauty's sake is reason enough to surrender to poster persuasion.
**Est: $1,200-$1,500.**

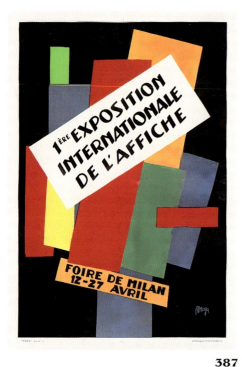

387

388

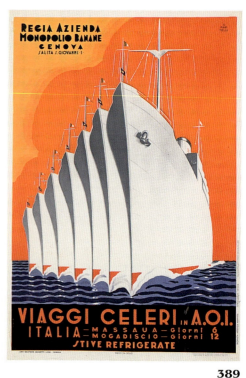

389

## MAGA AGENCY

**387. 1ère Exposition Internationale de l'Affiche.**
ca. 1927.
27³/₄ x 39¹/₂ in./70.4 x 100 cm
Maga, Milano
Cond B/Restored tears at folds.
It isn't often that we single out a graphic agency, but when an uncredited designer from an agency produces a work of such startling simplicity, then it's time to give credit where credit is due. For Italy's premiere International Poster Exposition, being held at the Milan Fair, we're given this Cubist evocation of cut-and-paste proportions, leaving the door open to any number of passerby interpretations while clearly inducing a sense of the pasted paper's necessity in adding much needed color to otherwise bleak surroundings. *Rare!*
**Est: $2,500-$3,000.**

## E. MARIEL

**388. Fête Annuelle de Charité.** 1904.
39³/₈ x 50⁷/₈ in./100 x 129.2 cm
Imp. L. Cassan Aîné, Toulouse
Cond B/Slight tears and stains at folds and edges.
A peculiar blend of Far Eastern and Byzantine elements coalesce to spawn a placid yet revelrous promotion for an annual charity festival sponsored by a Toulouse student association, whose intentions and ties to tradition are so profound that they spell out the purpose of their soiree in Latin on their overflowing chalice of human kindness.
**Est: $1,200-$1,500.**

## G. MARTELLI

**389. Viaggi Celeri in A.O.I.** 1936.
27¹/₄ x 39¹/₂ in./69.2 x 100.3 cm
Arti Graphishe Giuseppe Lang, Genova
Cond B+/Slight tears at edges.
This Geneva-based shipping line promises rapid transport to Red Sea and Indian Ocean ports of call—including Mogadishu, which at the time was the capitol of Italian Somaliland—and backs it up with a towering Art Deco fleet slicing its way through gently lapping waters. They also make mention of their refrigerated holds, which Martelli artfully reinforces with the sleekness of the ship's ice-white hulls contrasted off the overheated African skies.
**Est: $1,200-$1,500.**

# MATHER WORK INCENTIVE POSTERS

390

391

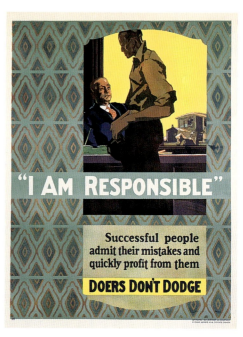

392

# MATHER: THE MASTER MOTIVATOR

The year is 1923. The war has been over for five years. The economy is booming. Workers, men and women, are streaming into cities from small towns and farms to make their fortunes working in factories and other expanding industries. And, Charles Howard Rosenfeld comes up with an idea to motivate these people to work harder, to get them to want to work harder to maximize profits for their bosses. His idea: a series of posters that extol the virtues of hard work and encourage the efforts of real team players. Rosenfeld was a "super salesman". He was convinced that he could motivate the workers. He knew that he could handle writing the messages, but was at a loss as to how to display them. Enter Charles Mather. Mather came from an old-line printing family in Chicago. Bored with run-of-the-mill printing assignments, he had to temporarily take leave from the company to explore the options of advertising. Their meeting was a marriage made in propaganda heaven. Rosenfeld had the entrepreneurial spirit and the writing skills, Mather the advertising perspective and printing skills. Together, they produced one of the most outstanding continuous series of graphically significant posters ever created in America.

The 1920s was a time when commercial advertising was becoming a major force in American society. It was also a time when advertising was thought to have a potentially utopian function. President Calvin Coolidge in a 1926 speech to the American Association of Advertising Agencies remarked that, "By changing the attitude of mind, it (advertising) changes the material condition of the people. . . . advertising ministers to the spiritual side of trade." Mather and Rosenfeld clearly understood this concept.

The extraordinary posters produced by Mr. Mather and Mr. Rosenfeld (actually invented by them, for nothing similar existed), took the idea of the poster in an entirely new direction. Instead of promoting particular products, they used this adverting medium to sell ideas, the aim of which was to modify or change attitudes and work practices in the American workplace. They called them "Constructive Organization Posters" and each year issued a catalogue showing the available images and claimed to have a poster to cure every "destructive practice among workers, from absenteeism to rudeness." Each poster contained Mr. Rosenfeld's text–he called them "messages"—and stunning graphic images created by one of the six talented Chicago-based commercial artists hired by Mr. Mather specifically for this purpose. They worked for him on a free-lance basis during the six years that these posters were produced. At times, these free-lancers were given assignments to produce illustrations to fit particular text messages. In other instances, they supplied drawings to fit appropriate text. And what is fascinating about this is the fact that between 1923 and 1929, the years the posters were produced, there were more than 350 images, never once repeating an illustration or a message. Certainly a steady source of income for a talented group of artists.

The catalogues, apart from showing the years' output of posters, provide fascinating insights into the concepts of business organization and worker relations that were prevalent at the time. As an example, the 1926-27 catalogue index notes: "Every known destructive practice among workers (and there are 136 different ones listed alphabetically) is covered by at least one poster, and usually by a series from which you can choose the most suitable to meet the condition of the moment. Should the trouble prove obstinate, follow up the first poster selected with one or more others in the series. In this way, the problem will be handled from every angle–no matter what posters you select for display, morale will be improved, turnover reduced, loyalty stimulated, results and greater profits insured for your firm." Not to mention more sales stimulated and greater profits for the Mather firm.

But, the messages would not have worked, if they worked at all, without the brilliant illustrations to catch the attention of the workers. Would anyone have stopped to read or even be attracted by some words posted on the wall? That's where the idea of an "advertising" poster came into play. Depending on the theme of the message being conveyed, the artists used bright bold images and colors to catch the eye and enliven the text. Their use of bright colors and masterly drawing techniques along the simple images they selected, such as animals, sports, trains and plains, street scenes, men and women, as well as many more significant subjects made these posters both powerful advertising devices and superb works of art. Preparation of the individual posters was truly a collaborative venture between writer and artist. Text and image were always conceived as an integral whole; the images always represented the story set out in the messages.

Over the six years that they were produced, the posters just seemed to get better and better, both in terms of the illustrations and the messages. Each year, the posters underwent a gentle tinkering; only the size remained the same: 36" x 44". The messages became shorter, simpler and less strident in tone. A graphic "style" for the year was set. Each year it was somewhat different. Background treatments changed, drawing techniques were modified and color palettes became brighter by the year. In this respect, by 1929, planes of pure color were used to delineate figures replacing more intricately drawn characters.

The end came for this series of posters in 1929. The Great Depression hit full force. There was no need to motivate people to work when there was no work available. There also wasn't any money available to buy the posters. So, production of the Mather Work Incentive posters stopped. And that is the great shame. For by that time, Mather, Rosenfeld and the artists had "gotten it right". One can only speculate on what would have followed.

The posters produced in 1927 are among the most unique and decorative of the entire series. They are also extremely rare and difficult to find. It was the only year where all the illustrations and text were placed against a colorful tapestry-like background. This set them off from all of the previously issued posters, making them extremely eye-catching and appealing to the workers for whom they were intended. The illustrations, while reduced in size, were made stronger and more dynamic through drawing techniques, portrayal of easily comprehended scenes and the use of bright colors. All of the text, the messages, was placed in "boxes" with contrasting colored background so that they could easily be read. The posters in this auction are perfect examples of what Mather intended when he began his poster production four years earlier. Strong, beautifully drawn illustrations with corresponding, integrated messages all put together with great design skill. Over the years, these posters have become recognized as outstanding examples of American graphic design. And, as Mather says in his sales catalogue, "they speak immediately and directly to the viewer." What more could one ask of a poster?

—From the introduction of the soon-to-be-published book, *Mather Work Incentive Posters*, by John Heller. Reproduced with kind permission of the author.

---

**Note:** Although only three posters in this series are signed (Nos. 393, 396 & 398), it's most probable that all are, in fact, the work of **Willard Frederic Elmes**.

**390. Beware the Red Beast!** 1927.
$35^5/8$ x $47^1/8$ in./90.5 x 119.7 cm
Mather & Company, Chicago
Cond A–/Unobtrusive tears in margins.
Just hearing the title brings thoughts of Communism to mind. However, the "Beast" here is no way ideological, but rather the very real industrial danger of fire. Though you have to admit that a crimson dragon does a rather nice job of encapsulating both possibilities.
**Est: $1,200-$1,500.**

**391. The Higher the Better.** 1927.
$35^1/2$ x $47^1/4$ in./90.2 x 120 cm
Mather & Company, Chicago
Cond B+/Restored tears, largely in top margin.
Paying attention is always a good idea, but there are a few more crucial situations where the need for it is as vital as in aerial stunt work, where the slightest lapse in concentration could result in the demise of an associate. Perhaps a tad overstated in terms of workplace detail, but these trapeze artists certainly deliver the goods when it comes to demonstrating the chain of dependence.
**Est: $1,200-$1,500.**

**392. "I Am Responsible".** 1927.
$35^5/8$ x $47^1/8$ in./90.5 x 119.3 cm
Mather & Company, Chicago
Cond A.
Owning up to one's mistakes is never an easy task. But this encounter between a clearly penitent employee and a strict, yet benevolent employer hits the nail right on the head without a single overstated note. And when it comes to catch-phrases, "Doers Don't Dodge" has to be considered one of responsibility's finest.
**Est: $1,200-$1,500.**

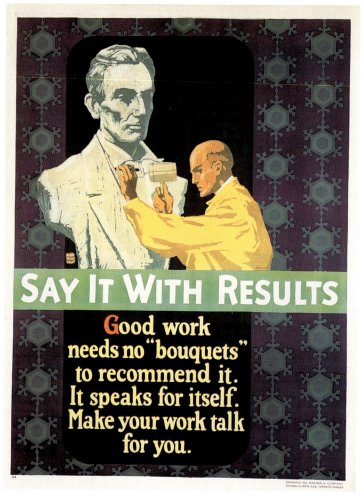

## MATHER (continued)

**393. Say It With Results.** 1927.
$35^3/4$ x $47^1/8$ in./90.8x 119.7 cm
Mather Co., Chicago
Cond A–/Tears at left edges.
A job well done is its own best reward. And this sculptor's attention to detail is nothing short of commendable. Of course, Elmes' inclusion of honest American iconoclasm is nothing short of genius in and of itself.
**Est: $1,300-$1,600.**

**394. Let's Learn to Listen!** 1927.
$35^3/4$ x $47^1/2$ in./90.6 x 120.7 cm
Mather & Co., Chicago
Cond A.
Athletics once more provide the bridge between ideology and implementation, demonstrating not only that pride can hinder constructively-dispensed criticism, but that every team needs a single guiding voice to dispense these words of wisdom.
**Est: $1,300-$1,600.**

**395. Is it True?** 1927.
35 x 47 in./90.1 x 119.4 cm
Mather & Co., Chicago
Cond A–/Unobtrusive tear at top edge.
Although the Mather messages were inspirational, there was such an earnest squareness about them that it must have been hard to avoid using a certain routine, pedestrian quality in their images. And though there's nothing exotic or even allegorical about this design, Elmes' potent sense of dismissive theatricality fantastically delivers the message of refusal to partake in idle gossip.
**Est: $1,200-$1,500.**

**396. It's up to You.** 1927.
$35^5/8$ x $47^1/4$ in./90.5 x 120 cm
Mather & Co., Chicago
Cond A.
Necessity may be the mother of invention, but only keen insight spawns innovation. The message of this poster may be simple, but the Mather reinforcement of efficient horse-sense (or horseless-sense in this particular case) keenly appeals to individual foresight.
**Est: $1,200-$1,500.**

**397. The Blind Trail!** 1927.
$35^1/2$ x $47^1/8$ in./90 x 119.7 cm
Mather & Co., Chicago
Cond A.
Or "Look Before You Leap!" These homesteaders obviously didn't do their research: Expecting a land of milk and honey, these poor pilgrims find themselves stranded in bone-dry desolation, the clear result of relying exclusively on the word of others. And the Mather parallel with regard to secondhand word-of-mouth makes it crystal clear that one can never collect too much personal data.
**Est: $1,300-$1,600.**

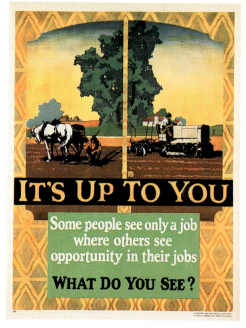

**398. Are You Ready?** 1927.
$35^3/4$ x $47^1/8$ in./90.6 x 119.2 cm
Mather & Co., Chicago
Cond A–/Unobtrusive tears in margins.
The use of sports-related images to connect a message attempting to make to its way into the psyche of the everyday viewer is a surefire approach. Not only have we accepted catch phrases from athletics as a part of our daily lexicon ("There's no 'I' in 'TEAM'", being the obvious example), but these images serve as an excellent metaphor in terms of individual excellence within a group structure. Elmes' tackle-dummy pounding stalwart does a superior job of drilling home the credo of preparedness.
**Est: $1,300-$1,600.**

**397**

**398**

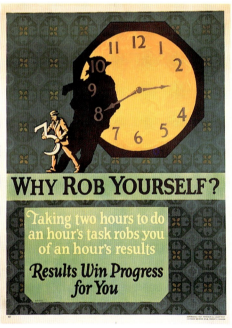

**399**

**400**

**401**

**399. Mending Beats Tearing.** 1927.
35¹/₂ x 47¹/₄ in./90.4x 120 cm
Mather & Co., Chicago
Cond A.
Whenever a particular profession was needed to reinforce a Mather missive, a salt-of-the-earth occupation always seemed to be the worker of choice. Here, hardworking fishermen are used to exemplify the need for prudent critical exchanges, placing the focus on the need for watchful maintenance over harsh replacements.
**Est: $1,200-$1,500.**

**400. See Them Stare!** 1927.
35¹/₂ x 47 in./90.2 x 119.4 cm
Mather & Co., Chicago
Cond A.
Who is that shadowy foreground figure? Who is that unkempt no-goodnic distracting the shiny, happy people with a decent work ethic from their appointed duties? It's a latecomer, that's who! An individual worthy of all the derision that may be heaped upon him. A wonderfully guilt-based promotion for personal accountability.
**Est: $1,200-$1,500.**

**401. Why Rob Yourself?** 1927.
35⁵/₈ x 47¹/₈ in./90.5 x 119.8 cm
Mather & Company, Chicago
Cond B+/Restored paper loss in upper left corner;
vertical tear at top center.
Though most Mather posters wear their literalness on their rolled-up sleeves, this design's literal sense of pilfering time elevates it into the realm of the blissfully silly. The thief in question is even wearing a kerchief to hide his identity! Not that the message of workplace dedication is one to be taken lightly; it's just nice to see a subtle sense of humor at play in a Mather creation.
**Est: $1,200-$1,500.**

**402**

**403**

## SASCHA MAURER (1897-1961)

**402. Flexible Flyer/Splitkein.**
23¹/₂ x 37 in./59.5 x 94 cm
Cond A.
Ref: PAI-XXI, 313
A brand of ski equipment advertises with a well-conceived design. The design uses the sleek, Hollywood-influenced style of enhanced realism that came into vogue during the 1940s. Maurer was best known for a series of posters he created for the New Haven Railroad and other New England clients.
**Est: $1,500-$1,800.**

## LUCIANO ACHILLE MAUZAN (1883-1952)

**403. Il Granatiere Rolland.** 1911.
40¹/₄ x 56 in./102 x 142 cm
G. Ricordi, Milano
Cond B/Slight tears at folds.
Ref: Mauzan, C11
A spectacularly unusual poster portrait of Napoleon I—at once commanding, concerned, befuddled, corpulent, searching, and ultimately resigned, a meeting ground of both potency and astonished defeat—promotes the Italian release of "Il Granatiere Rolland," directed by Luigi Maggi and produced by the Film d'Arte Itiliano, the Italian subsidiary of the ubiquitous Charles Pathé. The film tells the story of Napoleon's ill-fated Russian campaign as seen through the eyes of one of the soldiers in his "Grand Army". The movie is notable for its surprising production values for such an early film, most especially in the ignominious retreat of the French army, filmed in a snowy location in the Piedmont Alps of Northern Italy.
**Est: $3,000-$3,500.**

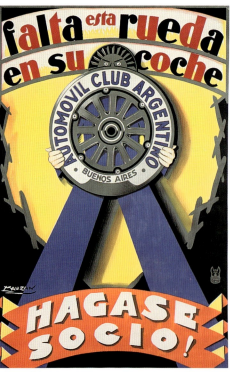

**404**

**406**

**404. Automovil Club Argentino.** ca. 1930.
39¹/₂ x 59⁵/₈ in./100.4 x 151.5 cm
Affiches Mauzan/Cosmos
Cond A–/Slight tears and stains at edges.
Ref: Mauzan, A307; PAI-XXXII, 134

A graphic figure with a head resembling a hood ornament and holding the tire-shaped logo of the national auto club as if it were a steering wheel urges Buenos Aires drivers to join.
**Est: $1,700-$2,000.**

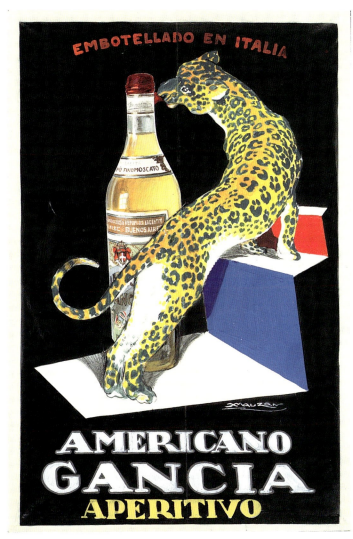

**405**

**407**

**408**

**405. Bertozzi.** 1930.
39¹/₄ x 55 in./99.7 x 139.7 cm
Mauzan Morzenti, Cernusco-Lombardone
Cond A.
Ref: Mauzan/Treviso, p. 76; Mauzan, A033 (var);
  Mauzan Affiches, p. 99; PAI XXIX, 499
Mauzan goes for a touch of the grotesque in publicizing
Bertozzi cheese, but does it with such chutzpah that

the overall effect is pleasing—so much so that this
represents the fourth edition of this particular design.
And with three judges putting their olfactory reputations
on the line, it can be safely assumed that although justice may be blind, it is quite keen in the other senses.
Mauzan produced well over 2,000 posters during the
course of his long, prodigious career. Born in France,
Mauzan would begin his life as an illustrator in Italy in
1909, working for Ricordi and other topnotch printing
firms. He remained there until 1927, when he and his
wife were invited to Buenos Aires. There he continued
a frantic pace of poster production until 1933, when
the Mauzans returned to France, where he would continue his work for the rest of his days. His boundless
imagination is a landscape of ingenious concepts and
incongruous associations working in harmony. He lays
on color freely, but what marks his designs as unique
is his sense of humor, by turns witty, grotesque, mad,
pungent, charming and openly affectionate.
**Est: $4,000-$5,000.**

**406. Hesperidina.** 1930.
29 x 43³/₈ in./73.7 x 110.2 cm
Affiches Mauzan, Buenos Aires
Cond B+/Slight tears and creases at folds and edges.
Ref: Mauzan, A388
It's time to wake up your appetite with Hesperdina, the
aperitif especially distilled to get you well on the road
to voracity. And if this rotund courtier is any indication,
it increases your hunger to a gluttonous degree. In
fact, I'd say it's a foregone conclusion that the turkey
before him will likely be turned into nothing more than
skeletal remains the second he has a moment to himself. But not to be selfish, this rosy-faced, eye-popping

gourmand invites us along the road to obesity with a
finger-wagging, "Now it's your turn." *Rare!*
**Est: $1,700-$2,000.**

*The following ten maquettes of Mauzan are from
his Argentine period, 1927-1933, and are all
from the artist's studio.*

**407. Americano Gancia.** ca. 1927.
20¹/₄ x 29³/₄ in./51.5 x 75.6 cm
*Gouache and ink maquette.* Framed.
Ref: Mauzan, A370 (var)
The original artwork for the Italian aperitif poster that
remained virtually unchanged on its lithographic journey. There's nothing particularly American about the
product, but Mauzan includes a dash of red, white and
blue for good measure. What he makes perfectly clear
with his gently lapping leopard is that Gancia is the
perfect potion to unleash your inner wildcat.
**Est: $4,000-$5,000.**

**408. Crying Time/Texte.**
20¹/₄ x 29³/₄ in./51.5 x 75.6 cm
*Gouache and ink maquette.* Framed.
Ref: Mauzan, M067
Waaaaaaaaaah! It's her dress and she'll cry if she
wants to! So cruel that it's funny. This eye-grabbing
maquette, either intended to promote ink, laundry
detergent or stain remover one would imagine, is even
kind enough to point out where the promotional lettering was intended to go. Never has a crybaby been so
appealing. Copyright seal and number, as well as
Mauzan's studio seal appear verso.
**Est: $2,000-$3,000.**

409

410

## MAUZAN (continued)

### 409. Centaur Refreshed.
20 x 29³/₄ in./50.8 x 75.6 cm
*Gouache and ink maquette.* Framed.
Ref: Mauzan, M012
This thirsty jockey certainly has no one but himself to blame for the parched state in which he presently finds himself, seeing as he is the only possible creature responsible for pushing himself to the point of dehydration. Mythically surreal, this brilliant artwork aptly shows the depths of Mauzan's creativity, where no combination or association of elements was too absurd or unimaginable.
**Est: $4,000-$5,000.**

### 410. Bilz/Queen of Beverages.
20¹/₈ x 30 in./51 x 76.2 cm
*Gouache and ink maquette.* Framed.
Ref: Mauzan, M011
All hail the Soda Queen! Created for Bilz carbonated beverages—but for some unknown reason never used as an actual poster—Mauzan conjures forth an amazing vision of blazing refreshment, combining an unlikely union of Carmen Miranda and an Aztec or Incan sun goddess to a startlingly brilliant conclusion.
**Est: $4,000-$5,000.**

### 411. Sipping Swimmer.
20¹/₂ x 29³/₄ in./52 x 75.5 cm
*Hand-signed gouache and ink maquette.* Framed.
Ref: Mauzan, M009
Between the parasol, the dip in the ocean and a refreshing beverage, you'd think this overheated beachgoer should be able to cool down. But the sunshine background expanse, unbroken by clouds of any stripe, makes us think that Mauzan may have placed his tippler in scorching terrain indeed. Even the fish look like they'd like to get their fins on some of the drink du jour.
**Est: $4,000-$5,000.**

411

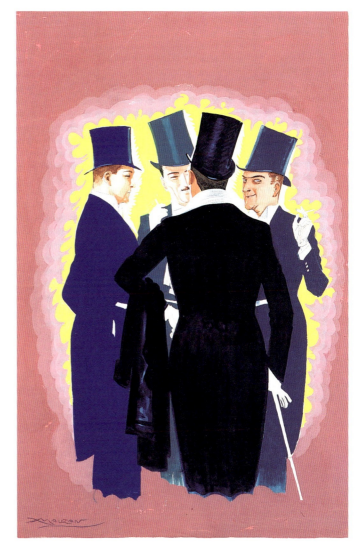

412

413

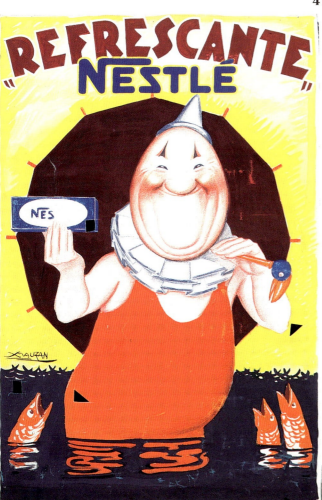

414

### 412. Fashionable Encounter.
20 x 30 in./50.8 x 76.2 cm
*Hand-signed gouache and ink maquette.* Framed.
Ref: Mauzan, M063
Sure, they look great, but this tête-à-tête quartet certainly seems to have mischief on their agenda. The elegant foursome was no doubt intended to promote a clothier with the insight to let Mauzan's rich gradations of blue send him hurling onto the cutting edge of advertising. Unfortunately, no such visionary tailor would appear to have existed.
**Est: $4,000-$5,000.**

### 413. Carnivore's Delight.
20 x 30 in./50.7 x 76.2 cm
*Hand-signed gouache and ink maquette.* Framed.
Ref: Mauzan, M003
It's never a good idea to catch a tiger by the tail, but getting one by the taste buds is a different story altogether. And this young butcher is so confident in the quality of his cured meats that he doesn't even mind that one of nature's fiercest predators is cozying up to him. It probably doesn't hurt that the little fella is just so darn cute.
**Est: $4,000-$5,000.**

### 414. Nestlé.
20 x 30 in./50.7 x 76.2 cm
*Hand-signed gouache and ink maquette.* Framed.
Ref: Mauzan, M247; PAI-XXVII, 499 (var)
Although chocolate isn't necessarily associated with the cooling properties one normally couples with summertime refreshment, it seems to be just the ticket for this bathing clown with a parasol straight out of "Mary Poppins," as well as the gaping goldfish clamoring for a morsel. It was Mauzan's habit to snip out pieces of his maquettes to pass along to the printers in order to provide a color guide for the finished poster; this can clearly be seen here with the small geometric pieces that have been removed from the orange, blue and yellow portions of the artwork.
**Est: $4,000-$5,000.**

**415**

**416**

**417**

**420**

## MAUZAN (continued)

**415. Shoe Polish Lounge.**
29³/₈ x 21¹/₄ in./74.5x 54 cm
*Gouache and ink maquette.* Framed.
Ref: Mauzan, M016
Who said laying down on the job was a bad habit? This toothsome gentleman's gentleman certainly has found a way around that admonition, thanks in large part to a pair of oversized shoe polish rounds. Though this particular design didn't wind up as an actual poster, the boot-buffing butler found his way onto a poster for another polish: Ecla (*see* Mauzan, A094), where he can be seen wearing the same outfit, down to the red-and-white checked house slippers. Though unsigned, this maquette has the copyright number and Mauzan's studio seal appearing verso.
**Est: $3,000-$4,000.**

**416. Elephant Shower.**
21³/₄ x 22⁷/₈ in./55.2 x 58.5 cm
*Hand-signed gouache and ink maquette.* Framed.
A playful pachyderm sprays himself with a trunkful of water, with indications that prismatic fractals may have been included in the back-splash had the maquette seen its way to poster conclusion. And what product was this elephant shower intended to promote? Raincoats? Tarp? Soap? It's hard to say for sure, but one thing is certain: Mauzan had a way of applying his vision to the most mundane product and make it

appear enigmatic. Whatever item to which it was intended, it most certainly would have benefited from Mauzan's imaginative association.
**Est: $2,000-$3,000.**

## MEDAILLE

**417. La Pêche/La Chasse.** ca. 1900.
Each: 19³/₄ x 26¹/₄ in./50.1 x 66.6 cm
Imp. Champenois (not shown)
Cond A–/Unobtrusive tears near paper edges.
Ref: PAI-III, 332
A pair of decorative panels that pretty much proves that there are elements of interior design to suit every taste. You say that allegorical representatives of flowers, seasons and the times of the day are too girlie for you? Well, how about a nice set of Byzantine ladies that embody the bounty of the great outdoors, respectively bordered by appropriate flora and appropriate game, from crabs and prawns to pheasant and squirrel. Manly enough for you? Never have fishing and hunting looked so good. These compositions were offered by Champenois as "estampes décoratives" in his catalogue for ten francs a pair (In comparison, Mucha pairs, such as "Plume et Primavere" and the two Brittany women sold for twelve francs).
**Est: $2,000-$2,500. (2)**

## LUCIEN METIVET (1863-1932)

**418. Eugenie Buffet/Ambassadeurs.** 1893.
30³/₄ x 41¹/₄ in./78 x 120 cm
Imp. Charles Verneau, Paris
Cond B–/Restored tears at folds and edges.
Ref: DFP-II, 574; Maîtres, 22; Musée d'Affiche, 68; Theaterplakat, 39; Gold, 170; PAI-XXX, 138
The image of Buffet walking down a snowy street, her hands stuffed into her pockets and eyes burning intensely, is one of the classics of poster art. "This is the earliest of three posters Metivet did for this chanteuse; in all cases, he puts her on ordinary Paris streets in the clothes of a Paris working girl, the persona she projected in her performances" (Gold, p. 118). This prolific magazine and book illustrator did few posters; most notably for Buffet and the winning entry in *Century's* Napoleon poster contest (*see* PAI-XXXIV, 44).
**Est: $3,000-$4,000.**

## LEOPOLDO METLICOVITZ (1868-1944)

**419. Distillerie Italiane.**
13³/₄ x 18¹/₂ in./33.7 x 47 cm
G. Ricordi, Milano
Cond A. Framed.
One of Italy's most prolific posterists, Metlicovitz was

418

419

421

**BULLIER**

Tous les
**JEUDIS
GRANDE FÊTE**
Samedis & Dimanches
**BAL**

422

**420. Lauris.**
31¼ x 43 in./79.3 x 109.2 cm
G. Ricordi, Milan
Cond B+/Slight tears at folds and edges.
Ref: PAI-IV, 51
A woman in classic garb set in front of the Athens sky-
line admires herself in a hand-mirror. The setting of
antiquity is obviously intended to show the classic
qualities of the fragrance, Lauris, made by the same
Paris firm that was responsible for the Fleurs de
Mousse perfume (see PAI-XXXV, 386).
**Est: $2,000-$2,500.**

**421. Abbazia.**
25 x 37¼ in./63.6 x 94.7 cm
Cond B+/Tears, largely in margins.
Abbazia is a fashionable tourist spot in the Piedmont
region of northern Italy, not far from Milan, where the
foothills of the Alps and many lakes and rivers create
an abundance of vistas such as this. Promoted here as
the "Pearl of the Adriatic," Metlicovitz does an admirable job of not letting his artistic whims get in the way,
allowing the beauty of the verdant quietude to speak
volumes for itself.
**Est: $1,200-$1,500.**

## GEORGES MEUNIER (1869—1942)

**422. Bullier.** 1895.
34¼ x 48¼ in./87 x 122.6 cm
Imp. Chaix, Paris
Cond B+/Slight tears at folds.
Ref: Meunier, 13; DFP-II, 580; Reims, 853; Maitres, 147;
    Gold, 142; PAI-XXXI, 535 (var)
Meunier gives us plenty of action in this poster for the
Bullier dance hall with this flirtatious dancer whose
cavorting earns her a tip of the hat from an equally
torqued male patron. *This is the larger format.*
**Est: $1,700-$2,000.**

born in the Adriatic port city of Trieste, and appears
to have become a painter and portraitist without any
formal training. In 1891, he showed up in Milan at
Ricordi's print shop as a lithography trainee, proving
to be such a quick study he was promoted to technical
director within a year. Though Metlicovitz was more
than capable of adjusting his style to the needs of his
clientele, his best works are highlighted by a fever-

pitch sense of fantasia, a palpable sense of sensual
mythology being unleashed on pedestrian paper. Case
in point this promotion for a Milanese distributor of
petroleum burning heating elements, who conjures
forth a sylphic embrace to promote the "economy of
oil." Is such a beautiful indulgence warranted for
lamps and heaters? The point is absolutely moot, as
we are simply fortunate enough to have had it occur.
**Est: $2,000-$2,500.**

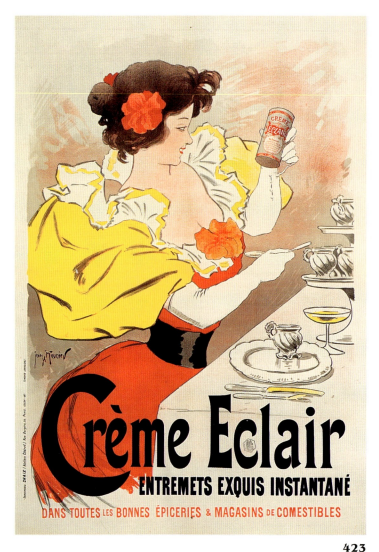

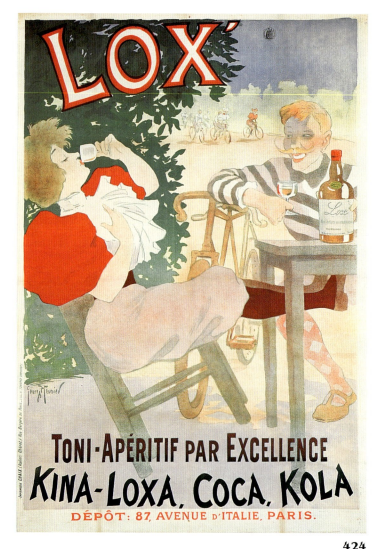

## MEUNIER (continued)

**423. Crème Eclair.** 1895.
$34^5/8$ x 49 in./88 x 124.5 cm
Imp. Chaix, Paris
Cond A.
Ref: Meunier, 15; Reims, 857; Gold, 52; PAI-XXXV, 387
Meunier, a Beaux-Arts trained painter and decorative artist, also designed 56 known posters, after the manner of Chéret in whose printing plant he produced most of them. What distinguishes Meunier, perhaps, is a particular lightness of spirit, as is evidenced in this poster for a latter-19th century Kool-Whip. "Thanks to this instant whipped-cream product, this woman escapes mess and bother. She can prepare elegant deserts in dinner dress: cinched waist, poufy sleeves, and flowers in her hair and decolletage—a veritable bell of the Belle Epoque" (Gold, p. 38).
**Est: $3,000-$4,000.**

**424. Lox.** 1895.
$33^1/2$ x $48^1/4$ in./85.3 x 122.6 cm
Imp. Chaix, Paris
Cond B+/Unobtrusive tears at stains and folds.
Ref: Meunier, 22; DFP-II, 586; Maindron, p. 91;
  Reims, 865; Wine Spectator, 25; PAI-XVI, 350
A pair of cyclists take a break with a refreshing drink. She's totally absorbed in the aperitif, he's totally absorbed in her—waiting with glee for the drink to take effect, no doubt. A wonderfully whimsical design from one of Chéret's most talented disciples.
**Est: $1,700-$2,000.**

**425. Fêtes Pour Soldats de Madagascar.** 1895.
$33^7/8$ x 49 in./88 x 124.6 cm
Imp. Chaix, Paris
Cond B+/Slight tears at folds.
Ref: Meunier, 17; DFP-II, 583; Reims, 861;
  PAI-XXXV, 388
Chéret's influence can once more be seen here in the exuberantly-sleeved mademoiselle with upswept hair and bared shoulders. She is beating a drum to announce a series of benefits sponsored by the

Parisian press on behalf of the troops occupying the faraway French colony of Madagascar.
**Est: $1,400-$1,700.**

**426. Nouveau Cirque/America!!!** 1895.
15 x 21 in./38.2 x 53.4 cm
Imp. Chaix, Paris
Cond B+/Slight tears at folds.
Ah, the French have always held America in such high esteem. This extravagantly staged train wreck—

unquestionably but a single example of an evening filled with "Exotic Buffoonery"—creates quite a slapstick splash for the Nouveau Cirque. No doubt, France's patron saint of comedy—the meritorious Jerry Lewis—would approve. *Rare!*
**Est: $1,000-$1,200.**

**427. Théâtre de l'Opéra/1er Bal Masqué.** 1895.
$34^1/8$ x $48^3/8$ in./86.7 x 123 cm
Imp. Chaix, Paris
Cond B+/Slight tears at folds.

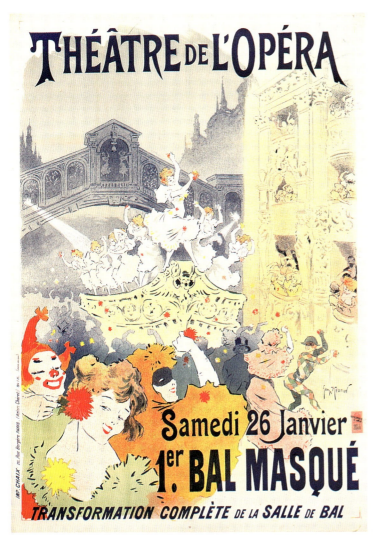

**427**

**428**

**429**

**430**

Meunier executed several designs for Christmas sales at the Place Clichy department store, all featuring a woman or girl on a rocking horse. This one is perhaps the liveliest and certainly one of the rarest. However, this time it's a rocking *mule* called upon to serve as the stationary steed, with a clown and a lady in red riding through a shopper's fantasy field of gifts represented by Japanese dolls, masks and assorted trinkets.
**Est: $1,700-$2,000.**

**429. Fêtes de Paris.** 1899.
33 1/8 x 49 in./84 x 124.4 cm
Imp. Chaix, Paris
Cond B+/Slight tears at folds.
Populated by a svelte mercantile super model embodying of the City of Lights—a benevolent deified embodiment of technological advancement accompanied by a minted image of legendary bourgeois and merchant leadership—this Meunier poster for the 1899 Paris festival wears its union of technology to beauty on its Art Nouveau sleeve. The event featured the unique pairing of the floral to the vehicularly illuminated. *Rare!*
**Est: $1,400-$1,700.**

**MISTI (Ferdinand Mifliez, 1865-1923)**

**430. Fête de Neuilly.** 1910.
15 1/8 x 23 1/8 in./38.5 x 58.7 cm
Atelier Misti, Neuilly s/ Seine
Cond A. Framed.
This trio of revelers, all smiles and sophistication, don't look like they're even close to calling it an evening as they make their way from the the annual fair in the Paris suburb of Neuilly, loaded down with loot from their visit—including a prize goldfish, which remains a carnival staple to this day. Misti was a busy poster artist who, between 1894 and 1914, designed more than 100 images—many for bicycles, as well as department stores, railroads, publishing clients and the Neuilly fair.
**Est: $1,200-$1,500.**

Ref (All Var but PAI): Meunier, Checklist; DFP-II, 582; Reims, 873; PAI-XXXIII, 448
The Théâtre de l'Opéra masked balls were always lavish events whose extravagance strained the limits of tasteful indulgence. But if there's any truth in advertising, this event pushed reason completely to the side as a flotilla of ballerinas arrives via a Grand Canal apparently diverted from Venice—along with the Rialto Bridge—for the amusement of the soirees loged revel-

ers. Meunier's design obviously got the job done as it was used again for the following two balls.
**Est: $2,000-$2,500.**

**428. A la Place Clichy/Etrennes.** ca.1896.
33 5/8 x 48 in./85.3 x 122 cm
Imp. Chaix, Paris
Cond B/Slight tears and stains at folds.
Ref: PAI-XXXI, 534

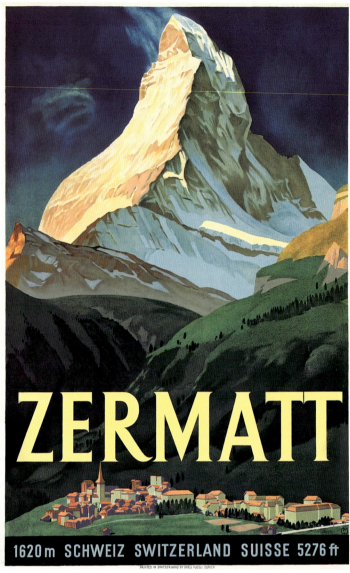

**431**

**435**

## MISTI (continued)

**431. Neuilly s/ Seine/Fête des Fleurs.** 1894.
$38^3/8$ x $58^1/8$ in./97.4 x 147.8 cm
Lith F. Appel, Paris
Cond B/Slight tears, stains and creases largely at folds.
It's rare to see people flocking to the suburbs for purely recreational business, but then again most bedroom communities don't offer anything nearly as lovely as this Neuilly flower festival. The entire design conveys a lovely florid commotion, but Misti saves a delicate, heavy-lidded enticement as the sunshiny centerpiece of his design. And take note: although carriages are permitted onto the grounds, it's more economical to make your way to the festival by pedestrian means.
**Est: $2,000-$2,500.**

**432. Le Vélo.** 1897.
$36^3/8$ x $50^5/8$ in./92.3 x 128.7 cm
Imp. P. Vercasson. Paris
Cond B+/Slight tears at folds.
Imaginative and lovely, this Misti promotion for *Le Vélo* provides a shadowy clandestine diversion for this radiant beauty whose Chinese lantern illuminated visage reinforces the emancipating contributions of the bicycle without giving into pedantic tendencies. Though mentioned only in the upside-down fine print near the paper's name, the publication also covered automotive events and sports as a whole, even though bicycling was its primary focus.
**Est: $1,500-$1,800.**

## PAUL MOHR

**433. Bicyclettes Dainty.** 1923.
31 x $46^1/2$ in./78.7 x 118.2 cm
Affiches Edia, Paris
Cond B+/Slight tears at folds.

**432**

Ref: PAI-XIX, 34
Depicting your bicycle as capable of circus stunts was one way of elevating it above merely, well, pedestrian riding. Fancifully costumed rider figures were another. This Cappielloesque design uses both.
**Est: $1,400-$1,700.**

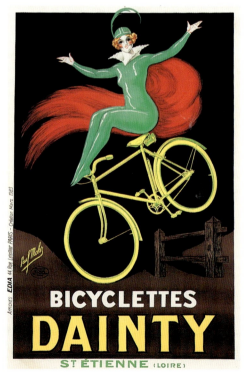

**433**

## ERNEST MONTAUT (1879–1936)

**434. Hurtu.**
$21^1/2$ x 16 in./54.5 x 40.8 cm
L. Marcel Fortin, Paris
Cond A.

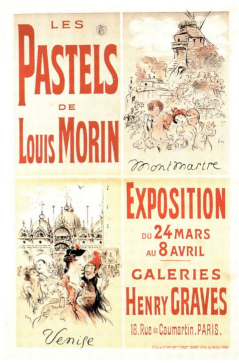

**434**

**436**

ÉVEIL DU MATIN   ÉCLAT DU JOUR   RÊVERIE DU SOIR   REPOS DE LA NUIT

**437**

## LOUIS MORIN (1855-1938)

**436. Les Pastels de Louis Morin.** 1898.
25³/₈ x 37 in./64.5 x 94 cm
Imp. Minot, Paris
Cond B/Slight tears and stains at folds and edges.
After trying his hand in architecture, sculpture and draftsmanship, Morin settled into a career as an illustrator and graphic artist, publishing sketches in *La Caricature* and *Le Chat Noir*, as well as writing and illustrating books of his own design. In addition to contributing to *Figaro illustrée, Paris illustré* and *Revue illustée*, he founded his own publication, *Revue des Quat' Saisons*. Also a performer and scenic designer for the *Chat Noir* cabaret, it can be said that Morin was a renowned artist in all his areas of accomplishment. And for an exhibition of his pastels at the Henry Graves galleries, Morin blows his own horn with fluffy aplomb, showing the distance between Montmartre and Venice is little more than geographic. *Rare!*
**Est: $1,500-$1,800.**

## ALPHONSE MUCHA (1860-1939)

**437. The Times of the Day.** 1899.
Each: 7¹/₄ x 23³/₈ in./18.5 x 59.3 cm
Imp. F. Champenois, Paris
Cond A. Framed.
Ref (All Var): Rennert/Weill, 62, Var. 1; Lendl/Paris, 71;
  Wine Spectator, 77; PAI-XXXIV, 481
"A quartet of barefoot young ladies represents the different times of the day. The borders are decorated in identical patterns, but the amber hues of the lines are changed slightly from panel to panel, and the criscross areas at the top have different floral panels. Each girl appears in an outdoor setting, with slender trees or tall flowers emphasizing her slim figure. . . . The borders are worked out in such an exquisite pattern that each picture appears to be mounted in an elaborate frame of its own, or else seen through a decorated window. Quite possibly Mucha's whole concept for the series was that of gothic stained-glass windows" (Rennert/Weill, p. 232). In this rare, smaller format, the names of the different times of day, which appeared in the larger size in the white margin below, are now centered in a special ornament filled box that has been added underneath each picture.
**Est: $14,000-$17,000.** (4)

A master of depicting automotive and aeronautic events, Montaut shows us his humorous side in this smaller, in-store display for Hurtu automobiles and bicycles. Both vehicles in the design are made by the Hurtu firm, which like many other companies began by manufacturing bikes and then added automobiles. Not that the transportation graphics are given short shrift, but it's the trio of characters that populate Montaut's creation that sets it apart: the buffoonish chauffeur who can't believe he's been nabbed for his unspecified infraction, the exalted officer who was certain he'd get his man atop a Hurtu and the bemused female passenger who's wise to the fact that boys will be boys. There's also a sly implication that had this gendarme not been atop a Hurtu, this motoring rapscallion may very well have escaped the clutches of justice. A delightful vehicular promotion.
**Est: $1,200-$1,500.**

## CARL MOOS (1878-1959)

**435. Zermatt.**
24¹/₄ x 39¹/₄ in./64.2 x 99.8 cm
Orell Fussli, Zürich
Cond A-/Slight tears at edges.
Breathtaking, isn't it? Sometimes natural grandeur—be it actual or artistically rendered—speaks volumes without a single descriptive. And Moos' awe-inspiring view of the Matterhorn as it dwarfs the Swiss village in the Valais canton is one such circumstance. Carl Moos was the son of Swiss painter, Franz Moos. Carl was trained and raised in Munich; he had a successful span of seven years of poster design there before returning for good to his more peaceful fatherland at the start of World War I.
**Est: $1,400-$1,700.**

438

439

440

## ALPHONSE MUCHA (continued)

### 438. Sarah Bernhardt/American Tour. 1896.
21 1/8 x 77 3/4 in./74 x 197.5 cm
Strobridge Lith. Co., Cincinnati
Cond A. Framed.
Ref: Rennert/Weill, 3, Var. 2; Lendl/Paris, 13;
    Masters 1900, p. 24 (var); PAI-XXXIV, 472
Sarah Bernhardt made one of her periodical tours of
the United States from January through June of 1896.
In the process, not only did she introduce American
audiences to her luminescent acting style, but also to
her personal posterist, Alphonse Mucha. She had the
"Gismonda" design (see PAI-XXX, 142) recreated at
Strobridge and used it throughout her American tour.
**Est: $8,000-$10,000.**

### 439. Medée. 1898.
29 3/4 x 81 in./75.6 x 205.7 cm
Imp. F. Champenois, Paris
Cond B/Unobtrusive tears at seam and edges.
Ref: Rennert/Weill, 53; Lendl/Paris, 7; DFP-II, 645;
    Mucha/Art Nouveau, 11; PAI-XXXII, 426
In this 2-sheet poster, "Mucha's exquisite design used
Medea's arm and the dagger as a giant exclamation
point, emphasized by the look of stark horror in her
face as she extracts gothic vengeance. It is one of his

most powerful posters and an unusual departure from
his normal choice of tranquil, sunny scenes" (Lendl/
Paris, p. 20).
**Est: $10,000-$12,000.**

### 440. Lorenzaccio. 1896.
14 1/4 x 40 1/4 in./36.2 x 102.2 cm
Imp. F. Champenois, Paris
Cond B-/Restored tears.
Ref: Rennert/Weill, 20; Lendl/Paris, 4; DFP-II, 626;
    Maitres, 144; Mucha/Art Nouveau, 7;
    PAI-XXXIV, 484
"The character of Lorenzaccio, in the play by Alfred
de Musset, is based on Lorenzo the Magnificent (1449-
1492), the most powerful of the Medicis, who ruled
the city state of Florence. In the play, Lorenzaccio
struggles desperately to save Florence, which had
grown rich during his reign, from the grip of a power-
hungry conqueror. Mucha represents this tyranny by a
dragon menacing the city coat of arms and portrays
Lorenzaccio pondering the course of his action. Sarah
Bernhardt adapted the play, first written in 1863, for
herself, and the new version, for which this poster was
produced, opened December 3, 1896. Never afraid to

tackle a male role, Bernhardt made Lorenzaccio into
one of the classic roles of her repertoire" (Lendl/Paris,
p. 18). *This is the smaller format.*
**Est: $3,000-$4,000.**

### 441. Vieillemard/Autumn. 1895.
15 x 20 in./38 x 51 cm
Vieillemard, Paris
Cond A/On board. Framed.
One of Mucha's early projects, commissioned by the
Vieillemard printing firm prior to the success of his
other seasonal personifications. And this is an Autumn
of a different stripe, far more substantial than forth-
coming incarnations. Though far more clad than any
of the following Falls, this particular courtesan exudes
a confident sensuality verging on the haughty. As she
sits near an overgrown fountain, directly making eye-
contact with the viewer in her overripe surroundings,
you get the distinct feeling that you're not in the presence of some virginal waif, but rather a woman of substance, one that time has aged to perfection, graphically
speaking that is. *Rare!*
**Est: $5,000-$6,000.**

**441**

**442**

**442. Bières de la Meuse.** 1897.
$39^5/_8$ x 59 in./100.6 x 149.8 cm
Imp. F. Champenois, Paris.
Cond A–/Unobtrusive folds; slight stains at edges. Framed.
Ref: Rennert/Weill, 27; Lendl/Paris, 37; Mucha/Art Nouveau, 23;
    Timeless Images, 36; Maitres, 182; DFP-II, 633; PAI-XXXII, 431
"The jovial beer drinker has her long flowing tresses adorned with some appropriate beer ingredients, including barley stalks and green hops, and field poppy flowers indigenous to northeastern France. This is another one of Mucha's characteristic designs featuring a beauty, semi-circular motifs, and artfully meandering hair" (Rennert/Weill, p. 126).
**Est: $15,000-$20,000.**

**443. Société Populaire des Beaux-Arts.** 1897.
$17^3/4$ x $24^1/4$ in./45 x 61.6 cm
Imp. F. Champenois, Paris
Cond A/Mounted on board. Framed.
Ref: Rennert/Weill, 23; Lendl/Paris, 38; DFP-II, 641; PAI-XXXIII, 459
"This society was founded by a Paris lawyer, Edmond Benoit-Levy, in 1894, with the purpose of popularizing art by holding *laterna magica* shows—what we would call today a slide presentation. . . . One of Mucha's traits was to personify ideas in supernatural beings who interacted with ordinary people. Here. . . the lovely female with the flamboyant crown of hair, leaning on a projection machine, symbolized art instruction by means of slides, while the young man in the foreground is a. . . student" (Rennert/Weill, p.116). Mucha uses an abundant amount of gold ink in the hair and elaborately-wrought frame.
**Est: $7,000-$9,000.**

**443**

444

445

446

## ALPHONSE MUCHA (continued)

**444. The Seasons/Winter.** 1896.
20³/4 x 39³/4 in./52.5 x 101 cm
Imp. F. Champenois, Paris (not shown)
Cond B+/Slight creasing at tears. Framed.
Ref: Rennert/Weill, 18; Lendl/Paris, 62 (var); Mucha/Art Nouveau, 44d; PAI-XXXIII, 462 (var)
"The idea of personifying the four seasons was nothing new—the printer Champenois had done it before with other artists—but Mucha breathed so much more life into it that this became one of the best-selling sets of decorative panels, and he was asked to repeat this theme at least twice more, in 1897 (*see* PAI-XXXIV, 416) and 1900 (*see* PAI-XIX, 445), and he also did another panel with only three of the seasons (*see* PAI-XXIX, 544) . . . . Winter, her brown hair barely visible as she is huddled in a long green cloak, snuggles by a snow-covered tree trying to warm a shivering bird with her breath" (Rennert/Weill, p. 90). This particular version appears without the French word for winter, *hiver*, at the poster's bottom area.
**Est: $10,000-$12,000.**

447

448

**445. Lefèvre-Utile/Sarah Bernhardt.** 1903.
19²/₃ x 27¹/₈ in./50.2 x 68.8 cm
Imp. F. Champemois, Paris
Cond A–/Slight creasing. Framed.
Ref: Rennert/Weill, 86; Lendl/Paris, 19; PAI-XXXIV, 476
"A sensitive portrait of Sarah Bernhardt in a wistful pose from one of her major stage successes, *La Princesse Lointaine*, is used here to promote Lefèvre-Utile's biscuits, with Sarah's own hand-written testimonial: "I haven't found anything better than a little LU—oh, yes, two little LU" (Lendl/Paris, p. 51). One of the earliest examples of a celebrity endorsement, proving that Sarah was not only a great actress, but a sharp business woman as well. *For another of her promotions, see Chéret's La Diaphane (No. 235).*
**Est: $14,000-$17,000.**

**446. Zdenka Cerny.** 1913.
43¹/₄ x 41⁷/₈ in./109.8 x 106.3 cm
V. Neubert, Smichov-Prague
Cond A. Framed.
Ref (All Var but PAI): Rennert/Weill, 102;
    Lendl/Paris, 88; Mucha/Art Nouveau, 39;
    Gold, 177; PAI-XXXV, 422
This poster was prepared for Ms. Cerny's European tour planned for the fall of 1914; when war broke out that spring, the tour was canceled, and the poster was not used. Cerny was the daughter of a Czech-American music teacher who befriended Mucha in Chicago in 1906. "Mucha worked from a photograph of Zdenka with a cello, but idealized her face by investing it with a spiritual quality, her love of music. He created a unique poster-portrait by adjusting the slant of her head, softening her expression, lightening the hair, lift-

ing the hand turning the sheet music, and elongating the body. Two circles, one with lilies symbolizing Zdenka's youthful innocence, the other with laurels of her past triumphs, complete the design suffused with warm light" (Mucha/Art Nouveau, p. 180). This is the image portion of the poster; normally the lower text-sheet accompanies its counterpart and proclaims the young musician to be "The Greatest Bohemian Violin-cellist" (*see* PAI-XXX, 144). *Hand-signed by Ms. Cerny.*
**Est: $3,000-$4,000.**

**447. Job.** 1898.
40¹/₄ x 59 in./102 x 150 cm
Imp. F. Champenois, Paris
Cond A–/Slight tape stains in bottom margin.
Ref: Rennert/Weill, 51; Lendl/Paris, 49; DFP-II, 634;
    Modern Poster, 9; Masters 1900, p. 18;
    Wine Spectator, 74; Gold, 2; PAI-XXXIV, 474
"In both of Mucha's posters for Job cigarette papers—this is the second; the first was done in 1896—he gives us women sensually involved in the act of smoking. Here, the figure is full-length, her abandoned hair an echo of the pale fabric volumes of her gown. As she watches the lazy waft of smoke, even her toes curl deliciously in pleasure. The artist's meticulous craftsmanship can be seen in such details as the gown's clasp (of Mucha's own design), and in the way he worked the product name into the background pattern" (Gold, p. 2). Mucha prepared still another preliminary design for the cigarette company, which apparently was never printed. We assume the two originals had such popular appeal that a third version was simply deemed unnecessary.
**Est: $7,000-$9,000.**

**448. Exposition de St. Louis.** 1903.
29¹/₂ x 40 in./75 x 101.6 cm
Imp. F. Champenois, Paris
Cond A. Framed.
Ref: Rennert/Weill, 87 Var. 1; Lendl/Paris, 43 (var);
    Mucha/Art Nouveau, 30; DFP-II, 650 (var);
    PAI-XXIX, 545
"The Mucha maiden holding hands with the Indian chief advertises the 1904 World's Fair at St. Louis, Missouri, and invites the French traveler to take a journey involving six days by steamer and one day by train. . . . The theme of the fair was science and industry, as shown in the circle at right. The star in it represents the rather unusual first day of the Fair, which demonstrated the sensitivity and scientific value of a rather new discovery of the time, the photocell. A photocell at the bottom of a long tube was aimed at a spot in the heavens where a bright star—Arcturus—would appear at the exact opening hour of the Fair. As the star's light reached the photocell at the precise moment, it activated a switch which lit all the lights in the fair grounds" (Rennert/Weill, p. 310). Note the interesting marketing approach for this World's Fair: Taking a typically American tack, comparative importance to prior fairs in Philadelphia, Paris and Chicago is made through that of size, in this particular case with real estate. This fair has the largest amount of real estate, in fact, twice the size of the 1893 Chicago show.
**Est: $12,000-$15,000.**

**449**

**450**

**451**

## MUCHA (continued)

**449. Flirt.** 1899.
$11^5/8$ x $24^3/4$ in./29.7 x 62.8 cm
Imp. F. Champenois, Paris
Cond A–/Slight stains at edges.
Ref: Rennert/Weill, 72; Lendl/Paris, 18 (var);
    L'Art du Biscuit, p. 9; Gold, 63; PAI-XXX, 44
This is the original printing of a point-of-purchase display in 1899; after the 1900 World's Fair in Paris, the poster was reprinted with an added line of text referring to a prize won by the product on that occasion. "To bring home the name of the product, Mucha created a discreet flirtation which embodies the 19th-century ideal of a romantic encounter: the girl demure and coy, the gentleman persuasive, the setting a fragrant garden. But he didn't forget the sponsor: The wrought-iron gate carries the name, and the girl's dress features a print pattern of the letters L-U, a subtle decorative reminder" (Gold, p. 46).
**Est: $4,000-$5,000.**

**450. The Flowers/Carnation.** 1900.
$17^1/2$ x $41^1/4$ in./44.5 x 104.6 cm
Imp. F. Champenois, Paris (not shown)
Cond A.
Ref: Rennert/Weill, 49b; Lendl/Paris, 69c;
    Mucha/Art Nouveau, 50c; PAI-XVI, 371
"The Flowers" set of decorative panels (*see* PAI-XXXI, 552) consisted of four stunning women intended to embody the Rose (*see* following lot), the Iris, the Lily and, shown here, the Carnation. The Carnation is the only brunette represented in a field of blondes, seen casting a coy glance over her shoulder. The pose was so enticing that she, alone amongst these four, was later used to advertise a commercial product (*see* R/W, 61) with only slight changes to detail.
**Est: $8,000-$10,000.**

**451. The Flowers/Rose.** 1900.
$17^1/2$ x 41 in./44.5 x 104.2 cm
Imp. F. Champenois, Paris (not shown)
Cond A.

Ref: Rennert/Weill, 49d; Lendl/Paris, 69a;
    Mucha/Art Nouveau, 50b; PAI-XXXIII, 465
One flower rises above the rest when the air is filled with romance: the rose. And Mucha's personification of that fleshy blossom stands on its own, "proud and closed in her strictly formal pose" (Mucha/Art Nouveau, p. 196). But lest we judge this constrained beauty too harshly, let's not forget that the rose, of all the avidly sought blooms, is the only one equipped with thorns to protect her from the uninvited. Mucha's alluring, yet restrained vision calls to the fore artistically what is often overlooked in casual observations of nature.
**Est: $8,000-$10,000.**

**452**

**452. Byzantine Heads.** 1897.
Each: $11^3/8$ x $13^3/4$ in./29 x 35 cm
Imp. F. Champenois, Paris (not shown)
Cond A. Framed.
Ref (All Var but First): Rennert/Weill, 40, Var 1.;
    Lendl/Paris, 67; Mucha/Paris, 37-38;
    Mucha/Art Nouveau, 48; PAI-XXXI, 549
"The mastery evident in creating two archetypes of the female form against a decorative background confirms Mucha's artistic maturity. Both women, portrayed in profile, have their heads decorated with beautiful jewelry, the richness and oriental nature of which suggested the name *Byzantine Heads* for the series. The

**453**

**454**

**455**

subtle differences in details between the paintings are worth noticing. For the first time there appeared the perfect form of Mucha's often-used motif, a circle framing each head interrupted by a strand of hair. With this device, it is as if Mucha's unreachable beauties have broken the magic border between themselves and their admirers and suggest the possibility that they might, perhaps, meet." (Mucha/Art Nouveau, p. 192).
**Est: $15,000-$18,000. (2)**

**453. Friendship.** 1904.
11⁵/₈ x 17⁵/₈ in./29.5 x 44.7
Cond A. Framed.
Ref: Rennert/Weill, 89; PAI-XXXII, 447 (var)
"One of the tangible proofs of Mucha's warm reception in the United States is the glowing tribute paid him by the *New York Daily News* on Sunday, April 3, 1904. The front page of the paper's Art Supplement contained a full-color reproduction titled, 'Friendship', and another page inside was devoted to articles about him and more reproductions of his work, as well as a caricature of Mucha by Berger. One of the homage paying appreciations was written by a former student who had met him in Paris, J. Hayden-Clarenden, who may not have been too sure of Mucha's origins—he erroneously identifies him as a 'Roumanian-French-man'—but was obviously sincere about his art: 'His beautiful study of Friendship . . . is a charming allegor-

ical sketch of America and France, and interprets in a truly poetic spirit the bond of sympathy between the old country and the new, the elder woman and the younger, as he had depicted them.' . . . This unusual campaign may be responsible for making the image so popular that it was issued separately as a lithograph for sale. Since there is no announcement to this effect in the paper on the day of publication, it must be assumed that a separate printing was undertaken later, in response to popular demand" (Rennert/Weill, p. 314).
**Est: $2,500-$3,000.**

**454. Lefèvre-Utile/Gaufrettes Vanille.** ca. 1896.
9 x 9 in./23 x 23 cm
Imp. F. Champenois, Paris
Cond A/P. Framed.
Ref (Both Var): Art et Biscuits, 66; Art du Biscuit, p. 86; PAI-XIV, 369
This design, using the face of a young woman from one of his Lefevre-Utile posters (see PAI-XXXI, 546) was also called into play as a box-top for tins of vanilla wafers, and, as seen here, in a rare larger format embellished with metallic gold ink. The added ornamental embellishments are pure Mucha. "One of Mucha's most personable young ladies, her hair cascading irrepressibly in fine style. . . Note the initials LU in that part of the golden ornamental border that protrudes

into the picture at right" (Rennert/Weill, p. 113).
**Est: $1,400-$1,700.**

**455. Portrait of a Lady in a Hat.** 1904.
28⁵/₈ x 45¹/₄ in./72 x 115 cm
*Hand-signed pastel painting.* Framed.
Ref: Mucha/Master, p. 195
Though the existence of this particular pastel is documented, no specific information is given other than when it was painted. But the year itself is significant, seeing as 1904 marks Mucha's departure from Paris for New York. Did he finish the portrait for a client before leaving for the United States? Or was it a commission he received upon arrival in America? It seems like a rather lightweight test of his talents seeing as one of his primary reasons for coming to the States was to raise large amounts of cash to further the scope of his artistic endeavors, a task he achieved by doing oil portraits of society ladies and not by doing such quick pastels. Could this be a working model to get the design down before committing the finished portrait? Sadly, at the present time, these questions remain unanswered. That, however, doesn't take a shred of soft beauty away from our mysterious poser, whose postimpressionistic presence and verdant enclosure are simply breathtaking.
**Est: $30,000-$40,000.**

456

457

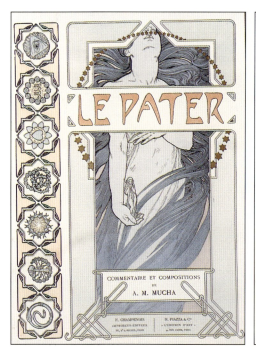

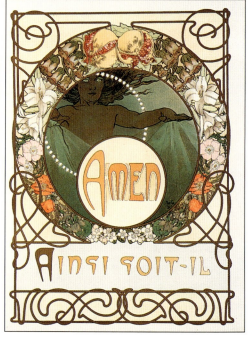

458

## MUCHA (continued)

**456. Paris 1900.** 1899.
$26^7/_8$ x $38^5/_8$ in./68.2 x 98 cm
Kunstanstalt G. Czeiger, Wien
Cond A–/Slight stains and creases, largely at edges.
Framed.
Ref: Rennet/Weill, 66; Lendl/Paris, 41; DFP-II, 649; PAI-XXXIII, 466

"Mucha's design shows a handsome youth lifting a veil off the standing lady—'Paris revealing Austria to the world,' according to contemporary publicity. The heraldic symbol of Austria-Hungary, a two-headed eagle, may be seen behind the girl's head on both sides" (Rennert/Weill, p. 248).
**Est: $6,000-$7,000.**

**457. C. S./Y.W.C.A.** 1922.
$7^1/_2$ x $11^3/_4$ in./19 x 29.8 cm
V. Neubert a Synové, Smíchov
Cond A. Framed.
Ref: Rennert/Weill 107, Var. 1; Lendl/Paris, 90;
PAI-XXXIII, 469
"This poster was used for fund raising for the Czechoslovak YWCA. . . . The movement came to Czechoslovakia after Alice Masaryk, the daughter of the first Czech president, Thomas Masaryk, became acquainted with

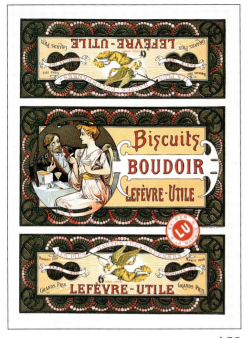

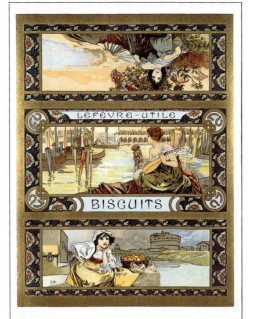

**459**

**460**

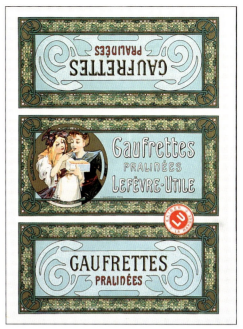

**461**

**462**

**463**

Mucha's typical attention to detail. And each of the designs is assigned a specific background color; in the case of this saucy affair, apricot is the color of choice. **Est: $1,000-$1,200.**

**460. Lefèvre-Utile/Mélange Italien.** 1901.
$8^1/_2$ x $11^1/_8$ in./21.6 x 28.2 cm
Cond A/P.
Ref: Art du Biscuit, p. 94; PAI-XIII, 339
Instead of settling on a central image to convey the romance of the cookies contained within, this design for "Mélange Italien" biscuits has three sides of the box covered with idealized women against the backdrops of Naples, Venice and Florence, each framed, as one might expect from the designer, in a highly decorative border. **Est: $1,400-$1,700.**

**461. Lefèvre-Utile/Gaufrettes Pralinées.**
$8^3/_4$ x $12^1/_4$ in./22.2 x 31 cm
Cond A/P. Framed.
Ref: PAI-V, 248 (var)
This biscuit exchange between two porcelain-skinned young ladies may well have been the first work by Mucha for Lefèvre-Utile. **Est: $1,000-$1,200.**

**462. Lefèvre-Utile/Biscuits Champagne.**
8 x $10^7/_8$ in./20.2 x 27.6 cm
Imp. Moderne, Nantes
Cond A/P. Framed.
Ref: Art du Biscuit, p. 90; PAI-XVI, 370 (var)
Cobalt sets off this soignée rendezvous, slyly demonstrating that dunking need not be exclusively a cookies and milk affair. **Est: $1,000-$1,200.**

## MAURICE NEUMONT (1868-1930)

**463. Funabules/Séverin.** ca. 1895.
$36^1/_4$ x $50^1/_4$ in./92 x 127.6 cm
Imp. Caby & Chardin, Paris
Cond B+/Slight tears at folds.
Though no tightrope walker is seen in this promotion for an entertainment destination that draws its name from that particular skill, it certainly would seem as if the Funabules have all the bases covered, from comedia dell'arte to musical merriment, with a touch of tragedy and barely concealed modesty thrown in for good measure. And Neumont conveys it all with colorful fanfare and a showman's panache. And their featured performer, Séverin, was the stage pseudonym of Armand-Jean de Malafayde, a native Bordeaux and film actor of some note. A lifelong Parisian, Neumont was a painter, lithographer and posterist best-known for his somber, moving political posters during World War I. Towards the end of his life, however, he returned to the form displayed here, as he became president of the Salon des Humoristes. **Est: $1,500-$1,800.**

its work while she stayed at the YWCA Settlement House in Chicago, where she was attending the University of Chicago during 1918 and 1919. . . . (A) Prague branch of the World YWCA was opened in May 1920 and achieved an enrollment of 500 in its first membership drive. . . . Mucha's poster was a part of the organization's efforts to enroll more members and find the funds to build more homes for girls in the major cities in the country" (Rennert/Weill, p. 356). *This is the smaller format.* Hardly larger than a standard sheet of writing paper, it was probably meant for use on bulletin boards and other eye-level display, or perhaps as a handbill. **Est: $4,000-$5,000.**

**458. Le Pater.** 1899.
$11^3/_4$ x $16^1/_8$ in./30.2 x 41 cm
*Hardcover illustrated book in excellent condition.*
Ref: Mucha/Art Nouveau, 72; PAI-XXXII, 580
"At this auspicious time, the turn of a century, Mucha wanted to deliver to future generations his reflections upon human life and man's place in the universe. He wished to present the way that leads man to a gradual ascent to the divine ideal. He determined to fulfill these goals in his own version of the Lord's Prayer" (Mucha/Art Nouveau, p. 233). The book, printed by F. Champenois and published by H. Piazza, to whom Mucha dedicated it, consists of a series of seven drawings. The seven verses of the prayer are each presented with three illustrations by Mucha, plus color title

page. Mucha felt that this was his supreme achievement as an illustrator, and to see this rare portfolio is to know it: The images abound in Byzantine symbolism, executed and decorated in the very best art nouveau style. *One of a total of 500 numbered copies; this is one of 100 copies printed on Japan paper.* **Est: $5,000-$6,000.**

**459. Lefèvre-Utile/Biscuits Boudoir.**
$8^1/_8$ x 11 in./20.7 x 28 cm
Imp. Moderne, Nantes
Cond A/P. Framed.
Ref: Art du Biscuit, pp. 92 & 93; PAI-XVI, 370 (var)
Think fast. When was the last time that you munched on a prepackaged cookie and thought to yourself, "My God, that packaging is absolutely exquisite!" Chances are that unless you're a fan of plastic wrap and elves who live in hollow trees that this situation has never occurred. Thank goodness we have this and the following four souvenirs from a more gentile period, where how the product was presented was equally as important as the product itself. Mucha designed these box tops for Lefèvre-Utile biscuits, each consisting of a central design and two-back-to-back trademarks, all printed on one sheet. In the individual distinguishing pictures, Mucha depicted fashionable social occasions at which biscuits are being consumed, mostly with wine. All of the background patterns, ornamental borders and decorative elements are executed with

**466**

**464**

**465**

## ERIK NITSCHE (1908-1998)

**464. Atoms for Peace: Nine Posters.** 1955–1960.
Each: 35$^1$/$_2$ x 50$^1$/$_4$ in./90 x 127.5 cm
R. Marsens, Lausanne
Cond A/Slight creases at the edges on 2 of the posters.
Ref (All Var): Modern American Poster, 82-84;
    Modern Poster, 209; Images of an Era, 22;
    PAI-XXVIII, 455
As one of the largest defense contractors in the United
States, General Dynamics built the first atom-powered
submarines and many other products of the nuclear
age. The company was understandably anxious to up-
grade its image and emphasize peaceful applications
of its capabilities, which is why it needed to make its
existence known at the first Atomic Energy Conference
in Geneva in 1955. With much of its work secret, an
exhibit of actual hardware would have been out of the
question; fortunately, General Dynamics found Erik
Nitsche to express its achievements and goals in
graphic terms. The result was "Atoms for Peace"—a
poster campaign that became a breakthrough in the
symbolic expression of the corporate image, with a
total of 29 images being created for the series. Born
in Lausanne to a family of American background,
Nitsche studied in his native city and in Munich. In
1934 he moved to the United States, where he became
a designer for major national periodicals including
*Life, Look* and *Vanity Fair,* and worked on film and
theatrical posters. He remained a top master of graphic
arts, versatile and adaptable, belonging to no particular school but always ready to find ingenious solutions
to design problems. In 1996 he was inducted into the
prestigious New York Art Directors' Club Hall of Fame.
*We are honored that he created the poster commem-
orating the PAI-XXIV sale.*
**Est: $2,500-$3,000.** (9)

**465. Exploring the Universe: Seven Posters.**
    1955–1960.
Each: 35$^1$/$_4$ x 50$^1$/$_8$ in./89.6 x 127.4 cm
R. Marsens, Lausanne
Cond A/P.
More Nitschean explorations of the positive side of
research and its inevitable applications, both atomic
and otherwise, to achieve a publicly palatable vision
of a new world order just around the corner.
**Est: $2,000-$2,500.** (7)

## STEFAN NORBLIN (1892-?)

**466. Gdnyia.** ca. 1950.
23$^3$/$_4$ x 33$^3$/$_4$ in./60.4 x 85.8 cm
Cond B/Restored tears at paper edges.
Gdynia, the north Polish port on the Baltic Sea and the
Gulf of Danzig, was originally a small German fishing
village transferred to Poland as part of the reparations
in World War I. It quickly became an important rail
center as well, with industries producing metals,
machinery and food products. Although the harbor
was heavily damaged in World War II, the city suffered
relatively little destruction, and by 1950, with most of
the harbor rebuilt, Gdynia was again an important
commercial port. Norblin's trilingual design makes it
abundantly clear that the "new" Baltic harbor is once
again open for business with this paean to industrial-
ized commerce.
**Est: $1,500-$1,800.**

## GASTON NOURY (1866-?)

**467. Le Père Didier/Affiches et Bouquins.**
15$^3$/$_4$ x 23$^5$/$_8$ in./40 x 60 cm
Imp. Bougerie, St. Denis
Cond B+/Slight tears and stains at folds.
Ref: Reims, 906
A quayside encounter between a young lithographic
aficionado and an estimable *bouquiniste.* Though
executed with an air and palette of established
respectability by Noury, it would appear as if both the
potential buyer and the seller have an eye for pretty
things. Noury was born and grew up in Elbeuf where
his grandfather was founder and director of the local
museum. Although his primary interests were painting
and drawing nature subjects, he created several
evocative posters of the era. Maindron (1896) indicates that the "young Noury" is one of the best illustrators of the period.
**Est: $800-$1,000.**

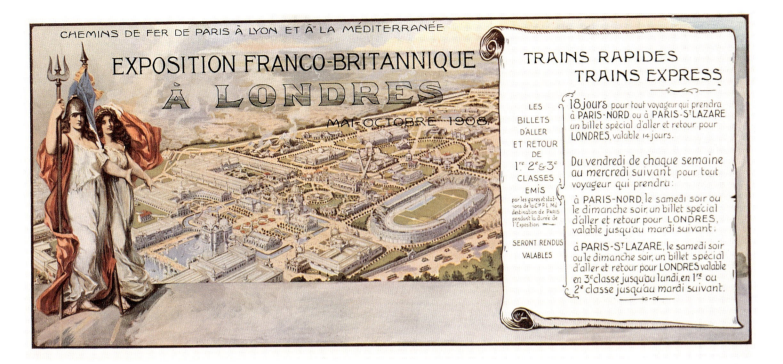

**469**

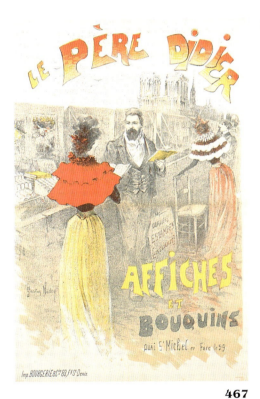

**467**

**468**

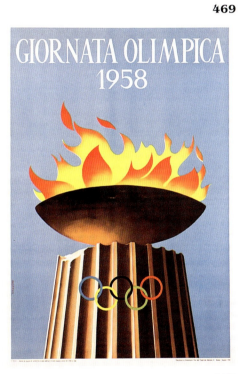

**470**

## EUGENE OGE (1869-1936)

**468. Dentifrices du Docteur Péterson.** ca. 1897.
$38^3/_4$ x $55^3/_8$ in./98.4 x 140.6 cm
Imp. Charles Verneau, Paris
Cond B/Tears and stains at folds and edses.
Ref: Ogé, 148; Health Posters, 228
This lad seems a bit young to have a medical degree—much less to stand as an expert witness before some form of inquiry—but you can't argue with the intensity of his passion towards the Doctor Peterson brand of dental products. Advertised as the "best and least expensive" toothpaste on the market, this young practitioner extols the virtues of the entire Peterson line—mouthwash, brushing powder and paste. Ogé's principal claim to fame was his long tenure as house artist for the printer Charles Verneau around the turn of the century; he also, however, produced numerous drawings that were well-received in fine-art circles. A retrospective exhibition of all his posters drew a large audience at the Bibliothèque Forney in Paris during the summer of 1998.
Est: $1,500-$1,800.

## OLYMPIC POSTERS

**469. Exposition Franco-Britannique.** 1908.
Artist: **Anonymous**
$13^3/_4$ x $6^1/_4$ in./35 x 16 cm
Cond A. Framed.
Ref: PAI-XXXIV, 491 (var)
This handbill for a Franco-British track and field warm-up exhibition prior to the 1908 London Olympics not only features the Rubanesque embodiments of the two nations competitive spirits, but also the Great Stadium at Shepherd's Bush, visible at right, complete with its infield swimming pool and cinder track. While the poster version simply announced the Exposition (*see* PAI-XXXIV, 491), this handbill promotes the train packages from Paris to London. This 1908 event ran for over three months—July 13th through October 29th. The special round-trip packages are for a two week stay. The Olympics were a much more leisurable event in 1908.
Est: $1,200-$1,500.

**470. Giornata Olimpica.** 1958.
Artist: **Gregori**
$37^3/_8$ x $39^1/_4$ in./69.5 x 99.6 cm
Vecchioni & Guadagno, Roma
Cond A.
The fiery cauldron of Olympic flame blazes brightly in this Gregori design for the 1958 "Olympic Days," preliminaries to the Rome Olympics of 1960. Gregori also designed a poster for the following year's event (*see* PAI-XXXI, 182), showing the passing of the Olympic torch from the ancients down to our time. *Rare!*
Est: $1,400-$1,700.

  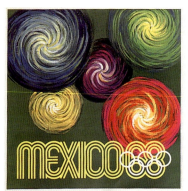 

**473**

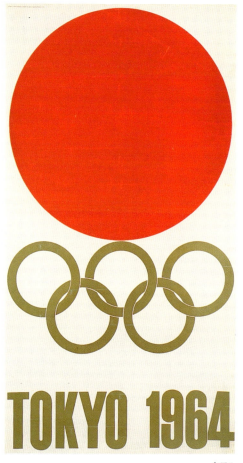

**471**

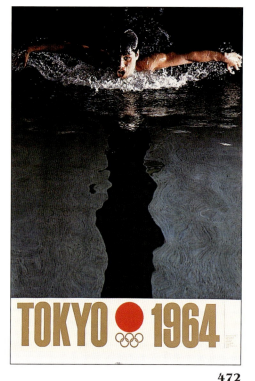

**472**

between the frothing butterfly stroke and glassine waters dazzles the eye with hypnotic simplicity.
**Est: $1,000-$1,200.**

**473. Mexico 1968: Four Posters.**
Artists: **Pedro Ramirez Vasquez, Eduardo Terrazas, Lance Wyman & Villazón**
Each: 35 x 35¼ in./89 x 89.5 cm
Impresos Automaticos de Mexico
Cond A.
Ref: Olympics, p. 91; PAI-XIV, 507 (var)
Although all the official posters for the XIXth Olympiad were the combined teamwork of three artists—Mexicans Vasquez and Terrazas collaborating with Wyman from the U.S.—one of these four designs is signed by an artist named "Villazón". All told, there were seventeen approved designs, most of them printed in more than one color scheme. Guided by the motto "Information, esthetics, functionalism," the trio of official artists incorporated native Mexican motifs into their designs, particularly the concentric patterning found in the art of the Cuichol Indians.
**Est: $2,000-$2,500.** (4)

**MANUEL ORAZI (1860-1934)**

**474. Thais.** 1894.
15⅛ x 41⅝ in./38.6 x 108 cm
Imp. Lemercier, Paris
Cond A.
Ref: Maindron, p. 97; French Opera, 34;
      Theaterplakat, 46; PAI-XXIX, 560
The mood of the poster perfectly matches that of the Massenet opera for which it was created. An excellent account of it is given by Broido. She also quotes Maindron's comment that this poster resembles "a papyrus, torn, eaten away by the centuries. Orazi has created a poster that is the first to have such a curious form." Exotic themes were a speciality of Orazi, an accomplished painter, illustrator and designer.
**Est: $1,400-$1,700.**

**474**

## OLYMPIC POSTERS (continued)

**471. Tokyo 1964 Olympics.**
Artist: **Yusaku Kamekura (1915-1997)**
21⅝ x 40½ in./55 x 103 cm
Toppan Printing Co.
Cond B/Slight stains and creases.
Ref: Olympics, p. 79; Takashimaya, 304; PAI-XIV, 506
Up until 1960, the custom was to have one official design for each Olympiad, plus one or at most two alternates for each separate event (like the Winter Games). For the 1964 Tokyo Olympics, Kamekura and his team prepared four posters of equal standing. This official poster features the rising sun over the interlocking rings, the image which, coincidentally, became the symbol of the 1964 games.
**Est: $800-$1,000.**

**472. Tokyo 1964 Olympics.**
Artist: **Yusaku Kamekura (1915-1997)**
28¾ x 40⅞ in./73 x 103.8 cm
Dai Nippon Printing Co., Japan
Cond A–/Slight tears, largely at edges.
Ref: Olympics, p. 81; Kamekura, 60;
      Plakatkunst, p. 161; PAI-XXXI, 189
Another of the official 1964 Olympic posters, focusing our attention on grace, strength and determination. These unifying factors set to the page by Kamekura define Olympic resolve with moments of motion frozen by the camera for eternity—grace of the photo direction of Jo Murakoshi and the skill of photographer Osamu Hayasaki. And in this piece, the contrast

**475. Theodora.** 1884.
34½ x 47¾ in./87.6 x 121.2 cm
Imp. Delanchy, Ancourt, Paris
Cond B+/Restored margins.
Ref: DFP-II, 672; Reims, 921; Abdy, p. 131;
      PAI-XXXIII, 482
Although mostly known as a master of subtle color shadings, Orazi could also surprise us with an entirely atypical design like this one for a play whose theme required a classicist approach. The description of this poster in the 1896 Reims catalogue indicates that the "byzantine mosaic decor" is by Orazi and the design is by Auguste François Gorguet (1862-1927). Maindron

476

477

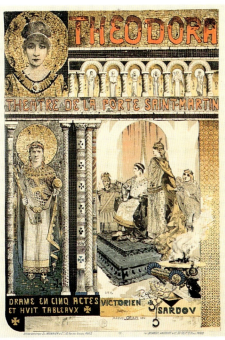

475

478

### 476. Parfums des Femmes de France.
$36^1/_4$ x $51^1/_4$ in./92 x 130 cm
Imp. Paul Dupont, Parsi
Cond A–/Slight tears at top edge.
Pal was wont to embody anything in the form of a woman; here, he legitimately was promoting a product that made it all but unavoidable. But the one area in which Pal excels, even surpasses those considered to be the greatest posterists of all time, is the sheer accessibility of his women, who in their admittedly idealized form still appear breathtakingly attainable. At least that's what the gifted Pal wanted us to believe. *For another treatment for the same perfume producers, see PAI-XX, 355. Rare!*
**Est: $3,000-$3,500.**

### 477. Folies-Bergère/La Loïe Fuller. ca. 1895.
$32^3/_8$ x $48^3/_8$ in./82 x 122.6 cm
Imp. Paul Dupont, Paris
Cond B–/Restored tears at folds and edges.
Ref: Wagner, 81; Reims, 944; Abdy, p. 59;
    Spectacle, 1145; Loie Fuller, 68; PAI-XII, 356
Colors were her specialty, and colors are what Pal gives us—stupendous, gorgeous colors that barely conceal Fuller's figure.
**Est: $2,000-$2,500.**

### 478. Les Fêtards.
$23^5/_8$ x $31^1/_2$ in./60 x 80 cm
Imp. E. Delanchy, Paris
Cond A.
Ref (All Var but Opera): French Opera, 44;
    Spectacle, 673; Gold, 160; PAI-XXX, 148
"The Palais Royal was an early version of a shopping mall—an arcade with a number of stores, a bistro or two, and even a theater, which on this occasion was presenting a light musical revue. Pal comes through, as usual, with a delectable dancing damsel, obviously one of the 'roisterers' of the title" (Gold, p. 112). This is the second edition of this design; the "d'après" designation denotes it as a printing based on Pal's initial design.
**Est: $1,000-$1,200.**

declared this important work "une affiche parfaite" (1886, p. 118), and Sagot, in his 1891 catalogue, said it exhibits a "Très belle composition" (no. 1256). It may well be the first poster ever done for Sarah Bernhardt.
**Est: $1,700-$2,000.**

## PAL (JEAN DE PALÉOLOGUE, 1860-1942)

A member of a Rumanian dynasty stretching back to Byzantine rulers, Pal was born in Bucharest, but started his artistic career in London as a magazine illustrator. In 1893, he moved to Paris, at first drawing illustrations. There then followed five years of intense activity in posters in which he produced some of the most sensuous designs ever used in advertising up to that time. His loving tributes to the female figure have become prized finds for the eclectic collector. Abandoning Paris as abruptly as he had London, Pal made his final move to the United States in 1900. There, he again worked for publications, and eventually wound up working for the auto, film and animation industries. He died in Miami in 1942. All posters presented here are from his Paris period, 1893-1900.

479

480

## PAL (continued)

**479. Olympia/La Fée des Poupées.** 1894.
31¹/₄ x 47⁷/₈ in./79.4 x 121.6 cm
Imp. Paul Dupont, Paris
Cond B+/Slight tears at folds.
Ref: Spectacle, 1280; Reims, 939; PAI-XXVI, 472
The Olympia is still one of the most popular variety showcases in Paris. For the October 16, 1894 opening of a ballet titled "The Fairy of the Dolls" playing at the venue, Pal created one of his strongest designs. The fairy's powers clearly include an ability to make the inanimate toys—a drumming soldier, Punchinello and a little princess—come to life!
**Est: $2,500-$3,000.**

**480. Whitworth Cycles.** ca. 1894.
56 x 83³/₈ in./142 x 211.8 cm
Imp. Paul Dupont, Paris
Cond B+/Slight tears at folds.
Ref: Maindron, p. 120; Reims, 958; V & A, 242; PAI-XXXII, 467
Pal executed a minimum of three designs for Whitworth Cycles, all of them featuring a gentleman cyclist showing his bike off to a group of six women either peering down from atop a wall (*see* PAI-XXV, 446), completely descended from their perch and showing more attention to the bike than its rider (*see* PAI-XXX, 289) or, in what would seem like the midway point in this poster narrative, with the women divided equally between wall and ground. In this two-sheet design, three women are still partially obscured behind the wall, while the others have convened around the rider and his Whitworth. Exactly what they are more enraptured with, bike or roguish rider, is left for the viewer to decide.
**Est: $2,000-$2,500.**

**481. A la Place Clichy/Exposition de Blanc.** 1899.
39³/₄ x 54³/₈ in./101 x 138.2 cm
Imp. Caby & Chardin, Paris
Cond B+/Slight tears at folds and edges.
Ref: Gold, 23; PAI-XXX, 91

481

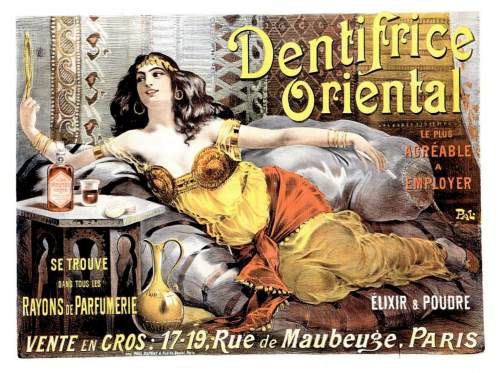

**484**

**483**

**485**

"Pal's portrayal of women were always flattering, nearly worshipful: perfect bodies, perfect faces, classic beauty. But where artists such as Mucha or Privat Livemont idealized women, Pal, with his realistic attention to detail, gave them a decidedly solid, earthly quality: These are women of flesh and blood. It's not clear whether Pal's design shows two salesgirls at the Place Clichy White sale packing up merchandise or a satisfied customer showing off her purchases at home, but in either case the women and the ruffed bed linens are equally appealing" (Gold, p. 17).
**Est: $1,700-$2,000.**

**482. Dentifrice Oriental.** ca. 1898.
57⁷/₈ x 42¹/₈ in./147 x 107 cm
Imp. Paul Dupont, Paris
Cond B/Unobtrusive tears, largely at folds and edges.
Ref: Grain de Beauté, 39; PAI-IX, 418
Since the toothpaste that he was trying to sell claimed to be "Oriental," Pal went to opulent excess to depict a sensuous, sultry charmer in her boudoir, admiring

her pearly smile in a mirror. One might speculate that this is what would've happened had Cecil B. DeMille been asked to direct a toothpaste commercial.
**Est: $3,000-$4,000.**

**483. Folies-Bergère/Tous les Soirs.**
57³/₈ x 44¹/₂ in./145.8 x 113 cm
Imp. Paul Dupont, Paris
Cond A–/Unobtrusive folds.
Ref (Both Var): Gold, 147; PAI-XXX, 151
"In the seven years Pal spent in Paris, the city's best known music-hall availed itself of his services at least a dozen times, recognizing his superior talent for showing women performers at their best. In this case, however, it's not the showgirls but the patrons who are being used to attract customers. Elegant and apparently out for the evening on their own, these two women assure prospective visitors of the showplace's high repute" (Gold, p. 103). *This is the rare larger format.*
**Est: $6,000-$8,000.**

**484. Olympia/"Mauvais Rêve."** ca. 1895.
30 x 46³/₄ in./76.2 x 118.8 cm
Imp. Paul Dupont, Paris
Cond B/Slight tears and stains at folds.
Ref: Reims, 943; Maindron, p. 102; DFP-II, 689;
PAI-XXXIV, 499
It appears that in the pantomime "Bad Dream," playing at the Olympia, Irma de Montigny played a boy's role, but there is decidedly nothing masculine about her lovely face and engaging smile.
**Est: $1,700-$2,000.**

**485. La République.** 1898.
44⁷/₈ x 63¹/₈ in./114 x 160.3 cm
Imp. Chardin, Paris
Cond A–/Slight tears at folds and edges.
Ref: DFP-II, 694; PAI-XXVIII, 475
The allegorical Marianne with a French tricolored rosette in her hair, holds a laurel branch in one hand and a rolled up copy of the Constitution in the other—representatives all of the lofty aims espoused by this political daily.
**Est: $1,200-$1,500.**

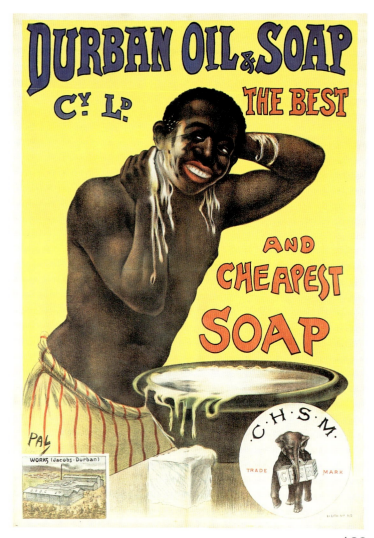

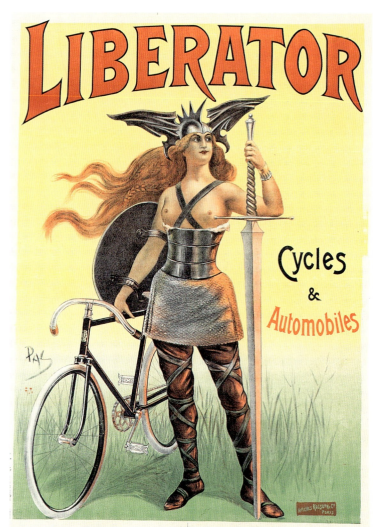

**486**

**487**

## PAL (continued)

**486. Durban Oil & Soap.**
44 x 61$^1$/$_2$ in./111.8 x 156.2 cm
La Lithographie Nouvelle, Asnières
Cond B/Slight tears and stains at folds.
Even with all the atrocious exaggerations we're exposed to on a daily basis, it's an astonishing sight to behold to the contemporary eye to watch a black person washing away their pigment. But, once upon a time, it was the advertising norm, to show just that in order to demonstrate a product's cleansing power. And Pal proves that he's no exception to the rule with his poster for the Durban soap and oil line, complete with an inset of the company factory in Jacobs-Durban. Also note that credit is given to Louis Charbonnier—a posterist of some merit himself—for executing this Pal design on lithographic stone. *Rare!*
**Est: $2,000-$2,500.**

**487. Liberator Cycles & Automobiles.** ca. 1899.
41 x 56$^3$/$_4$ in./104 x 144.2 cm
Affiches Kossuth, Paris
Cond B+/Slight tears at folds.
Ref (All Var but PAI): DFP-II, 696; Bicycle Posters, 48;
    Petite Reine, 33; PAI-XXX, 292
Faced with the concept of "Liberator," other designers might have thought of a male figure (as, in fact, can be seen on the firm's logo), but Pal finds a way to inveigle one of his curvaceous beauties into the scene. A most definitive signs of the popularity of this design is the fact that abundant reprintings were executed by several different printing firms utilizing the talents of various other posterists to do nothing but redraw Pal's original artwork, such as this Charles Tichon variant or another by Émile Clouet (*see* PAI-XXXI, 580). What remains identical in every version is the resolute "Don't mess with me, Mister" look of the sturdy "Soldat Gaulois," standing guard with her awesome armory of sword and shield and Liberator helmet, and, of course, Liberator bicycle. Rarely has the saying "If it ain't broke, don't fix it" been applied with such resolute beauty.
**Est: $1,500-$1,800.**

**488**

**489**

**488. Le Mémorial de Saint-Hélène.** ca. 1893.
36$^7$/$_8$ x 54$^1$/$_8$ in./93.6 x 137.4 cm
Imp. Paul Dupont
Cond B–/Stains at folds.
Ref: Reims, 947
An unusually sedate promotion from Pal, advertising the release of the historical serialized novel , "The Memorial of Saint Helena," featuring a dejected and brooding Napoleon under the watchful eye of a skeptical captor. Not to say that the treatment isn't com-

pletely appropriate, taking into consideration that the lonely island exile became his home after his defeat and surrender to the British at Waterloo. He would spend his remaining years there, quarreling with the British governor, Sir Hudson Lowe, and dictating his memoirs. After long suffering from cancer, he died May 5, 1821. It's interesting to note that a colored engraving was included with every installment of the story.
**Est: $1,200-$1,500.**

491

492

490

**489. Le Secret de Germaine.** ca. 1895.
31³/₈ x 48¹/₂ in./79.6 x 123.2 cm
Imp. Paul Dupont, Paris
Cond B/Slight tears at folds and stains at edges.
Ref: Reims, 952
Born in 1847 in a small village, Louis Boussenard would go on to create an oeuvre that earned him the nickname the "Jules Verne of Loiret," a well-earned sobriquet seeing as his novels also revolved around eccentric voyages throughout the world and perilous adventures. It's impossible to say what precipitated this hell-hound attack, but what a savage—not to mention flesh-flashing—way to promote "Germaine's Secret," a Boussenard novel making its debut in the Petite Republique. Pal was no stranger to creating exceptional promotions for Boussenard's work: He designed the astonishing poster for a stage adaptation of the author's most famous work, "Le Tour du Monde d'un Enfant de Paris" (see PAI-XXXV, 431). *Rare!*
Est: **$1,700-$2,000.**

**490. L'Opéra Comique/Sapho/Emma Calvé.** 1897.
38³/₄ x 53¹/₄ in./98.4 x 135.3 cm
Imp. F. Hermet, Paris
Cond B–/Slight tears at folds. Framed.
Ref: Affiche Opéra, 52; PAI-XVI, 405
A smashing poster for the Massenet opera, "Sapho," starring the famed Emma Calvé, beautifully designed—and decorously so in light of the potentially salacious subject matter—by Pal. Colorfully audacious lettering adds to the impact.
Est: **$1,400-$1,700.**

## MAXFIELD PARRISH (1870-1966)

**491. Ferry's Seeds.** 1921.
20³/₈ x 27¹/₂ in./51.8 x 69.8 cm
Rusting Wood, N.Y.
Cond B/Slight tears and stains, largely at edges. Framed.
Ref: Parrish/Japan, 102; Parrish, p. 112; PAI-XXIX, 576
All along we've been told that silver bells and cockle shells had been instrumental in the success of the output of Mary's garden, when all along the truth was that the key was Ferry's Seeds. An absolutely charming Parrish rendering of a little lady patiently waiting for her seeds to sprout with a classic repose greater than her years would deem possible. On at least one other occasion, the artist found his advertising inspiration in a nursery rhyme (see PAI-XXIV, 469), dropping the product name into the singsong to delightful effect. American artist Maxfield Parrish is known and loved for the illustrations—romanticized landscapes and comic fantasies—he created for popular magazines at the turn of the century: Scribner's, Colliers, Lippincott's and such. Every now and then he executed posters for them, conceived more or less as covers and about the same size. His fame was ensured with 25 years of illustrations for calendars produced in vast runs by both Edison Mazda and the publishers Brown & Bigelow. With the notable exception of the "Dutch Boy" that became synonymous with Colgate's cleanser, Parrish contributions to advertising were rare.
Est: **$7,000-$9,000.**

## RENÉ PÉAN (1875-1940)

**492. Olympia.** 1899.
34 x 48 in./86.4 x 122 cm
Imp. Chaix, Paris
Cond B/Restored tears, largely in top text area.
You can't help but notice that Pean may have appropriated a few stylistic elements from Chéret in this design for the renowned Paris music hall—the flouncing chorines, the sophisticated woman with the opera glasses, the admiring gentlemen, all set into motion with a spectacular use of color. But unlike his master, Pean gives the scene more substance, a heightened realism that still maintains the potential for attainable decorous revelry.
Est: **$1,700-$2,000.**

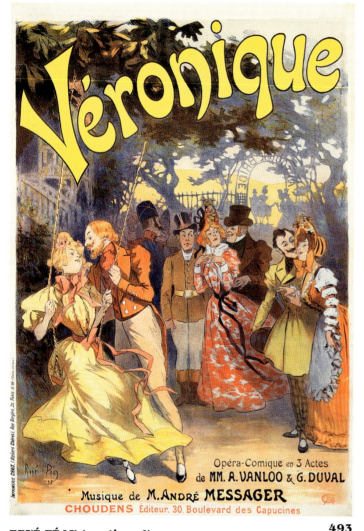

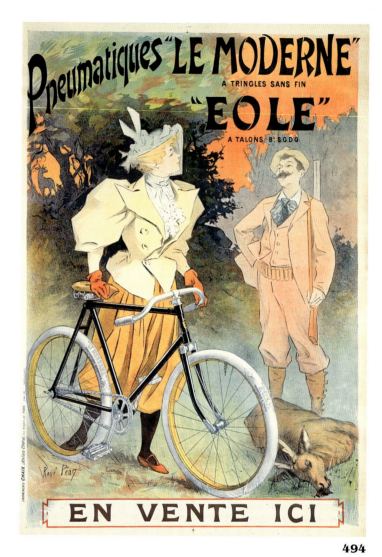

**493**

**494**

## RENÉ PÉAN (continued)

**493. Véronique.** 1898.
33¹/₂ x 47⁷/₈ in./85 x 121.7 cm
Imp. Chaix, Paris
Cond A.
Ref: Spectacle, 125
The third of the Pean advertisements in this auction
for musical extravaganzas at the Théâtre des Bouffes-
Parisiens. This time out it's "Véronique," which opened
on December 10, 1898, that takes center stage. Though
the fanciful specifics of the comic-opera have long
since faded, the arboreal courtship would seem to indicate another "Happily Ever After" affair—except for
the sourpuss at center, that is.
**Est: $1,400-$1,700.**

**494. Pneumatiques "Le Moderne"/"Eole".** 1896.
34¹/₄ x 48³/₄ in./87.2 x 124 cm
Imp. Chaix, Paris
Cond B+/Slight tears at folds and edges.
Ref: Petite Reine, 16 (var)
You'd think that this frilly cyclist might be a little impressed with the hunting prowess of the gentleman that
has engaged her along her pathless jaunt. But it's he
who seems to be astonished by her pneumatic choice—
or should I say choices, seeing as she has opted for
two different tires to provide the smooth ride such a
delicate wildflower requires: the "Eole" brand to the
fore, the "Le Moderne" tire aft. A slightly unlikely
scenario, but an ideal one that manages to kill two
promotional birds with one well-placed stone.
**Est: $1,700-$2,000.**

**495. Shakspeare!** 1899.
23⁵/₈ x 31¹/₂ in./60 x 80 cm
Imp. Chaix, Paris
Cond A.
Ref: Spectacles, 126
To bark or not to bark, that is the question. Taking
namesake inspiration from The Bard on Avon, this
classy little pup is placed in the spotlight as the title
character in "Shakspeare!," the comic-operetta that
opened at the Bouffes-Parisiens on November 23, 1899.
**Est: $1,000-$1,200.**

**495**

**496. Le Soleil de Minuit.** ca. 1898.
33³/₄ x 48³/₄ in./85.7 x 123.8 cm
Imp. Chaix, Paris
Cond A.
Ref: Spectacle, 124b
A promotional triptych from Pean for "The Midnight
Sun," a light-opera that premiered at the Théâtre des
Bouffes-Parisiens in October of 1898. It can't be deter-
mined which northern landscape this "Sun" chose to
rise upon, but these frothy scenes make it clear that
the sunny flirtations on display were sure to melt the
hearts of even the stuffiest patron of the arts.
**Est: $1,400-$1,700.**

**496**

## EDWARD PENFIELD (1866–1925)

**497. Harper's/November.** 1893.
11¹/₂ x 16¹/₂ in./29 x 42 cm
Cond A–/Unobtrusive tear upper left corner. Framed.
Ref: Lauder, 144; DFP-I, 327
Harper's posters from their first year of publication—
1893—are particularly rare. We see here that right
from the get-go, Penfield went for an immediate association between the reader's social circles and the
magazine, while also showing that no matter where it

**498**

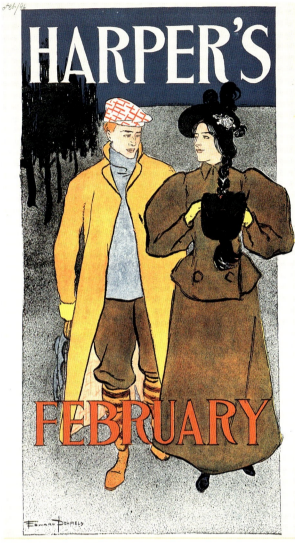

**499**

**497**

**500**

is that you feel you need to be, there's always time to pick up a copy of Harper's.
**Est: $1,000-$1,200.**

**498. Harper's/January.** 1895.
$12^3/8$ x $17^3/8$ in./31.5 x 44.2 cm
Cond B+/Slight tears and stains at edges. Framed.
Ref: DFP-I, 340; Reims, 1257; Lauder, 1611 PAI-XXXIV, 97
Once more, Penfield expresses the Harper's upscale

association. Here, a copy of the magazine carried by the woman appears to be sufficient grounds to facilitate an introduction.
**Est: $800-$1,000.**

**499. Harper's/February.** 1896.
$10^3/4$ x $18^1/2$ in./27 x 47 cm
Cond A. Framed.
Ref: DFP-I, 337; Lauder, 154; Reims, 1270;
    PAI-XXXIV, 110

Penfield is one of America's premier posterists. For a ten-year period, from 1891 to 1901, he was an art director at Harper's, and from 1893 he produced a series of monthly posters for its magazine. These were largely used as in-store displays for bookshops as well as newsstands. Most are deliciously irrelevant; all are interesting. The sporting young couple on their way to the skating rink are the epitome of the 1890s smart set.
**Est: $800-$1,000.**

**501**

**503**

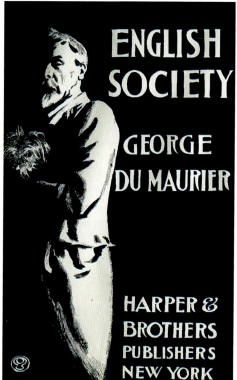

**502**

**AIR FRANCE EASTERN AIR LINES**

**DEUX RÉSEAUX - UN SEUL BILLET**

**504**

## PENFIELD (continued)

**500. Harper's/August.** 1899.
12 x 11$^1/8$ in./30.6 x 28.2 cm
Cond B/Slight tears and stains at fold and upper right corner. Framed.
Ref: DFP-I, 404; Lauder, 224; PAI-XXVII, 559
The most intriguing aspect of many Penfield designs is what the artist chooses to withhold from the viewer. It's almost as if he gives one a well-executed framework which allows an individual to create a unique story around the image. Here, it's unclear what the relationship is between the woman at the reins and the gentleman doffing his boater to her as he waits, suitcase in hand, at a trolley stop. There are several scenarios which could play themselves out, but no matter what tale evolves, it's certain that the couple has attracted each other's attention, and in the process, engaged the curiosity of the passer-by.
**Est: $1,000-$1,200.**

**501. Country Carts: Four Posters.** 1900.
Each: 22$^1/8$ x 15$^5/8$ in./56.2 x 39.6 cm
Published by R. H. Russell, New York
Cond B+/Slight tears and stains at edges.

Ref: PAI-XXXIV, 506
Throughout his illustrative life, Penfield "incorporated coaches in some of his Harpers' posters, as well as in the work for other clients. Studying coach design and history was a favorite hobby, and he later became a collector of these vehicles, and wrote about them for Outing. The unfinished manuscript of a book on coaches survives among his family papers" (Penfield, p. 13). This attraction to early vehicular transport wends its way across these four decorative panels, titled "Country Carts Series #1," no doubt part of a larger portfolio devoted to horse drawn conveyance. Though Penfield renders every horse and driver with masterful surety, it's his attention to detail—in this particular case to the finer points of the Exercising, Hackney, Kentucky Breaking and Meadow Brook carts —that makes him a superior chronicler of his time
**Est: $1,500-$1,800.** (4)

**502. English Society.** 1897.
12$^1/4$ x 19$^1/2$ in./31 x 49.5 cm
Cond A. Framed.
Ref: Lauder, 204; DFP-I, 370
For a volume of sketches focusing on the Victorian lifestyle drawn from illustrator and novelist George De Maurier's (1834-1896) work in Punch, as well as other sources, Penfield takes a stylistic turn, focusing on the brooding artist behind the drawings in a woodblock print-inspired black-and-white encounter of the artist emerging from the shadows. Stark and striking.
**Est: $600-$800.**

506

507

505

## LETEZIA PITIGLIANI (1935- )

**503. Harbor Festival.** 1978.
59<sup>1</sup>/4 x 44<sup>3</sup>/4 in./150.5 x 113.6 cm
Cond A.
What a difference a few decades make. Whereas this Pitigliani vision of a post-Bicentennial Harbor Festival taking place in and above the waters of lower Manhattan

must have been an out-and-out celebration of technological progress and transportational superiority at the time of its printing, it now appears as if it might be a glimpse into a Department of Homeland Security's "Worst Case Scenario" mockups. But what a spectacular window this opens up, a jubilant look back to when the Twin Towers stood tall and the most horrific prospect one faced in Manhattan was a lack of seaport parking.
**Est: $700-$900.**

## PLAQUET

**504. Air France/Eastern Air Lines.** 1950.
24<sup>5</sup>/8 x 39<sup>1</sup>/4 in./62.5 x 99.5 cm
Perceval, Paris
Cond A.
Ref: PAI-XXII, 478
We rarely see Air France posters promoting the company's commercial shipping services. This image is by Plaquet, who was responsible for at least three other designs for the airline between 1949 and 1952. Interlocking rings in the colors of the French and American flags symbolize a tie-in with Eastern Airlines, while the globe shows the extensive network of routes available as a result of the venture. Created in France with English text for use in the U.S.
**Est: $1,000-$1,200.**

## MAX PONTY (1904-1972)

**505. Navigation Paquet/Le Maroc. Les Canaries.**
24<sup>3</sup>/8 x 39<sup>1</sup>/4 in./62 x 99.8 cm
Imp. Hachard, Paris
Cond A–/Slight creases in background.
Ponty's known designs are few, but more than suffice to establish him as a foremost Art Deco posterist. Here he turns his geometric attention to the Paquet line's Moroccan and Canary Island service, softening the angularity of the festivities with the inclusion of a well-toned beachgoer rejoicing in the ship's sunset

arrival. "Packets" are small ships that carry mail and small cargo in addition to passengers. Often, in the glory days of ocean travel, these ships were the only means to reach small ports or remote destinations where the big liners wouldn't stop.
**Est: $1,200-$1,500.**

## LA PORTE

**506. L'Eclair.**
15<sup>1</sup>/4 x 23<sup>1</sup>/8 in./38.8 x 59.6 cm
Oil on canvas. Framed.
"'L'Eclair' was an independent, politically oriented journal which devoted a lot of effort to advertising by means of posters and, in fact, held one of the most hotly contested competitions for the best poster of the year" (Gold, p. 68). There's nothing to indicate that this angelic vision of journalism in the name of political fortitude ever made its way to a poster conclusion, but the spirit of independent honesty breezes off this la Porte work with an impossible-to-dismiss sense of whisper-soft idealism and cherubic integrity.
**Est: $5,000-$6,000.**

## LEO PUTZ (1869-1940)

**507. Moderne Galerie.** 1906.
31<sup>1</sup>/2 x 42<sup>3</sup>/4 in./80 x 108.5 cm
Reichhold & Lang, München
Cond A–/Restored tears at edges.
Ref: DFP-III, 2615; Takashimaya, 109; PAI-XIV, 414
His credentials are impeccable: studies at the Munich Academy and at the Julian in Paris; member of the Secession in Berlin, Vienna and Munich, work on the Jugend. Most active as a painter, Putz nevertheless produced a few posters, of which this one is probably the best known, an allegory with a water nymph carrying an oversize oyster shell. A cool grey-green sea color pervades the design.
**Est: $2,000-$2,500.**

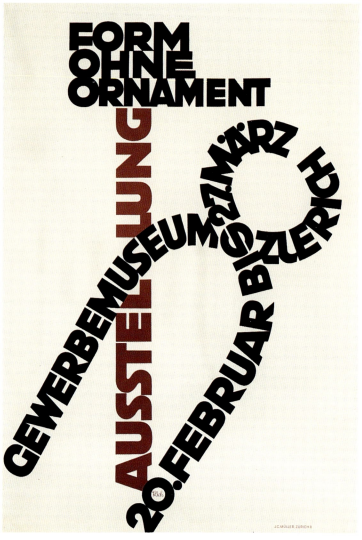

**508**

**511**

**509**

**510**

## WALTER RACH

**508. Ausstellung/Form Ohne Ornament.** 1927.
35¹/₄ x 50¹/₂ in./89.6 x 128.4 cm
J. C. Müller, Zurich
Cond B/Restored tears, largely at edges.
Ref: Margadant, 43
Ironically, words fall dismally short of describing this Rach design for an exhibition of artwork focusing on "Form Without Ornamentation" at Zurich's Gewerbemuseum even though the poster's tools are comprised solely of words. "Memorable" and "fiercely creative" are but two of the exclamatory descriptives that hopelessly don't do justice to this hammer-and-tongs creation. *Rare!*
**Est: $2,000-$2,500.**

## LESLIE RAGAN (1897-1972)

**509. A Century of Service/Norfolk and Western.** 1938.
21¹/₈ x 27⁷/₈ in./56 x70.8 cm
Cond A.
Ref: PAI-XXXI, 600
The past is the present, while the dream of a yet-to-be-realized powerful engine rides like a phantom on the smoke of the technological marvel of a coal-burning locomotive in a scene from the 1830s, the very first decade of railroading in the United States. Ragan, an Iowa native who studied painting and illustration in Chicago before moving to New York City, spent most of his career creating posters for the Norfolk & Western and the New York Central railroads.
**Est: $1,200-$1,500.**

## JACQUES RAMEL (1913-1999)

**510. Monaco Grand Prix 1956.**
31¹/₄ x 46³/₄ in/79.4 x 119 cm
Imp. A.D.I.A., Nice.
Cond A.
Ref: Ferrari, p. 213; PAI-XXV, 9
Ramel, who contributed several strong designs for the Grand Prix, gives only a hint of the ambience by showing an imposing Monaco structure suspended in space above the racers. The featured driver appears to be the popular Alberto Ascari in his red Ferrari 500; the race was actually won by a Maserati driven by Stirling Moss.
**Est: $2,500-$3,000.**

## HENRI RAPIN (1873-?)

**511. Exposition des Arts Décoratifs.** 1925.
31 x 46³/₄ in/79 x 118.7 cm
Imp. Lapina, Paris
Cond B+/Unobtrusive folds; slight stains at edges.
Ref: PAI-XXIV, 482
The 1925 Exposition Internationale des Arts Décoratifs

**513**

**512**

**514**

business trip to Paris, he met Felician Rops who persuaded him to attend the Academy at Liège . . . Rassenfosse at first designed small graphic works like ex libris and letterheads, then went on to book illustrations and magazine cover designs. His posters have a directness and simplicity that bring them an immediate attention" (Wine Spectator, 102). *Hand-signed.*
**Est: $5,000-$6,000.**

### RAY-LAMBERT

**513. Nouilles Lagelouze.** 1921.
31¹/₈ x 47 in./79 x 119.2 cm
Edition Publie Tout, Paris
Cond A–/Unobtrusive folds.
This somnambulant gourmand seems virtually powerless to fend off the urge to indulge in a late-night plate of Lagelouze pasta. Which brings to mind the following query: Is the up-top text, "You'll wake up at night to eat Lagelouze noodles," merely a promotional indulgence or is it a subliminal command destined to invade our slumber? What a delicious quandary. It's interesting to note that the Bibliothèque Nationale lists this artist alphabetically under "Lambert (Ray)," and then advises the reader to proceed to the entry for "Raylambert." However, these volumes don't go as far as the letter "R."
**Est: $1,200-$1,500.**

### LOUIS J. RHEAD (1858–1926)

**514. The Century/Midsummer Holiday Number.**
1894.
19⁵/₈ x 14³/₈ in./49.7 x 36.5 cm
Cond A–/Unobtrusive tears at edges. Framed.
Ref: Lauder, 46; Margolin, 53; PAI-XXXIV, 133
Rhead cleverly unifies the Art Nouveau work for *The Century* by echoing the woman's auburn tresses in the orange trumpets and roses which surround her and then reflecting the wave of her hair in the lines of the stylized sky. Rhead was one of the first poster artists to gain an international reputation. Born in England, he was quite active in London, New York and Paris with equal success; his exhibition of posters in New York in 1895 was America's first, and was well received. He was heavily influenced by Grasset, whom he admired and met while in Paris.
**Est: $2,000-$2,500.**

et Industriels Modernes was the exhibition that crowned the Art-Deco trend of the period, gave it its name and sent it forth to dominate applied arts for the next decade. One can hardly blame the financial organizers for not realizing all that in advance. Unlike Loupot's poster for the event itself (*see* PAI-XXVIII,386), this design announcing the bond issue is monumental rather than *moderne*—not surprising since it was created by a Salon member who won medals for his paintings in 1904 and 1910 and was an officer in the Legion of Honor. Rapin groups heroic figures representing the participating nations at the top of a ziggurat shape containing all the details; the large grey space serves as a foil for the flags' bright colors. Credit is also given to "C. Boignard" in the lower-left margin.
**Est: $1,200-$1,500.**

### ARMAND A. L. RASSENFOSSE (1862-1934)

**512. Genièvre La Croix.**
24 x 18³/₄ in./61 x 47.6 cm
Lith. Bénard, Liège
Cond A–/Unobtrusive folds. Framed.
Sometimes all the humanitarian aid a person needs is a good stiff drink. Of course, Rassenfosse is far too civilized for that, so he trots out a gentile cafe scene for the entire family, including a waiter who doesn't appear to be a stranger to the juniper-based beverage being touted here. "Armand Rassenfosse . . . was expected to follow in the footsteps of his father, a prosperous merchant in Liège, pursuing his penchant for drawing and engraving only as a hobby. But on a

**516**

**517**

**515**

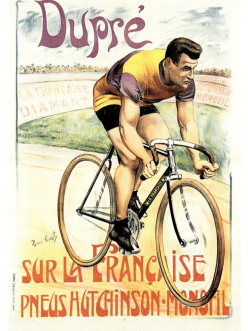

**520**

## HENRI RIVIÈRE (1864-1951)

**515. Chat Noir.** 1896.
$16^{1}/_{2}$ x $23^{1}/_{4}$ in./42 x 59 cm
Cond A–/Slight tears.
The Chat Noir cabaret presents an impressive evening of spectacle within their entertaining confines, but this poster, and its passle of playfully yowling felines on the rampage, doesn't fail in an infotainment level either. Rivière, a leading print maker and illustrator, was, along with Willette, Caran d'Ache and Steinlen, associated early on with the Chat Noir cafe and journal founded in Montmartre by Rodolphe Salis in 1881/ 1882. As secretary and one of the illustrators of the journal and as inventor of the venue's shadow theater, Rivière exercised a great deal of influence on the artistic environment of the Chat Noir.
**Est: $1,000-$1,200.**

## MANUEL ROBBE (1872-1936)

**516. Plasson Cycles.** 1897.
$35^{3}/_{4}$ x $49^{7}/_{8}$ in./90.8 x 126.6 cm
Imp. Bourgerie & Cie, Paris
Cond B/Restored tears at folds and edges. Framed.
Ref: Petite Reine, 34; Gold, 70; PAI-XXXIII, 31
"In 1851, Amelia Bloomer took a step towards emancipation by appearing in public in loose pants gathered at the knee—the first sensible public costume for some of the sports and athletics in which women were now hesitantly taking part. The term 'bloomers' came into the language at this time, and as we can see here, they were ideally suited to biking" (Gold, p. 50). Robbe, a prolific printmaker, produced only a handful of posters, two being for the Plasson bicycle. In this one, a chivalrous chap gives his best gal a push to help her get rolling. By the time he created his next Plasson design, men were altogether absent and sisters were doing the cycling for themselves (see PAI-VII, 390).
**Est: $1,700-$2,000.**

## GEORGES ROCHEGROSSE (1859–1938)

**517. Automobile Club de France/3eme Exposition.** 1901.
$36^{1}/_{4}$ x $50^{1}/_{8}$ in./92 x 127.3 cm
Imp. Barreau, Paris
Cond A.
Ref (All Var): DFP-II, 752; Auto Show III, 37; PAI-XXVI, 42
For the third ACF expo to be held at the Grand Palais, the club chose a painter in the classic vein to give the event an aura of prestige. As expected, Rochegrosse

provided a grandiose allegory that achieves the desired effect impressively. Most interestingly he uses an oversized gear wheel to create a Mucha-like halo behind the automotive queen and then reflects the image in the pattern of her gown. *This is the smaller version.*
**Est: $3,000-$3,500.**

## NORMAN ROCKWELL (1894-1978)

**518. Four Freedoms.** 1943.
Each: $39^{3}/_{4}$ x $55^{1}/_{2}$ in./101 x 141 cm
U.S. Government Printing Office, Washington D. C.

SAVE FREEDOM OF SPEECH

BUY WAR BONDS

SAVE FREEDOM OF WORSHIP

EACH ACCORDING TO THE DICTATES OF HIS OWN CONSCIENCE

BUY WAR BONDS

OURS...to fight for

FREEDOM FROM WANT

OURS...to fight for

FREEDOM FROM FEAR

**518**

EDISON MAZDA LAMPS

EDISON MAZDA LAMPS

**519**

1903 CALENDRIER DE LA VIE ILLUSTRÉE 1903

**521**

LES BOUCHONS-TOKIO

savignac

**522**

Cond B+/Unobtrusive tears along folds.
Ref: Rockwell's America, pp. 204-207;
    Rockwell Illustrator, pp. 143-149;
    American Posters, p. 24; PAI-XXXIV, 523
The Four Freedoms is probably the most ambitious and serious work by the most famous American illustrator of the 20th century. In addition to major advertising campaigns, his talent was also employed by the U. S. government for support of the Second World War effort. It was FDR who had distilled the cause for which

we were fighting into Four Freedoms. Only Rockwell could have represented such big ideas in his homey, folksy way without over-sentimentalizing or trivializing them. He undertook the paintings on his own initiative; it was only after he had failed to interest the Office of War Information in them and they had been published in the Post that the government saw their potential and used them in poster campaigns for both the general war effort and War Bonds. The Treasury Department also took the originals on tour; seen by 1.2 million people, they helped sell $132 million in bonds. The original paintings form the centerpiece of the Rockwell Museum in Stockbridge, Massachusetts, as well as that of the smashingly successful tour of this artist's work. *This is the larger format of the series.*
**Est: $1,500-$2,000. (4)**

**519. Edison Mazda Lamps: Two Posters.** 1920.
Each: $18^1/_2$ x $29^1/_4$ in./47 x 74.4 cm
Cond B/Slight tears near edges.
Ref: PAI-XXXIII, 519 & 520
Edison Mazda, a division of General Electric, was a brand name attached to any manufacturer through the auspices of National Mazda, having gone through a rigorous testing process at the National Plant in Euclid, Ohio. From 1910 through the 1930s, the National Mazda name was an appellation associated with excellence and GE masterfully used it to its best advantage: Not only an exceptional marketing tool, the submission process was a shrewd corporate maneuver which allowed General Electric to precisely examine their competitor's latest innovations. Of course, all of this sounds supremely opportunistic and crassly capitalistic when contrasted off homespun Rockwellian portraiture—be it an elderly couple quietly enjoying "Life's Evening Time" or the wholesome harmony of "The Melody

of Music and The Melody of Light.". And that, ladies and gentleman, is why the world has graphic artists—to put a personal face to a cold commercial world. And no one did that better during his day than Rockwell.
**Est: $2,000-$2,500. (2)**

## PRIVAT RONZAGUE

**520. Dupré/sur la Française.** ca. 1909.
$43^3/_4$ x $62^1/_4$ in./111.4 x 158 cm
Imp. Paul Dupont, Paris
Cond A.
It's all velodromatic business in this Ronzague design for the Française "Diamond" bicycle, a bike outfitted with superior Hutchinson tires. Despite the fact that Monsieur Dupré isn't one of the all-time greats in the pantheon of cyclists, he still was good enough to be crowned the victor of the 1909 World Sprint Championship.
**Est: $2,000-$2,500.**

## AUGUSTE ROUBILLE (1872-1955)

**521. Calendrier de la Vie Illustrée/1903.** 1902.
16 x $11^1/_2$ in./40.5 x 29.2 cm
Cond A. Framed.
Roubille, one of the great caricaturists of the time and a frequent contributor to such humor magazines as *Le Rire*, *Le Sourire* and *Cocorico*, spins a four-panel journey that follows a fashionable young lady through the seasons in this 1903 calendar for *La Vie Illustrée*. The style isn't far from hieroglyphic, but the stylized pastoral quality works wonderfully. The inclusion of a pair of background companions—most especially the dogs for the days of winter and the Pan-ish gentleman of spring—bring additional depth to the poster.
**Est: $800-$1,000.**

**523**

**524**

**525**

**526**

Au revoir et merci Monsieur Savignac.

upe

## RAYMOND SAVIGNAC (1907-2002)

**522. Les Bouchons-Tokio.** 1999.
19⁵/₈ x 24 in./50 x 61 cm
Mourlot, Paris (blind stamp)
Cond A/P.
Ref: Savignac, 158
Savignac was the *enfant terrible* of French poster art,
who, along with Bernard Villemot, had more impact on
that country's graphics of the past 40 years than any
other artist. As for his style, there are no displays of
technical virtuosity that might compete with the wit—
only disarmingly simple, almost childish brushwork,
basic colors and uncluttered design. For example,
there's something a little, well, screwy about this Savignac poster for a wine bar in Tokyo. And delightfully
so, with his His-and-Hers corkscrew pair making an
intoxicating couple, blissfully aware that their duties
release nothing but merriment and revelry.
**Est: $1,000-$1,200.**

**523. Tintin Orange.** 1962.
63 x 45³/₄ in./160 x 116 cm
Imp. Henon, Paris
Cond A.
Ref: Savignac, 77; Savignac/Japan, 22; PAI-XXVI, 530
An established celebrity is always a good way to place
the public's attention directly on your product. From
the The Osbornes peddling Pepsi products to Jeanne
Granier peddling wine (*see* PAI-XXVI, 200), it's a surefire technique. Not only is international cartoon sensation Tintin used by Savignac in this advertisement, he's
promoting his own soft drink, Tintin Orange, produced
by the Tintin Drink Society of Paris. This pasteurized
and carbonated orange beverage is made with "pure
sugar" for "kids from 7 to 77." Savignac borrows the
intrepid Belgian teenage reporter directly from his creator, Georges Remi Hergé, whom he credits on the
poster with "d'Après Hergé." Tintin's come along way
since his debut in the pages of *Le Vingtieme Siecle* in

1929. Beginning in 1930, the comic strips were put into book form and gained near-global popularity in 1958
when they were translated into other languages. Savignac presents the amateur sleuth taking a break from
one of his adventures to split a bottle of his namesake
pop with his constant companion, Snowy (or Milout in
the original French), who so enjoys it that he holds his
beloved bone with his ear as to not interfere with his
quality refreshment time. *This is the smaller format.*
**Est: $2,000-$2,500.**

**524. Loterie Nationale.** 1972.
45³/₄ x 61³/₄ in./116.2 x 157 cm
Lalande-Courbet, Wissous
Cond A.
Ref: Savignac, 280
It might be a slightly uphill battle, but these three wise
men-cum-santas appear more than ready for the task.
Covering both the Christmas and Epiphany lottery

**528**

drawings, these magi bear the gifts that anyone was sure to appreciate: Not gold, frankincense and myrrh, but sacks of cold hard cash.
**Est: $1,200-$1,500.**

**525. Orangina.** 2001.
27¹/₂ x 40⁷/₈ in./70 x 103.6 cm
Idem Editions, Paris

Cond A/P.
Ref: Savignac, 75 (var)
*One of a special-edition printing of 300 copies from a Savignac maquette executed in 1964.*
The next time that someone tells you that something —money pops immediately to mind—doesn't grow on trees, tell them that you might not be so sure. And as proof, offer-up the example of this Savignac poster for Orangina, an advertisement that the bottled beverage's refreshing nature comes directly from the branch. Chances are that this is the reason that Orangina is "better than soda."
**Est: $800-$1,000.**

**526. Au revoir et merci Monsieur Savignac.** 2002.
157¹/₂ x 117¹/₂ in./400 x 303 cm
Union de la Publicite Exterieure
Cond A.
Though Americans may have grown to take the litho-graphically superior for granted, it's quite obvious that the French have not. This incredible 8-sheet testimonial—measuring 10 x 13 feet—serves as a touching reminiscence to the warm feeling and deep gratitude felt by all Frenchman for this artist who so enlivened their existence for such a long period of time. A few months after his passing, this design was placed on the billboards of France. What contemporary artist in any country would command such a tribute today? And adding to the poignant nature of this poster is that this is the Savignac creation that launched the artist, both as a posterist and into the hearts of his countrymen, a poster whose importance Savignac himself made clear in the first words of his autobiography: "I was born at the age of 41, weaned on the udder of the Monsavon cow." There's almost a bittersweet feel to the stance of the cow now, as if she's also saying "au revoir" to her creator. It's safe to say that this billboard is otherwise totally unavailable today . . . and that it will be prized by collectors for many years to come.
**Est: $4,000-$5,000.**

## PIERRE SEGOGNE (?-1958)

**527. Jean Borlin: Two Maquettes.** 1925.
Each: 7 x 10 in./17.7 x 25.3 cm
*Hand-signed goauche, pencil and ink maquettes.*
Framed.
Though this pair of Segogne maquettes present the talents of the founder of the Ballet Swedois with more background detail and facial distinction than the Colin study of the same artist (*see* Lot 287), this pair of geometrically slicive works still leaves a great deal of interpretation open to the viewer. Perhaps this indicates that the ethereal nature of Borlin's choreography was something that could only be hinted at in any other medium outside of the dance. The one constant: Borlin himself, an androgynous anchor amidst a maelstrom of unleashed creativity.
**Est: $5,000-$6,000.** (2)

## G. SEIGNAC

**528. Emprunt National.** 1920.
30¹/₄ x 46³/₈ in./76.8 x 117.8 cm
Imp. Joseph-Charles, Paris
Cond A.
Ref: PAI-XXXI, 644
The bountiful harvest of peace is reaped—in more ways than one—in this image for what was to be the last national bond drive of the post-World War I era. Though it's possible to interpret the work in two ways—a return of dividends or an entrusting of one's financial future —the feeling of prosperity flowing off the Seignac design comes much more from the rosy-cheeked embodiments of France and the United States than it does from the overflowing coffer. The unsullied *paysanne* was Seignac's allegorical contribution to the national drive, utilizing her services several times, always with her apron overflowing with the abundant harvest, her hair interwoven with poppies and wheat, her nationalist color scheme seemingly more a necessity than an overt act of patriotism.
**Est: $1,200-$1,500.**

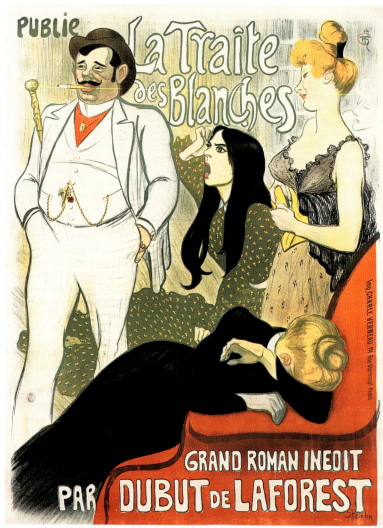

529

534

## SCOTTI

**529. Mar del Plata.**
29 x 43¹/₄ in./73.6 x 110 cm
Grafico Argentino, Buenos Aires
Cond B–/Restored tears.
Graphic shorthand is the order of the day in this
Scotti Art Nouveau tourism poster for the Argentine
getaway on the Atlantic Ocean. Founded in the 1850s
and currently playing host to two universities, Mar del
Plata is one of the most popular seaside resorts in all
of South America. Scotti's two-dimensional trio sums
up the three elements that have made Mar del Plata a
thriving metropolis: a thriving fishing industry, an
urban sophistication and a great beach scene.
**Est: $2,000-$2,500.**

## BEN SHAHN (1898-1969)

**530. A View from the Bridge.** 1955.
14 x 22 in./35.5 x 56 cm
Artcraft Litho., New York
Cond A/P.
Ref: Shahn, 163; PAI-XXXII, 101
"Shahn's ability to express emotion in hands is wonderfully affirmed in . . . the central figures in this poster
. . . The lettering of the play's title illustrates the integral
role Shahn's calligraphy played in many of his compositions, particularly as contrasted with the dull perfection of the machine-lettered message below" (Shahn,
pp. 114 & 136). A work of perfect simplicity that subtly underscores the thematic duality of isolation and
passion in Arthur Miller's classic tale of latent sexual
obsession, paranoia, envy, and even homophobia.
**Est: $700-$900.**

## KENNETH DENTON SHOESMITH
(1890-1939)

**531. Ligne Cunard/"Mauretania" at Cherbourg.**
38¹/₂ x 28³/₄ in./97.7 x 72 cm
Cond B/Unobtrusive tears, largely near edges.
Ref: PAI-XXII, 103 (var)

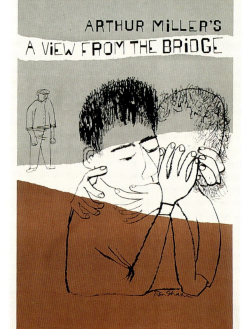

530

532

It's rare that we're given a night scene in ship portraiture. Here, the red-stacked *H.M.S. Mauretania* is
ablaze with lights in the Cherbourg harbor. Completed
in 1907, the liner inaugurated Cunard's first sailing
out of the port of Southampton and started calling on
Cherbourg in 1911. The most popular ship to ever sail
the North Atlantic, she continued crossing and cruising
until September 26, 1934. On that day, the *Queen*

*Mary* was launched, and "The Grand Old Lady" set out
from New York on her final voyage. "It should be noted
that despite the popularity of the *Queen Mary* and her
consort the *Queen Elizabeth*, both these ships were
products of the Great Depression, constructed to carry
thousands of passengers across the Atlantic. . . . More
likely than not it was their immense size . . . that had
captured the minds of the many, whereas the vintage
of ship to which the Mauretania belonged marked

"MAURETANIA" AT CHERBOURG     CUNARD LINE

**531**

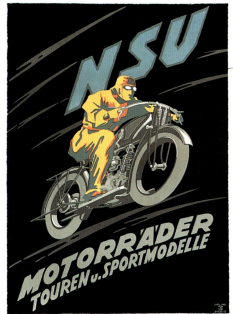

**533**

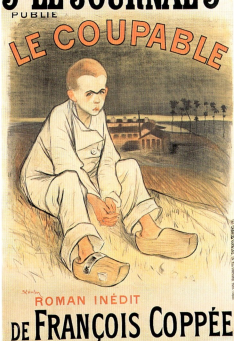

**535**

**536**

the zenith in class, sleekness, decor and clientele" (Passenger Liners, p. 50). A pupil of Fred Taylor and a sailor by training, Shoesmith was a brilliantly talented English painter, posterist and decorative artist who died before he was fifty. *This is the larger format with text in English.*
**Est: $2,500-$3,000.**

## ALBERT STAEHLE (1899-1974)

**532. New York World's Fair 1939.**
19⁵/₈ x 29⁵/₈ in./49.7 x 75.7 cm
Grinnell Litho. Co., NYC
Cond B+/Slight tears at folds. Framed.
Ref: Trylon, p. 39; PAI-XXXI, 566
Fireworks, brilliant lighting and a happy wave from an official hostess greet us at the Fair's opening ceremonies. An image befitting "the grandest illusion of the century" (Trylon, p. 39) that was The World of Tomorrow.
**Est: $1,500-$1,800.**

## VON LOEWE STEGLITZ

**533. NSU/Motorräder.**
26⁷/₈ x 35³/₄ in./68 x 90.8 cm
Cond A.
At the turn of the 19th century, the small factory town of Neckarsulm, in southern Germany, was the home of a company that manufactured automatic knitting machines, as well as a successful line of bicycles that went by the name "Neckarsulm Strickmaschinen Union" ("Neckarsulm Knitting-machine Union"). An accurate name to be sure, but quite a mouthful for the non-German speaking client. Hence, they eventually adopted the initials NSU. They would go on to manufacture a line of popular lightweight street motorcycles, a mode of transport that never really caught on in the United States. But as this Von Loewe Steglitz design shows, we as a nation may very well have missed out on a good thing—a ride that provided the speedy intensity craved by thrill-seekers with the lightweight stability that made them an ideal urban transport as well.
**Est: $1,200-$1,500.**

## THÉOPHILE-ALEXANDRE STEINLEN (1859-1923)

**534. Le Journal/La Traite des Blanches.** 1899.
47¹/₄ x 62³/₄ in./120 x 159.4 cm
Imp. Charle Verneau, Paris
Cond A–/Unobtrusive folds.
Ref (All Var): DFP-II, 793; Bargiel & Zagrodzki, 35B;
    Crauzat, 512; Gold, 90; PAI-XXX, 210
"Quite a few literary works of this era first saw the light of day as installments printed in daily or weekly papers . . . A major novel appearing in a trickle would hold readers for several months, with the hope that (readers) would get used to the paper's other features and remain loyal afterwards. The lure of a new sensational novel was often used to advertise the paper itself. And sensational is the word for this poster advertising installments of 'White Slavery.' It depicts a heartless pimp with three of his victims. One is arguing passionately for her freedom, one seems resigned to her fate, and one in utter despair. In Steinlen's original version, the willing prostitute had her breasts bared, but there was an adverse reaction to the poster, and this censored version was hastily substituted" (Gold, p. 66). *This is the larger format without Le Journal text banner at top.*
**Est: $6,000-$7,000.**

**535. Le Journal/Le Coupable.** 1896.
38¹/₂ x 60¹/₂ in./97.8 x 153.6 cm
Imp. Charles Verneau, Paris
Cond B/Tears and stains, largely at edges.
Ref: Bargiel & Zagrodzki, 26; Maîtres, 134;
    Crauzat, 498; DFP-II, 788; PAI-XXI, 410
The novel that the newspaper is publishing in serialized form tells the story of a boy from an orphanage. Steinlen reinforces the drabness of the child's life by using a largely monochrome background. In English, the novel's title was The Guilty Man. *This is the complete, two-sheet poster.*
**Est: $2,000-$2,500.**

**536. A Natural Woman.**
19¹/₈ x 25³/₄ in./48.5 x 65.4 cm
*Charcoal drawing.* Framed.
Wonderful in its simplicity and disarming in its honesty, this Steinlen charcoal study of the female form shows just how distorted our contemporary view of femininity has become. Not that there's any need to apologize for the body that one was born with, but this woman defies the boyish quality today's fashion has become obsessed with. Here's the real deal—full hips, curvaceous, sturdy and graceful, a woman of substance, freed from the constraints of period corsets and girdles, artistically permitted to indulge in the miracle of womanhood. Beautiful. *Estate stamp verso.*
**Est: $3,000-$3,500.**

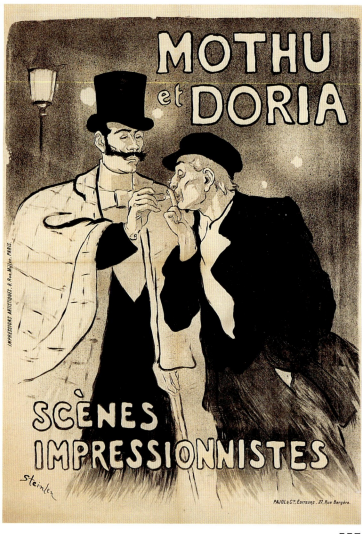

**537**

**541**

**538**

**539**

## STEINLEN (continued)

**537. Mothu et Doria. 1893.**
36¹/₈ x 50 in./92 x 127 cm
Impressions Artistiques, Paris
Cond B+/Unobtrusive folds.
Ref (All Var but PAI): Bargiel & Zagrodzki, 12A.2;
    Crauzat, 490; DFP-II, 780; Maitres, 46; PAI-XXXI, 72
A gentleman rather disdainfully proffers a light to a
lowly ruffian on the street in this poster for a pair of
singers. We get just the right hint of the social ten-
sions of the period. *This is the rare black and white
proof of the design.*
**Est: $5,000-$6,000.**

**538. Studies in Femininity.**
10 x 14 in./25.3 x 35.5 cm
*Ink and crayon artwork.* Framed.
This double-sided artwork shows Steinlen exploring
feminine mystique with agile surety, placing facets of
the female form—naked and clothed, facial and cor-
poreal—in sketch form to paper, attempting to artistically dissect the components of womanly allure in
order to best comprehend—and in the process, most
efficiently utilize—the powerful draw of the female of
the species. Interestingly enough, Steinlen appears to
have happened upon an image he would later use in a

fully-formed poster as the hat wearing woman—both
on the front of the sheet and the sole figure to appear
verso—seems to be the model for the passenger in
the Motocycle Comiot design (*see* PAI-XXVIII, 53).
*With Steinlen Estate Stamp.*
**Est: $3,000-$4,000.**

**539. The Labors of Man.**
9¹/₂ x 13¹/₂ in./24 x 34.3 cm
*Crayon artwork.* Framed.
Not only a talented artist, Steinlen was a keen
observer of the human condition. In opposition to the

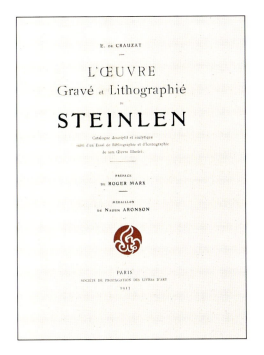

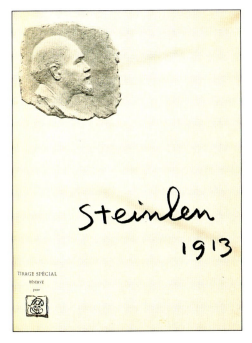

**540**

female sketches he set down (*see* previous lot), here he sets his sights on a more working class subject: the common man. Far more brutish and oafish than what we were privy to in the prior drawings, the work is nonetheless sympathetic, not so much a judgment as an investigation. And though there is a certain lumbering quality to the featureless figures that lumber above his head, this seated man is a study in world-weariness —corpulent and sedentary, a product of the working class he has been cast into. *Steinlen Estate Stamp appears in the lower right corner.*
**Est: $3,000-$4,000.**

**540. L'Oeuvre Gravé et Lithographié de Steinlen.**
1913.
9³/₄ x 13 in./24.8 x 33 cm
Ref: PAI-XXIX, 641(var)
*Steinlen's personal copy of the catalogue raisonné of his work by E. de Crauzat.*
This deluxe edition, in leather binding, consists of 232 pages plus a special suite of 17 full-page etchings and lithographs. Printed on chine paper, this very special edition was created for the Society of XX and offered, with dedication of its president, to Steinlen. Published

by the Société de Propagation des Livres d'Art of Paris, it contains a preface by Roger Marx and is the only complete catalogue raisonné of all the artist's work on paper. An interesting aspect is the many handwritten additions and corrections made by Steinlen, largely involving titles and dates. This is a most special reference and art work for the serious Steinlen collector.
**Est: $12,000-$15,000.**

## STENBERG BROTHERS
**(Vladimir, 1899-1982; Georgi, 1900-1933)**

**541. Chicago.** 1929.
24³/₄ x 37 in./61.7 x 94 cm
Cond B/Restored tears, largely at edges.
Ref: Stenberg/MoMA, p. 68; Russian Films, p. 50
"A Chicago mobster . . . makes advances to Roxie . . ., the beautiful wife of a cigar-stand owner Amos. . . . When she accepts an invitation to the mobster's house, he tries to rape her. She kills him in self-defense, but must stand trial for murder. A crooked lawyer . . . guarantees to win the case, but asks for a huge sum of money. Amos solves the dilemma by stealing the money from the lawyer's own safe. The lawyer wins

the case, but suspecting that he is about to be paid in his own money, alerts the police. The poster shows Amos trying to deal with Chicago's shady side, while Roxie laughs heartlessly at his efforts" (Russian Posters, p. 50). Though not a direct copy, the story line certainly would seem to be the inspiration for the Kander and Ebb musical of the same name, first brought to the public's attention by Bob Fosse and now, at the time of this writing, a top Oscar contender. The Stenberg Brothers were Russian designers and poster artists who embraced Constructivism and became major figures in the avant-garde of Soviet art during the turbulent revolutionary era after 1917. "While techniques of film and photomontage were the point of departure for their posters, the . . . brothers, masters of color and lithographic process, preferred to draw their images. The facilities available for printing photographic images simply did not give them the sharpness and color they desired. However, the photographic quality of their renderings was achieved with a primitive method of projecting film and photographic images to the desired size and then drawing over them" (Modern Poster, p. 30).
**Est: $14,000-$17,000.**

542

543

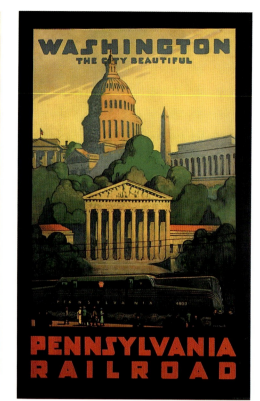

544

545

## DIMITRI STELLETSKI (1875-?)

**542. Matinée au Profit des Artistes Russes.**
$31^1/4$ x $47^5/8$ in./79.4 x 121 cm
Imp. Lapina, Paris
Cond B/Slight stains and creases. Framed.
Ref: DFP-II, 802; PAI-II, 229
Stelletski, who studied at the St. Petersburg Academy of Art before moving to Paris, was much influenced by the decorative style of Russian painting and icons and the Byzantine elements found in them. This poster announces a performance for the benefit of Russian students residing in Paris. Note that Auguste Rodin was honorary chairman and also delivered the keynote address.
**Est: $800-$1,000.**

## SYLVIO

**543. Roland Dorsay et ses Cadets.** 1932.
$31^1/2$ x $47^3/8$ in./80 x 120.5 cm
France Affiches, Paris
Cond B–/Restored tears, largely at folds and edges.
Ref: PAI-XIII, 433
If listening to a Salabert album of jazz courtesy of Roland Dorsay and His Cadets was even half as swank and swingin' as the graphic experience portrayed here, then that audiophile was in for a musical treat indeed. Sylvio does an incredible job of setting an Art Deco tone that generates a palpable excitement without the assistance of a single riff or syncopated melody.
**Est: $1,400-$1,700.**

## GRIF TELLER

**544. Pennsylvania Railroad/Washington.**
$24^3/4$ x $39^1/2$ in./62.8 x 100.3 cm
O. Co., Clifton, N.J.
Cond B/Restored tears, largely in borders.
Ref: PAI-XXXII, 86
The stacked perspective may not be geographically accurate, what with every monument and important landmark in the District of Columbia being visible from a single vantage point. But, it does, however, make for a compelling and persuasive poster for the Pennsylvania Railroad's service to the Nation's Capital. The locomotive seen in the foreground is a Type GG-1 electric engine, the first of its series and the product of Raymond Loewy, one of the first major proponents of streamlining in industrial design. The DC run origi-

nated out of New York and represented the only portion of the Pennsylvania line run exclusively on electricity. In fact, it is still utilized today by Amtrak for its high-speed service between the Eastern meccas.
**Est: $1,700-$2,000.**

## H. TOCHTERMANN

**545. Volksflugtag.** 1935.
$34^5/8$ x $48^1/2$ in./88 x 123.2 cm
Cond A.
A poster for a Munich for a day of man celebrating his conquest of flight features the image of a Heinkel 70 aircraft—one of the most advanced single engine monoplanes of its day and used by Lufthansa as a mail plane. The Tochtermann design also prominently features the insignias of both Lufthansa and the Nazi party amidst the textual specifics of aerial daring and mastery. "To-day's fast, streamlined turban engines owe a great deal more than is generally appreciated to that aristocrat of Germany's aircraft industry, Professor Ernst Heinkel, who combined exceptional foresight with immense tenacity of purpose. . . . The He 70 transport . . . set such an unrivaled standard of clean modern design that Rolls-Royce bought . . . one as a flying test-bed for their Kestrel V engine" (*History of Aviation*, by John W. R. Taylor and Kenneth Munson, p. 337). Twice listed on the poster is the name of German flying ace Ernst Udet, the youngest and second-highest scoring German flyer of World War One. A general in the Luftwaffe during World War II, Goering made Udet the scapegoat for the debacle of the Battle of Britain, and he was forced to commit suicide in 1941.
**Est: $1,700-$2,000.**

## HENRI DE TOULOUSE-LAUTREC (1864-1901)

**546. The Chap Book.** 1896.
$23^7/8$ x $15^7/8$ in./60.5 x 40.3 cm
Imp. Chaix, Paris (not shown)
Cond A–/Slight stains on right side.
Ref: Wittrock, P18A; Adriani, 139-I; Wagner, 24 (var); DFP-II, 846 (var); Wine Spectator, 51 (var); PAI-XII, 418
Commissioned by Stone & Kimball (the Chicago publisher of The Chap Book) from La Plume (which provided the design by Lautrec), this poster was never used in the United States; possibly it was intended to

promote the magazine's sale in France only. "The Irish American Bar at 33 rue Royale was furnished in gleaming mahogany, and had a Chinese-Indian bar-keeper called Ralph, who with stoical calm served the British jockeys and trainers and local coachmen who frequented the bar. Here, too, the florid figure of Tom . . . . the Rothschild's coachman, a particular favorite with Lautrec for his supercilious manner . . . is visible among the customers being served by Ralph with a special concoction" (Adriani, p. 196). Julia Frey makes it clear that the subject of this poster was also a home-away-from-home for Lautrec: He "let people know he could be found every afternoon in a certain bar. For several years from 1894 onwards, it was the Irish and American Bar. . . . There, it is said, Henry presided over the clients in the bar as he had over his house guests, insisting to Ralph . . . that people he didn't like not be admitted" (Frey, p. 390). *This is the rare proof before the addition of letters.*
**Est: $35,000-$40,000.**

**547**

**548**

**546**

**548. Jane Avril.** 1893.
35 x 48¹/₈ in./89 x 123.2 cm
Imp. Chaix, Paris
Cond B/Restored tears; image and colors excellent.
    Framed.
Ref: Wittrock, P6B; Adriani, 11-I; Wagner, 7;
    DFP-II, 828; Maitres, 110 (var); Wine Spectator, 41;
    PAI-XXVII, 602

Ebria Feinblatt indicates, with good reason, that this "is universally considered his most brilliant and successful design" (Wagner, p. 22). Toulouse-Lautrec shows "Jane Avril on stage doing her specialty, which, according to contemporaries, was essentially a cancan that she made exotic by making a pretense of prudery—the 'depraved virgin' image aimed at arousing the prurience in the predominantly male audience. The sexual innuendo was captured by the artist by contrasting the dancer's slender legs with the robust, phallic neck of the bass viol in the foreground—a masterly stroke that not only heightens our perception but also creates an unusual perspective: we see the performer as an orchestra member would, and this allows Toulouse-Lautrec to show, as if inadvertently, how tired and somewhat downcast she looks close-up, not at all in keeping with the gaiety of the dance that is perceived by the audience. It is clear, as Maindron has pointed out, that she is dancing entirely for the viewer's pleasure, not hers, which makes it a highly poignant image. Seemingly without trying, Toulouse-Lautrec not only creates a great poster but makes a personal statement: Only a person who really cares about his subject as a human being would portray her with such startling candor" (Wine Spectator, 41).
**Est: $50,000-$60,000.**

**547. Aristide Bruant Dans Son Cabaret.** 1893.
37¹/₂ x 52¹/₄ in./95.2 x 122.7 cm
Imp. Edw. Ancourt, Paris
Cond A–/Slight tears at seam and edges.
Ref: Wittrock, P9C; Adrianni, 130; Maitres, 82;
    DFP-II, 827; PAI-XXXIII, 577

Bruant was a strong, forceful, and in many ways vulgar entertainer of intimate cabarets—the kind of places where fashionable society went "slumming" for thrills. Lautrec captures this brutal quality of the entertainer and the disdain with which he treated his audiences by having him show us the broad of his back, with his red scarf forming an exclamation point on it. The pose itself makes a complete, self-contained statement— Toulouse-Lautrec at his very best.
**Est: $60,000-$70,000.**

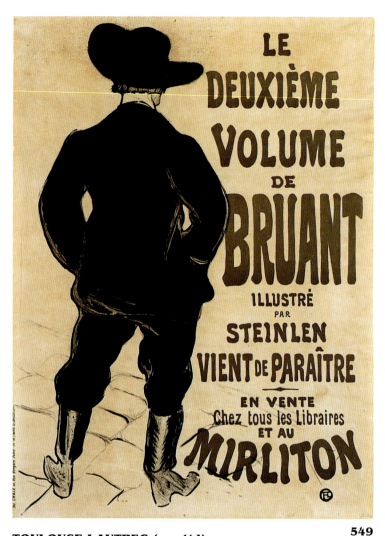

## TOULOUSE-LAUTREC (cont'd)

**549. Le Deuxième Volume de Bruant/Mirliton.** 1893.
23⁵/₈ x 31⁷/₈ in./60 x 81 cm
Imp. Chaix, Paris
Cond B–/Restored tears, largely near edges. Framed.
Ref: Wittrock, P10C; Adriani, 57-IV; DFP-II, 832; PAI-XXXII, 537
In one version of this poster, we see the *chansonnier* with text announcing the opening of his new cabaret (*see* PAI-XXXII, 536). In this one, the sale of a songbook by Bruant, illustrated by Steinlen, is promoted and we're reminded that we can hear it all at the Mirliton. Both are distinguished by Bruant's insolent stance: The point made is that we can recognize the famous performer not only despite his turning his back to us, but *because* of it. Who else would have the audacity to be so rude?
**Est: $7,000-$9,000.**

## HENRI DE TOULOUSE-LAUTREC (1864-1901)

**550. La Vache Enragée.** 1896.
23¹/₂ x 32¹/₈ in./59.7 x 81.5 cm
Imp. Chaix, Paris
Cond A–/Horizontal fold. Framed.
Ref: Wittrock, P27A; Adriani, 165-II; Abdy, p. 85; DFP-II, 844; Wagner, 26;
    PAI-XXXII, 535 (var)
This poster advertises Willette's magazine, *La Vache Enragée,* which lasted for only a single year. Wittrock, who rates the rarity of this state as "uncommon," also indicates that "the image in the poster was drawn by Toulouse-Lautrec in imitation of the style of A. Willette" (p. 808). This is one of the few Lautrec posters with movement: the runaway cow is the centerpiece of a remarkable caricature depicting sheer panic in some, curious complacency in others—an obvious reflection of the world that swirled around the artist. Explains Julia Frey in her wonderful biography of the artist, "Henry shows a *vachalcade,* the cavalcade of starving, angry artists for whom the magazine was spokesman, attacking Senator Béranger, whose morals squad was trying to censor them" (Frey, pp. 421-22).
**Est: $32,000-$36,000.**

**551. Marcelle Lender, en Buste.** 1895.
10¹/₂ x 13⁷/₈ in./26.7 x 35.2 cm
Cond B+/Slight tears, largely at edges. Framed.
Ref: Wittrock, 99-IV; Adriani, 115-IVa; PAI-XXI, 440
Parisian actress Marcelle Lender (1862-1926) had been appearing in a

**552**

**553**

Lender as the Galaswintha at the court of King Chilpéric. It was not so much the flimsy plot of this medievel farce as the actress . . . who led Lautrec to sit through the operetta nearly twenty times. Always watching from the same angle, from one of the first tiers on the left, he would lie in wait with his sketch pad . . . No other lithograph is printed with such a wealth of subtle color combinations" (Adriani, p. 157). *This is the edition that appeared in the German journal, Pan.*
**Est: $12,000-$15,000.**

**552. May Belfort.** 1895.
$23^1/_2$ x 32 in./59.7 x 81.3 cm
Kleinman, Paris
Cond A. Framed.
Ref: Wittrock, P14B; Adriani, 136-IV; DFP-II, 837; Wagner, 16; PAI-XXXIV, 575
"In the poster Belfort is framed by long black curls under an enormous cap, her hands hiding most of a yellow-eyed kitten. Lautrec presents her on a diagonal plane, her brilliant orange-red dress slanting to the left, her shoulder brought forward in the picture plane to place her in a frontal position. The flat sweep of her gown bellow the frilled, green-splattered sleeves is, taken by itself, merely a red sail or banner" (Wagner, p. 27). Julia Frey's excellent biography gives some interesting background to this: " May Belfort, whom Henry represented in at least ten works, had gained a reputation for corrupt innocence by appearing onstage dressed as a baby holding a black kitten in her arms, and 'miaowing or bleating' her popular song, 'Daddy Wouldn't Buy Me a Bow-Wow,' whose lines had a double meaning which was not lost in the French-speaking audience: 'I've got a pussycat, I'm very fond of that.'" (Frey, p. 382).
**Est: $35,000-$40,000.**

**553. May Milton.** 1895.
23 x $29^7/_8$ in./58.4 x 75.3 cm
Cond A. Framed.
Ref: Wittrock, P17, trial proof; Adriani, 134-II, trial proof
According to Adriani, "May Milton was an English dancer with a pale, serious face and strong chin who appeared at the Moulin Rouge." Toulouse-Lautrec is almost brutally frank in depicting her face, neither pretty nor youthful, and pointing out the inappropriateness of the white debutante's dress with puffed sleeves which she wore on stage. Yet the point is made with such gentle irony that it may have been missed, or ignored, by the performer herself, as she apparently used the poster for personal publicity. *This is the rare trial proof in olive-green only.*
**Est: $18,000-$22,000.**

**554**

series of comic operas, principally at the Théâtre des Variétés, since 1889. Utterly enamored with the performer, Lautrec did many drawings of her—alone and with co-stars—in many of her roles. Here, she is depicted in her role in *Chilpéric*, an operetta-revue that was revived at the Variétés in 1895. The main attraction in *Chilpéric* was the bolero, danced by Marcelle

**556**

**557**

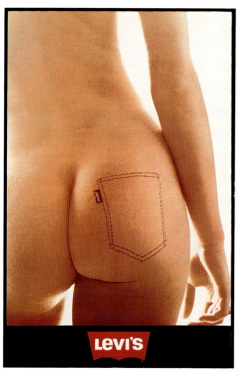

**555**

**558**

## FERNAND TOUSSAINT (1873-1955)

**554. Café Jacqmotte.** 1896.
33 x 41¹/₄ in./83.8 x 105 cm
O. De Rycker, Bruxelles
Cond A–/Unobtrusive folds.
Ref: DFP-II, 1131; Belle Epoque 1970; Reims, 1504;
   Wagner, 100; Timeless Images, 47;
   Masters 1900, p. 96; PAI-XXXIV, 581
Toussaint had a long and productive career in Belgium

as a painter, but unfortunately produced few posters. And of these, the Café Jacqmotte, with its rich color contrasts and its strong design, is his very best. It's the color combinations which makes this poster stand out. Everything is luminous and flowing, giving form and grace to this rare and impressive composition. The poster was printed by Toussaint's friend, O. de Rycker,

the master lithographer of Brussels, "who could achieve the nuances of luminous mother-of-pearl (Jacqmotte) or colored dreams (Le Sillon) . . . Toussaint could also compose in sonorous letters like sounds of a gong (Le Sillon) or in a continuous and modulated sound like music (Jacqmotte)" (Belle Epoque 1970, p. 84).
**Est: $15,000-$18,000.**

## IDA VAN BLADEL (1931- )

**555. Levi's.** 1971.
25 x 37 in./63.5 x 94 cm
Vita Nova, Holland
Cond A/P.
Ref: V & A, 215; Gallo, p. 276; Belgique/Paris, 150;
Affiches Belges, 26 ; PAI-XXXIV, 585
Years before an under-aged Brooke Shields scandalously confessed that nothing came between her and her Calvins, Van Bladel showed the world that slipping into a pair of Levi's was as good as slithering into a very tight second skin. A directly clever, succinct statement. The Antwerp-born designer was the art director at Young & Rubicam International in Brussels where this remarkable poster was created.
**Est: $1,200-$1,500.**

## JEAN-DOMINIQUE VAN CAULAERT (1897-1979)

**556. Mistinguett/Théâtre Mogador.** 1937.
45³/4 x 61¹/4 in./116.2 x 155.5 cm
Atelier Girbal, Paris
Cond A-/Unobtrusive stains. Framed.
Ref: PAI-XXXV, 399
With the trademark sophistication and refinement for which his celebrity portraits were known, Van Caulaert paints Mistinguett in her rags-before-riches street urchin personae for an appearance in *ça c'est Parisien* at the Théâtre Mogador. Van Caulaert's specialty was portraits —barely a luminary of his time escaped his particular brand of immortality. His imagination and skill were as powerful as his ability to capture a personality.
**Est: $1,700-$2,000.**

## J. PAUL VERREES (1889-1942)

**557. Join the Air Service.** 1917.
25 x 37 in./63.3 x 94 cm
Ketterlinus, Philadelphia
Cond A.
Ref: Looping the Loop, 71; PAI-XXXII, 65
An imaginative recruiting poster for pilots in World War I, with a very good representation of the flimsy biplanes they were expected to fly. Verrees was born in Belgium and came to the U.S. in 1909; this poster was considered one of his finest, and one of the best aviation posters ever designed anywhere.
**Est: $2,500-$3,000.**

## MARCEL VERTES (1895-1961)

**558. Frou Frou.** 1922.
62³/4 x 47 in./159.4 x 119.5 cm
H. Bataille, Rouen-Paris
Cond B/Restored tears.
Ref: PAI-XXXI, 696
A charming design for a satirical magazine. Every element works—the flirty miss, the ogling oldster, the prototypical battle-ax—even the handle of his umbrella enjoys the view. And the coloring is perfection as well —zesty background, proper seductress-scarlet, envy-green wife. The poster is for the postwar revival of the publication, which enjoyed its original run between 1900 and 1914. Vertès, a highly talented painter and illustrator, was born in Budapest. After an initial stint designing political posters in his home town following World War I, he settled in Paris, chronicling the city life during the Roaring Twenties. Later, he would relocate once more, this time to the United States.
**Est: $3,500-$4,000.**

**559. Lily Pons.**
41 x 78³/4 in./104 x 199 cm
Tooker Litho. Co., N.Y.
Cond B/Stains at folds.
A light-as-air watercolor confection calls the viewer's attention to Lily Pons, the "World's Greatest Coloratura Soprano," whose lilting talents arrived in the public ear via the grace of Columbia Records. Lily Pons (1898-1976) had one of the great operatic careers of the 20th century, enchanting audiences with her crystalline voice, lovely stage personality and great offstage chic. After her unheralded 1931 debut at New York's Metropolitan Opera in "Lucia," where the audience literally roared their approval, she became front page news throughout the country and suddenly, the petite-framed, 22-inch-waisted singer became a national sensation.
**Est: $1,000-$1,200.**

## EMILIO VILA (1887-1967)

**560. Napierowska.**
12 x 17¹/2 in./30.5 x 44.5 cm
*Hand-signed watercolor and ink maquette.* Framed.
Renowned for her appearance in Louis Feuillade's 1915 classic "Les Vampires" and referred to by certain members of the French press as "une vamp sensuellement viperine," Napierowska is portrayed by Vila with unflinching sensuality, every inch an opulent diva. Another in a line of effortlessly elegant work from the prolific Moroccan-born Spanish artist who produced several posters for the nascent film industry during his time in Paris.
**Est: $1,700-$2,000.**

561

562

563

564

### EUGENE VAVASSEUR (1863-?)

**561. Marque l'Aigle.**
$60^3/8$ x $44^1/2$ in./153.3 x 113.2 cm
Imp. des Arts Industriels, Paris
Cond B/Slight tears and stains at folds.
An amazing poster for a brand of rubber footwear that uses the unfortunate state of an aged military man and Vavasseur's slicing wit to spectacular proportions. Just take a gander at the lower left text being perused by the soaking poodle: "What used to comfort me in my pitiful fate was that I had feet that were safe from any moisture. Only here, for little expense, is the admirable Eagle shoe that gives everyone the same immunity. Now what's the use of me being an amputee?" Funny and disturbing all at the same time. As a posterist, Vavasseur was well known for his invention of humorous characters, as well as contributing drawings to such periodicals as *La Caricature, La Silhouette* and, under the pseudonym Ripp, to *L'Eclipse, La Gaudriole* and *La Revue Illustrée*.
**Est: $2,500-$3,000.**

### VIC

**562. IIIe Salon de la Gastronomie.**
$30^3/4$ x $46^3/4$ in./78 x 118.7 cm
Imp. Delanchy-Dupre
Cond B-/Restored tears; stains at edges.
Vic's poster advises us to "Run to Luna Park" for the third annual gastronomic fair being held there. And it seems like fairly sound advice, seeing as the poster's charging gigantic gourmand appears to be prepared to eat and drink anything he can get his voracious hands on.
**Est: $800-$1,000.**

### BERNARD VILLEMOT (1911-1989)

**563. Get.** ca.1954.
63 x $45^5/8$ in./160 x 115.8 cm
Imp. S. A. Courbet, Paris
Cond A-/Unobtrusive tears at folds and edges.
Ref: PAI-XIX, 511
As effectively as Villemot distilled the essence of orange into his sun-drenched images for Orangina, for this mint-flavored drink he evokes a cool world of blue and green. The childish shapes and naive perspective are as refreshing and dreamlike as the colors. With the utmost economy—two stylized tree, two bottles—we are presented with a storybook scene: the bottles, tilted just so, seem to be having a romantic conversation in the shade of the tree.
**Est: $1,200-$1,500.**

**564. SGTM/Marseille.**
$24^1/2$ x 39 in./62.2 x 99 cm
Tolmer, Paris
Cond A.
A poster that shows simultaneous restraint—for Villemot—and a complete emblematic dedication to promotional identity adversities the Marseille-based General Society of Maritime Travel's ports of call with little more than a reflective sunburst and vessel of striking replication.
**Est: $1,000-$1,200.**

**566**

**565**

## JACQUES VILLON (1875-1963)

**565. Inquiétude.** 1901.
10¹/₄ x 13³/₈ in./26 x 34 cm
Imp. Chaimbaud, Paris
Cond A/P. Framed.
Villon was an important figure in the history of modern art and a quintessential figure in the bohemian scene of fin-de-siècle Paris. A cubist painter, illustrator and printmaker, he created only some six posters—all graced by his superb drawing and observation of character. His talents change the introspective woman gracing this complete song sheet for a piano waltz by Gaston Roux into a bittersweet monument to solitude. His pensive sitter perfectly embodies the name of the music it has been paired with: "Concern." Tender and touching.
**Est: $1,400-$1,700.**

**567**

## KONSTANTIN VYALOV (1900-1976)

**566. Kogda Probuzhdayutsya Mertvyye
(When The Dead Wake Up).** 1935.
42¹/₂ x 27⁵/₈ in./108 x 70 cm
Cond B+/Slight tears at edges.
Ref: PAI-XXX, 683
A jarring round of billiards promotes the 1935 re-release of a Sovkino antichurch comedy originally titled *St. Jorgen's Day*. This "sonorized" version of the film (when it was first released, it played as a popular silent film since Soviet conversion to sound was still a few years off) was issued at a time when antichurch senti-ment was so prevalent among the politically correct of

the day that the mere mention of a saint's name in the title—even though meant facetiously—may have been too much for the censors to swallow; thus, its new name. The story follows two escaped convicts in an unnamed Western country who disguise themselves as nuns. With the police hot on their trail, they duck into a church where they discover in the midst of their concealment that the following day is the feast of St. Jorgen, a celebration that includes a processional through the town featuring a worthy maiden who has been chosen as the "bride" of the saint. Being crafty sorts, one of the crooks decides to deck himself out in fancy clerical garb and emerges from the church the next morning declaring to be St. Jorgen come back to Earth. Before the church elder can take action, the phony saint and his sidekick have been embraced by the gullible townsfolk. The chief of police recognizes the pair and tells the elder, who not wanting to disap-point a congregation that has embraced this "miracle," offers them a passport and safe conduct out of town once the parade is over if they promise never to return. They play one more prank on the pious hypocrite before they leave: they take that year's designated bride—none other than the priest's daughter.
**Est: $4,000-$5,000.**

## WARNER & MAY-GIL

**567. Engagez-Vous.**
25¹/₂ x 38⁷/₈ in./64.8 x 98.7 cm
Wallon, Vichy
Cond B+/Slight tears and stains, largely at folds.
Army recruiting meets Art Deco. This poster to encour-age young men to enlist in France's Army Signal Corps does a stylish job of combining very few elements—transmission wires, radio equipment, a dedicated moni-tor who verges on the cyber-science fictional and a lone dove—in a decidedly sleek manner to arrive at an end that is at once informative, elegant and immediate.
**Est: $1,000-$1,200.**

568

570

## WILLIAM WELSH (1889-?)

**568. Pullman/Vacation Lands Are Calling.** 1936.
20$^1$/8 x 26$^1$/4 in./51 x 66.5 cm
Charles Daniel Frey Co., Advertising, Chicago
Cond A–/Slight stains at edges. Framed.
Ref: PAI-XXXIV, 606
Repetition was Welsh's lithographic bread and butter. Most obviously he uses it here with a quartet of gulls to give his design a bit of motion. But more subtly, take a look at the whitecaps and the pattern of the horizon wavelength—even the shadow of his slender artist seems to echo the pattern in the surf-battered rocks. All of this is secondary, of course, to the central figure of the series—a strong, independent, emancipated woman relishing her free time courtesy of Pullman. Kentucky-born Welsh was trained throughout the United States and in Paris as well. Accomplished and lauded as both a painter and an illustrator, his work can be seen in the Chicago Art Institute, in the mural decorations for the Men's Cafe in Chicago's Palmer House Hotel and on numerous covers of the *Woman's Home Companion*. And for Pullman, of course.
**Est: $1,200-$1,500.**

## JACQUES WELY (ca. 1875-1910)

**569. Les Desmoiselles des St. Cyriens.** 1898.
23$^1$/2 x 31$^7$/8 in./59.7 x 81 cm
Imp. Ed. Delanchy, Paris
Cond A.
Ref: French Opera, 50; PAI-XXXV, 502
Everything appears as prim and proper as can be—I mean, seriously, it takes a rather oversexed imagination to infer anything from a salute and a shuttlecock. But looks can be deceiving. "A girls' boarding school is conveniently located near the aristocratic officers' training school, Saint-Cyr. In the risqué plot typical of French operettas of the time, the heroine is not only in-

volved romantically with a cadet, but is also faced with the prospect of an inheritance—provided she competes in a nude beauty contest" (French Opera, p. xxiv).
**Est: $700-$900.**

## JUPP WIERTZ (1881-1939)

**570. Deutsche Kunstflug-Meisterschaff.** 1936.
22 12 x 33$^1$/4 in./57.2 x 84.5 cm
Cond A.
High above a freshly-completed stretch of the Autobahn, the German Aerobatics Championship begins to play itself out thanks to Wiertz's elegant rendering of a participating Jungmeister Bu-133. The craft is considered to be one of the finest aerobatic machines ever created. On a darker note, the Bu-133 was also widely used by the "Luftsportverband," a clandestine association of flying schools used by the Third Reich to train future Luftwaffe fighter pilots. Wiertz, born in Aachen, studied in Berlin and became one of the most famous German poster masters of his era. He worked from an independent studio beginning in 1914, mainly for the German railroads and the travel industry.
**Est: $1,000-$1,200.**

## ADOLPH L. WILLETTE (1857-1926)

**571. League Populaire Antialcoolique.**
25$^3$/4 x 39$^1$/4 in./65.3 x 99.6 cm
Imp. Réunies, Lyon
Cond B+/Unobtrusive folds.
An arresting admonition from Willette, a successful painter who in 1887 switched to drawing, lithography and poster design. Executed on the behalf of the Popular Anti-Alcohol League, the design wins absolutely no points for subtlety. However, even before one's eyes reach the supporting text, the poster's message is crystal clear, with the "Voluntary Slave" having chained himself to the bar rail as the ghoulish barkeep tops off

the drinker's glass with his poison of choice. The temperance message below, intended to obliterate the "Great Enemy of the Working Class," is even more to the point, pointing out all of the things that are left behind in a bar (health, reason, money and time) and a long list of the people and mind-expanding opportunities that are cheated in the process. Willette became a frequent contributor to satirical publications such as "Le Rire" and "Chat Noir," even founding three of his own magazines, as well as being one of the founders of "Les Humoristes."
**Est: $1,200-$1,500.**

569

572

573

### JEAN D'YLEN (1866-1938)

**572. Bitter Sectrestat.** 1924.
$77^3/_4$ x $96^1/_2$ in./197.5 x 245.1 cm
Imp. Vercasson, Paris
Cond B/Restored tears, largely at seam.
After several years as a designer of jewelry, d'Ylen became a full-time posterist in 1919 and signed an exclusive contract with Vercasson in 1922. He may have owed the job offer to the fact he was a sincere admirer and disciple of Cappiello, who was the previous star of the Vercasson shop, and thus the firm was assured of an uninterrupted flow of designs of unbridled exuberance which had been Cappiello's trademark. A fine example is this 2-sheet, larger format poster for Bitter Secrestat gentian, the motivating force behind this geriatric jig, as well as for the flush that graces this prancing oldster's cheeks. And as tempted as one might be to polish-off both bottles in one's possession, the text virtuously reminds us to "Give (one) to your best friend."
**Est: $3,500-$4,000.**

**573. Chantier Houiller.** 1924.
42 x $62^3/_4$ in./106.7 x 159.4 cm
Imp. Vercasson, Paris
Cond A-/Slight creases.
Not a promotion for a single coal-producing enterprise, but rather for the need to support existing and future carboniferous sites in their domestic and industrial mining efforts. Conceptually, this cart-topping miner works on both an exultant and disbelieving level. The fact that the Brussels advertising agency, Ferdi, also gets credit indicates that this was a design intended for both Belgian and French posting.
**Est: $2,000-$2,500.**

571

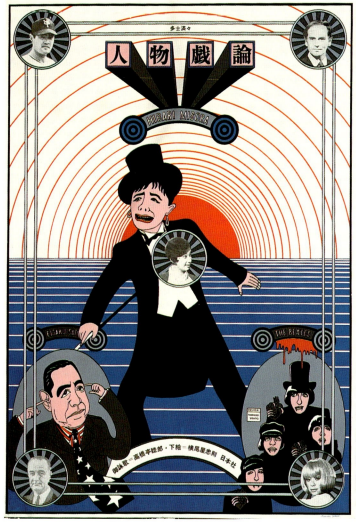

574

575

## TADANORI YOKOO (1936- )

### 574. Hibari Misora.

28³/₄ x 40³/₈ in./73 x 102.5 cm

Cond A–/Slight stains at edges.

*Hand-signed, silk-screen poster.*

"Enka" music can best be described as Japanese blues, melancholy strains overflowing with yearning for loves lost and one's home town. And Hibari Misora is probably the most famous Enka performer to have ever lived. She began singing as a Kyoto teenager in the 1950s and continued right up to her sudden death in 1989. She was only 52 years old. She is often thought of as having comforted Japan through the difficult recovery from the devastation of the war years, and her name, which one has to assume is a stage name even though no data to the contrary exists, roughly translates to "Skylark (in the) Beautiful Sky". She made more than 300 records and recorded more than 1,400 songs in her life. Yokoo concocts a multi-cultural graphic stew to set the legendary entertainer in the public's eye, complete with a cameo of Lyndon Johnson and a rather derisive appearance by The Beatles, here transformed into "The Beates," a quartet of heart-nabbing vampires.

**Est: $1,500-$1,800.**

576

**578**

**579**

**575. Koshimaki-Osen.** 1968.
29$^1$/$_2$ x 41$^3$/$_8$ in./74.8 x 1052 cm
Cond A–/Slight stains at edges.
Ref: Yokoo, 26; Tadanori Yokoo, 541 (var)
*Hand-signed, silk-screen poster.*
Sexual innuendo abounds in this Yokoo poster for Koshimaki-Osen (literally translated: "Loincloth Hermit"), a theatrical event by the Gekidan Kara-kumi troupe not open to those under the age of eighteen, a fact spelled out on the out-sticking tongue lower right. Artistically-directed by troupe leader Kara Juro, Gekidan Kara-kumi were the Japanese avant-garde performers of their time. For example, they would, for a lark, go into Ginza, the most expensive and tawny shopping district in Tokyo and just set up a tent and perform. Kara was a very famous actor, playwright and screen-play writer, and is considered one of the founders of the Little Theater Movement (shogekijo). Shogekijo grew out of the younger theater practitioners' disillusionment with the Western-influenced style of the 1960s and their attempt to give contemporary theater a distinctly Japanese feel. "The posters Yokoo created

**577**

for the troupe reflected Kara's intentions exactly. The fake design and garish color combination of this poster, with a peach and a rose-motif hanafuda taken straight from a box of bargain-size matches, the rising sun pattern, the billowing awning from a tenement house and the pattern made up of female nudes flying through the air in a manner reminiscent of something out of a Superman comic, exactly communicate the scandalous, antagonistic and unique content of the play . . . It was after the appearance of this poster that many people first started to become interested in the plays of the 'Jokyo Gekijo'" (Yokoo, p. 8).
**Est: $1,200-$1,500.**

## ZIG (Louis Gaudin, ?-1936)

**576. Mistinguett.** 1928.
46 x 61$^1$/$_4$ in./117 x 155.6 cm
Imp. H. Chachoin, Paris
Cond B–/Slight tears at top folds and top text. Framed.
Ref: PAI-XXXII, 568
Mistinguett, queen of the French music-hall, had a way of outliving her designers. After her favorite, Gesmar, died in 1928, she switched to Zig. The artist had been a habitué of Montmartre cabarets where he sang and recited at the drop of a beret. Both of them affected a flamboyantly showy style, which exactly suited the Miss persona, and after he proved himself with set and costume designs, she ultimately trusted him with the design of her posters. Here, Zig gives us Mistinguett as a country girl complete with a basket of flowers. Beyond its graphic flair, it's Zig juxtaposing the star's saucy sexiness with naïf trappings—like Brigitte Bardot in her gingham bikini—that makes the image so effective.
**Est: $4,000-$5,000.**

**577. Casino de Paris/Mistinguett/Paris Qui Brille.** 1931.
29$^3$/$_4$ x 85 in./75.6 x 216 cm
Centrale Publicité, Paris
Cond B+/Slight tears and stains.
Ref: PAI-XXXI, 13
Zig's poster for Mistinguett's "Paris Dazzles" revue more than lives up to its designation: a bejeweled Mistinguett, pink-tinged feather in one hand, reins of her playful team of blue horses in the other, spotlit against a black background. This is the larger format.
**Est: $3,000-$4,000.**

**578. Casino de Paris/Mistnguett/Paris Qui Brille.** 1931.
15$^1$/$_2$ x 35 in./39 x 88.8 cm
Central Publicité, Paris
Cond A.
Ref: Folies-Bergère, 67; Delhaye, p. 35; PAI-XXXI, 14
In this poster for the revue "Paris Dazzles" at the Casino de Paris, Zig depicts Mistinguett perched on a stool, with the city at her feet, displaying most of her visible assets. Setting off all that skin: long red gloves, oodles of dripping jewelry and an insouciant little hat. This is the smaller format.
**Est: $2,500-$3,000.**

**579. Le Beguin Americain.**
10$^1$/$_2$ x 15$^7$/$_8$ in./26.8 x 40.2 cm
*Gouache, pencil and metallic silver costume design.* Framed.
The word "béguin" has many possible interpretations. It can mean a woman's extravagant hairdo. Or it can be a particularly intense momentary passion. It's also a person who is nothing more than a desirable object. Or it can just mean plain, old "fancy." Absolutely every one of these potential definitions apply to this Zig presentation of an outfit that only a showgirl could love. In what seems to be a feather-star-and heart adorned bathing suit, this "Fancy American" maiden is but one of the titillating countries that must have been on display in "The International" revue, a title mentioned by name under this get-up's appellation.
**Est: $1,400-$1,700.**

# BOOKS AND PERIODICALS

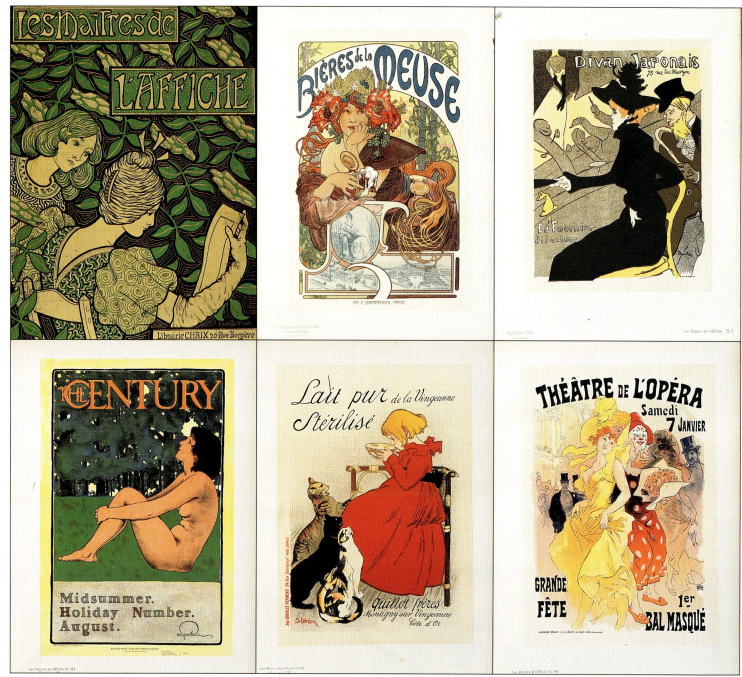

**580. Les Maitres de l'Affiche, 1896-1900.**
Each: 11³/₈ x 15³/₄ in./29 x 40 cm
Published by Librairie Chaix, Paris
Ref: Maitres; PAI-XXXII, 569
*All 256 Plates. In five volumes, each with the Paul Berthon-designed covers. Introductory text pages by Roger Marx.* Excellent condition, with tissue overlays. Slight foxing on six supplemental plates.
This series of original lithographic reproductions of posters—four plates were mailed to subscribers each month for five years, with sixteen supplements—crowned the affichomanie at the end of the 19th century. Alain Weill makes two interesting observations about this series. Its appeal, in part, was due to its manageable size: "At the time posters posed a problem which, moreover, has still not been solved: how to

keep and enjoy a collection consisting of very large prints which one has to preserve rolled or flat in some cabinet . . . (This book) provided a reduction of the most valued and consequently the most widely known posters, thus enabling collectors and other interested people to examine quickly and easily the main works of the current advertising production." Weill notes that one month's offerings (4 prints) could be had at the same price as an original poster by Lautrec, Mucha or the other greats of the poster pantheon: "This is not at all surprising since the posters were printed in great quantities on ordinary paper and, to boot, the one-time art and plate costs were assumed by the company whose product it advertised; the dealers paid printers only for the overrun they wished to acquire. Hence, we must consider it normal that *Les Maitres*

*de l'Affiche*, specially produced by means of lithography on quality paper, was offered for sale at the price of an original poster. The people did not perceive these two types of products as being in competition. They were infatuated with small prints and with this kind of compilation" (Maitres/Images Graphique edition, pp. 4 & 5). *At a time when individual plates are selling well above $2,000, it isn't far fetched to say that a complete set is unlikely to ever be offered again. Collectors beware!*
**Est: $40,000-$50,000.**

For other publications, see Mucha's *Le Pater* (Lot 458) and Crauzat's catalogue raisonné of *Steinlen* (Lot 540)

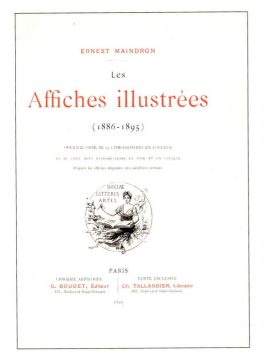

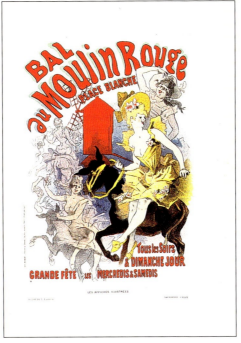

**581**

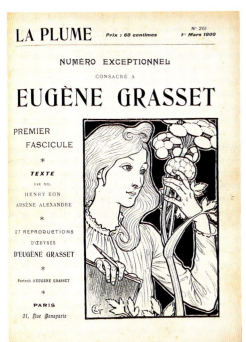

**582**

**583**

**581. Les Affiches Illustrées 1886-1895,
    by Ernest Maindron.**
9 x 12¹/₂ in./23 x 30.7 cm
Published by G. Boudet, Paris, 1896.
Hardcover binding in overall excellent condition; slight
tears in tipped-on covers.
Ref: PAI-XXXIII, 618 (var)
256 pages, with 64 color reproductions, 102 in black-
and-white.
Limited, numbered edition of 1,025 copies.
Probably the single most important reference work in
the field of poster art; the French text is erudite and
enthusiastic, the reproductions sumptuous and plenti-
ful. Contains the most complete listing of Chéret
posters (882 of them) prior to the Broido update. *This
is Steinlen's personal copy, dedicated to him by the
publisher, Boudet.*
**Est: $3,000-$4,000.**

**582. La Plume/Grasset.** 1900.
7 x 10 in./18 x 25.3 cm
3 issues in hardcover binding.
These numbers were devoted to the work of Eugène
Grasset, and they contain critiques, biography and
approximately 100 illustrations covering the entire
spectrum of the decorative art of this Art Nouveau
master.
**Est: $600-$800.**

**583. Das Moderne Plakat, by Jean-Louis Sponsel.**
    1897.
8¹/₂ x 10⁷/₈ in./21.2 x 27.7 cm
Verlag von Gerhard Kuhtmann, Dresden
Ref: PAI-XXIII, 538
A country-by-country survey of posters, published in
Germany in 1897. Its wide scope required a total of
316 pages and 318 illustrations, including 52 plates in
color. Coming a year after Mandron's 1896 classic,
this monumental work is further proof of the worldwide *affichomanie* ("poster craze") of the period. A
rare and valuable reference for the serious collector.
**Est: $1,700-$2,000.**

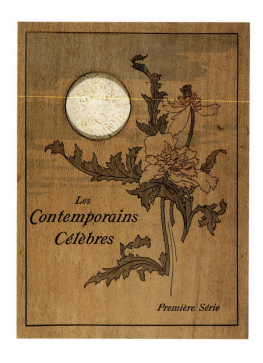

**584**

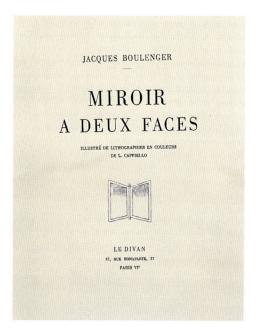

**585**

**586**

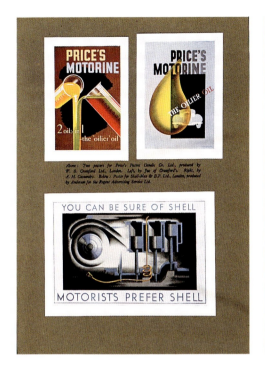

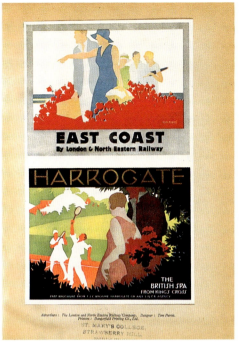

**587**

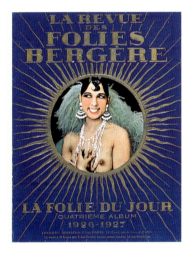
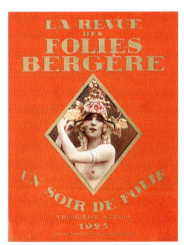

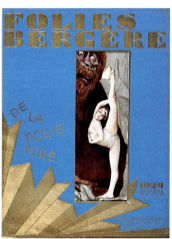

**588**

## BOOKS AND PERIODICALS (cont'd)

**584. Les Contemporains Célèbres.** 1904.
10 x 12³/₄ in./25.2 x 32.4 cm
Published by Publications Octave Beauchamp &
G. de Malherbe, Paris
Excellent condition; hardcover binding.
Ref: PAI-XXXII, 589
A volume published by Lefèvre-Utile and Octave Beauchamp, Paris, and distributed by G. de Malherbe, containing portraits, biographies, signed testimonials and some of Cappiello's finest caricatures of contemporary celebrities. You might be asking yourself just what do Sarah Bernhardt, Anatole France, Réjane, Granier, Massenet, Bartholdi and the Queen of Madagascar have in common? The answer is quite simple: They all love Lefèvre-Utile biscuits, of course.
**Est: $2,000-$2,500.**

**585. Miroir a Deux Faces, by Jacques Boulenger,**
**illustrated by Leonetto Cappiello.** 1933.
8 x 10¹/₄ in./20.2 x 26 cm
Published by Editions du Divan, Paris
Boxed set; excellent condition.
Ref: PAI-XXXII, 591 (var)
*Deluxe edition: Includes original signed preparatory pencil drawing by Cappiello.*
One of only 12 copies printed on Montval velin with addition of color progression proofs, and with dedication by the author. Total number of entire edition was only 80 copies!

The two volumes contain 33 color lithographs executed directly on stone by Cappiello.
The artist's acute eye compliments the narrative, one whose two faces of the same mirror represent the romantic novel's dual protagonists' memoirs—the first volume recounting the man's recollections, while the second relates the parallel memories of past events from the woman's point of view.
**Est: $4,000-$5,000.**

**586. Schnackenberg: Kostume/Plakate und**
**Dekorationen, by Oskar Bie.** 1922.
10 x 13 in./25.5 x 33 cm
Published by Musarion-Verlag, München.
Hardcover binding; cover slightly soiled.
Ref: PAI-XXX, 644
Schnackenberg was an unusual graphic artist—a cultured and sophisticated esthete who created only a handful of posters, mostly for his acquaintances in Munich theatrical circles. His sense of design was highly individual, a quaint amalgam of caricature and fantasy that he called "suggestive dreams." This is the only known book to date that focuses exclusively on the works of the great German artist, displaying the spectacular sweep of his lithographic and decorative mastery, as well as his costume designs, in forty full-page illustrations, most of which are in color.
**Est: $1,200-$1,500.**

**587. 18 Publicity Annuals.** 1924-1948.
8¹/₈ x 11³/₈ in./20.5 x 29 cm
Published by The Studio, London
All in hardcover bindings, except 1932.
Over 1,000 poster illustrations; replete with articles on posters and their artists. The titles and editors changed—1924: *Posters and their Designers*, by Sydney R. Jones; 1925: *Art & Publicity*, by Jones; 1926-1929: *Posters & Publicity*, edited by Jones, Harrison and Mercer & Gaunt; 1930-31: *Modern Publicity*, edited by Mercer & Gaunt; *1932-1948: Modern Publicity*: 10 annual volumes. Includes tip-on reproductions and an index to each volume. An incredible library for the serious collector!
**Est: $4,000-$5,000.**

**588. Folies-Bergère: 12 Programs. 1926-1936.**
Each: 9³/₈ x 12³/₈ in./23.8 x 31.4 cm
Each in excellent condition; in presentation carton.
All the great music hall stars of the '20s and '30s are represented in these lavishly-illustrated programs: Joséphine Baker, Betty Campson, Glenn Ellyn, Les Dodge Twins, Chrysis, Suzy Beryl and Miss Bluebell.
*Due to the risqué nature of the illustrations, you must be 18 years old to view them!*
**Est: $2,500-$3,000.**

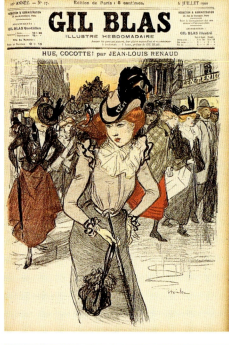

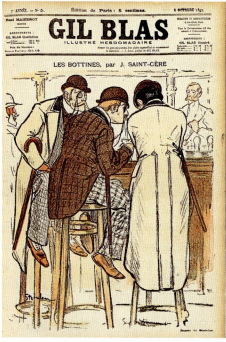

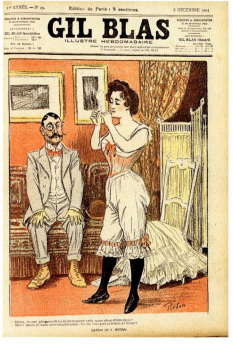

589

**589. Gil Blas: 1891-1901.**
10$^1$/$_2$ x 15$^3$/$_8$ in./26.5 x 39 cm
Five leather bound volumes; overall excellent condition;
slight staining at paper edges.
Contains short stories, social commentary, music and
poetry, but most importantly, about 1,000 illustrations
of which more than 300 are color illustrations by
Steinlen. Featured artists include Balluriau, Guillaume,
Guydo, Grün, Bernard, Redon, Poulbot, Bac and other
designers well-known to poster collectors.
**Est: $8,000-$10,000.**

**590. Le Rire: 1894-1919.**
9 x 11$^7$/$_8$ in./22.5 x 30 cm
Overall excellent condition; bound in 25 volumes.
Ref: PAI-XXXIV, 618 (var)
*One of the largest collections of this important jour-
nal ever assembled.*

This is the famous satirical weekly to which Lautrec
contributed drawings, mostly in color and all 18 appear
here. Also important (and delightful!) are the numerous
fine caricatures by Cappiello, including his first published
work—sketches of Puccini and Novelli—in the July 2,
1898, issue. Other artists represented include some of
the top posterists of the period: Hermann-Paul, Jossot,
Léandre, Forain, Willette, Valloton, Métivet, Roedel,
Faivre, Steinlen and Roubille. *An incredible find!*
**Est: $7,000-$9,000.**

**591. L'Assiette au Beurre: 1901-1909.**
10 x 12$^1$/$_2$ in./25.5 x 32 cm
8 volumes, numbers 1-416, in publisher's original yearly
embossed bindings, with monthly decorative wrappers.

This was surely the most hard-hitting of all the political
and social satire journals of the period. It was almost
entirely visual, with each 16-page issue consisting
mainly of full page drawings, half of which were in
color. The serious (abuses of power by business, army,
landlords, etc.) was tempered by more light-hearted,
but sharp examinations of mother-in-laws, cuckolds,
feminists, actresses, sportsmen, etc. Poster collectors
will recognize the work of Edouard Bernard, Jules
Chéret, Cappiello, Hermann-Paul, Iribe, Jossot, Léandre, Lefèvre, Meunier, Orazi, Poulbot, Redon, Savignol,
Steinlen, Villon, Widhopff and Willette. Yearly indexes
provided in this deluxe edition. *Must be seen!*
**Est: $7,000-$9,000.**

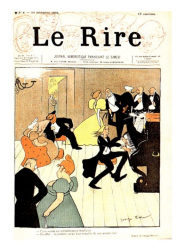

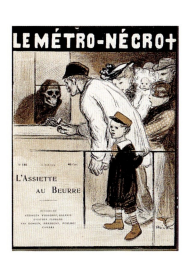

# BIBLIOGRAPHY

The following is a list of books used in the preparation of this catalogue. In the interest of brevity, these works have been abbreviated in the Reference ("Ref:") section of the description of each lot. The abbreviations can be found below accompanied by the work's full title, publisher's name, city and date of publication. It should be noted that we have made no reference to the many magazines and annuals which are essential tools in this area, such as *The Poster, Estampe et Affiche, La Plume, Arts et Metiers Graphiques, Vendre, Das Plakat, Gebrauchsgraphik* and *Graphis Posters*.

NOTE: References to prior PAI books are limited to the last auction in which the poster was offered. We refer readers to our book, *Poster Prices VII*, which gives the complete record of each poster offered at the first 36 PAI sales.

**Abdy**
*The French Poster*, by Jane Abdy. Clarkson N. Potter. New York, 1969.

**Absinthe**
*Absinthe: History in a Bottle*, by Barnaby Conrad III. Chronicle Books, San Francisco, 1988.

**Absinthe Affiches**
*L'Absinthe: Les Affiches*, by Marie-Claude Delahaye. Musée de l'Absinthe, Auvers-sur-Oise, 2002.

**Adriani**
*Toulouse-Lautrec: The Complete Graphic Works*, by Götz Adriani. The catalogue raisonné, featuring the Gerstenberg collection. Thames & Hudson, London, 1988.

**Affiche Opéra**
*L'Affiche Opéra*. Catalogue of the exhibition at the Musée de la Seita, Paris, Oct. 1894-Jan. 1985.

**Affiche Réclame**
*Quand l'Affiche Faisait de la Reclame!* Editions de la Réunion des Musées Nationaux, Paris. 1991.

**Affiches Azur**
*Affiches d'Azur—100 Ans d'Affiches de la Côte d'Azur et de Monaco*, by Charles Martini de Chateauneuf. Editions Gilletta, Nice, 1992.

**Affiches Riviera**
*Affiches de la Riviera*, by Annie de Montry, Françoise Lepeuve & Charles Martini de Chateauneuf. Editions Gilletta, Nice-Matin, 2001.

**Air France**
*Air France/Affiches/Posters 1933-1983*, by Jérôme Peignot. Fernand Hazan, Paris, 1988.

**Ailes**
*Voici des Ailes, affiches de cycles*. Catalogue from the exhibition at the Musée d'Art ey d'Industrie, Saint-Ätienne, May 3-September 22, 2002.

**Ali d'Italia**
*Ali d'Italia: Manifesti Dipinti Sul Vulo In Italia, 1908-1943*. Edited by Maurizio Scudiero and Massimo Cirulli. Publicity Print Press, New York, 2000.

**Alimentaires**
*Un Siècle de Reclames Alimentaires*, by F. Ghozland. Editions Milan, 1984.

**Alo**
*Alo/Affiches Touristiques*, by Georges Hallo and Claude Finon. Editions Clouet, Paris, 2002.

**Alpes**
*Les Alpes à l'Affiche*, by Yves Ballu. Editions Glenat, Grenoble, 1987.

**American Posters**
*Posters American Style*, by Therese Thau Heyman. Harry N. Abrams, New York, 1998.

**American Railroad**
*Travel by Train: The American Railroad Poster*, 1870-1950, by Michael E. Zega and John E. Gruber. Indiana University Press, Bloomington, 2002.

**Art & Auto**
*L'Art et Automobile*, by Hervé Poulain. Les Clefs du Temps, Zoug, 1973.

**Art Deco**
*Art Deco Graphics*, by Patricia Frantz Kery. Harry N. Abrams, New York, 1986.

**Art du Biscuit**
*L'Art du Biscuit*, by Patrick Lefèvre-Utile. Éditions Hazan, Verona, 1995.

**Art et Biscuits**
*L'Art et les Biscuits: La publicité de la firme Lefèvre-Utile de 1897 à 1914*. Edited by Georges Herscher. Editions du Chêne, Paris, 1978.

**Auto Posters**
*100 Years of Auto Posters*, by Dominique Dubarry. Maeght Editeur, Paris, 1991.

**Auto Show I**
*1er Salon de l'Affiche Automobile*. Catalogue of the exhibition, compiled by Jacques Perier, and sponsored by the Automobile Club de France, Paris, October 1978.

**Auto Show II**
*2eme Salon de l'Affiche Automobile*. Catalogue of the exhibition at the Musée de l'Affiche, Paris, September to October 1979. Edited by Jacques Perier.

**Auto Show III**
*L 'Automobile et la Publicité*. Catalogue of the exhibition at the Musée de la Publicité, Paris, 1984.

**Avant Garde**
*The 20th Century Poster—Design of the Avant Garde*, by Dawn Ades. The catalogue-book of the exhibition of the Walker Art Center, Minneapolis, 1984. Abbeville Press, New York, 1984.

**Bargiel et Zagrodzki**
*Steinlen-Affichiste. Catalogue Raisonné*, by Réjane Bargiel and Christophe Zagrodzki. Editions du Grant-Pont, Lausanne, 1986. (Distributed in the United States by Posters Please, Inc., New York City).

**Baumberger**
*Otto Baumberger 1889-1961*. Catalogue of the exhibition of Baumberger posters held at the Museum für Gestaltung Zurich, May-July 1988, and subsequently in Basel and Essen.

**Belgique/Paris**
*L'Affiche en Belgique 1880-1980*. Catalogue of the exhibition at the Musée de l'Affiche, Paris, 1980. Text by Alain Weill.

**Belle Epoque 1970**
*La Belle Epoque—Belgian Posters*. The catalogue-book of the touring exhibition of the Wittamer-De Camps collection. Text by Yolande Oostens-Wittamer. Grossman Publishers, New York, 1971.

**Berthon & Grasset**
*Berthon & Grasset*, by Victor Arwas. Academy Editions, London; Rizzoli, New York, 1978.

**Bicycle Posters**
*100 Years of Bicycle Posters*, by Jack Rennert. Harper & Row, New York, 1973.

**Bouvet**
*Bonnard: The Complete Graphic Work*, by Francis Bouvet. Rizzoli, New York.

**Broders**
*Voyages: Les Affiches de Roger Broders*, by Annie de Montry and Françoise Lepeuve. Syros-Alternatives, Paris, 1991.

**Broders Travel**
*Roger Proders/Travel Posters*, by Alain Weill and Israel Perry. Queen Art Publishes, New York, 2002.

**Broido**
*The Posters of Jules Chéret: 46 Full Color Plates and an Illustrated Catalogue Raisonné, 2nd ed.*, by Lucy Broido. Dover Publications, N.Y., 1992.

**Brown & Reinhold**
*The Poster Art of A. M. Cassandre*, by Robert K. Brown and Susan Reinhold. E. P. Dutton, New York, 1979.

**Brussels**
*Homage to Brussels: The Art of Belgian Posters 1895-1915.* Catalogue of the 1992 exhibition at the Jane Voorhees Zimmerli Art Museum at Rutgers University, New Brunswick, New Jersey.

**Buffalo Bill**
*100 Posters of Buffalo Bill's Wild West*, by Jack Rennert. Darien House, New York, 1976.

**Buffalo Bill/Legend**
*Buffalo Bill's Wild West: An American Legend*, by R.L. Wilson, with Greg Martin. Random House, New York, 1998.

**Cappiello**
*Cappiello.* Catalogue of the exhibition at the Galerie Nationale du Grand Palais, Paris, 1981.

**Cappiello/St. Vincent**
*Leonetto Cappiello–dalla pittura alla grafica.* Catalogue of the exhibition in Centro Culturale Saint-Vincent. Text by Raffaele Monti & Elisabeth Matucci. Artificio, Firenze, 1985.

**Carlu**
*Jean Carlu.* Catalogue of the exhibition of the Posters of Jean Carlu at the Musée de l'Affiche, Paris, 1980.

**Cassandre/Suntory**
*Cassandre: Every Face of the Great Master, 1901-1968.* Catalogue of the exhibition held at the Suntory Museum, Osaka, June-August, 1995.

**Chaumont/Exposons**
*Exposons Affichons: 300 affiches d'expositions.* Catalogue for the 5th annual Poster Festival of Chaumont, France. Includes a section on "L'Affiche pour l'affiche" (Posters on Posters) from the Rennert collection. Somogy, Paris, 1994.

**Chemins de Fer**
*100 Ans d'Affiches des Chemins de Fer*, by Pierre Belves. Edition NM— La Vie du Rail, Paris, 1980.

**Chocolate Posters**
*Chocolate Posters*, by Israel Perry and Alain Weill. Queen Art Publishers Inc., New York, 2002.

**Cirque**
*Le Cirque Iconographie.* The circus poster catalogue of the Bibliothèque Nationale, Paris, 1969.

**Colin**
*100 Posters of Paul Colin*, by Jack Rennert. Images Graphiques, New York, 1977.

**Colin Affichiste**
*Paul Colin: Affichiste*, by Alain Weill & Jack Rennert. Editions Denoel, Paris, 1989.

**Color of Spain**
*El Color de España/The Color of Spain: Tourism, Festivities and Exhibitions from 1890 to 1940*, by Jordi Carulla and Arnau Carulla. Postermil, Barcelona, 2000.

**Côte Belge**
*Affiches de la Côte Belge 1890-1950*, by Marie-Laurence Bernard. The collection of Roland Florizoone. Uitgeverij Marc van de Wiele, Brugge, 1992.

**Crauzat**
*L'Oeuvre Gravé et Lithographié de Steinlen*, by E. de Crauzat. Société de Propogation des Livres d'Art, Paris, 1913. Reprinted by Alan Wofsy Fine Arts, San Francisco, 1983.

**Czwiklitzer**
*Les Affiches de Pablo Picasso*, by Christopher Czwiklitzer. Art-C.C., Bâle-Paris, 1970.

**Darracott**
*The First World War in Posters*, by Joseph Darracott. Dover Publications.

**Deco Affiches**
*Affiches Art Deco*, by Alain Weill. Inter-Livres, Paris, 1990.

**Delhaye**
*Art Deco Posters and Graphics*, by Jean Delhaye. Academy Editions, London, 1977.

**DFP-I**
*Das Frühe Plakat in Europa und den USA.* Volume I. British and American Posters. Edited by Ruth Malhotra and Christina Thon. Mann Verlag, Berlin, 1973.

**DFP-II**
*Das Frühe Plakat in Europa und den USA.* Volume II.French and Belgian Posters. Edited by Ruth Malhotra, Marjan Rinkleff and Bernd Schalicke. Mann Verlag, Berlin, 1977.

**DFP-III**
*Das Frühe Plakat in Europa und den USA.* Volume III. German Posters. Edited by Helga Hollman, Ruth Malhotra, Alexander Pilipczuk, Helga Prignitz, Christina Thon. Mann Verlag, Berlin, 1980.

**España**
*España en 1000 Carteles*, by Jordi Carulla and Arnau Carulla. Postermil, Barcelona, 1995.

**Femme s'Affiche**
*La Femme s'Affiche.* Catalogue of the exhibition of the Kellenberger collection held in Montreux, 1990.

**De Feure**
*Georges De Feure: Maitre du Symbolisme et de l'Art Nouveau*, by Ian Millman. ACR Editions, Courbevoie (Paris), 1991.

**Fix-Masseau**
*Pierre Fix-Masseau: Affiches 1928-1983.* Catalogue of the exhbition at the Bibliothèque Nationale, Paris, 1983.

**Folies-Bergère**
*100 Years of Posters of the Folies Bergère and Music Halls of Paris*, by Alain Weill. Images Graphiques, New York, 1977.

**French Opera**
*French Opera Posters 1868-1930*, by Lucy Broido. Dover Publications, New York, 1976.

**Frey**
*Toulouse-Lautrec: A Life*, by Julia Frey. Viking Penguin, New York, 1994.

**Gallo**
*The Poster in History*, by Max Gallo. American Heritage Publishing, New York, 1974.

**Gold**
*First Ladies of the Poster: The Gold Collection*, by Laura Gold. Posters Please Inc., New York City, 1998.

**Golf**
*L'Affiche de Golf/Golf Posters*,by Alexis Orloff. ƒditions Milan, Toulouse, 2002.

**Gourmand**
*Un Voyage Gourmand: 60 affiches de gastronomie*, by Alain Weill. Catalogue of the exhibition at the Musée-Galerie de la Seita, Paris, 1984.

**Grain de Beauté**
*Grain de Beauté–Un Siecle de Beauté par la Publicité*, by Claudine Chevrel and Béatrice cornet. Somogy Editions d'Art, Paris, 1993.

**Health Posters**
*Posters of Health*, by Marine Robert-Sterkendries. Therabel Pharma, Brussels, 1996.

**Hohlwein 1874-1949**
*Ludwig Hohlwein 1874-1949: Kunstgewerbe und Reklamekunst*, by Volker Duvigneau and Norbert Gota. Klinkhardt & Bierman, Munich, 1996.

**Hohlwein/Stuttgart**
*Ludwig Hohlwein: Plakate der Jahre 1906-1940.* Catalogue of the Hohlwein exhibition at the Staatsgalerie Stuttgart in Germany, March-April 1985. Text by Christian Schneegass.

**Iconography of Power**
*Iconography of Power: Soviet Political Posters Under Lenin and Stalin*, by Victoria E. Bonnell. University of California Press, Berkeley, 1997.

**Images of an Era**
*Images of an Era: The American Poster, 1945-1975.* Catalogue of the exhibition of the Smithsonian Institution, Washington. D.C., 1975.

**Ives**
*Pierre Bonnard/The Graphic Art,* by Colta Ives, Helen Giambruni and Sasha M. 1989-1990. Harry N. Abrams, New York, 1989.

**Kamekura**
*Exhibition of Works by Yusaku Kamekura.* Catalogue of the exhibition held at the Kirin Plaza, Osaka, 1988.

**Karcher**
*Memoire de la Rue–Souvenirs d'un imprimeur et d'un afficheur.* Illustrated book of the archives of the Karcher printing firm of Paris with introduction by Alain Weill. WM Editions, Paris, 1986. (Distributed in the U.S.A. by Posters Please, Inc., New York with a translation of text and the addition of an index).

**Lauder**
*American Art Posters of the1890s* (The Leonard A. Lauder Collection). Catalogue of the exhibition of the Metropolitan Museum of Art, New York, October 1987—January 1988. Text by David W. Kiehl. Harry N. Abrams, New York, 1987.

**Lendl/Paris**
*Alphonse Mucha: La Collection Ivan Lendl.* Catalogue of the exhibition at Musée de la Publicité, Paris, 1989. Text by Jack Rennert. Editions Syros/Alternatives, Paris.

**Litfass-Bier**
*Litfass-Bier: Historische Bierplakate-Sammlung Heinrich Becker.* Edited by Gerhard Dietrich. Plakat/Konzepte, Hannover, 1998.

**Loie Fuller**
*Loie Fuller: Magician of Light.* Catalogue of the exhibition at the Virginia Museum, Richmond, 1979.

**Looping the Loop**
*Looping the Loop: Posters of Flight,* by Henry Serrano Villard and Willis M. Allen, Jr. Kales Press, San Diego, California, 2000.

**Maindron**
*Les Affiches Illustrées, 1886-1895,* by Ernest Maindron. G. Boudet, Paris, 1896.

**Maitres**
*Les Maitres de l'Affiche 1896-1900,* by Roger Marx. Imprimerie Chaix, Paris 1896-1900. Reprinted as Masters of the Poster 1896-1900 by Images Graphiques, New York, 1977, and The Complete "Masters of the Poster," by Dover Publications, New York, 1990.

**Mangold**
*Burkhard Mangold (1873-1950).* Catalogue of the exhibition at the Kunstgewerbemuseum, Zurich, 1984.

**Margadant**
*Das Schweizer Plakat/The Swiss Poster, 1900-1983,* by Bruno Margadant. Birkhaus Verlag, Basel, 1983.

**Margolin**
*American Poster Renaissance,* by Victor Margolin. Watson-Guptill Publications, New York, 1975.

**Marques**
*Images de Marques/Marques d'Images: 100 marques du patrimoine français,* by Daniel Cauzard, Jean Perret and Yves Ronin. Editions Ramsay, Paris, 1989.

**Marseille**
*Marseille s'Affiche–Regards sur la Provence,* by Patrick Boulanger. Editions E.E.M.P., Marseilles, 1996.

**Marx**
*Bonnard: Lithographie,* edited by Claude Roger-Marx. Monte Carlo, 1952.

**Masters 1900**
*Masters of the Poster 1900,* by Alan Weill. Bibliothèque de l'Image, Paris, 2001.

**Mauzan**
*The Posters of Mauzan–A Catalogue Raisonné,* by Mirande Carnévalé-Mauzan. Exclusive North American distribution by Posters Please, Inc., New York, 2001.

**Mauzan Affiches**
*Mauzan: Affiches/Oeuvres Diverses,* by A. Lancellotti. Casa Editrice d'Arte Bestettie Tumminelli, Milan, ca. 1928.

**Mauzan/Treviso**
*Manifesti di A. L. Mauzan,* by Antonio Mazzaroli. Editrice Canova, Treviso, 1983.

**Menegazzi-I**
*Il Manifesto Italiano,* by Luigi Menegazzi. Electa Editrice, Milan, ca. 1976.

**Meunier**
*Georges Meunier–affichiste 1869-1942.* Catalogue of the exhibition at Bibliothèque Fourney, Paris, 1978.

**Modern American Posters**
*The Modern American Poster,* by J. Stewart Johnson. Catalogue of the Japanese exhibition of the posters from the N.Y. Musuem of Modern Art collection, 1983-84. Little Brown, Boston, 1983.

**Modern Poster**
*The Modern Poster,* by Stuart Wrede. Catalogue of the exhibition at the Museum of Modern Art, New York, 1988. New York Graphic Society/Little Brown and Co., Boston, 1988.

**Moderno Francés**
*El Cartel Moderno Francés.* Catalogue for the Colin, Carlu, Loupot and Cassandre exhibition at the Museo Nacional Centro de Arte Reina Sofia, Madrid, 2001.

**Montagne**
*La Montagne s'Affiche,* by Daniel Hillion. Editions Ouest-France, Rennes, 1991.

**Mouron**
*A. M. Cassandre,* by Henri Mouron. Rizzoli, New York, 1985.

**Mucha/Art Nouveau**
*Alphonse Mucha: The Spirit of Art Nouveau.* Catalogue of the touring exhibition organized by Art Services International, Alexandria, Virginia, 1998. Edited by Victor Arwas, Jana Brabcovà-Orlikovà and Anna Dvoràk.

**Mucha/Master**
*Alphonse Mucha: The Master of Art Nouveau,* by Jiri Mucha. Hamlyn Publishing Group, Feltham, 1967.

**Murray-Robertson**
*Grasset: Pionnier de l'Art Nouveau,* by Anne Murray-Robertson. Bibliothèque des Arts, Paris/Editions 24 Heures, Lausanne, 1981.

**Musée d'Affiche**
*Musée d'Affiche.* Catalogue for the inaugural exhibition titled Trois Siècles d'Affiches Françaises, Paris, 1978.

**Negripub**
*Negripub: L'image des Noirs dans la publicité,* by Raymond Bachollet, Jean-Barthelemi Debost, Anne-Claude Lelieur and Marie-Christine Peyrière. The book of the exhibition at the Bibliothèque Forney, 1992. Editions Somogy, Paris.

**Olympics**
*L'Olympisme par l'Affiche/Olympism through Posters.* International Olympic Committee, Lausanne, 1983.

**Operetta**
*Operetta: A Theatrical History,* by Richard Traubner. Doubleday & Company, Inc., Garden City, New York, 1983.

**PAI – Books of the auctions organized by Poster Auctions International, Inc.**

**PAI-I**
*Premier Posters.* Book of the auction held in New York City, March 9, 1985.

**PAI-II**
*Prize Posters.* Book of the auction held in Chicago, November 10, 1985.

**PAI-III**
*Poster Impressions.* Book of the auction held in New York City, June 1, 1986.

**PAI-IV**
*Prestige Posters.* Book of the auction held in New York City, May 3, 1987.

**PAI-V**
*Poster Pizzazz.* Book of the auction held in Universal City, California, November 22, 1987.

**PAI-VI**
*Poster Splendor.* Book of the auction held in New York City, May I, 1988.

**PAI-VII**
*Poster Potpourri.* Book of the auction held in New York, November 13, 1988.

**PAI-VIII**
*Poster Treasures.* Book of the auction held in New York, May 7, 1989.

**PAI-IX**
*Poster Palette.* Book of the auction held in New York, November 12, 1989.

**PAI-X**
*Elegant Posters.* Book of the auction held in New York, May 20, 1990.

**PAI-XI**
*Poster Passion.* Book of the auction held in New York, November 11, 1990.

**PAI-XII**
*Poster Panache.* Book of the auction held in New York, May 5, 1991.

**PAI XIII**
*Poster Jubilee.* Book of the auction held in New York. November 10, 1991.

**PAI-XIV**
*Poster Extravaganza.* Book of the auction held in New York May 3, 1992.

**PAI XV**
*Rarest Posters.* Book of the auction held in New York, November 8, 1992.

**PAI-XVI**
*Poster Parade.* Book of the auction held in New York, May 2. 1993.

**PAI-XVII**
*Poster Classics.* Book of the auction held in New York, November 14, 1993.

**PAI-XVIII**
*Winning Posters.* Book of the auction held in New York, May 1, 1994.

**PAI-XIX**
*Prima Posters.* Book of the auction held in New York, November 13, 1994.

**PAI-XX**
*Poster Panorama.* Book of the auction held in New York, May 7, 1995.

**PAI-XXI**
*Timeless Posters.* Book of the auction held in New York, November 12, 1995.

**PAI-XXII**
*Positively Posters.* Auction held in New York City, May 5, 1996.

**PAI-XXIII**
*Poster Delights.* Auction held in New York City, November 10, 1996.

**PAI-XXIV**
*Poster Pleasures.* Auction held in New York City, May 4, 1997.

**PAI-XXV**
*Sterling Posters.* Auction held in New York City, November 9, 1997.

**PAI-XXVI**
*Postermania.* Auction held in New York City, May 3, 1998.

**PAI-XXVII**
*Poster Ecstasy.* Auction held in New York City, November 8, 1998.

**PAI-XXVIII**
*Poster Vogue.* Auction held in New York City, May 2, 1999.

**PAI-XXIX**
*Posters for the Millennium.* Auction held in New York City, November 4, 1999.

**PAI-XXX**
*Poster Allure.* Auction held in New York City, May 7, 2000.

**PAI-XXXI**
*Poster Power.* Auction held in New York City, November 12, 2000.

**PAI-XXXII**
*Dream Posters.* Auction held in New York City, May 6, 2001.

**PAI-XXXIII**
*Swank Posters.* Auction held in New York City, November 11, 2001.

**PAI-XXXIV**
*Poster Pride.* Auction held in New York City, May 5, 2002.

**PAI-XXXV**
*Posters Perform.* Auction held in New York City, November 10, 2002.

**Parrish**
*Maxfield Parrish*, by Coy Ludwig. Watson-Guptill Publications, New York, 1973.

**Parrish/Japan**
*Maxfield Parrish: A Retrospective.* Exhibition catalogue published by Brain Trust Inc., Tokyo, 1995.

**Passenger Liner**
*Era of the Passenger Liner*, by Nicholas T. Cairis. Pegasus Books, London, 1992.

**Penfield**
*Designed to Persuade: The Graphic Art of Edward Penfield.* Catalogue of the exhibition at The Hudson River Museum, Yonkers, New York, 1984. Text by David Gibson.

**Petite Reine**
*La Petite Reine: Le Vélo en Affiches à la fin du XIXeme.* Catalogue exhibition of bicycle posters of the end of the 19th century held at Musée de l'Affiche, Paris, May to September, 1979.

**Plakat Schweiz**
*Das Plakat in der Schweiz*, by Willy Rotzler, Fritz Schörer and Karl Wobmann. Edition Stemmle, Zurich, 1990.

**Plakate München**
*Plakate in München 1840-1940.* Catalogue of the exhibition of Munich posters at the Münchner Stadtmuseum, 1975-76.

**Plakatkunst**
*Plakatkunst von Toulouse-Lautrec bis Benetton*, by Jürgen Döring. Edition Braus und Museum für Kunst und Gewerbe, Hamburg, 1994.

**Plakatkunst 1880-1935**
*Plakatkunst 1880-1935*, by Christiane Friese. Klett-Cota, Stuttgart, 1994.

**Presse**
*Affiches de Presse.* Catalogue of the exhibition at the Musée de la Seita, Paris, February-March, 1984.

**Price**
*Posters*, by Charles Matlack Price. George W. Bricka, New York, 1913.

**Rawls**
*Wake Up, America! World War I and the American Poster*, by Walton Rawls. Abbeville Press, New York, 1988.

**Reims**
*Exposition d'Affiches Artistiques Françaises et Etrangères.* The catalogue of the November 1896 exhibition held in Reims. Reissued in a numbered edition of 1,000 copies by the Musée de l'Affiche in 1980.

**Rennert/Weill**
*Alphonse Mucha: The Complete Posters and Panels*, by Jack Rennert and Alain Weill. G. K. Hall, Boston, 1984.

**Ricordi**
*Grafica Ricordi: Dal Manifesto Storico all produzione d'avanguardia*, by Giovanni Sangiorgi, Giorgia Mascherpa and Giulia Veronesi. Ente Premi, Roma, Ricordi, 1967.

**Rockwell Illustrator**
*Norman Rockwell, Illustrator*, by Arthur L. Guptill. Watson-Guptill, New York, 1946.

**Rockwell's America**
*Norman Rockwell's America*, by Christopher Finch. Readers' Digest/Harry N. Abrams, B.V., The Netherlands, 1976.

**Rogers**
*A Book of the Poster*, by W. S. Rogers. Greening & Co., London, 1901.

**Russian Films**
*Film Posters of the Russian Avant-Garde*, by Susan Pack. Benedikt Taschen Verlag, Koln, Germany, 1995.

**Salon des Cent**
*Le Salon des Cent: 1894-1900.* Affiches d'artistes, by Jocelyne Van Deputte. Catalogue of the exhibition held at the Musée Carnavalet, Paris, 1995.

**Salon des Cent/Neumann**
*Le Affiches du Salon des Cent.* Catalogue of the exhibition at Fondation Neumann, Gingins, Switzerland, 2000, and Musée des Arts Décoratifs, Bordeaux, 2001.

**Savignac**
*Savignac.* The catalogue raisonné published to coincide with the Bibliothèque Fourney retrospective. Paris Bibliothèques, 2001.

**Schardt**
*Paris 1900,* by Hermann Schardt. G P. Putnam's Sons, New York, 1970; reprinted in 1987 by Portland House, New York. (Originally published as Paris l900: Französiche Plakatkunst, Belser Verlag, Stuttgart, 1968.)

**Shahn**
*The Complete Graphic Works of Ben Shahn,* by Kenneth W. Prescott. Quadrangle/New York Times Book Co., New York, 1973.

**Sorlier**
*Chagall's Posters: A Catalogue Raissonné,* edited by Charles Sorlier, Crown Publishers, Inc., New York, 1975.

**Spectacle**
*Les Arts du Spectacle en France—Affiches Illlustrées 1850-1950,* by Nicole Wild. The catalogue of the Bibliothèque de l'Opera (part of the Bibliothèque Nationale), Paris, 1976.

**Stenberg/MoMA**
*Stenberg Brothers: Constructing a Revolution in Soviet Design.* Catalogue of the exhibition at the Museum of Modern Art, New York, 1997. Edited by Christopher Mount.

**Takashimaya**
*The Poster 1865-1969.* Catalogue of the exhibition which opened at the Takashimaya Art Gallery, Nihonbashi, Tokyo, April 18, 1985, and consisted largely of posters from the Deutsches Plakat Museum of Essen, Germany.

**Le Tennis**
*Le Tennis à l'Affiche 1895-1986,* by Jean-Pierre Chevallier. Albin Michel, Paris, 1986.

**Theaterplakate**
*Theaterplakate: ein internationaler historischer berblick,* by Hellmut Rademacher. Edition Leipzig, Leipzig, 1990.

**Timeless Images**
*Timeless Images.* Catalogue of the touring Exhibition of posters in Japan, 1984-85. Text by Jack Rennert; in English and Japanese. Exclusive American distributor: Posters Please, Inc., New York City.

**Tolmer**
*Tolmer: 60 ans de création graphique dans l'Ile St. Louis.* Catalogue of the exhibition at the Bibliotèque Fourney, Paris, 1986.

**Train à l'Affiche**
*Le Train à l'Affiche: Les plus belles affches ferroviaires française,* by Florence Camard and Christophe Zagrodzki. La Vie du Rail, Paris, 1989.

**Trylon**
*Trylon and Perisphere/The 1939 New York World's Fair,* by Barbara Cohen, Steven Heller and Seymour Chwast. Harry N. Abrams, New York, 1989.

**V & A**
*The Power of the Poster,* edited by Margaret Timmer. Book of the exhibition at the Victoria & Albert Museum, London, 1998. V & A Publications, London, 1998.

**Villemot**
*Les affiches de Villemot,* by Jean François Bazin. Deno'l, Paris, 1985.

**Voyage**
*L'Invitation au Voyage,* by Alain Weill. Somogy, Paris, 1994.

**Wagner**
*Toulouse-Lautrec and His Contemporaries: Posters of the Belle Epoque from the Wagner Collection.* Book of the exhibition at the Los Angeles County Museum of Art, 1985.

**Wagons-Lits**
*125 Years International Sleeping Car Company,* by Albert Mühl and Jurgen Klein. The history in text and graphics of the Wagons-Lits company, with text in German, French and English. EK-Verlag GmbH, Freidburg, 1998.

**Wallonie**
*L'Affiche en Wallonie: A travers les collections de la Vie Wallonne.* Edited by the students of the seminaire d'Esthetique de l'Université de Liège, 1980.

**Weill**
*The Poster: A Worldwide Survey and History,* by Alain Weill. G.K. Hall, Boston, 1985.

**Wine Spectator**
*Posters of the Belle Epoque: The Wine Spectator Collection,* by Jack Rennert. The Wine Spectator Press, New York, 1990.

**Wittrock**
*Toulouse-Lautrec: The Complete Prints,* by Wolfgang Wittrock. 2 volumes. Sotheby's, London, 1985.

**Word & Image**
*Word & Image.* Catalogue of the exhibition at the Museum of Modern Art, New York, edited by Mildred Constantine. Text by Alan M. Fern. New York Graphic Society, Greenwich, Connecticut, 1968.

**Yokoo**
*100 Posters of Tadanori Yokoo,* by Koichi Tanikaw. Images Graphiques, New York, 1978.

**Yokoo/Graphic Works**
*Tadanori Yokoo–All About Tadanori Yokoo and his Graphic Work.* Kodansha, Tokyo, 1989.

# POSTER PRICES VII

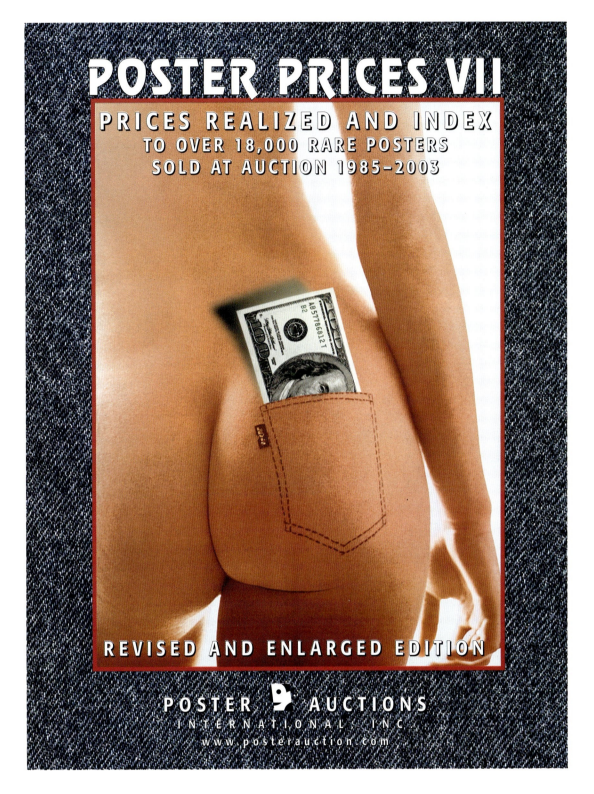

The revised and expanded 224-page book, your index
and price guide to more than 18,000 posters offered
by PAI at its first 36 auctions, will be published July 30, 2003.
It is absolutely essential for any collector and we urge you
to order it now. The price is $50 ($60 foreign).

# TITLES IN THE POSTER ART LIBRARY

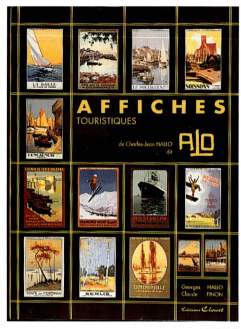

**B481**

**B486**

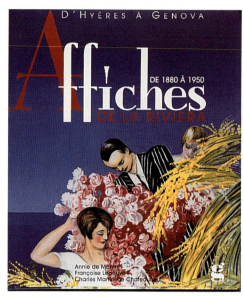

**B472**

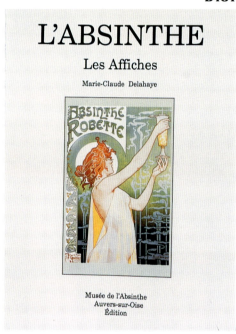

**B479**

**B394**

**B436**

**B481. ALO: Affiches Touristiques,**
by Georges Hallo and Claude Finon.
9 x 12 in./22.8 x 31 cm. Hardcover; 132 pages.
French text. Total of 170 posters, in color, featuring all
the travel destinations of the French railways. With
biography and index. **$50.**

**B486. ROGER BRODERS: Travel Posters,**
by Alain Weill. 8$^1$/$_8$ x 10$^3$/$_4$ in./20.6 x 27.3 cm.
Hardcover; 102 pages; text in English & French.
100 posters in full color. Broders' posters, from 1922
to 1932, made their mark on the history of travel
posters by creating some of the most stunning images
of his time. Weill's commentary is excellent. **$45.**

**B472. AFFICHES DE LA RIVIERA de 1880 à 1950,**
by Annie de Montry, Françoise Lepeuve and Charles
Martini de Chateauneuf. 9$^1$/$_2$ x 11 in./24 x 28 cm.
Hardcover; 280 pages; 524 color plates; text in English & French.
This is the revised and expanded edition of the previ-
ously-released *Affiches d'Azur*, covering posters for
the world-renowned region from Toulon to Genova,
encompassing the Var and the Alpes-Maritimes states
of France, as well as Monaco and Nice. A delightful
pictorial tour. **$70.**

**B479. L'ABSINTHE: LES AFFICHES,**
by Marie-Claude Delahaye.
6 x 8$^1$/$_4$ in./15 x 21 cm. Softcover; 288 pages.
A very complete and erudite look at Absinthe posters,
with all such images in full color, from Livemont to
Cappiello to Thiriet and others. Biographies of artists;
information on printers. Text in French. **$40.**

**B485. CHOCOLATE POSTERS,**
by Alain Weill. 10$^1$/$_2$ x 13$^3$/$_4$ in./26.6 x 27.2 cm.
Hardcover; 144 pages; text in English & French.
The 165 color plates cover the chocolate posters from
Bouisset, Cappiello, Grasset, Steinlen, Mucha, Loupot,
Cassandre and many others. **$45.**

**B436. LOUPOT: L'Art de l'Affiche,**
by Christophe Zagrodzki. 8$^1$/$_2$ x 10$^1$/$_2$ in./22 x 27 cm.
Hardcover; 128 pages; 200 color plates; text in French.
The catalogue raisonné of the brilliant colorist's work,
featuring all of his Swiss and French Art Deco master-
pieces. **$40.**

**B136. THE POSTERS OF JULES CHÉRET,**
by Lucy Broido. Revised edition of catalogue raisonné
of Chéret's posters. 356 black-and-white photos;
46 color plates. Softcover; 124 pages. **$18.**

**B394. HERBERT LEUPIN,**
by Karl Luond and Charles Leupin.
9 x 11$^3$/$_4$ in./22.8 x 29.8 cm. Hardcover; 316 pages;
text in German. All 367 posters of this prolific Swiss
artist shown chronologically and in color. **$90.**

**B302. POSTERS OF THE BELLE EPOQUE:**
**The Wine Spectator Collection,** by Jack Rennert.
10 x 13 in./25 x 33 cm. Hardcover; 256 pages;
220 color reproductions of some of the finest turn-of-
the-century posters, from Chéret to Cappiello, with
annotations to each poster. **$75.**

**B476. TRAVEL BY TRAIN,**
by Michael E. Zega and John E. Gruber.
11 x 11 in./28 x 28 cm.
Hardcover book, in English, with 164 poster images
and excellent descriptive and historical text that finally
gives the American railroad posters of 1870-1950
their due. **$50.**

**B471. MASTERS OF THE POSTER 1900,**
by Alain Weill.
Text in English/French/Italian.
8$^3$/$_4$ x 11$^1$/$_2$ in./22.2 x 29.2 cm.
Softcover; 250 pages; 350 color plates.
Alain Weill has updated the 1896-1900 "Maitres de
l'Affiche" and not only expanded it up to 1914, but
corrected the bias of the former work by making it far
more inclusive of other countries and artists. As Weill

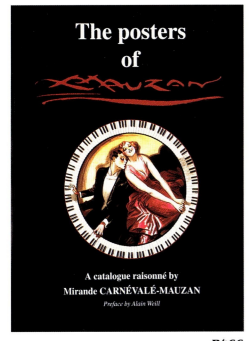

**B466**

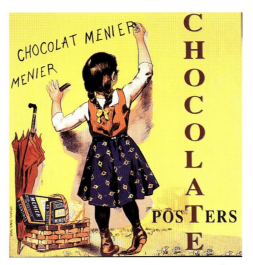

**B485**

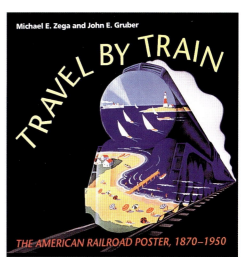

**B476**

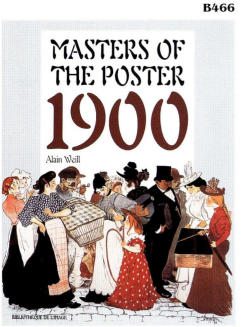

**B471**

**B136**

**B302**

says, "Here . . . the reader can quite simply admire a series of beautiful posters. This is, in the end, what we really have to offer for, if 1900s posters are still extremely popular even today, then this is because they are above all superb pieces of decorative art." A wonderful pictorial book of some of the finest posters ever created. **$50.**

**B466. THE POSTERS OF MAUZAN,**
by Mirande Carnévalé-Mauzan.
$9^3/_8$ x $12^5/_8$ in./24 x 32 cm. Over 500 color illustrations; 224 pages; Softcover; text in English. Includes biography, essays on his early Italian film posters, his commercial posters in Italy, Argentina and France, as well as Mauzan delving into his own work with extracts from his notebooks and other writings. Complete annotations and index. The definitive work on this most imaginative of posterists. **$50.**

---

# CONDITIONS OF SALE

The Conditions of Sale in this catalogue, as it may be amended by any posted notice during the sale, constitutes the complete terms and conditions under which the items listed in this catalogue will be offered for sale. Please note that the items will be offered by us as agent for the consignor.

Every potential buyer should read these Conditions of Sale and it will be agreed, acknowledged and understood by such buyer that said buyer has consented to each and every term and condition as set forth herein.

## 1. Authenticity and Terms of Guarantee.

For a period of five years from the date of this sale, Poster Auctions International, as agent, warrants the authenticity of authorship of all lots contained in this catalogue as described in the text accompanying each lot.

This warranty and guarantee is made only within the five year period and only to the original buyer of record who returns the purchased lot in the same condition as when sold to said buyer; and, it is established beyond doubt that the identification of authorship, as set forth in the description in this catalogue as may have been amended by any posted signs or oral declarations during tire sale, is not correct based on a reasonable reading of the catalogue and the Conditions of Sale herein. Any dispute arising under the terms in this paragraph will be resolved pursuant to final and binding arbitration at the American Arbitration Association.

Upon a finding by an Arbitrator in favor of buyer, the sale will be rescinded and the original purchase price, including the buyers premium, will be refunded. In such case, Poster Auctions International and the purchaser shall be deemed released of any and all claims that each may otherwise have had against the other arising out of the sale of such item.

The benefits of any warranty granted herein are personal to the buyer and are not assignable or transferable to any other person, whether by operation of law or otherwise. Any assignment or transfer of any such warranty shall be void and unenforceable. The purchaser refers only to the original buyer of the lot from Poster Auctions International and not any subsequent owner, assignee, or other person who may have or acquire an interest therein.

It is understood, in the event of disputed authenticity of authorship of any lot results in a rescission of the sale and restitution of the original price and premium paid by such purchaser, stated aforesaid, such restitution is buyer's sole remedy and Poster Auctions International disclaims all liability for any damages. incidental, consequential or otherwise, arising out of or in connection with any sale to the buyer.

Poster Auctions International has provided as much background information for each item listed in this catalogue as possible and has made reasonable efforts to insure the accuracy of the descriptions provided; but Poster Auctions International disclaims any warranty with regard to such descriptions and statements which accompany the listings in this catalogue, including but not limited to, the year of publication, the size, the condition, the printer, the references or any other background information or fact. Accordingly, buyer has due notice that any such information and/or descriptions cannot and will not be considered as material facts to this transaction and will root affect any sales herein.

**On the fall of the gavel, THE SALE IS FINAL.**

**All items are sold AS IS.**

The consignor warrants good title to the buyer. Poster Auctions International and the consignor make no representations or warranty that the buyer acquires any reproduction rights or copyright in items bought at this sale.

Any statements made by Poster Auctions International, whether in this catalogue or by its officers, agents or employees, whether oral or written, are statements of opinion only and not warranties or representations of material facts as to each arid every transaction herein.

## 2. Auctioneers Discretions.

Poster Auctions International has absolute discretion to divide any lot, to combine any of them, to withdraw any lot, to refuse bids and to regulate the bidding. Poster Auctions International reserves the right to withdraw lots at any time prior to or during the sale. The highest bidder acknowledged by the auctioneer will be the purchaser of the lot. Any advance made on an opening bid may be rejected if the auctioneer deems it inadequate. In the event of any dispute between bidders, or in the event of doubt as to the validity of any bid, the auctioneer shall have the final decision either to determine the successful bidder or to re-offer and re-sell the lot in dispute. If any dispute arises after the sale, the auctioneer's sale record shall be deemed the sole and conclusive evidence as to the purchaser of any lot or item.

## 3. Transfer of title and property.

Upon the fall of the auctioneer's hammer, title to the offered lot shall pass to the highest bidder, who may be required to sign a confirmation of purchase; and, shall be required to pay the full purchase price. The purchaser shall assume full risk and responsibility for the lot purchased upon the fall of the auctioneer's hammer. Poster Auctions International, at its option, may withhold delivery of the lots until funds represented by check have been collected or the authenticity of bank or cashier checks has been determined. No purchase shall be claimed or removed until the conclusion of the sale. In the event Poster Auctions International shall, for any reason whatsoever, be unable to deliver the lots purchased by the buyer, its liability shall be solely limited to the rescission of the sale and refund of the purchase price end purchaser's premium.

Poster Auctions International disclaims all liability for damages, incidental, consequential or otherwise, arising out of its failure to deliver any lots purchased. Poster Auctions International does not charge extra or sell separately any frame if a poster is so offered; but it is clear that it is the poster and not the frame which is being offered for sale. Poster Auctions International shall not be responsible for any damage to the frame or to any poster within the frame. Generally, framed posters offered for sale were received framed, photographed that way, and Poster Auctions International can make no warranty or representations regarding the condition of the poster in unseen areas of any such frame. All items are sold strictly as is and the purchaser assumes full risk and responsibility for the purchased lot upon the fall of the hammer, as stated aforesaid.

All lots shall be paid for and removed at the purchaser's risk and expense by noon of the second business day following the sale. Lots not so removed will, at the sole option of Poster Auctions International and at purchaser's risk and expense, be stored at Poster Auctions International's office or warehouse or delivered to a licensed warehouse for storage. Purchaser agrees, in either event, to pay all shipping, handling and storage fees incurred. In the case of lots stored at Poster Auctions International's own warehouse, the handling and storage fee will be an amount equal to 2% of the purchase price for each such lot, per month, until removed, with a minimum charge of 5% for any property not removed within thirty days from the date of the sale.

In addition, Poster Auctions International shall impose a late charge, calculated at the rate of 2% of the total purchase price per month, if payment has not been made in accordance with these Conditions of Sale.

Poster Auctions International may, on the day following the sale, remove all unclaimed lots to its offices or warehouse.

Unless purchaser notifies Poster Auctions International to the contrary, purchaser agrees that Poster Auctions International may, at its discretion, use purchaser's name as buyer of the item sold. If the purchaser fails to comply with one or more of these Conditions of Sale, then, in addition to any and all other remedies which it may have at law or in equity, Poster Auctions International may, at its sole option, cancel the sale without notice to the buyer. In such event, Poster Auctions International shall retain as liquidated damages all payments made by the purchaser, or sell the item and/or lots and all other property of the purchaser held by Poster Auctions International, without notice. Such liquidation sale shall be at standard commission rates, without any reserve. The proceeds of such sale or sales shall be applied first to the satisfaction of any damages occasioned by the purchaser's breach, and then to the payment of any other indebtedness owing to Poster Auctions International, including without limitation, commissions, handling charges, the expenses of both sales, reasonable attorneys fees, collection agency fees, and any other costs or expenses incurred thereunder. The purchaser hereby waives all the requirements of notice, advertisement and disposition of proceeds required by law, including those set forth in New York Lien Law, Article 9, Sections 200-204 inclusive, or any successor statue, with respect to any sale pursuant to this section.

## 4. Buyer's Premium

A premium of 15% will be added to the successful bid price of all items sold by Poster Auctions International. This premium shall be paid by all purchasers, without exception.

### 5. Order Bids
Poster Auctions International shall make reasonable efforts to execute bids for those not able to attend the auction; and act on the prospective purchaser's behalf to attempt to purchase the item desired at the lowest price possible, up to the limit indicated by purchaser in writing as if the purchaser were in attendance. Poster Auctions International shall not be responsible for any errors or omissions in this matter. Poster Auctions International reserves the right not to bid for any such purchaser if the order is not clear; does not arrive in sufficient time; the credit of the purchaser is not established prior to the sale; or, for any other reason in its sole discretion. An Order Bid Form shall be provided on request.

### 6. Sales Tax
Unless exempt by law, prior to taking pssession of the lot, the purchaser shall be required to pay the combined New York State and local sales tax, or any applicable compensating tax of another state, on the total purchase price.

### 7. Packing and shipping
Packing and/or handling of purchased lots by Posters Auctions International is performed solely as a courtesy for the convenience of purchasers. Unless otherwise directed by purchaser, packing and handling shall be undertaken at the sole discretion of Poster Auctions International. Poster Auctions International, at its sole discretion as agent of the purchaser, shall instruct an outside contractor to act on its behalf and arrange for or otherwise transport purchased lots. Charges for packing, handling, insurance and freight are payable by the purchaser. Poster Auctions International shall make reasonable efforts to handle purchases with care, but assumes no responsibility for damage of any kind. Poster Auctions International disclaims all liability for loss, or damages of any kind, arising out of or in connection with the packing, handling or transportation of any lots/items purchased.

### 8. Reserves.
All lots are subject to a reserve, which is the confidential minimum below which the lot will not be sold. Poster Auctions International may implement the reserve by bidding on behalf of the consignor. The consignor shall not bid on consignor's property.

### 9. Notices and jurisdiction.
(a)     All communications and notices hereunder shall be in writing and shall be deemed to have been duly given if delivered personally to an officer of PAI or if sent by United States registered mail or certified, postage prepaid, addressed as follows:

From:    Poster Auctions International
To:    _____(Seller)
    _____
    _____
From:    _____(Seller)
To:    Poster Auctions International
    601 W. 26th Street
    NewYork, NewYork 10001

or to such other address as either party hereto may have designated to the other by written notice.

(b)     These Conditions of Sale contain the entire understandings between the parties and may not be changed in any way except in writing duly executed by PAI and buyer.

(c)     These Conditions of Sale shall be construed and enforced in accordance with the laws of the State of New York.

(d)     No waiver shalt be deemed to be made by any party hereto of any rights hereunder, unless the same shall be in writing and each waiver, if any, shall be a waiver only with respect to the specific instance involved and shall in no way impair the rights of the waiving party or the obligations of the other party in any other respect at any other time.

(e)     The provisions of these Conditions of Sale shall be binding upon and inure to the benefit of the respective heirs, legatees, personal representatives and successors and assigns of the parties hereto.

(f)     The Conditions of Sale are not assignable by either party without written permission of the other party; any attempt to assign any rights, duties or obligations which arise under these Conditions without such permission will be void.

---

# DESCRIPTION OF THE POSTERS

I. Artist's name.
Unless otherwise indicated, the artist's name, mark or initials appear on the poster.

2. Year of the Poster.
The year given is that of the publication of the poster, not necessarily the date of the event publicized or the year that art for it was rendered.

3. Size.
Size is given in inches first, then centimeters, width preceding height. Size is for entire sheet, not just the image area.

4. Printer.
Unless otherwise indicated, the name of the printer is that which appears on the face of the poster. It should be kept in mind that frequently the establishment credited on the poster is, in fact, an agency, studio or publisher.

5. Condition of the Poster.
We have attempted a simplified rating of all the posters in this sale. It should be kept in mind that we are dealing in many cases, with 50 to 100-year-old advertising paper. The standards of the print collector cannot be used. Prints were, for the most part, done in small format, on fine paper, and meant to be immediately framed or stored in a print sleeve or cabinet. A poster, for the most part, was printed in a large format, on the cheapest possible paper, and was meant to last about eight weeks on the billboards.

Most important to the condition of a poster—not eight weeks but often eighty years later—is the image of the poster: is that image (the lines, the colors, the overall design) still clearly expressed? If so, it is a poster worth collecting.

While details of each poster's condition are given as completely and accurately as possible, blemishes, tears or restorations which do not detract from the basic image and impact should not seriously impair value.

All posters are lined, whether on linen or japan paper, unless otherwise indicated. But please note that posters received in frames are not inspected out of their frames and therefore no warranty can be made about them.

All photos are of the actual poster being offered for sale. A close look at the photo and a reading of the text should enable the buyer who cannot personally examine the item to make an intelligent appraisal of it.

The following ratings have been used:

Cond A     Designates a poster in very fine condition. The colors are fresh; no paper loss. There may be some slight blemish or tear, but this is very marginal and not noticeable. A+ is a flawless example of a poster rarely seen in such fine condition. A– indicates there may be some slight dirt, fold, tear or bubble or other minor restoration, but most unobtrusive.

Cond B     Designates a poster in good condition. There may be some slight paper loss, but not in the image or in any crucial design area. If some restoration, it is not immediately evident. The lines and colors are good, although paper may have yellowed (light-stained). B+ designates a poster in very good condition. B– is one in fairly good condition. The latter determination may be caused by heavier than normal light-staining or one or two noticeable repairs.

Cond C     Designates a poster in fair condition. The light-staining may be more pronounced, restorations, folds or flaking are more readily visible, and possibly some minor paper loss occurs. But the poster is otherwise intact, the image clear, and the colors, though possibly faded, still faithful to the artist's intent.

Cond D     Designates a poster in bad condition. A good part of such poster may be missing, including some crucial image area; colors and lines so marred that a true appreciation of the artist's intent is difficult, if not impossible. There are no D posters in this sale!

The above condition ratings are solely the opinion of Poster Auctions International, and are presented only as an aid to the public. Prospective purchasers are expected to have satisfied themselves as to the condition of the posters. Any discrepancy relating to the condition of a poster shall not be considered grounds for the cancellation of a sale.

Some other notes and designations relating to the condition of a poster:

Framed     Where a poster is framed, this is indicated. In many cases, we have photographed the poster in the frame and the dimensions given are those which are visible within the matting or edges of the frame.

Paper     All posters in this sale are linen- or japan-backed unless the designation "P" appears.

6. Bibliography.
An abbreviation for each reference (Ref) is given and can be found in the complete Bibliography. The reference is almost always to a reproduction of that poster. If a "p." precedes it, it means the reproduction or reference is on that page; if number only, it refers to a poster or plate number. Every effort has been made to refer to books that are authoritative and/or easily accessible.

7. Pre-Sale Estimate
These estimates are guides for prospective bidders and should not be relied upon as representations or predictions of actual selling prices. They are simply our best judgment of the fair market value of that particular poster in that condition on the date it was written.

# THE POSTER ENCYCLOPEDIA

## MISSING ANY BOOKS?

These hardcover, auction catalogues form an essential encyclopedia for the poster collector. Each illustrates over 500 posters, with full annotations, bibliography, estimates and prices realized. Price of individual volumes: **$40** each ($45 foreign).

**SPECIAL OFFER:** All 28 previous catalogues (Auctions I–XXXV, excluding out-of-print volumes I, II, III, VI, VII, XIV, and XV) for only **$700** ($775 foreign).

# POSTER AUCTIONS INTERNATIONAL, INC.

601 WEST 26TH ST., NEW YORK, N.Y. 10001

TEL (212) 787-4000. FAX (212) 604-9175

www.posterauctions.com          Email: info@posterauctions.com

# POSTER PERSUASION
## ORDER BID FORM

Please bid on my behalf on the following lots up to the price shown. I understand that all bids are subject to the Conditions of Sale which are printed in the Catalogue.

Poster Auctions International will make every effort to execute bids for those not able to attend and act on the prospective purchaser's behalf to try to purchase the item desired at the lowest price possible up to the limit indicated by purchaser below as if the purchaser were in attendance, but Poster Auctions International cannot be responsible for any errors or omissions in this matter. Poster Auctions International may reserve the right not to bid for any such party if the order is not clear, does not arrive in sufficient time, or the credit of the purchaser is not established, or for any other reason in its sole discretion.

The purchase price will be the total of the final bid and a premium of 15% of the final bid together with any applicable sales tax. Unsuccessful bidders will not be informed but may telephone for sales results.

_____    Date _____
                        (Signed)

NAME  _____

ADDRESS _____

City _____State _____Zip _____

TEL: Home: (        ) _____ Office: (        ) _____ FAX: (        ) _____

BANK: Name _____Telephone (        ) _____

      Address _____

      Account Number _____Officer _____

REFERENCE _____

| Lot # | Artist | Title | BID (excluding premium) |
|-------|--------|-------|-------------------------|
| _____ | _____ | _____ | $ _____ |
| _____ | _____ | _____ | $ _____ |
| _____ | _____ | _____ | $ _____ |
| _____ | _____ | _____ | $ _____ |
| _____ | _____ | _____ | $ _____ |
| _____ | _____ | _____ | $ _____ |
| _____ | _____ | _____ | $ _____ |
| _____ | _____ | _____ | $ _____ |
| _____ | _____ | _____ | $ _____ |

# YES, you CAN
## be with us on May 4.

If you cannot attend our New York sale in person, you can nonetheless take advantage of these rare offerings.

# BID by MAIL, FAX or PHONE
## with confidence.

Simply fill out the form on the reverse side of this page, indicating your maximum bid for each desired lot. It should be in our New York offices no later than Friday, May 2.

You may indicate an "either-or" bid if you want to purchase only a portion of the items on your wish list. You may also indicate a maximum total dollar amount. We execute your bid on your behalf at the lowest price possible.

To bid by telephone, simply fill in the lot numbers and indicate the phone number where we can reach you on Sunday, May 4. When your lot number comes up, we'll call you.

*Either way, you bid with confidence:* We execute your bid on your behalf at the lowest possible price.

### DON'T MISS OUT ON THE POSTER YOU WANT
### just because you can't be in New York.

**REMINDER:** You can view all the posters at The International Poster Center, 601 W. 26th Street, New York City from April 15 to May 3. Hours: 9–5 Monday–Friday; 10–6 Saturday and Sunday.

*We are a bidder-friendly organization!*